Founding Editor: J. R. MULRYNE
General Editors:
JAMES C. BULMAN, CAROL CHILLINGTON RUTTER

The Winter's Tale

Already published in the series

Geraldine Cousin *King John*
Anthony B. Dawson *Hamlet*
Jay L. Halio *A Midsummer Night's Dream* (2nd edn)
Stuart Hampton-Reeves and Carol Chillington Rutter The *Henry VI* plays
Bernice W. Kliman *Macbeth* (2nd edn)
Alexander Leggatt *King Lear*
James Loehlin *Henry V*
Scott McMillin *Henry IV, Part One*
Lois Potter *Othello*
Hugh M. Richmond *King Henry VIII*
Margaret Shewring *King Richard II*

Shakespeare in Performance

The Winter's Tale

MARY JUDITH DUNBAR

with a chapter by
CAROL CHILLINGTON RUTTER

Manchester University Press
Manchester and New York

Distributed in the United States exclusively
by Palgrave Macmillan

Copyright © Mary Judith Dunbar 2010

The right of Mary Judith Dunbar to be identified as the author of all of this work except Chapter IX has been asserted by her in accordance with the Copyright, Designs and Patents Act 1988.

Chapter IX: Copyright © Carol Chillington Rutter 2010

The right of Carol Chillington Rutter to be identified as the author of Chapter IX of this book has been asserted by her in accordance with the Copyright, Designs and Patents Act 1988.

Published by Manchester University Press
Oxford Road, Manchester M13 9NR, UK
and Room 400, 175 Fifth Avenue, New York, NY 10010, USA
www.manchesteruniversitypress.co.uk

Distributed in the United States exclusively by
Palgrave Macmillan, 175 Fifth Avenue, New York,
NY 10010, USA

Distributed in Canada exclusively by
UBC Press, University of British Columbia, 2029 West Mall,
Vancouver, BC, Canada V6T 1Z2

British Library Cataloguing-in-Publication Data
A catalogue record for this book is available from the British Library

Library of Congress Cataloging-in-Publication Data applied for

ISBN 978 0 7190 2741 3 hardback

First published 2010

The publisher has no responsibility for the persistence or accuracy of URLs for any external or third-party internet websites referred to in this book, and does not guarantee that any content on such websites is, or will remain, accurate or appropriate.

Typeset by Action Publishing Technology Ltd, Gloucester
Printed in Great Britain by MPG Books Group, UK

CONTENTS

List of illustrations *page* vii
Series editors' preface xi
Acknowledgements xiii
Note on the text xxi

Introduction: 'This wide gap of time': Theatrical issues and performance history 1

I Granville Barker's production at the Savoy Theatre, 1912 32

II Postwar renewal: Peter Brook's production at the Phoenix Theatre, 1951 62

III Trevor Nunn's production with the Royal Shakespeare Company, 1969–71 85

IV Audrey Stanley's production with the Oregon Shakespearean Festival, 1975 110

V Jane Howell's television production for the British Broadcasting Corporation, 1980 134

VI Peter Hall's production at the National Theatre, 1988 151

VII Reinvention and cultural translation: Ingmar Bergman's production with the Royal Dramatic Theatre of Sweden, 1994–95 174

VIII Declan Donnellan's production with the Maly Drama Theatre, St Petersburg, 1997 194

IX	**'A world ransomed, or one destroyed':** **English *Tale*s at the millennium** by Carol Chillington Rutter	213
	Notes	243
	Appendix	258
	Bibliography	263
	Index	279

LIST OF ILLUSTRATIONS

1 Herbert Hewetson as Time. Directed by Harley Granville Barker, Savoy Theatre, London, 1912. By permission of the Shakespeare Birthplace Trust   *page* 50

2 H. O. Nicholson as the Old Shepherd, Cathleen Nesbitt as Perdita, Dennis Neilson-Terry as Florizel, Stanley Drewitt as Camillo. Directed by Harley Granville Barker, Savoy Theatre, London, 1912. By permission of the Shakespeare Birthplace Trust   52

3 Lillah McCarthy as Hermione, Esmé Beringer as Paulina, Henry Ainley as Leontes, Cathleen Nesbitt as Perdita, Stanley Drewitt as Camillo, Charles Graham as Polixenes, Dennis Neilson-Terry as Florizel. Directed by Harley Granville Barker, Savoy Theatre, London, 1912. By permission of the Shakespeare Birthplace Trust   57

4 John Gielgud as Leontes, Flora Robson as Paulina, Lewis Casson as Antigonus. Directed by Peter Brook, Phoenix Theatre, London, 1951. Angus McBean Photograph. Copyright © Harvard Theatre Collection   74

5 Diana Wynyard as Hermione and John Gielgud as Leontes. Directed by Peter Brook, Phoenix Theatre, London, 1951. Angus McBean Photograph. Copyright © Harvard Theatre Collection   83

6 Barrie Ingham as Leontes, Judi Dench as Hermione, Richard Pasco as Polixenes. Directed by Trevor Nunn, Royal Shakespeare Company, Royal Shakespeare Theatre, Stratford-upon-Avon, 1969. Photograph by Thomas F. Holte. Tom Holte Theatre Photographic Collection. Copyright © Shakespeare Birthplace Trust   91

7 David Bailie as Florizel and Judi Dench as Perdita. Directed by Trevor Nunn, Royal Shakespeare Company, Royal Shakespeare Theatre, Stratford-upon-Avon, 1969. Photograph by Thomas F. Holte. The Thos F and Mig Holte Photographic Collection. Copyright © Shakespeare Birthplace Trust   102

8 Le Clanché du Rand as Hermione, Peter Silbert as
   Polixenes, Todd Reichenbach as Mamillius, James
   Edmondson as Leontes. Directed by Audrey Stanley,
   Oregon Shakespearean Festival, 1975. Photograph by
   Hank Kranzler. By permission of the Oregon
   Shakespeare Festival   118

9 Le Clanché du Rand as Hermione, Randi Douglas as
   Paulina, James Edmondson as Leontes. Directed by
   Audrey Stanley, Oregon Shakespearean Festival, 1975.
   Photograph by Hank Kranzler. By permission of the
   Oregon Shakespeare Festival   128

10 Carmi Boushey as Perdita, Le Clanché du Rand as
   Hermione, James Edmondson as Leontes. Directed by
   Audrey Stanley, Oregon Shakespearean Festival, 1975.
   Photograph by Hank Kranzler. By permission of the
   Oregon Shakespeare Festival   130

11 Eileen Atkins as Paulina and Tim Pigott-Smith as Leontes.
   Directed by Peter Hall, National Theatre, London, 1988.
   Photograph by John Haynes. By permission of
   John Haynes   165

12 Kristina Törnqvist as Perdita, Kristina Adolphson as
   Time, Jakob Eklund as Florizel. Directed by
   Ingmar Bergman, the Royal Dramatic Theatre of Sweden,
   Stockholm, 1994. Photograph by Bengt Wanselius. By
   permission of Bengt Wanselius   188

13 Natalia Akimova as Hermione, and members of the
   court. Directed by Declan Donnellan, the Maly Drama
   Theatre, St Petersburg, Russia, 1997. Photograph by
   Victor Vasilyev. By permission of the Maly Drama
   Theatre, St Petersburg   205

14 Alexandra Gilbreath as Hermione, Antony Sher as Leontes,
   Geoffrey Freshwater as Camillo, Ken Bones as Polixenes,
   Emily Bruni as Mamillius, and members of the court.
   Directed by Gregory Doran, Royal Shakespeare Company,
   Royal Shakespeare Theatre, Stratford-upon-Avon, 1999.
   Photograph by Malcolm Davies. Copyright © Shakespeare
   Birthplace Trust   226

15 Stephen Rashbrook as Cleomenes, Steven Elliott as Dion, Joe Dixon as Camillo, Nick Sampson as Archidamus, and members of the court. Directed by Nicholas Hytner, National Theatre, London, 2001. Photograph by Philip Carter. Copyright © Philip Carter   226

16 Tam Williams as Mamillius. Directed by Edward Hall, Propeller, Watermill Theatre, Newbury, 2005. Photograph by Robert Day. Copyright © Robert Day   227

17 Richard McCabe as Autolycus, with revellers in Bohemia. Directed by Adrian Noble, Royal Shakespeare Company, Royal Shakespeare Theatre, Stratford-upon-Avon, 1992. Photograph by Malcolm Davies. Copyright © Shakespeare Birthplace Trust   228

18 James Tucker as Young Shepherd. Directed by Edward Hall, Propeller, Watermill Theatre, Newbury, 2005. Photograph by Christopher Kennedy. Copyright © Christopher Kennedy   229

SERIES EDITORS' PREFACE

Recently, the study of Shakespeare's plays as scripts for performance in the theatre has grown to rival the reading of Shakespeare as literature among university, college and secondary-school teachers and their students. The aim of the present series is to assist this study by describing how certain of Shakespeare's texts have been realised in production.

The series is not concerned to provide theatre history in the traditional sense. Rather, it employs the more contemporary discourses of performance criticism to explore how a multitude of factors work together to determine how a play achieves meaning for a particular audience. Each contributor to the series has selected a number of productions of a given play and analysed them comparatively. These productions – drawn from different periods, countries and media – were chosen not only because they are culturally significant in their own right but also because they represent something of the range and variety of the possible interpretations of the play in hand. They illustrate how the convergence of various material conditions helps to shape a performance: the medium for which the text is adapted; stage-design and theatrical tradition; the acting company itself; the body and abilities of the individual actor; and the historical, political, and social contexts which condition audience reception of the play.

We hope that theatregoers, by reading these accounts of Shakespeare in performance, may enlarge their understanding of what a play-text is and begin, too, to appreciate the complex ways in which performance is a collaborative effort. Any study of a Shakespeare text will, of course, reveal only a small proportion of the play's potential meaning; but by engaging issues of how a text is translated in performance, our series encourages a kind of reading that is receptive to the contingencies that make theatre a living art.

J. R. Mulryne, Founding Editor
James C. Bulman, Carol Chillington Rutter, General Editors

ACKNOWLEDGEMENTS

Since performance of a Shakespeare play is a richly collaborative living art, in writing about *The Winter's Tale* in performance I have sought to learn from and give voice to the work of actors, directors, designers, and other theatre professionals whose labor and interpretative discoveries have made it possible for audiences to experience the play's multiple potentialities in the theatre. I have tried to do this in part by quoting from my interviews with theatre artists engaged in some of the most significant twentieth-century productions of *The Winter's Tale* as well as by connecting scholarly research to my direct experience of those productions I was able to see in performance. For her generous scholarly collaboration, I am exceptionally grateful to Carol Rutter, theatre scholar and performance critic *extraordinaire*, for the book's final chapter, in which she draws upon her first-hand experience of the play in performance to give us a comparative analysis of eight of the most important British productions of *The Winter's Tale* from the turn of the late twentieth century into the early twenty-first century.

I am additionally indebted to the work of other Shakespeare scholars and critics, including those whose engagement in performance criticism has been part of the collaboration between the academy and the theatre that has become a vital part of Shakespeare scholarship. Performance critics and scholars writing about *The Winter's Tale* owe a particular debt to Dennis Bartholomeusz, whose *The Winter's Tale in Performance in England and America 1611–1976*, with its critically fine and detailed stage history, I have long admired. Since performance history and criticism is always a work in progress, I hope this book may augment his in a number of distinctive ways. This volume extends study of *The Winter's Tale* in performance from the last quarter of the twentieth century into the first decade of the twenty-first century, and it particularly focuses in depth on a select number of major twentieth-century productions. The Introduction contains a brief account of landmark productions of *The Winter's Tale* prior to the twentieth century and thus offers historical context and perspective from which to evaluate the achievements of the play's later productions. My approach primarily uses critical analysis of significant productions that particularly illuminate the interpretative and theatrical challenges *The Winter's Tale* presents. For that purpose I have done fresh archival research and give detailed assessments of important twentieth-century productions in individual chapters, including two on major late twentieth-century productions of *The Winter's Tale* outside England and North America – those by the Royal Dramatic Theatre of Sweden (directed by Ingmar Bergman) and by the Maly Drama Theatre of Europe (directed by Declan Donnellan). I have also made extensive use of my interview material unavailable elsewhere.

Special gratitude to those directors, actors, and other professionals who generously gave illuminating interviews from which they have allowed me to cite in this book. Among those directors I was able to interview whose productions of *The Winter's Tale* are the subject of chapters of this book are Trevor Nunn, Peter Hall, and Audrey Stanley. The Maly Dramatic Theatre's Artistic Director Lev Dodin (in an interview in St Petersburg conducted on my behalf by Naum Pinkhasik), and Natalia Kolotova, the Maly's Company Manager and Assistant Director (in a separate interview conducted on my behalf by Karina Chumakova) each commented on *The Winter's Tale* production (1997) directed by Declan Donnellan with the Maly company. Jane Howell allowed me to cite her words about her British Broadcasting Corporation production from a letter and from an interview she gave to Mary Maher, who helpfully shared both with me. Donya Feuer, choreographer for Ingmar Bergman's 1994–95 production of *The Winter's Tale*, gave me detailed insight into the integral relation of her movement work to the play's unfolding dramatic action. Among those actors who kindly granted permission to quote from their interviews, which were unforgettably engaging and insightful, are Judi Dench, Barrie Ingham, James Edmondson, Le Clanché du Rand, Tim Pigott-Smith, Eileen Atkins, Ken Stott, and Pernilla August.

Performance work is often particularly revelatory in the process of rehearsal, as is learning from actors when they are teaching as well as on stage. I count among my valued teachers those whose work, owing to limitations of scope and space, I have been able to refer to only very briefly in this book, if at all; but they have immensely enriched my understanding of *The Winter's Tale*. I am especially indebted to Patrick Stewart for many important conversations about his exceptionally striking work as Leontes in the 1981–83 Royal Shakespeare Company production of *The Winter's Tale* (directed by Ronald Eyre); the conversations took place both during the opening run of the production in 1981 at the Shakespeare Memorial Theatre in Stratford-upon-Avon and especially during his two-week residency at Santa Clara University in April 1983, just after he had concluded, at the Barbican in London, the two-year run of that production – making new discoveries even through the time of the last performance. I am very fortunate as well to have worked as Dramaturg for the 1990 Shakespeare/Santa Cruz production that was finely directed by Sara Pia Anderson. Former Royal Shakespeare Company actor Paul Whitworth played Leontes; Paul's probing questions in rehearsals and astonishingly fresh work on the part further opened up a spectrum of possibilities I had not before envisaged. I had the additional joy in that production's rehearsals of learning by working with Olivia Virgil Harper as Paulina, Danny Scheie as the Young Shepherd, Jack Zerbe as Antigonus, Peter Jacobson as Autolycus, and Tim Fullerton as Florizel. I am also immeasurably grateful to my close colleagues Fred Tollini, SJ, and Equity actor Aldo Billingslea for all I learned from them while I acted as Dramaturg for Tollini's production of *The Winter's Tale* at Santa Clara University in 2000. Aldo's powerful Leontes richly deserved the praise he received from Stephen Booth, veteran of many productions of *The Winter's Tale*, who found Aldo's Leontes one of the best he had ever experienced.

Strong thanks, as well, to other actors, directors, designers, and theatre staff whose performance work and interviews, which have significantly enlarged my perceptions of *The Winter's Tale*, I would love to have been able to cite had the scope of this book made it possible. I have learned much from those actors and directors with whom I spoke who were involved in the Royal Shakespeare Company productions directed by John Barton and Trevor Nunn in 1976, with special thanks to Ian McKellen for his responses to my questions concerning his impressive Leontes; by Ronald Eyre in 1981–83; by Terry Hands in 1986–87; by Adrian Noble in 1992; and by Gregory Doran in 1999. Terry Hands in 1987 and Gregory Doran in 1999 (premiere 10 December 1998) not only gave interviews but generously gave me opportunities to learn by observing rehearsals at London's Barbican Theatre when their productions of *The Winter's Tale* were being transferred from Stratford-upon-Avon. I also honour what I learned from conversations with company members in productions at the Stratford Festival, Stratford, Ontario, Canada, in 1986, directed by David William; by the New York Shakespeare Festival in 1989, directed by James Lapine (with particular thanks to Diane Venora, who played Hermione); at the Globe Theatre, London, in 1990, directed by David Freeman; by the English Shakespeare Company in 1990, directed by Michael Bogdanov; by the Cornerstone Theater Company, Los Angeles, in 1991, directed by Bill Rauch; and by the Shakespeare Repertory, Chicago, in 1994, directed by Barbara Gaines. I am deeply thankful for conversations at the Oregon Shakespeare Festival (Ashland) with many actors and theatre professionals who have been involved in productions directed there by Libby Appel in 1990, by Fontaine

Syer in 1996, and by Michael Edwards in 2002, as well as for valuable interviews with each of those directors and actor and dramaturg Barry Kraft. I am, furthermore, grateful to those associated with the Utah Shakespeare Festival, including actor Gary Armagnac, for conversations about *The Winter's Tale* directed by James Edmondson for that festival in 1996.

Performances and rehearsals continually open our awareness of interpretative possibilities. I was fortunate to live in England in the 1960s and 1970s during an important time of experimentation and change in styles of Shakespearean production and in new British drama, and my teaching in London (full-time for the University of London Institute of Education and part-time for the University of London Extra-Mural Department) included exploration of dramatic texts in relation to performance. Special thanks to my colleague from those years and still a great friend, Margaret Cottier, with whom to discuss performance is wonderfully to widen one's perception of it; I found very helpful indeed her detailed notes on the Maly production of *The Winter's Tale* when it was performed in England in the spring of 1999. My friend the late Maurice Daniels, formerly of the RSC, clarified many points about lighting design in his astute reading of a draft of my chapter on Trevor Nunn's 1969–71 production and he also helped facilitate my observation of rehearsals with the RSC and the National Theatre. Rehearsals are fertile sites for discovery and create an immediate need for detailed textual investigation and for exploring theatrical challenges. I am enormously grateful to Peter Hall for allowing me to be present in workshops and rehearsals for the National Theatre's 1988 season of late plays, and am additionally thankful for the valuable conversations I had with Roger Warren during that season and with Tony Church about his Antigonus in Hall's *Winter's Tale*.

I am, furthermore, greatly indebted for inspiration to those teachers whose scholarship has connected literary criticism to their commitment to drama in performance. As a Fulbright scholar at the University of Bristol I studied Greek and Shakespearean drama with H. D. F. Kitto and modern drama with Ronald Gaskell, from whom I received generous guidance indeed, as I did at Stanford when I completed doctoral work with Ronald Rebholz. I participated as a Fellow of the Institute for Renaissance Studies in a valuable course led by Homer Swander in connection with the Oregon Shakespeare Festival. The 1982 Humanities Institute on Shakespeare in Performance at the Folger Shakespeare Library led by Bernard Beckerman and Cary Mazer further challenged my explorations of complex relations between text and performance. I am indebted to the Folger Institute of Renaissance and Eighteenth-Century Studies and to a grant from the National Endowment for the Humanities (NEH) for making it possible for me to participate in what for many of us in that 1982 Institute was a seminal time, and to the NEH for a later Summer Stipend in support of my research for this book. I celebrate colleagues from that seminar at the Folger with whom it has been possible to journey further, including Ellen O'Brien and Bernice Kliman. I am very grateful to Bernice for sharing experiences of productions of *The Winter's Tale* in New York, for sending performance notes, and for her astute reading of a draft of my chapter on Jane Howell's British Broadcasting Corporation production.

Other colleagues with whom I have exchanged ideas at meetings of the Shakespeare Association of America, International Shakespeare Association, and Modern Language Association deserve specific thanks. Peter Donaldson, Herb Coursen, and Mary Maher all helpfully responded to early versions of my chapter on Howell's production. Gene England sent perceptive and detailed notes regarding his experience while in London of the Maly Drama Theatre production of *The Winter's Tale*. Phil McGuire has given astute and witty advice. Barbara Hodgdon's stimulating notes and questions on a draft of my chapter on Ingmar Bergman's production still keep me thinking. Michael Warren and Audrey Stanley each read drafts of certain chapters with care. I am delightedly grateful, too, to have benefited since the early 1980s from their splendid scholarly and creative work at the University of California, Santa Cruz, and from a rich harvest of conversations with them about texts and performances at Shakespeare/Santa Cruz.

My colleagues at Santa Clara University have abundantly supported me and the research for this book. Particular thanks to Don Dodson and the Provost's office for grants that have helped to fund this project, and to the Dean's office and to English Department chairpersons past and present for additional research support. I appreciate the encouragement of colleagues with whom I teach in the English Department and Women's and Gender Studies Program; those with whom I work closely in the Department of Theatre and Dance, in which my Shakespeare courses are cross-listed; and those, including André Delbecq, who are trusted companions in the Ignatian Faculty Forum. Heartfelt gratitude to Juan Velasco and Eileen Elrod for their invaluable gifts of deep listening, loving kindness, and healing laughter that have supported me in this project and beyond it. Craig Gower of the Communication Department gave fine advice on techniques and terms of television production. With extraordinary generosity, Dan Maloney in Media Services has many times given kind and skilled help, as has his colleague Ruth Ellison. Elwood Mills, with meticulous attention to detail at a high level of photographic art, expertly facilitated my use of the photographs in the book. Karen Fox took special initiative to give me detailed reports on performances of the Maly Drama Theatre's production of *The Winter's Tale* and to connect me with research assistants in Russia; my thanks to Karina Chumakova, Alex Gorshkov, and especially, for her extensive and insightful research, to Natalia Alexandrova.

For their resourceful research assistance and strong interests in *The Winter's Tale* it is a delight to thank my students Maureen McDonnell, Megan Tracy, Olga Kuskova, Allia Homayoun, Jennifer BeVard (with whom I worked on a Faculty and Student Research Assistant Program grant), Emily McMullen, Julie Jigour, and Sara Barrantes. I continue to have animating conversations about this book project with Maureen, now herself a university professor and scholar of Shakespeare in performance. Olga, with whom I worked on a Dreher Internship Grant for faculty and student collaborative research, gave important assistance with Russian translation of many sources used in my chapter on the Maly Drama Theatre production of *The Winter's Tale*. She also facilitated the interview with Lev Dodin in St Petersburg conducted by Naum Pinkhasik, and its translation by Katherine Kuskova; strong thanks to each of them.

My research has greatly benefited from the kind and knowledgeable assistance of librarians and archivists, including Sylvia Morris, Helen Hargest, and others at the Shakespeare Centre Library, Stratford-upon-Avon, whose Curator of the Royal Shakespeare Company collection, David Howells, gave permission to use references to archival materials related to the 1969–71 production of *The Winter's Tale* directed by Trevor Nunn. Particular thanks, too, to Niky Rathbone at the Birmingham Shakespeare Library, who gave permission to quote from the Gordon Crosse Theatrical Diaries; to Claire Hudson and Andrew Kirk at the Victoria and Albert Theatre Museum, and its Archivist and Conservation Manager, Guy Baxter, who gave the permission of the Museum, as owner of the material, for me to refer to two unpublished sources related to *The Winter's Tale* – the Account Book from Harley Granville Barker's 1912 production and the promptbook for the 1951 production directed by Peter Brook. Kit Leary of the Oregon Shakespeare Festival (OSF) archives has been especially helpful over the years, and I additionally thank her and her administrative colleague Eddie Wallace for facilitating permission to use archival materials and reproduce photographs from Audrey Stanley's 1975 production. I also gratefully acknowledge archivists at the National Theatre, National Sound Archive of the British Library, University of Bristol Theatre Collection, and Stratford Festival Archives (Canada), as well as librarians and staff of the Folger Shakespeare Library, the Harvard Theatre Collection of Widener Library, the Horace Howard Furness Memorial Library of the University of Pennsylvania, the Lincoln Center Library, and the Library of Santa Clara University. I have been thankful over the years for the expert and kind assistance I have received from Santa Clara University librarians; it has been particularly extensive from Leanna Goodwater, Cindy Bradley, and Carolee Bird.

I am indebted to other persons who enabled me to use valuable resources in my research for this book. I thank Ulla Åberg, Head of the Drama Department for the Royal Dramatic Theatre of Sweden, for permission to use quotations from the production script, interviews, programme, *Dramat* magazine, and Lyric Opera Surtitles Program Script File Header, all related to the production of *The Winter's Tale* directed by Ingmar Bergman and presented at the Brooklyn Academy of Music in 1995. Margarita Bergman, widow of Paul Britten-Austin, in correspondence facilitated by her son Thom Britten-Austin, graciously gave permission for me to quote from Paul Britten-Austin's translations of the *Songes* of Carl Jonas Love Almqvist used for those surtitles at the Brooklyn Academy of Music. Natalia Kolotova, Company Manager and Assistant Director of the Maly Drama Theatre of Europe, St Petersburg, granted permission to use references to the production script, programme, other archival documents, and her interview concerning *The Winter's Tale* directed in 1997 by Declan Donnellan. I also thankfully acknowledge the following: The Society of Authors as the Literary Representatives of the Estate of Harley Granville Barker for permission to use short extracts from Barker's *More Prefaces to Shakespeare*, Edward M. Moore, ed., Princeton: Princeton University Press, 1974; Cambridge University Press for permission to use short extracts from Dennis Bartholomeusz' *The Winter's Tale in Performance in England and America 1611–1976* (published 1982); and Independent Television for permission to quote from London Weekend Television's 1988 South Bank Show (produced and directed by Chris Hunt and edited and presented by Melvyn Bragg) about the 1988 National Theatre season of Shakespeare's late plays directed by Peter Hall. I warmly thank the photographers (credited in the List of Illustrations) and archivists who supplied photographs and granted permission for me to reproduce the photographs in this book.

I strongly appreciate the staff at Manchester University Press for expert work on the production and publication of this book. I am, in addition, especially fortunate to have Jim Bulman as my editor; for his acutely perceptive comments on individual chapters as well as on my full typescript at varying stages, and for his astute and extremely valuable editorial guidance, I am deeply grateful. There are two more persons whose highly skilled and immensely sustaining support helped me to complete this book. I am unendingly thankful to Molly Edgar, who brought years of keenly perceptive study of literature and a specific interest in *The Winter's Tale* to her spirited dedication to this book project together with her exceptional clarity, wit, computer savvy, and legendary problem-solving abilities. She meticulously checked myriad aspects of typescript style and formatting; she also did detailed document preparation and indexing, getting at least twice as much superb quality work done at any working session as I thought possible. Linda Houghton Madsen, with immeasurable generosity, drawing on her years of experience in editing and publishing, gave careful and imaginatively engaged comments on multiple drafts and also undertook the lengthy and challenging work of obtaining permissions clearance involving text and archival material, interviews, and photographs. For her compassionate accompaniment and encouragement throughout the entire process of completing this book I have profound and enduring gratitude.

NOTE ON THE TEXT

All quotations from the text of *The Winter's Tale*, unless otherwise noted or within a direct quotation from another author, are from the edition of *The Winter's Tale* edited by Stephen Orgel (Oxford: Oxford University Press, 1996). When references to this edition are from its Introduction, its footnotes, or its Appendix A, B, or C, the brief form of reference is to Orgel, ed., followed by the page number.

All quotations from the First Folio of *The Winter's Tale* are from *The Norton Facsimile: The First Folio of Shakespeare*, 2nd ed., based on Folios in the Folger Shakespeare Library Collection, prepared by Charlton Hinman, with a new introduction by Peter W. M. Blayney, New York: Norton, 1996.

All quotations from the texts of Shakespeare's plays except *The Winter's Tale*, unless otherwise noted or within a direct quotation from another author, are from *The Norton Shakespeare*, 2nd ed., based on the Oxford Edition, General Editor, Stephen Greenblatt (New York and London: Norton, 2008).

Every effort has been made to obtain permission to reproduce the illustrations in this book and to secure any required permission to cite from sources. If any proper acknowledgement has not been made, copyright-holders are invited to contact the publisher.

INTRODUCTION

'This wide gap of time': Theatrical issues and performance history

A 'very great play': Marjorie Garber's estimation in 2004 of *The Winter's Tale* (828) testifies to the play's major revaluation in the wide gap of time since Dryden's charge, in 1672, that like *Love's Labour's Lost* and *Measure for Measure*, the play was 'either grounded on impossibilities, or at least, so meanly written, that the Comedy neither caus'd your mirth, nor the serious part your concernment'.[1] Many contemporary critics and theatre artists would agree with Garber. Though in each age, as Stephen Orgel points out, *The Winter's Tale* has had both supporters and detractors (Orgel, ed., 1), during the second half of the twentieth century the proportion of critics who held the play in high esteem significantly increased.[2] Earlier critics had stimulated the reassessment. As Maurice Hunt notes, in the later 1930s it began to be argued that by the time of *The Winter's Tale* (1610–11) 'Shakespeare gathers in and recapitulates the experience of his own great tragedies in order to move beyond them' to renewal ('*The Winter's Tale': Critical Essays*, 20). Subsequent critics have demonstrated that in *The Winter's Tale* Shakespeare also drew transformatively on his earlier work in the comedies as well as on romance traditions and the emergent genre of tragicomedy.[3] By 1969, Ernst Schanzer judged that recent criticism was 'yielding to a juster appreciation of the play's greatness. Its construction is coming to be seen not as clumsy and artless but as entirely purposeful and carefully planned, the proper vehicle for the play's significances' (45). Such a shift in critical judgement has been part of a growing reappraisal of the late plays; Charles Frey demonstrated in his 1980 analysis of views of *The Winter's Tale* that in the previous few decades 'no group of Shakespeare's plays' had 'increased more in public and scholarly esteem' (1).

[1]

Revaluation of *The Winter's Tale* has been happening not only in scholarship and criticism; it has also been happening in the play's recent performance history. Significant productions have shown, as R. P. Draper puts it, 'what most of all needed to be demonstrated – its essential stageworthiness, while also demanding that it be taken seriously' (75). Rediscovery of the play's theatrical strengths was made possible in part by the movement in twentieth-century Shakespearean production away from illusionist theatrical production styles, which in various forms had dominated the English stage from the time of Dryden, becoming increasingly elaborate through most of the nineteenth century. Such complicated scenography did not well accommodate the conventions of Shakespearean drama. This study therefore begins with a defining moment: the production of *The Winter's Tale* by Harley Granville Barker, whose Shakespeare season at the Savoy Theatre in 1912 was the most important early twentieth-century expression in British Shakespeare production of the break from illusionism. As Dennis Kennedy writes of Barker's achievement,

> *The Winter's Tale* offered a chance to show the power of taking an unbroken text swiftly, to show the value of open staging, and to concentrate on Shakespeare's own method of characterization. Perhaps for the first time since the closing of the theatres [1642], Shakespeare was presented on a commercial London stage in a manner designed to exhibit his craftsmanship as a dramatist. (*Granville Barker*, 124)

Barker's production opened up a space for revaluation of *The Winter's Tale*. Though its reception involved some negative criticism which, as Kennedy puts it, was often 'hostility to the play', he concludes: 'Most spectators, sometimes despite themselves, felt excited by the vitality and strength of *Winter's Tale*' (*Granville Barker*, 123, 135–6).

'No play of Shakespeare's boasts three such women' as Hermione, Paulina, and Perdita, wrote Granville Barker in his acting edition of the play; his statement marks an early stage in yet another important reason for ongoing reassessment of *The Winter's Tale*: rethinking of the women's roles (repr. *More Prefaces*, 23). Lillah McCarthy, Hermione in the 1912 production, had an acting style which resisted the previous era's Victorian norms for women's behaviour. Barker repudiated sentimental prettiness and recitation of set speeches in directing Perdita, and the role of Paulina gained in long overdue respect. Such reassessment arises from the cultural matrix in which both criticism and theatrical production not only participate but are shaping forces. Barker and McCarthy – who were married to each other from 1906 until 1917 – were aligned with progressive voices in the debate over questions emphasized by the 'new woman' movement[4] and integral to the 'new drama' being written and produced by both Barker and George Bernard Shaw. The 'woman question', as it was called, was spurred on by the 1889 London production of Ibsen's *A Doll's House*. Emerging ever more strongly in the 1890s, questions involving gender challenged foundational 'institutions, assumptions and beliefs, particularly those centring on sexuality, marriage, and family life' (Caine, 134). Such questioning, more far-reaching than that typical of mid-Victorian feminism, shaped the conflicts in Barker's *The Marrying of Ann Leete* (written in 1899, first produced 1902); 'you want a new world ... you new woman', says Ann's brother (Kennedy, *Granville Barker*, 12). In Shaw's *Man and Superman* (1905) McCarthy played the leading role of Ann Whitefield, about whom she later wrote: 'She was a "new woman" and she made a new woman of me.'

> The men – the conventional men who had made women after their own imagining and according to their predilections – disapproved of Ann: unladylike! She was insistent when she should have been submissive. What is to become of the home? She had a will of her own instead of one of theirs ... Mrs. Pankhurst, who Heaven knows never lacked resolution, herself told me that Ann Whitefield had strengthened her purpose and fortified her courage. (McCarthy, 63–4)

McCarthy later recalled that her work as Ann Whitefield would have turned her into a suffragette if she had not already been one (148).[5]

Advocacy for women's right to vote intensified with the formation of the Women's Social and Political Union (WSPU) in 1903, led by the Pankhurst family; and it continued to build in campaigns from 1905 to the time of the First World War, with suffrage for women over the age of thirty finally granted in Britain in 1917. In 1907, Barker, with McCarthy in the leading role, directed *Votes for Women!* written by the American actress Elizabeth Robins, who in 1891 had played the title role in the

Independent Theatre production of *Hedda Gabler* (Beckson, 165–6) and was on the board of the WSPU (Kennedy, *Granville Barker*, 58). The role of suffragette was one with which Lillah McCarthy strongly identified: 'I had walked in processions. I had carried banners for Mrs. Pankhurst and the Cause' (McCarthy, 148). The suffrage campaign in Britain was at its height in 1912–13, coinciding with Barker's production of *The Winter's Tale* (McDonald, *'New Drama'*, 4). On the day Barker's production of *The Winter's Tale* opened (21 September 1912), suffragists protested during a speech by Lloyd George (*Westminster Gazette*, 23 September 1912, 8). The WSPU had denounced the force-feeding of suffragettes (Mrs Leigh and Miss Evans) in prison earlier in the month (*Westminster Gazette*, 5 September 1912, 5). The day after *The Winter's Tale* opened, it was reported that Mrs and Miss Pankhurst were threatened with expulsion by French Police should they demonstrate when Prime Minister Asquith was passing through Paris (*Observer*, 22 September 1912). 'If there were ... a female suffrage agitation in Sicilia', one reviewer quipped, 'Paulina was certainly its prime mover'. He went on to ask: 'Is Mr. Barker (by choosing this play) seeking to rope in Shakespeare on the side of the Suffrage angels?' (*Referee*, 22 September 1912, 3).

Revaluation of Paulina's role has continued, with outstanding women actors contributing to a growing understanding of its importance. Refusing stereotypes of termagant or shrew, some of the actors studied in this book have, in differing ways, shown Paulina's wit, rhetorical power, and moral courage: Flora Robson (Phoenix Theatre, 1951), Elizabeth Spriggs in 1970–71 and Brenda Bruce in 1969 (Royal Shakespeare Company (RSC), 1969–71), and Eileen Atkins (National Theatre, 1988). Spriggs particularly highlighted Paulina's becoming Leontes' spiritual guide; Atkins in addition detailed Paulina's simultaneous role as the King's political counsellor. Paulina's prominence in the play has also been firmly established by a wide range of other distinguished performances, including ones by Peggy Ashcroft (Shakespeare Memorial Theatre, 1960), Barbara Leigh-Hunt (RSC, 1976), Sheila Hancock (RSC, 1981), Susan Wright (Stratford, Ontario, Canada, 1986), Tamu Gray (Oregon Shakespeare Festival, 1996), and Estelle Kohler (RSC, 1999).

The dynamism in performance that comes from rethinking the principal women's roles makes vividly clear that in the play's multiple turning points, particularly in the trial and statue scenes, the actions of Hermione and Paulina provide the crucial counterforce to Leontes. Each woman articulates a powerful critique of his violent injustice; each goes on to offer, in differing ways, thoroughly unsentimental compassion once Leontes' full acknowledgement of his destructiveness is clear. In criticism, as in theatrical production, there is a tendency for focus to be so strongly placed on Leontes' psychological journey that the women's parts, and the play's social and political dimensions, are not given their full weight. The British director Sara Pia Anderson emphasized, in talking with the cast of the production she guest directed in 1990 for Shakespeare/Santa Cruz, that the play does not revolve only around Leontes. It is not one person's story, she said; it explores the dynamics in families and in how we act in communities.[6] Hermione and Paulina, faced with Leontes' tyrannical abuse of power, strongly contest it and, in solidarity, resist it. Resistance is played out on a smaller but significant scale in the sub-plot when Perdita, having encountered Polixenes' patriarchal rage, protests: 'I was not much afeared, for once or twice / I was about to speak and tell him plainly / The selfsame sun that shines upon his court / Hides not his visage from our cottage, but / Looks on alike' (IV.iv.439–43). Resilient, she acts in opposition to his rage, claiming agency in actions which help bring about her own marriage. The women's choices are critical to the spiritual regeneration not only of Leontes but of themselves and of their kingdoms.

Feminist criticism, particularly from the 1970s onward, has responded to the potential of the *Winter's Tale* text to raise questions involving gender relations and power imbalances, and to scenes opening up space for women's voice and agency: Hermione's brilliant rhetoric, defending herself at trial (III.ii); Paulina's courage in speaking truth to power when she confronts Leontes and his courtiers, bringing Hermione's baby from prison to him and defending the Queen against charges of adultery (II.iii); her even more forceful daring to name Leontes 'tyrant' (III.ii.173) toward the end of the trial scene – the very charge he had hoped to clear by staging the trial. Paulina in V.i is given the role both of spiritual and political counsellor – a woman's role which may be without precedent in early modern English drama (see Asp, 145). She wins from Leontes, over the objections of his courtiers, the 'office / To choose you a queen' (V.i.77–8) – a power normally reserved for patriarchal control over royal succession. Hermione, speaking to Perdita toward the end of the statue scene, voices her agency: 'For thou shalt hear that I, / Knowing by Paulina that the oracle / Gave hope thou wast in being, have preserved / Myself to see the issue' (V.iii.125–8). Given such crucial scenes, by the end of the dramatic action, gender and power relations – though still working within patriarchal structures – have been significantly renegotiated. Critical debate continues to probe to what extent the play suggests that its patriarchal world has been reformed. Janet Adelman (*Suffocating Mothers*) and Carol Neely (*Broken Nuptials in Shakespeare's Plays*) see in the play a significantly greater degree of reform than do Valerie Traub (*Desire and Anxiety*) and Peter Erickson (*Patriarchal Structures in Shakespeare's Drama*).[7]

The Winter's Tale puts under a critical lens the potentially tragic consequences for women, family, and the state of patriarchal efforts to control women's bodies and speech. That such early modern cultural anxieties are deeply embedded in social structures may help explain the suddenness with which Leontes' jealousy can erupt, and certainly its ever-more-violent growth over the course of three acts. Related male attempts to regulate midwifery and childbirthing practices also drive Leontes' behaviour in the sequence of scenes from II.i through the trial, beginning with his violent disruption of the community of women gathered around Hermione, who 'rounds apace' (II.i.16). Sara Pia Anderson, when directing the 1990 Shakespeare/Santa Cruz production, said she was keenly aware of the contrast between the 'very female world' at the beginning of Act II, scene i and the world of Leontes and his Lords. She staged the women's space on the opposite side of the circular playing area from which (stage right) the men – Leontes, Antigonus, and Lords – broke into the vital community of the women and Mamillius. The quiet intimacy of Mamillius telling his winter's tale in Hermione's ear is disrupted by the harsh tones of Leontes' demands and accusations: 'Give me the boy. I am glad you did not nurse him. / Though he does bear some signs of me, yet you / Have too much blood in him' (II.i.56–8). Contemporary scholarship locates this scene in male anxieties about the impossibility, in the early modern period, of proving biological paternity, and in related cultural debates about increasing patriarchal attempts to control practices of birth and lactation (Paster, 164).

Hermione refuses to be silent in the face of Leontes' accusation of adultery, claiming voice in her own defence far more than does either Hero or Desdemona in comparable scenes of public shaming (*Much Ado About Nothing*, IV.i, and *Othello*, IV.i, respectively). When Leontes delivers his charge, 'for 'tis Polixenes / Has made thee swell thus' (II.i.61–2), Hermione immediately contradicts it: 'But I'd say he had not' (62). When Leontes escalates the charges – 'She's an adultress ... / More, she's a traitor' – followed by the harsh coinage, 'bed-swerver' (II.i.88–9, 93; see Orgel, ed., p. 123, n. 93), Hermione counters with even more force: 'No, by my life, / Privy to none of this' (95–6). That the personal is the political, in Adrienne Rich's famous phrase, is evident in *The Winter's Tale* in a double sense. Leontes' tyrannical domestic behaviour becomes far more dangerous when allied to his tyrannical behaviour as King – a point underscored to me in an interview with Tim Pigott-Smith, who played Leontes in Peter Hall's 1988 production (National Theatre). Leontes acts unilaterally on his politicized personal definition of Hermione as a 'traitor' (II.i.89), arresting her as a political prisoner. When Hermione requests that 'My women may be with me, for you see / My plight requires it' (II.i.117–18), she implies her right to female birth attendants, as was the norm in England for women in the early modern period. That her women's community is now so brutally contained, her birthing chamber a prison, is an indictment of Leontes' violation of birthing rituals and locates the play on the progressive side of a cultural debate which could well have been familiar to Shakespeare's audiences.

Cultural contestation becomes, increasingly, sharply gendered in II.iii. Hurling misogynist epithets at Paulina, Leontes particularly uses those which attack Paulina's power of speech, calling her 'Dame Partlet' (75), and threatening Antigonus for his refusal to 'stay her tongue' (109), that tongue of the prattler, 'Lady Margery, your midwife there' (159). The term 'midwife', and its relation to the term 'gossip', is illuminated by Caroline Bicks's examination of the cultural contestation in early modern England over midwifery and childbirth practices (see her 'Midwiving Virility in Early Modern England' and *Midwiving Subjects in Shakespeare's England*). Paulina tells Leontes she has come 'About some gossips for your highness' (II.iii.41), using the word 'gossips' in its early, spiritual sense, implying that Leontes should designate godparents for the baptism of his baby. But the word 'gossip', Bicks explains, 'came to mean both a female birth attendant and a female tattler' ('Midwiving Virility', 50), and it is this latter sense, especially, which Leontes seizes upon. By the mid-sixteenth century in England, licensing of midwives involved an oath which makes clear, as Bicks puts it, 'that paternity was fashioned by the words of two women: the mother and the midwife' ('Midwiving Virility', 52). Since women's speech thereby had power to name patriarchal lineage, it aroused acute male anxiety. 'Paulina was not present at Perdita's birth', as Bicks points out, but 'her narrative contradicts the King's tale of an adulteress wife and a bastard daughter' ('Midwiving Virility', 52). Leontes, conflating the term 'midwife' with the misogynist idea of the tattler, attempts to discredit Paulina's testimony as to his baby's paternity. At trial, the oracle discredits Leontes' accusations.

At trial, furthermore, Hermione names the 'immodest hatred' with which Leontes has denied her the 'childbed privilege' (III.ii.100–1). Gail Paster cites a relevant passage from William Gouge's *Domesticall Duties* (dated 1622, but reflective of attitudes also in earlier circulation): 'To lay this [accusation of infidelity] to a wives charge unjustly, is at any time a most shamefull and odious reproach: but in the time of childbirth whether just or unjust, a thing too too spiightfull and revengeful' (quoted in Paster, 272).

It is 'precisely the nature of Leontes' tyranny', Paster argues, 'to insist upon his power over the customary forms of female agency and management in birth, to effect his personal will even against local privilege – here metonymized by the privilege of childbed from which he hales Hermione for her trial' (271). Remarkably, Hermione's speech has such cogent power that she is able to prevent Leontes' public shaming from defining her. Through her own voice she claims agency, in part changing the place of her circumscribed suffering into a space both for political critique and for self-definition.

Keen awareness of the costs to Hermione and Paulina of patriarchal power may be among the factors leading to a tendency in theatrical production, especially since the later 1980s, toward darkened endings which emphasize remembrance of loss. Other factors may include a contemporary post-Freudian awareness, as Gary Waller points out, that 'the family is by no means idealized in the late plays. While many critics used to see the family as a symbol of stability in the comedies and romances, it can also be seen as yet another site of instability, a place where there is contestation between generations ... and where harmonies are tentative' (62). Waller's point is relevant to the National Theatre production in 1988, directed by Peter Hall; of the major British productions analysed in this volume, it offered the darkest, most problematized ending. Ingmar Bergman's Swedish production, in 1994, presented an enigmatic ending that was even darker and more tentative. By no means, however, are darkened endings the only option for those engaged in questions of gender and power, or for twentieth- and twenty-first-century performance of *The Winter's Tale*. When joy is presented at its most profound, as in Audrey Stanley's 1975 Oregon Shakespearean Festival production, it does not exclude remembered sorrow. Such joy is firmly grounded in the scene's complex tones; it offers, to use Tolkein's phrase, 'joy poignant as grief' (68).

Mingled tragicomic tones offer a wide range of performance possibilities not only for the play's ending but also for other of its most challenging theatrical sequences. To judge from its reception in criticism and its performance history, the play poses problems for theatrical interpreters that give rise to the following questions: How might performers work with the complex interactions in the early part of Act I, scene ii to make convincing the swift inception of Leontes' jealousy and, toward the end of the trial scene (III.ii), his sudden beginnings of repentance? Following that major turning point, in what ways might the series of transitional sequences – the famous First Folio (1623) stage direction for Antigonus, '*Exit pursued by a Beare*', and Time as Chorus – be effectively produced? How might directors and performers keep alive the varied styles, energies, and myriad shifts of action in the very long pastoral sequence in Bohemia (IV.iv), including its final complications, role-playing, and costume changes? How might an actor work with the challenge of presenting Hermione like a statue (V.iii)? What might be not only the visual design but also the placement onstage affecting focus on both the statue and those responding to it? How might directors and actors orchestrate the statue scene's dynamics and its series of discoveries while modulating its complex tones of joy and of sorrow?

Involving both practical stagecraft and matters of interpretation, decisions about how to meet each of these theatrical challenges involve experimenting with their dramatic functions and exploring the meanings which emerge in rehearsal and performance. Evidence from twentieth-century performances suggests that not only can these challenges be effectively met in the theatre, but they can be met in a strikingly wide range of ways. These myriad performance possibilities arise in part from what Raymond Williams called the 'relatively open form' of Shakespearean drama, 'multivocal' and 'interactive' ('Afterword', in Dollimore and Sinfield, eds, 237). Furthermore, as Terry Eagleton has argued, performances cannot fully or 'mechanically' be 'extrapolated' from readings of a play's editions, but result from the specific labours involved in particular theatrical productions (65). An important qualification to Eagleton's statement has been made by W. B. Worthen: 'It is not the case that *no* relationship can be "extrapolated", only that all the relationships between texts and performances are contingent, a function of the intervening practices of production, practices which transform the text into a new representation of the work' (*Shakespeare and the Authority of Performance*, 21). *The Winter's Tale*, first produced in 1610–11 in particular political and theatrical conditions of the early seventeenth century, has an ever-changing 'after life' (Jonathan Miller's term; *Subsequent Performances*) that is embedded in cultural history and must be understood as intertwined with its multiple reproductions in texts from the First Folio of 1623 onward and in the theatre.

Theatrical issues and the question of genre

Each of the play's challenges with which theatrical interpreters must engage involves the play's dramatic conventions and thus its genre and tragicomic mingling of tones. The First Folio's inclusion of *The Winter's Tale* among the comedies is intelligible in terms the Renaissance inherited from antiquity: *prima turbulenta, tranquilla ultima* (at first turbulent, in the end tranquil) was Donatus' formulation of Terence's dictum about classical comic form (Cunningham, 164, 259). But the action of *The Winter's Tale* is far more complex, its generic boundaries more fluid, than such a formula can indicate. Precisely when 'turbulence' begins, for example, is debatable: most interpreters see none in the play's first scene, and many, like Schanzer (introd. Penguin ed., 22), see 'tranquillity' continue in the second scene until Leontes speaks 'Too hot, too hot!' (I.ii.107). (That phrase is followed by a colon in the First Folio, whereas Orgel uses an exclamation mark; differences in punctuation can affect interpretation.) Furthermore, is the play's ending tranquil? Much turbulence has been overcome, but the concluding multiple reunions also contain past and present pain.

Renaissance conceptions of genre, 'inclusive' rather than 'exclusive', differ both from Donatus' formulation and from many recent ones. As Stephen Orgel has argued, a 'mixture of genres' was 'an essential element of the theatrical experience for Shakespeare's audience, and by the time *The Winter's Tale* was written tragicomedy had been established through an extensive critical debate as a dramatic genre of unquestionable seriousness' (Orgel, ed., 3–4). In *The Winter's Tale*, furthermore, Shakespeare pushed the boundaries even of this emerging genre, if we compare it to John Fletcher's simple definition of tragicomedy in his preface to his play *The Faithful Shepherdess* (1608): it 'wants [lacks] deaths, which is enough to make it no tragedy, yet brings some near it, which is enough to make it no comedy' (quoted in McDonald, *Bedford Companion*, 178). Such a formula fails to account for the action of *The Winter's Tale*, in which some deaths are averted, but two deaths, those of Mamillius and Antigonus, are final.

Orgel points out how problematic for Shakespeare's last plays is the term 'romance', with its nineteenth-century connotations. Dowden, though not the first to apply the term to the plays (Coleridge earlier called *The Tempest* a romance), gave the category wide currency beginning in the 1870s and, with it, his idea of the plays' supposed 'sweet serenity' (quoted in Orgel, ed., *The Winter's Tale*, 2–3). Stanley Wells cautions that the term 'romance' was never used in Shakespeare's day about a play ('Shakespeare and Romance', 49); Stephen Orgel goes further and warns of the term's 'ultimate inadequacy as a critical category for Shakespearian drama' (Orgel, ed., 3). These are important caveats and may help critics shift from a broad classification to emphasis on how deeply Shakespeare changes what he uses of the conventions of Hellenistic romance. Deriving in part from the *Odyssey* and plays like Euripides' *Alcestis*, these conventions were largely transmitted through Renaissance English adaptations of them in pastorals, epics, and 'novels' like Robert Greene's *Pandosto*, Shakespeare's primary source for *The Winter's Tale*. In the play, Shakespeare transforms such conventions in order to explore political, moral, and philosophical problems, as did his predecessors – e.g., Sidney, in the *Arcadia* (1590, augmented 1593), and Spenser, in *The Faerie Queene* (1590, Bks I–III; 1596, Bks I–VI (I–III revised)).[8]

Since Hellenistic and Renaissance uses of romance stories involve tragicomic events and tones, as do Renaissance pastorals, the conventions of their genres are interrelated. Barbara Mowat, in *The Dramaturgy of Shakespeare's Romances*, recognizes the connection between tragicomedy and romance; she states that *The Winter's Tale* enacts a distinctive 'variety of tragicomedy' and that 'in the Romances, Shakespeare blends tragic and comic views' (27, 93). Joan Hartwig, in *Shakespeare's Tragicomic Vision*, prefers the term tragicomedy, since it is at least a Renaissance term, one given for a genre of drama whose emergence in England was stimulated by the translation (anonymous) in 1602 of Guarini's 1590 *Il Pastor Fido*. Guarini's play, which 'established tragicomedy as a serious genre in the Renaissance', as Orgel points out, 'was itself a pastoral', and 'for most of the dramatists of Shakespeare's age, pastoral was the mode in which tragedy and comedy became inseparable' (Orgel, ed., 37).

Dramatic conventions are linked to a play's mode; as its title suggests, *The Winter's Tale* deliberately presents itself, at moments, as an improbable fiction. When the oracle is fulfilled and the lost daughter found, a gentleman asked to relate the news says 'such a deal of wonder is broken out within this hour that ballad-makers cannot be able to express it', adding it is 'so like an old tale that the verity of it is in strong suspicion' (V.ii.23–5, 28–9; cf. 60). Peele refers to 'a merry winters tale' and 'an old wives winters tale' to 'drive away the time', in his *Old Wives Tale* (quoted in Pafford, liii, n. 3). Shakespeare plays ironically with the notion that so-called old wives' tales, winter's tales, could be derided as groundless; Lady Macbeth scorns Macbeth's fears of Banquo's ghost as if they were passions that 'would well become / A woman's story at a winter's fire' (*Macbeth*, III.iv.63–4). The story proves true. Differently, so does the tale Mamillius proposes to tell: 'A sad tale's best for winter; I have one / Of sprites and goblins.' 'There was a man –' he begins, 'Dwelt by a churchyard –' (II.i.25–30). His tale 'mirrors that of the play', as Schanzer comments; by the end of Act III, 'Leontes has become the man who dwelt by a churchyard, and even of the sprites and goblins we have had a glimpse in the vision of Antigonus' (III.iii.15–36; Schanzer, 8–9).

Shakespeare's strategic evocation of the idea of a tale is at once witty and serious, and can disarm disbelief. As Hermione embraces Leontes in the final scene, Paulina says, 'That she is living, / Were it but told you, should be hooted at / Like an old tale' (V.iii.115–17). When that which needs to be dramatized is beyond naturalistic probability, *The Winter's Tale* reminds us that stories can point beyond themselves. Strategies later theoreticians call metatheatrical bring to the foreground a spectator's awareness of being in a theatre, with all its artifice. Double awareness can both create aesthetic distance and draw hearers closer to an imaginative grasp of what is beyond literal representation. When Hermione's fidelity, not subject to ocular proof, is on trial, she refers to the impossibility of showing her inner truth and her grief in a fiction (including the present dramatic action) because they are 'more / Than history can pattern, though devised / And played to take spectators' (III.ii.34–6). As Hermione's lines suggest, *The Winter's Tale* tells of suffering, a winter of the heart and of the kingdom. To probe just such a tale, though, the play's mixture of tones and genres skilfully avoids the melodramatic effects that ensue if tragicomedy and romance story, with their sudden changes, are crudely handled. Shakespeare's use of his narrative source material involves the additional challenge of transforming not only its quality but also its medium; in the theatre, narrative structures must become dramatic.

In *The Winter's Tale*, Shakespeare uses theatrical artifice – sudden jealousy and repentance, the bear, Time as Chorus, the statue – not for its own sake, but because it is intrinsic to the play's complex ideas and dramaturgical strategies. Such dramaturgy makes possible rapid juxtapositions, mingled tones, evocations of wonder, and variations in aesthetic distance. Its overt theatricality and deliberate grotesquerie (as in the bear's pursuit of Antigonus and the Young Shepherd's account of it) at times usefully prevent audiences from full tragic involvement. But in a number of important instances, particularly in the statue scene, heightened theatricality increases a scene's emotional power, as Roger Warren persuasively argues in *Staging Shakespeare's Late Plays* (6).

Theatrical issues, political contexts, and Shakespeare's transformation of his major source

Many of *The Winter's Tale*'s most challenging features with which theatrical interpreters must engage – the suddenness of Leontes' jealousy, the bear, the Chorus of Time, the statue scene – are not to be found in the play's major source, Robert Greene's apparently popular prose narrative, *Pandosto*. Published first in 1588, it had been printed in five editions prior to the first documented performance of *The Winter's Tale* approximately twenty-three years later (cf. Orgel, ed., 234). 'The Triumph of Time', Greene's subtitle, and his title page motto – '*Temporis filia veritas*' (Truth, daughter of Time) – remain in Greene's narrative mere maxims whose relation to his story is undeveloped. Shakespeare, however, transformed those themes in *The Winter's Tale* as part of a complex, dynamic action in which time, cyclical as well as linear, is embedded in human generative, destructive, and regenerative powers. Time's 'joy and terror' (IV.i.1) are central to the play's dramaturgy; the Chorus makes a strategic apologia for the play's dramatic art, which involves changes and combinations of tragic and comic perspectives. Arguably, the play's mixed genres have their analogue in *Pandosto*, but, in Greene's handling, the mix is exceedingly crude: 'to close up the comedy with a tragical stratagem – he [Pandosto] slew himself' (*Pandosto*, 1595 ed., repr. Orgel, ed., 274). Leontes' extreme sorrow, in contrast, yields to possibilities of renewal, though remembrance of tragic loss tempers comic potentiality. Correspondingly, it is striking that Greene has no equivalent of the statue scene; when Queen Bellaria hears of her son's death, she dies and is not restored.

Shakespeare's relation to his sources is often most revealing where he most differs from them. Greene supplies plausible (though mistaken) motivation for Pandosto's jealousy: his wife Bellaria entertains his friend Egistus 'so familiarly that her countenance bewrayed [*sic*] how her mind was affected towards him, oftentimes coming herself into his bedchamber to see that nothing should be amiss to mislike him'. Between wife and friend grew 'such a secret uniting of their affections that the one could not well be without the company of the other'. Their 'custom' of walking in the garden, 'where they two in private and pleasant devices would pass away the time' explains why 'a certain melancholy passion entering the mind of Pandosto drave him into sundry and doubtful thoughts'. The doubt grows over a long time: 'These and suchlike doubtful thoughts a long time smothering in his stomach began at last to kindle in his mind a secret mistrust which, increased by suspicion, grew at last to a flaming jealousy that so tormented him as he could take no rest' (repr. Orgel, ed., 236).

Pandosto's jealousy is not only rationalized, it is also far less politically dangerous than that of Leontes. Greene makes only a few brief connections between the irrational passion of a king and the danger that he will become a tyrant (Orgel, ed., 238, 270). In *The Winter's Tale*, however, Leontes' tyranny is brought to the foreground, evoking Jacobean political conflicts over James I's attempts to revive monarchical absolutism (see Orgel, ed., 12–15). When his lords try to dissuade him from sending Hermione to prison – as Antigonus says, 'lest your justice / Prove violence' (II.i.127–8) – Leontes retorts: 'Why, what need we / Commune with you of this, but rather follow / Our forceful instigation?' In the next statement he insists, as did James I, on the King's right to unilateral decision making: 'Our prerogative / Calls not your counsels, but our natural goodness / Imparts this' (II.i.161–5). This politically charged moment connects the play to early Jacobean cultural struggles over monarchical absolutism, with Leontes taking James I's point of view (cf. Orgel, ed., p. 127, n. 163–5). Orgel has argued that Leontes' assertions 'that he is not accountable to his advisers, and his lords' and Paulina's equally tenacious questions and protestations, are informed by a debate that persisted throughout James's reign. It is to the point that Leontes is, in the dramatic contest, ultimately the loser' (Orgel, ed., 14). Leontes seeks for divine 'confirmation' (II.i.180), perhaps to mystify his authority and to quell criticism: to 'Give rest to th' minds of others' (191). Whereas Greene's oracle pronounces 'Pandosto treacherous' (repr. Orgel, ed., 246), Shakespeare's oracle specifically names 'Leontes a jealous tyrant' (III.ii.131).

By inventing the characters of Paulina, especially, and her husband Antigonus, Shakespeare greatly sharpens focus on political and moral dilemmas raised by Leontes' tyranny. Antigonus, charged with being a traitor unless he obeys the King's order to leave the newborn baby to chance in a remote place, swears obedience on Leontes' sword of state. Acting as an instrument of Leontes' tyrannical will, Antigonus, when he abandons Perdita, is destroyed in the process. Paulina opposes Leontes more consistently and courageously than do her husband and the other lords, whom she confronts: 'Fear you his tyrannous passion more, alas, / Than the Queen's life?' (II.iii.28-9). When she dares to tell Leontes that his cruel treatment of Hermione 'something savours / Of tyranny' (II.iii.118-19), she comes near to levelling the charge monarchs had long sought to avoid or suppress. Leontes indeed calls Hermione's trial in part to 'be cleared / Of being tyrannous' (III.ii.4-5). Since his actions go on to confirm his tyrannical behaviour, however, Paulina voices her accusation forcefully towards the end of the trial scene, three times: 'tyrant' (173); 'Thy tyranny' (177); 'O thou tyrant' (205).

These political conflicts involve not only kingship but gender. When Leontes attempts to silence Paulina's forceful speech, his accusations against her are loaded with misogynist rhetoric: 'A mankind witch!'; 'A callet / Of boundless tongue, who late hath beat her husband / And now baits me!' (II.iii.67, 90-2). Leontes berates Antigonus with failing to rule his wife (46, 74-5, 79, 108-9) and threatens to have Paulina 'burnt' (113). Greene has no equivalent of this scene, nor of Paulina's role when Leontes begins to take her as his counsellor at the end of the trial scene. Especially revealing of the play's concerns involving gender and power, as well as its historical context, is the first part of Act V, scene i, which is entirely without a parallel in Greene's story. In it, Paulina's tough counsel is political as well as spiritual. Though not given an official title, Paulina becomes Leontes' chief counsellor, and Leontes, over opposition from his lords, gives her the power to 'choose' him 'a queen' (V.i.77-8). Anxieties over royal succession during Elizabeth's reign had not been forgotten; they echoed in the lords' concern over Leontes' 'fail of issue' (V.i.27). That Paulina is given control over this central concern of patriarchy, the very issue of 'issue' – the birth of heirs – could have struck many in the Jacobean audience with a force hard for current audiences to imagine. And at a stroke this concern over patriarchal succession connects the first scene of the fifth act to the first three acts, for Leontes' sexual jealousy has been an obsession with legitimacy as well as with possession and control of the female erotic body. His violence against Hermione, and against a 'brat' he fears is 'the issue of Polixenes' (II.iii.92-3), is fuelled by specific patriarchal anxieties, with their cultural roots.

Events in James I's reign, moreover, would have given *The Winter's Tale* 'an eerie topicality', Orgel suggests, by the time of its revival by the King's Men for a court performance in late 1612 or 1613 to celebrate the forthcoming wedding of James I's daughter Princess Elizabeth to Prince Frederick the Elector Palatine (Orgel, ed., 16). The topic of royal marriages had circulated throughout the decade (since James I's accession in 1603), with negotiations for the marriages both of Princess Elizabeth and of James I's son, Prince Henry. The sudden death of the young Prince (November 1612) could have been recalled in the death of Mamillius, who was also thought 'of the greatest promise' (I.i.33–4) for the kingdom's future. Also alive in historical memory was the trial (1536) of Elizabeth's mother, Anne Boleyn, on Henry VIII's false charges of adultery; that trial may have had its disturbing resonances in Leontes' accusations and trial of Hermione. Furthermore, suspicions of illegitimacy, involving accusations of bastardy, had plagued Elizabeth I's reign, as they did the infant Perdita: six times in II.iii Leontes refers to the infant as 'bastard' (75, 139, 154, 160 twice, 174). Moreover, charges of bastardy were also raised against King James (see Orgel, ed., 29). The issue of Perdita's legitimacy thus had its immediate Jacobean correlates, which in turn echoed centuries of dispute about legitimate heirs to the English throne.[9]

Far from merely thrusting onstage 'some ridiculous, incoherent story' (Dryden, 206), Shakespeare changes Greene's story to create a play with effective dramaturgical strategies and resonance in its social and political contexts. Shakespeare makes Leontes' jealousy more irrational and more of a political threat than was Pandosto's. He invents the symbolic episode of the bear when he could easily have adopted Greene's tactic of simply having the baby's boat wash ashore. For serious thematic purposes and as a defence of his dramaturgy, Shakespeare presents audiences with 'th'argument of Time' (IV.i.29), though the Chorus is not necessary for sheer narrative plot information, which is conveyed in the next scene. And although Shakespeare's pastoral scenes are bucolic, they are also full of the darker energies of the con man Autolycus and the Dionysiac satyrs (characters who have no significant parallel in *Pandosto*).[10] Most striking of all, with no antecedent in Greene's tale, Shakespeare creates the statue scene.

The wonder the statue arouses in its spectators was held by Renaissance theorists to be an aesthetic effect of tragicomedy. As Shakespeare creates the scene, such an aesthetic is connected to the play's spiritual perspectives, to the importance it gives to its women characters, and to its partial – though crucial – reform of relations concerning gender and power. The statue would not move if the King had not repented of his abuses of power and if his female counsellor had not courageously acted to oppose yet also to guide him, helping to shape his, and the kingdom's, possible future. Nor would the statue move if a woman had not chosen to do so. Hermione gains newness of life from the daughter she 'preserved' herself to see (V.iii.127–8); so does the realm, whose lineage depends, now, upon a female heir to the throne, Perdita. Her brother lost for ever, it is she who now 'makes old hearts fresh' (I.i.37). Unlike *Pandosto*, the 'tale' grounds its improbabilities not in mere arbitrary turns of fortune but in specific human choices.

Early seventeenth-century performance history

The first extant printed version of *The Winter's Tale* is in the First Folio of 1623. Shakespeare was probably writing *The Winter's Tale* in late 1610 or early 1611; our sole piece of external evidence for the play's date is Simon Forman's journal, in which he records seeing the play in performance at the Globe, 15 May 1611. In Orgel's judgement, 'there is no reason to doubt that the play was new to the stage in the season when Forman saw it in 1611' (Orgel, ed., 80). Forman's is the only written account we have from a witness to the play's Globe performance, but unfortunately it provides mainly a reductive and partial plot summary, of interest particularly for his view of Autolycus: 'Remember also the rogue that came in all tattered like colt-pixie' (repr. Orgel, ed., 233). Forman apparently saw in Autolycus' disguise something of a colt-shaped folklore goblin; the *Oxford English Dictionary* defines colt-pixie as a 'mischievous sprite' and also cites Drayton: 'of purpose to deceive us'. Forman reduces the action with Autolycus to a simplistic moral: 'Beware of trusting feigned beggars or fawning fellows' (repr. Orgel, ed., 233). His comment may suggest, however, that Autolycus was in part recognizable as a type of contemporary vagabond. The character is also a creation 'from the underworld of Elizabethan cony-catching pamphlets, which inform his language as they provide sources for his trickery' (Orgel, ed., 51). Robert Greene was the author of several of the most popular of such pamphlets; Shakespeare's artistry transformed them as well as Greene's *Pandosto*. Shakespeare crafted *The Winter's Tale* with detailed working knowledge of the theatres in which it could be performed. His stagecraft accommodates rapid changes of time and place that facilitate performance of *The Winter's Tale*, with its sixteen-year 'wide gap of time' and two major locations needed to develop a double plot of two generations. The play calls upon actors to present the story in diverse modes, from the formal couplets in which the emblematic figure of Time directly addresses spectators, to the compressed, often extraordinarily complex styles of Leontes' speeches that explore his psyche and passions with intense particularity, sometimes inwardly, at other times in tortured asides to the audience, impassioned and/or witty. Actors could also on occasion play self-reflexively with the theatrical medium, as when Leontes speaks to the offstage audience: 'And many a man there is, even at this present, / Now, while I speak this, holds his wife by th'arm, / That little thinks she has been sluiced in's absence' (I.ii.190–2). Such presentational modes, in which actors can address audiences directly, are an advantage that can be strategically exploited by an actor such as Autolycus, for example: 'I see this is the time that the unjust man doth thrive ... Sure the gods do this year connive at us, and we may do anything extempore' (IV.iv.669–73).

The Winter's Tale was performed in differing theatrical spaces; its dramaturgy enables such flexibility, and, for all its command of visual presentation, the play requires no highly elaborate staging or machinery. It was performed in the public outdoor open-air amphitheatre of the Globe; it was also performed using indoor spaces like great halls, particularly in the second Blackfriars and at court, probably in the Banqueting House in the palace at Whitehall. Surviving records, though they are few (as for many Renaissance plays), suggest the relative popularity of the play in the early seventeenth century (cf. Orgel, ed., 1). There is a record of a court performance on 5 November 1611, before King James I, most likely in the Banqueting House (see Orgel, ed., 80, n. 1). Subsequent early seventeenth-century records are for performances at court in 1612–13, 1618, possibly 1619, 1623–24, and 1633–34; records note that the last of these, performed for the early

Caroline court, was 'likt' (Turner and Haas, 798–9).

In the following account of ways *The Winter's Tale* may have been staged in Shakespeare's time, the focus will be on the Globe, but possible differences between stagings at the Globe and at the Blackfriars will be selectively noted, always bearing in mind the many uncertainties in scholarly accounts of early Shakespearean staging.[11] The Blackfriars attracted a greater proportion of the moneyed classes than did the Globe, and catered to the wealthier members of its audience, placing them in seating near the stage; at the Globe, by contrast, the least affluent – 'groundlings' who stood in the yard surrounding the thrust platform stage – were closest to it. They might have had to endure physical discomfort and bad weather, but they could be what Gurr and Ichikawa call 'the most active participants in the game of playing' (*Staging*, 37). It is tempting to speculate that an actor in the role of Autolycus would have used differing tonalities, strategies, and improvisatory gambits when interacting with the audience members nearest him in each of these differing venues. Certainly he could have used the large stage posts which held up the canopy over the thrust stage at the Globe to hide from the Young Shepherd (Clown) when eavesdropping on him (e.g., IV.iii.31–48); the indoor stage at the Blackfriars had no need for similar posts, but an aside from Autolycus to the audience could suggest his eavesdropping without such physical concealment.

The 'eyeball-to-eyeball two way relation between actor and audience', as Michael Billington puts it, requires a 'presentational style of acting in which speeches and emotions are shared with the audience'; he adds that, in his experience of the reconstructed Globe, 'spectators, conditioned by illusionist theatre to sit watching plays in silence, enjoy being involved' (in Wells and Orlin, eds, *Shakespeare: An Oxford Guide*, 597). Whether seated or standing, in the Globe 'you were never more than thirty-five feet from the stage platform, and most people were much closer, but from every position you could see most of the other gazers and gapers' (Gurr and Ichikawa, 4). Audience members' vivid perception of other spectators can greatly heighten the sense of interactive participation in the performance event, while simultaneously raising the possibilities of metatheatrical awareness. In daylight at the outdoor Globe such consciousness is particularly strong. In Gurr's view, although the light was not as strong in the candlelit Blackfriars, 'at neither playhouse was there any thought of using darkness to conceal the playgoers from the players and from themselves' (*Playgoing*, 47). Furthermore, compared to the estimated size of the Globe amphitheatre, approximately 100 feet in outside diameter (Orrell, 'Designing the Globe', in Mulryne and Shewring, 57–9; cf. Gurr, *Playgoing*, 18), the smaller size of the hall – 66 feet by 46 feet – in which the second Blackfriars was set up could contribute, by its relative intimacy, to audience members' strong alertness to one another (Gurr and Ichikawa, 31).

Though they could have given rise to different opportunities and effects in performance, both the outdoor and indoor playing spaces used by Shakespeare's company shared freedom from painted scenery and elaborate sets; thus changes in location of time and place, created especially through language, could proceed unimpeded. Movable properties, hanging cloths, and costumes were additional signifiers, often symbolic as well as functional. For the trial scene of *The Winter's Tale*, for example, a large throne with canopy could have been carried on.

> Thrones for judges to sit on when hearing legal cases, or the 'chair of state' on which the supreme judge, the king, sat, were major symbols of authority. Besides the gilded wooden chair on which the authority figure sat, they were backed by a 'cloth of estate', with the royal arms, and a small canopy overhead. This whole 'state' was positioned on a dais several steps high, so that the authority figure's head could be on a level with the person standing in front of him. (Gurr and Ichikawa, 57)

Faced with an overpowering display of power, a young male actor performing Hermione could have drawn upon all his highly trained rhetorical skill to oppose the King's show of authority, pointing out that Leontes himself has authorized the charges by his dark imaginings, his 'dreams' (III.ii.79), building the argument until referring judgement to the higher authority of Apollo's oracle. Whether the symbolic property representing the oracle would have been onstage from the scene's beginning, as Alan Dessen has argued is an option ('Massed Entries', 125), or brought on after Hermione's reference to it (III.ii.113), it is a potent counter-symbol to the King's throne.

Conventions of symbolic visual presentation provide a context in which to weigh any appeal to realist literalism in arguments that the bear pursuing Antigonus must have been a live trained animal from the bear-baiting ring near the Globe. Though the issue cannot be settled with certainty, evidence is strong, as Schanzer has pointed out, that actors performed bears, and there is no evidence that live bears were used on the Elizabethan stage (192, n. 57). The inventory for the Admiral's Men on 10 March 1598 gives among the properties and costumes 'a beares skyne' (see Rutter, ed., *Documents*, 136). Moreover, as Biggins argues, certain theatrical texts, like Jonson's *Masque of Augurs*, make it clear from 'various humorous references' to 'three dancing "Beares"' that those roles were performed by actors. Lines suggest an actor's 'antics' for the bear in *Mucedorus*, which was performed by the King's Men in the presence of James I at Whitehall in 1610–11 (Biggins, 3–4). M. C. Bradbrook judged that in *The Winter's Tale* 'the bear that is summoned by the hunting horns in fulfilment of Apollo the hunter's decree is a human bear. How otherwise could the play be repeated anywhere but on Bankside?' (209). 'Certainly not at Whitehall before the King', added Bartholomeusz (13). Nevill Coghill not only sensibly argued that a bear cannot be a dependable performer but also made a good case for the actor-bear's dramatic purpose: in his pursuit of Antigonus, 'the terrible and the grotesque come near to each other in a *frisson* of horror instantly succeeded by a shout of laughter; and so this bear, this unique and perfect link between the two halves of the play, slips into place and holds' (35). Biggins agreed but added his experience of alternative effects: 'I have seen performances of *The Winter's Tale* in which the audience reacted perfectly seriously to the bear's brief appearance and Antigonus' hasty departure; the laughter came with the entrances and speeches of the Shepherd and the Clown' (6). Shakespeare's tragicomic use of the bear has its analogues; Louise Clubb points out that bears in pastoral plays from the European continent are simultaneously tragic and comic (17–30). As Orgel notes, Clubb shows that the bear is 'a tragicomic topos in sixteenth-century continental drama, a generic commonplace' (Orgel, ed., 37).

Shakespeare's tragicomic mingling of tones in *The Winter's Tale* is at its most profound in the *tour de force* of its statue scene, in which words are in counterpoint with silence and with a sustained and serious use of visual spectacle. Staging at the Globe could support such focus on heightened visual presentation. The Globe's platform stage had a back wall (the *frons scenae*) with what Andrew Gurr calls 'a door on each flank and a wider curtained space in the center, which was used for major entrances and occasionally for set-piece scenes' ('The Shakespearean Stage', 85, 99). It is probable, as Gurr and Ichikawa argue, that the statue would have been presented in the central space opening, which could be used for 'discoveries' (Gurr and Ichikawa, 2, 6–7, 46, 171; Gurr, *Rebuilding*, 89). Behind the central 'discovery space', which would have been covered with a stage hanging or curtain, could have stood '*Hermione (like a Statue:)*' – to cite part of the First Folio massed entry stage direction at the beginning of Act V, scene iii. Just before Paulina's lines 'Behold, and say 'tis well. / I like your silence; it the more shows off / Your wonder' (V.iii.20–2), Paulina could have pulled aside the curtain to reveal Hermione. That the statue could be displayed, or discovered, in this position would have made spectators aware that Hermione was the centre of the scene – even if, before Hermione later moved and came further forward, they were among that minority of viewers for whom the sight lines to the central opening were somewhat impeded. For them, the scene's visually descriptive language (e.g., V.iii.23–103) would have prompted their imaginative grasp of the action. These same viewers could have had a clear view of the onstage spectators – those actors further down on the platform stage, which projected almost half-way into the yard – whose responses to the statue are crucial to the dynamics of the scene. Even the Blackfriars' smaller stage – about 20 feet in width and depth – occupied nearly half the width of the hall, so that the audience would have been near to the onstage spectators (Gurr and Ichikawa, 32). In proscenium picture-frame theatres, by contrast, it can be challenging to position actors so that audiences can not only focus on Hermione but also be acutely aware of the responses of Leontes and the court.

The size and enclosed space of the Blackfriars may have been an advantage in enabling concentration upon the silences in the statue scene. Peter Hall, judging the Cottesloe to be approximately the same size the Blackfriars had been, speculated as much when directing *The Winter's Tale* in 1988 both for the small Cottesloe and for the much larger Olivier theatre (Warren, 146). Similarly, it may have been possible in the Blackfriars for hearers to pay greater attention to nuances of the music used when Paulina asked for music to awaken Hermione, her command 'Music; awake her – strike!' (V.iii.98) prompting musicians to strike strings of the viol (Orgel, ed., 275). The impact and significance of music in the statue scene, signalling healing and restoration, would not, however, have been lost in the Globe. Music for the satyrs' dance and for Autolycus' vigorous songs could have had equal impact, though in distinctive ways, in both theatrical spaces.

In *The Winter's Tale*, multiple *coups de théâtre* – especially in the statue scene – depend on willingness to awake faith in the art of theatre and the living art of the actor, as well as in the presentational art of the statue which, we discover, is an art that nature makes. In both the Globe and the Blackfriars, then, it is not surprising that the iconographic figure of Time, turning his emblematic hourglass at the exact middle of his speech of rhymed couplets ('I turn my glass', IV.i.16), could persuade hearers of his argument. His speech is not mere plot summary; it points to the significance of the play's theme of 'joy and terror', of time as witness to human error and as revealer of truth. 'Truth, daughter of Time', the ancient aphorism Greene cited on the title page of *Pandosto* but barely explored, is thematically central to *The Winter's Tale*, crystallized in the speech of Time, the Chorus. Moreover, the Chorus is a witty defence of the very dramatic strategies the play employs; it gives the playwright the power to 'o'erthrow law' and custom, including the neo-classicism emerging in Shakespeare's day. Unfortunately, it is a speech which, after the closing of the theatres in 1642, does not seem to have been heard again in a major production on the English stage until Charles Kean's *Winter's Tale* in 1856, over two hundred years later.

Restoration and eighteenth-century performance history

After the reopening of the British theatres in 1660, following the English civil war, *The Winter's Tale* was not produced until nearly the mid-eighteenth century, when it had a short run at Goodman's Fields in 1741. Shifts in critical taste and theatrical conditions, which were the context for Dryden's 1672 attack on the play after the restoration of the monarchy, intensified with the growth of neo-classicism. Pope so dismissed the art of *The Winter's Tale* that he declared that only 'perhaps a few particular passages, were of his [Shakespeare's] hand' (Preface to his edition of Shakespeare, quoted in Muir, *Sources*, 25). In the eighteenth century, *The Winter's Tale* survived mainly in truncated adaptations whose titles focused on the pastoral: Macnamara Morgan's *The Sheep-Shearing: Or Florizel and Perdita* (1754), which eliminates Leontes and Hermione, and thus the main tragic action, and David Garrick's *Florizel and Perdita, a Dramatic Pastoral, In Three Acts* (first produced 1756), which long held sway and influenced subsequent versions.

Garrick adhered to what he considered the unities of time, place, and action; his adaptation drastically cut and rewrote the play to fit neo-classical tastes. He set his play entirely in Bohemia, conveying what happened in Sicilia in the first three acts merely through dialogue between Camillo and a Gentleman. He brought the penitent Leontes to Bohemia by storm after Paulina earlier escaped there to save her life; Bohemia could thus become the location for Garrick's rewritten statue scene. His revised language is moralizing, sentimental, pious, and bound by concerns regarding social class. Moreover, Garrick's play is thoroughly depoliticized; there is no reference by Paulina to Leontes' tyranny. Her verbal strength is largely reduced, as is the power of her choices and those of Hermione. Garrick keeps the statue an object of mystery; he cut the lines that make it clear that Hermione has chosen to preserve herself to see the issue of the oracle. Furthermore, immediately after Paulina prompts Hermione to turn, following the line 'Our Perdita is found', Garrick adds lines that valorize the match between Perdita and Florizel in terms of blood and breeding: 'and with her found / A princely husband, whose instinct of royalty, / From under the low thatch where she was bred, / Took his untutor'd queen' (64). Hermione asks for blessing 'Upon their princely heads'. Though women could now play the roles themselves, as they could not in Shakespeare's day, gone are the intense moments focused on the reunion of mother and daughter. Gone, too, is Perdita's growth in self-assurance; Garrick gives her a speech in which she apologizes for her lowliness: 'I am all shame ... how to put on / This novel garment of gentility' (66). Gone, furthermore, is Leontes' line about the magic not only of Paulina's art, but of bodily touch: 'If this be magic, let it be an art / Lawful as eating' (V.iii.110–11). Hermione is given a pious speech to Leontes: 'Let purer thoughts, unmix'd with earth's alloy, / Flame up to heav'n, and for its mercy shewn, / Bow we our knees together.' In turn, she is put back on the metaphoric pedestal in Leontes' apostrophe to her: 'Thou matchless saint! – Thou paragon of virtue!' (64–5). It is a line John Philip Kemble retained nearly fifty years later, reinforcing a mould for Hermione that was to take over a century to break.

Nineteenth-century performance history

John Philip Kemble, who first staged *The Winter's Tale* in 1802 at Drury Lane and revived it in 1807 and 1811 at Covent Garden, carefully prepared three separate versions for his productions, recording scenic arrangements and movements for actors, especially for his own work as Leontes, in several detailed promptbooks. Kemble was the 'first actor-manager in the English theatre who systematically published his acting versions' (Shattuck, 'Shakespeare's Plays', p. 1910). Though he used far more of the Shakespearean text than had Garrick, restoring much of the content of the first three acts, Kemble nevertheless made numerous cuts in both major parts of the play. One of his notable excisions was the Chorus of Time: that presentational device did not, he felt, suit the picture-frame stage. According to Bartholomeusz, the text Kemble altered both for proscenium staging and to meet 'the expectations of nineteenth-century audiences' was 'used for half a century, with very few modifications by Young (1819), Macready (1823), Vandenhoff (1834), and Phelps (1845)'. Phelps, however, eliminated Garrick's and Kemble's sentimental piety from the concluding speech of Leontes and 'mercifully preferred Shakespeare's own' words (Bartholomeusz, 43).

Kemble saw the play as a tragedy, a view commonly held at the time and a valuable corrective to eighteenth-century emphasis – like Garrick's – upon the pastoral, though neither Garrick nor Kemble seemed in touch with the mingled tones of the play. All of Kemble's promptbooks, Shattuck tells us, 'call for the "Stage-cloth" – i.e., the green carpet which signified "tragedy"'. The growing scenic elaboration so characteristic of the nineteenth century is also evident from these promptbooks. The sets numbered eleven (for fifteen scenes); the Wister promptbook records 'eighty supernumeraries' and indicates that in the trial scene there were 'more than forty-five characters present' (Shattuck, *Kemble Promptbooks*, vol. 9, iii–iv). Kemble's acting style suited his taste for impressive, formal stage pictures; William Hazlitt characterized his deliberate movement by comparing him, as Shattuck puts it, 'to a marble statue'. Hazlitt's comment was that 'the least trip in his gait, or discomposure of his balance, would be sure to fracture some of his limbs' (quoted in Shattuck, 'Shakespeare's Plays', p. 1909). Despite that critique, Hazlitt – though far more of the romantic temper than Kemble – found his Leontes deeply engaging. In his perceptions of Kemble's acting we see Hazlitt's own fascination with details of character and the passions. Hazlitt found Kemble 'superior to every other actor' in portraying those characters whose development is dominated by 'one sentiment or exclusive passion'; and Hazlitt saw in Leontes such a character. In Leontes 'the growing jealousy of the King', wrote Hazlitt, 'and the exclusive possession which it at length obtains of his mind, are marked in the finest manner'. Focusing on Leontes' speech to Camillo that begins 'Is whispering nothing?' (I.ii.281–93), Hazlitt thought that as the speech developed, 'every proof tells harder, his conviction becomes more rivetted at every step of his progress, and at the end his mind is wound up to a frenzy of despair'. In playing 'such characters', Kemble's 'excellence', judged Hazlitt, 'consists entirely in the increasing intensity with which he dwells on a given feeling or enforces a predominant passion' (Hazlitt, *Collected Works*, in Waller and Glover, eds, vol. 11, 205–7). Hazlitt's focus on Kemble's ability to portray intense passion partly parallels his impression of Leontes' style in his essay on *The Winter's Tale* from his 1817 *Characters of Shakespear's Plays:*

> Even the crabbed and tortuous style of the speeches of Leontes, reasoning on his own jealousy, beset with doubts and fears, and entangled more and more in the thorny labyrinth, bears every mark of Shakespear's peculiar manner of conveying the painful struggle of different thoughts and feelings, labouring for utterance, and almost strangled in the birth. (Hazlitt, *Collected Works*, in Waller and Glover, eds, vol. 1, 324)

Hazlitt's judgement about the play, perhaps based in part on his experience of Kemble's performance, is, unfortunately, a minority view in the nineteenth century – that *The Winter's Tale* was, to quote him, 'one of the best-acting' of Shakespeare's plays (Hazlitt, *Collected Works*, in Waller and Glover, eds, vol.1, 325).

Hazlitt's contemporary, Samuel Taylor Coleridge, 'paid relatively little attention to the plays as works for the stage', according to R. A. Foakes, largely because of their 'cavalier treatment' (15) in productions of his day. Yet Coleridge has had a far greater influence on Shakespearean criticism than has Hazlitt. Notes from Coleridge's 1813 lecture comparing *The Winter's Tale* and *Othello* suggest that his mind, at work on the subject of passions, was more analytical than Hazlitt's. Examining the language of I.ii in *The Winter's Tale*, Coleridge thought that both Polixenes' 'obstinate refusal to Leontes' and his later 'yielding to Hermione' were 'well calculated to set in nascent action the jealousy of Leontes' (quoted in Foakes, 174). The 'first working' of such jealousy, thought Coleridge, showed overtly in Leontes' 'At my request he would not' (I.ii.86). Coleridge anatomized Leontes' passion: 'Excitability by the most inadequate causes: "too hot! too hot!"'; 'Eagerness to snatch at proofs'; 'Grossness of conception, and a disposition to degrade the object of it; sensual fancies and images: paddling, pinching'; 'Shame of his own feelings exhibited in moodiness and soliloquy'. Coleridge recognized, too, the linguistic obscurity due to the 'violence of the passion forced to *utter* itself, and therefore catching occasion to ease the mind by ambiguities, equivoques, talking to those who cannot, and who are known not to be able to understand what is said – a soliloquy in the mask of dialogue' (quoted in Foakes, 174). Whatever the dangers of Coleridge's method of focusing on individual characters, his openness to the style used to express Leontes' states of mind is a long way from neo-classical efforts to 'improve' Shakespeare's language. So, too, is Coleridge's interest in what Foakes calls 'the way Shakespeare's plays achieve organic growth and unity' (18), however problematic as well as stimulating these critical criteria have been. Coleridge distanced himself from an insistence on the neo-classical unities which, although they had begun to be challenged in the late eighteenth century, still remained a force in his day. Coleridge's understanding of Leontes' passion perhaps has more affinities with the acting style of William Charles Macready than with Kemble's.

Macready, for his productions of *The Winter's Tale* from 1823 to 1843, made few changes to the scenographic style used by Kemble, but many to his acting style. Macready's portrayal of Leontes, as Bartholomeusz puts it, 'was startling in its emotional realism': 'unpredictable', 'magnificently physical', 'moving in its abandon' (65). A critic in *The Times* found Macready's acting had 'less of dignity than that of the late Mr Kemble' and instead had 'a much greater portion of energy and fire'. Macready presented a Leontes, according to this critical account, whose jealousy, 'gradually ripening into a conviction of his consort's guilt', was 'traced through all its tortuous ramifications' (quoted in Bartholomeusz, 66). A reviewer in the *Morning Herald* thought that Macready had a talent 'for the familiar rather than the sublime'. In 'scenes of domestic feeling, even to its strongest emotions,' Macready 'very seldom fails' (quoted in Bartholomeusz, 66).

Helen (Helena) Faucit, Macready's Hermione for two productions in 1837 and a third in 1843, wrote a detailed recollection of their work in *The Winter's Tale*. Macready's response in the statue scene as she descended and moved toward him was at first to stand 'speechless, as if turned to stone; his face with an awestruck look upon it'. Paulina urged him to 'present your hand' (V.iii.107). 'Tremblingly he advanced, and touched gently the hand held out to him. Then, what a cry came with, "O, she's warm!"' (Faucit, 389–90). No pious additional lines like those Garrick had written were given her to say when she was reunited with Leontes; she instead saw the potential in her silence and in the physical embrace with Leontes: 'It was such a comfort to me, as well as true to natural feeling, that Shakespeare gives Hermione no words to say to Leontes, but leaves her to assure him of her joy and forgiveness by look and manner only, as in his arms she feels the old life, so long suspended, come back to her again' (390).

Helen Faucit's finely detailed reflections have both progressive and problematic elements when viewed from a contemporary feminist perspective. She makes an important advance in emphasizing that Paulina (a role she played in 1835 to Macready's Leontes) has a 'most important part in the drama' and 'should be impersonated in any adequate representation of the play by an actress of the first order. She is a woman of no ordinary sagacity, with a warm heart, a vigorous brain, and an ardent temper' (353–4). Faucit validates Paulina's 'hot anger', 'clear common-sense' and 'fearless courage'. Some of her statements about Hermione, however, adhere more to restrictive Victorian ideas of women's behaviour. Her interpretation of the moment when Leontes orders that she be taken away to prison is that Hermione 'attempts no remonstrance. She accepts her fate meekly.' Faucit here does not register the implied critique and resistance in Hermione's lines to Leontes: 'I never wished to see you sorry; now / I trust I shall' (II.i.123–4). Instead, she writes that Hermione says the lines 'bending with a low reverence to the king' (352). About the trial scene, she says, with knowledge born of experience, it is 'a scene which makes a large demand upon the resources of the actress, both personal and mental'. Acknowledging that Hermione has been 'placed in a most ignominious position', she summarizes how the Queen should respond: 'Hermione must be shown to maintain her queenly dignity, and to control her passionate emotion under an outward bearing of resigned fortitude and almost inconceivable forbearance' (359). This portrait, with its echoes of Victorian traditional precepts for women, occludes many alternative ways to perform Hermione's trial scene speeches. Precisely because Helen Faucit's interpretation was only a subtler version of conservative ideals of female behaviour than Garrick's 'paragon of virtue', her views suggest how hard it was for traditional expectations to loosen their hold.

Indeed, such expectations largely influenced the Hermione of Mrs Kean (Ellen Tree) in Charles Kean's 1856 production of *The Winter's Tale*. Bartholomeusz' apt judgement is that despite the so-called 'Hellenic' scenography, 'Mrs Kean's Hermione was a Victorian heroine' (87). Ellen Terry, who at the age of eight played Mamillius in that same 1856 production, in her later memoirs made a witty objection that as Hermione, despite the 'classical' production style, Mrs Kean was 'bunched out by layer upon layer of petticoats'. At the same time, Ellen Terry's praise for Mrs Kean's acting reveals the Victorian heritage of expectations for women: Mrs Kean's voice, Terry writes, was 'full of pathos', and her acting had 'dignity, simplicity, and womanliness' (15). We know less about Mrs Kean's acting than about Helen Faucit's, not only because Mrs Kean did not write about her own work but also because the focus of the reviewers was primarily on the elaborate spectacle Charles Kean had set out to create. His production took so-called 'archaeologically' detailed scenography to the extreme. Moreover, as Bartholomeusz points out, though Kean's project was to create a detailed 'historical period' for the play, 'he never asked himself whether it was Shakespeare's aim to write period plays' (81). Kean cut the text heavily (nine hundred lines from Acts IV and V alone), making way for the time it took to move his elaborate sets and painted backdrops. At least three hundred performers were involved in the 'Arcadian' dances and 'Dionysian' revels of satyrs and men. Though many reviewers were mesmerized by the lavishness of the spectacle, notes of protest began to appear: 'In the play itself', wrote a reviewer for *The Times*, 'there is nothing to suggest excessive splendour of decoration' (quoted in Frey, 29).

In the first major production of *The Winter's Tale* in England in the twentieth century, in 1906, Beerbohm Tree, as Gordon Crosse put it, 'thought that he was honouring' Shakespeare 'by embellishing his works'. But, concluded Crosse: 'Intending to praise Shakespeare he came near to burying him under a mountain of magnificence' (*Fifty Years of Shakespearean Playgoing*, 43). In comparison to Kean, Tree had his own commitment to a different kind of spectacular realism: though his production had more strengths than have commonly been recognized, it pushed hyper-illusionism to its limits on the picture-frame stage, with a live donkey, two live doves, and a running stream in the pastoral scene – as Bartholomeusz puts it, a 'heavy investment in bucolic detail'. It all made for 'a very slow progress through the verse' (Bartholomeusz, 127), even though, in the interests of his spectacle, Tree cut almost half the play's lines (Kennedy, *Granville Barker*, 123). It was precisely this tradition of detailed theatrical illusionism and drastically altered texts epitomized by Tree and Kean against which Harley Granville Barker reacted in his production of *The Winter's Tale* in 1912. Barker's production remains a critical turning point not only in the history of staging *The Winter's Tale* but in the history of twentieth-century Shakespearean production.

CHAPTER I

Granville Barker's production at the Savoy Theatre, 1912

> To the imagination, it looks as if he had invented a new heaven and a new earth. (George Bernard Shaw, interviewed about Barker's production of *The Winter's Tale*, *Observer*, 29 September 1912, 9)

> The performance seemed to me to be a riper and juster piece of Shakespearian criticism, a clearer perception and grasping of the Shakespearian idea, than I have seen hitherto in print or on the stage. (John Masefield, Letter to *The Times*, 27 September 1912, 7)

Amid the fierce critical contestation aroused by Harley Granville Barker's 1912 production of *The Winter's Tale*, George Bernard Shaw and John Masefield were among the progressive critics who understood the production's importance in staging and interpretation; it has, indeed, become a major landmark in critical and theatre history. Nearly three-quarters of a century after its first performance, Dennis Kennedy judged it 'one of the four or five most important Shakespearian productions' of the twentieth century (*Granville Barker*, 136). Shaw and Masefield, writing within days of its opening at London's Savoy Theatre on 21 September, came to Barker's defence amid the extraordinary critical controversy provoked chiefly by the production's non-illusionist eclectic scenery, its costumes, and the unaccustomed speed of the actors' speech. Shaw stressed the importance of Barker's staging, Masefield his breakthrough in critical interpretation. Masefield furthermore attributed to the stage a privilege traditionally reserved for the study: he saw performance as an act of criticism. Masefield and Shaw were joined by Desmond MacCarthy, who judiciously supported 'the way in which the dramatic quality of the words was realized by the actors' (*Eye-Witness*, 3 October 1912, 501).

Barker's break from the strictly framed action of the proscenium stage and its traditions of elaborate pictorial realism (illusionism) is what prompted Shaw's perception of 'a new heaven and a new earth'. Asserting 'the importance of the revolution that Barker has effected in the lighting and general aspect of the stage', Shaw noted: 'He has got rid of the footlights, and apparently trebled the spaciousness of the stage, though the actual addition consists only of a strip formerly occupied by the orchestra and the front row of the stalls' (*Observer*, 29 September 1912, 9). The crucial 'strip' was an apron stage – a partial thrust platform added to the proscenium theatre's main stage. Shaw's rhetoric of praise should not mislead us on this point: an apron was not Barker's invention, though his uses of it were particularly skilful. Barker spoke of an 'atrophied "apron"' surviving in some older proscenium theatres, 'but no one ventured out on it' (*Associating with Shakespeare*, 14). Renewed uses of apron staging, as Cary Mazer has pointed out, were 'the product of Edwardian avant-garde experimentation' (*Shakespeare Refashioned*, 134).[1]

For *The Winter's Tale* at the Savoy, the curved apron stage enabled actors to address audiences directly; asides, soliloquies and numerous scenes were presented close to spectators. John Palmer felt himself 'in direct, almost personal, contact with the players. Gone was the centuries-old, needless and silly illusion of a picture stage.' Palmer, however, realized that Barker was able to restore only 'a few essential points of the Elizabethan' style of production and acting (*Saturday Review*, 28 September 1912, 391). Barker retained traces of Edwardian pictorialism, for example, at times designating scenic locations, despite his crucial shift from detailed scenic representation (Mazer, *Shakespeare Refashioned*, 139–40, 150). According to Lewis Casson, Barker told him after the Savoy season that he wished he had used simpler staging (Casson and Thorndike, 'Recollections of Harley Granville-Barker').[2] Barker knew, too, that adding an apron could not create the ideal space for playing Shakespeare that he wanted; by the time he wrote *The Exemplary Theatre* (1922), Barker pointed out the limitations of adding a platform 'as a structural afterthought' to a proscenium stage (*The Exemplary Theatre*, 204). Yet Palmer's response in 1912 captures what was crucial at that historical moment to a keen and sympathetic observer. He emphasized, as did Shaw and others, not what was residual but what was emergent, not what was limited but what was advantageous. Barker's experiment with apron staging allowed him to offer what he considered a principle of Shakespearean theatre – close communication from actor to audience.

Amid Edwardian debates about staging Shakespeare, Barker situated himself in ways both principled and pragmatic between traditionalists and Elizabethanist reformers. He argued in his 1923 Introduction to *The Players' Shakespeare* that 'it should be possible – and it is necessary – to distinguish between the artistic essentials and the merely incidental features of the stage for which Shakespeare designed his plays' (*More Prefaces*, 48). One reason Barker objected to the traditionalist practice of detailed pictorial realism is that it violated one such artistic essential: it 'will detract from the importance of the actors' (*More Prefaces*, 49). But he also objected to attempted replication of 'incidental features' of the supposed Elizabethan stage – attempts he thought marred the work of reformers, including William Poel. Such 'accidentals', Barker contended, 'since we cannot convert ourselves into Elizabethans – we should find standing quite vexatiously between us and the *essentials* of the stagecraft' (*Associating with Shakespeare*, 17). Barker acknowledged his debt to Poel (in whose productions he had played Richard II in 1899 and Edward II in 1903), yet argued in a letter to the press:

> Tapestry curtains hung round? Well, tapestry is apt to be stuffy and – archaeological. We shall not save our souls by being Elizabethan. It is an easy way out, and, strictly followed, an honourable one. But there's the difficulty. To be Elizabethan one must be strictly, logically or quite ineffectively so. And, even then, it is asking much of an audience to come to the theatre so historically-sensed as that. (*Play Pictorial*, 21:126, January 1913, iv)[3]

Barker's approach was bold, yet a strategic compromise given the dilemma of staging Shakespeare in a proscenium theatre like the Savoy. Responding to his critics, he argued in the same letter to the *Play Pictorial* that since 'a new formula, a new convention, has to be found, the audience must learn to see, even as we learn to work in it'. He added: 'I assure you that such experiments aren't easy.' Disavowing both pictorial realism and antiquarian Elizabethanism, he wanted 'something that will reflect light and suggest space; if it's to be a background permanent for a play (this, for many reasons, it should be), something that will not tie us too rigidly indoors or out' (*Play Pictorial*, iv). As one major way to 'reflect light and suggest space' in *The Winter's Tale*, Barker used a white background for Leontes' palace. White 'was the first note struck', as one reviewer put it: 'A white curtain, and across the space belonging to the orchestra the stage was built out in a white platform. When the curtain rose you were looking at a scheme of decoration in white and gold' (*Daily Telegraph*, 23 September 1912).

To increase non-illusionistic brightness and, Barker said, to pick out bright colours, he used mainly what he called 'perfectly white light'.[4] Among notable variations for dramatic purposes was the dark scene of Leontes' torment ('Nor night nor day no rest', II.iii.1), lit almost entirely by a brazier. Having eliminated the footlights, Barker used front-of-house lighting 'from the auditorium', he said in interview, 'to give us as much reflected light as possible' (*Evening News*, 24 September 1912, 4). Two box lights hung from front centre of the upper circle and there were 'six cylinder lights at the front of the dress circle', according to Mazer. Additionally, there were 'four white arc lamps directly above the mainstage', and 'two side lamps, one in each "stage" box, i.e., the boxes closest to the stage which overlooked the extended apron stage' (Mazer, *Shakespeare Refashioned*, 135). Barker was not the first to use front-of-house lighting,[5] but he used it to great effect.

The stage architecture Barker created for his experimental *The Winter's Tale*, the first play in his Savoy Shakespeare season, was fundamentally the same as for his subsequent two Savoy Shakespeare productions – *Twelfth Night*, opening 15 November 1912, and *A Midsummer Night's Dream*, opening 6 February 1914. As Kennedy describes the architecture, upstage was a 'large raised acting area' bordered by an arch. 'Four steps lower and downstage' was 'a center space, on the main stage floor', which 'extended to the permanent proscenium arch' (*Granville Barker*, 124–5). Two steps below this main stage was the curved apron stage, thrusting out 12 feet deep at its centre.

One primary function of this stage architecture was articulated by the production's costume designer, Albert Rothenstein (who changed his name in 1916, during World War I, to Rutherston). Describing his joint work with Norman Wilkinson, who was responsible for the 'decoration' of the play, Rothenstein wrote that they used

> what may be described as two forms of decorative scene, namely, front curtains and built scenes, the latter occupying the whole of the existing [proscenium] stage proper, the former acting as backgrounds for the short front stage scenes [played on the apron]; a double stage after the manner of the Elizabethan Theatre was used, thus making it possible to give a Shakespeare play, with its many changes of scene and action, without pause, and without cutting down the text. ('Decoration in the Art of the Theatre', 18-19)

For *The Winter's Tale*, the large raised upstage area was used for the only two full-stage sets ('built scenes'). One, formed by a rear colonnade of six white, tall rectangular pillars, between which hung gold curtains, suggested Leontes' palace – 'rather an arrangement of line and colour than anything real' (*Daily Telegraph*, 23 September 1912). Slight alterations were made for the trial scene, and interior locales were suggested by rearranging or resetting furniture. The second set, its bold, simplified lines suggesting a thatched cottage, was background for the pastoral scenes. Scenes in these settings interchanged with scenes presented in front of painted drop curtains (cloths). Among those cloths listed in the production's Account Book (in the Theatre Museum, London),[6] one of them was white (used for several scenes, among them for Time in IV.i, for IV.ii, and for V.ii); some had abstract decoration or suggestions – not full representations – of place (e.g., prison), colour (e.g., silver, gold) or season (e.g., winter, summer). According to Norman Marshall, these drop curtains were far from austere; rather, they were of 'expensive materials, frequently silk' (151); Rothenstein said they 'fell in broad folds', their designs 'painted on [by hand] with dyes' ('Decoration', 19). 'As to scenery, as scenery is mostly understood – canvas, realistically painted – I would have none of it,' wrote Barker in his preface to his 1912 acting edition (*More Prefaces*, 24–5). Rothenstein and Wilkinson emphasized what they and Barker called 'decoration', as distinct from detailed verisimilar 'realism'. Arguing for the 'frankly artificial', Rothenstein opposed what he saw as the danger of 'naturalistic representation': 'No attention will have been paid to that all important relation between actor and background' ('Decoration', 15, 18).

To the extent that the bold pattern, line, and colour of some exotic costumes and properties called too much attention to themselves, however, Rothenstein and Wilkinson may have partially misjudged that right relation of actor to decor. One critic who found much to praise wrote: 'Details disturbed you, seemed too large, and so the whole scene became unquiet and distracting' (*Daily Telegraph*, 23 September 1912). Even an admirer of Barker like Bridges-Adams remembered years later that the 'first appearance of Miss Lillah McCarthy under a tremendous gold umbrella was so stunning that I cannot remember as much of her Hermione as I would like to' (*The Lost Leader*, 10–11). In some instances, the brilliance of the 'decoration' risked taking away the focus on the actor that Barker wanted to achieve.

Other debates about 'decoration' were partly, of course, fuelled by traditionalist objections. What some English reviewers called 'bizarre' and 'extravagant', as Dennis Bartholomeusz points out, 'would have delighted Matisse or Picasso' (163). Objections were judiciously answered by P. G. Konody, art critic for the *Observer*. He acknowledged that 'Mr. Rothenstein uses a palette of unprecedented daring.'

> He does not shrink from contrasting the most vivid hues of magenta, lemon yellow, emerald green, scarlet, and so forth. But vivid colours set boldly side by side without intervening neutral passages of neutral [*sic*] colour are not necessarily inharmonious, though it is infinitely more difficult to create harmony out of them. Considering the boldness of his attempt, he has been remarkably successful. His combinations of vivid hues have often a certain piquant sharpness, and only very rarely degenerate into crudeness. (29 September 1912, 9)

Konody knew that the decorative style was not meant to replicate a period style in detail, but to use elements of it in fresh ways. The costumes, he wrote, 'hold that suggestion of the late Renaissance which is indicated by the mention, in the play, of Giulio Romano, to whom is attributed the supposed life-like effigy of Hermione' (*Observer*, 29 September 1912, 9). Barker had asserted in his preface to the acting edition that he and Rothenstein took inspiration from Giulio Romano's work (*More Prefaces*, 24). One hopes they had a measure of Shakespeare's witty tongue-in-cheek reference to the artist; at least it was 'just to give one's imagination the key', stated Barker, that he named the production's decorative style 'Renaissance-classic' (*More Prefaces*, 24).

The costumes were more eclectic than 'historical' period labels suggest. 'Writing with what now seems baffling imprecision', declared Max Rutherston in 1988, 'Mr. Walkley of *The Times* called the design of *The Winter's Tale* "Post-Impressionist Shakespeare"' (*Albert Rutherston*, 9–10). Desmond MacCarthy objected to Walkley's label at the time. As secretary to the exhibition 'Manet and the Post-Impressionists' (November 1910, Grafton Galleries, with works by Gauguin and Cézanne), MacCarthy, with Roger Fry, had named the exhibition (Kennedy, *Granville Barker*, 134 and 217, n. 3), in effect creating the term Walkley appropriated. 'The qualities which the dresses lacked', wrote MacCarthy, 'were precisely those which Post-Impressionism has emphasised; synthesis, simplicity, generalisation, were not their strong points. They were amusing and fantastic, rococo, elaborate, Aubrey Beardsley, childish, sophisticated, eclectic, baroque, gaudy, what you will, but Post-Impressionist they were not.' Whether or not individual tastes were pleased, MacCarthy continued, the decor and costumes had an 'important quality: they suggested an imaginary world detached from historic time and place'. MacCarthy's defence rested on his assumption that *The Winter's Tale* 'is a fairy story' (*Eye-Witness*, 3 October 1912, 500). Whether or not one agrees with that assumption, MacCarthy did, however, target the difference between imaginative artistry and pseudo-historical detailed representation (as in Charles Kean's elaborate 1856 production).

Konody defended the eclectic design of the production as suitable for a play which includes a Delphic oracle, a Sicilian king, and an imagined coast of Bohemia; it belongs, he argued, 'to no specified time' (*Observer*, 29 September 1912, 9). At their best, the costumes had dramatic functions appropriate to character in a given moment. Hermione's grey cloak and grey silk trial-scene dress, for example, hung in simple folds; Leontes exchanged the richly lined silks and brocades of his Acts I–III costumes for plain black fine wool in Act V. Konody praised Time, in 'bright blue ... standing statuesquely against the expanse of heavy white curtain'. He reserved highest praise for the 'white, gold-curtained' palace, the drop-scenes, and the 'admirable lighting', emphasizing that 'everything *helps* the action': 'This, after all, should be, and is, the aim of all so-called modern stage "reformers"' (*Observer*, 29 September 1912, 9).

Continuity of action, one of Barker's major reformist aims,

was integral to his determination to use as full a text of the play as possible. Laurence Binyon registered the importance of these related aims; after seeing *The Winter's Tale* he wrote to Barker: 'O, the joy of the briskness and continuity of it all! The relief to have no footlights, no beastly tootlings between the acts, no drawling of voices and dragging of feet! It must electrify people to find that a Shakespeare play makes sense when not gutted of vital parts' (quoted in McCarthy, 159). Because Barker had eliminated delays needed for changing elaborate sets and had alternated between playing on the apron and on the main stage, action could move rapidly without any need to eviscerate the text merely to save time. The playing time for Barker's production was approximately three hours, with one fifteen-minute interval (intermission) at the end of Act III (Edward Moore, introd. to *More Prefaces*, 13). Barker cut very little of *The Winter's Tale*; conflicting accounts put the number of cuts at between six and twenty lines. One witness who saw the production, the critic for the *Outlook*, put the number at fourteen and one-half lines; Dennis Kennedy judged that cuts totalled approximately fifteen lines (*Granville Barker*, 216–17, n. 2). These estimates seem likely in view of passages marked with square brackets in Barker's acting edition (though acting editions are not infallible guides to performance).[7] Barker presented audiences with the first opportunity since the seventeenth century to experience a performance based on a nearly full text of *The Winter's Tale* in a major British or North American production.

Edwardian traditionalists were wedded to heavily cut and rearranged nineteenth-century texts that enabled time for elaborate scenic changes, practices evident in Beerbohm Tree's production of *The Winter's Tale* (at His Majesty's, 1906), the last major London production prior to Barker's. Opposing these practices and supporting Barker's reforms was a critic who recalled in 1912 his earlier review – titled 'Mangling Done Here' – of Mary Anderson's production of *The Winter's Tale* (Lyceum, 1887): 'during seventy minutes out of the three hours the curtain was down; one-third of the work omitted' (*Westminster Gazette*, 23 September 1912, 2). Barker partly allied his reforms with those of Edwardian Elizabethanists like Poel, certainly with Poel's call for performance to be based on unabridged texts (which Poel often failed to do in practice; see Speaight, esp. 98–101, 197–8, 258–63). Negotiating cultural debates between traditionalists and reformers, Barker responded to the controversy surrounding his production of *The Winter's Tale*: 'There is no Shakespearean tradition. At most we can deduce from a few scraps of knowledge what Elizabethan methods were ... We have the text to guide us, half a dozen stage directions, and that is all. I abide by the text and the demands of the text, and beyond that I claim freedom' (Barker, letter to the *Daily Mail*, 26 September 1912, 4).

Even Barker's strong commitment to text was very slightly constrained by his concern that Edwardian audiences might be offended by bawdy language. Because of that concern, he seems to have made two minor cuts (if one can judge from square brackets in the acting edition). Lines immediately before, after, and including Leontes' 'No barricado for a belly' (I.ii.199–204) and Autolycus' 'to geld a codpiece of a purse' (IV.iv.605–9) are bracketed. Barker justified his few additional cuts largely on pragmatic grounds of their presumed obscurity to audiences – lines involving Polixenes' reference to 'sneaping winds' (I.ii.12–14), for example, and Autolycus' word play on giving 'the lie' (IV.iv.718–21). However, he distinguished such cuts from passages he retained in which he found 'an intentional obscurity' suggesting Leontes' mental torment; these, such as Leontes' 'Affection! – thy intention stabs the centre' (I.ii.137), he considered 'a quite legitimate dramatic effect' ('On Cutting Shakespeare', a letter to the *Nation*, 27 September 1919, 767, quoted in *More Prefaces*, 13). He explained the point more fully in his acting edition: 'There is a most daring piece of technique by which twice or three times an actual obscurity of words (their meaning could never have been plain to any immediate listener) is used to express the turmoil of his [Leontes'] mind' (*More Prefaces*, 24; cf. his introd. to *Prefaces to Shakespeare*, 12). Barker insisted that these passages functioned dramatically, and he did not cut them. His Leontes, Henry Ainley, apparently proved such language, if not clear, at least playable: 'He took us through the tortures of Leontes and the involved speech that expresses those tortures at a pace that covered the ground very fast, while never losing the dramatic effect' (*Observer*, 22 September 1912, 10).

Though it has been given less scholarly attention, Barker's critical interpretation of *The Winter's Tale* is as important as his staging of it. Since he dates his preface to his acting edition 'July, 1912', he almost certainly wrote the preface while preparing the production. The edition was published in time to be sold at performances in the Savoy. As in his later *Prefaces to Shakespeare*, Barker confronts problems of dramatic construction, bringing to them his combined critical acumen and theatrical experience. Posthumously reprinted in *More Prefaces to Shakespeare*, Barker's preface to *The Winter's Tale* remains an important critical commentary.[8]

Critics from Ben Jonson onward have objected to *The Winter's Tale* because it departs from classical norms of drama, with its wide-ranging time and place, its mingling of tones, its supposed improbabilities. Barker defended the play's dramatic technique. He took the critical position, unusual at the time, that the play is at once a tragicomedy and a 'masterpiece' (*More Prefaces*, 19). Unlike Dowden, he did not dismiss the play as a falling off from the dramatist's heights. Barker argued: 'The technique of it is mature, that of a man who knows he can do what he will, lets himself in for difficulties with apparent carelessness, and overcomes them at his ease' (*More Prefaces*, 19).

The first difficulty, of course, is how to present Leontes' jealousy. Barker replied to those who objected to the lack of detailed and explicit motivation: 'Jealousy upon any foundation is less than jealousy, or more. Leontes has, as far as we can see, hardly the shadow of an excuse for his suspicion.' Since, unlike Othello, Leontes has no Iago to deceive him, there might seem a vacancy in the text. But Barker argued, 'and yet not vacant, but finely filled, for the wanton malice that is Iago the jealous man can only find, but finds surely, in his own heart' (*More Prefaces*, 21).

Neither Barker's comments nor contemporary reviews tell us at what point Leontes' jealousy was first suggested in Barker's production. The First Folio gives stage directions for Leontes in Act I, scene ii only in two places. The first is the entry – *'Enter Leontes, Hermione, Mamillius, Polixenes, Camillo'*. The second is the *'Exit'* after Leontes says to Camillo, 'I will seem friendly, as thou hast advised me' (line 346 in the Orgel edition). Barker's acting edition is not, however, simply a reprint of the play's text from the First Folio, and it is uncertain what other texts might have been used in preparing it. It does not use the Folio's massed entries; it contains some modernized punctuation, occasional emendations of previous editors, and added stage directions which, while shorn of the elaborate spectacle to which he was so opposed, do show traces of older editorial traditions. Among the most significant added stage directions, reproduced below in square brackets as in the acting edition, are two related to the presentation of Leontes' jealousy in I.ii. After Hermione's 'We'll thwack him hence with distaffs', there is the added direction '[*They pace away from* LEONTES.]'. The next editorial insertion (with no closing square bracket) is '[LEONTES *comes towards them*'. This insertion is just after Hermione's lines to Polixenes: 'If you first sinned with us and that with us / You did continue fault and that you slipped not / With any but with us.' (Stage directions and lines cited as in acting edition, 6, 8.) A photograph in the production's Account Book shows Henry Ainley, as Leontes, behind Hermione and Polixenes, watching them. As Dennis Kennedy points out, we cannot be certain that a photograph represents a particular performance moment (*Looking at Shakespeare*, 20–4); but this photograph may corroborate the inserted stage direction in the acting edition.

The two inserted stage directions resemble stage practices in certain previous productions. Macready, playing Leontes in his own productions of *The Winter's Tale* (1823 and 1843), had been upstage and came downstage toward Polixenes and Hermione on her line, 'Of this make no conclusion, lest you say / Your queen and I are devils' (I.ii.80–1). In addition, Bartholomeusz (138) notes that in Winthrop Ames's production at the New Theatre (New York) in 1910, Leontes approached Polixenes and Hermione and overheard her say, 'Th'offences we have made you do we'll answer' (I.ii.82). In Barker's production did Leontes overhear and misunderstand Hermione's line to Polixenes when he moved towards them? Or, if he did not overhear, did he misinterpret what he saw? Those questions cannot be answered with certainty.

Though often lacking important particulars, many reviews of Barker's production suggested that the inception of Leontes' jealousy was convincing. Rupert Hyde wrote: 'There is something ominous in the show of friendship between the two kings.' Citing Polixenes' opening lines, Hyde's perception was that 'Polixenes wants to get out of it'. Hyde continued: 'In no scene does Shakespeare create his atmosphere with greater skill. He does not use portents or witches' cauldrons to arouse foreboding. But, first by the over-civility, then by Leontes romping jealousy [*sic*] with his child, while Hermione and Polixenes flirt quite harmlessly, Shakespeare reveals himself a master' (*T. P.'s Weekly*, 4 October

1912, 423). In *Blackwood's Magazine*, a critic argued, 'The jealousy of Leontes is the more violent for the very reason that it is baseless. That which has been imputed as a fault is one of the virtues of the play' (November 1912, 692).

Reviewers of Henry Ainley's Leontes focused on his ability to express irrational passion; few thought that his initial scene was unconvincing, and many found his subsequent scenes (including his repentance) compelling. Cathleen Nesbitt, who played Perdita, remembered Ainley, as the jealousy developed, 'like a great tiger pacing to and fro' (*Listener*, 13 January 1972, 51). For the scene (II.iii) beginning 'Nor night nor day no rest', the brazier had been lit in the middle of the darkened stage, and as one critic described it, 'the snarling, skulking wolf of a jealous king, and raging, mocking Paulina and the shocked and awkward lords are seen in the red light that picks them out and passes them back into the shadows as the terrible action flames into fury or sinks back into shame' (*Observer*, 22 September 1912, 9).

Critical debate about Ainley's Leontes centred on the speed of his verse speaking, and that of the production overall; according to one disparaging critic, the production ran like the 'Margate express' (*Daily Mail*, 23 September 1912). Also typical of conservative responses was that of J. E. Harold Terry: 'It is a thousand pities that all save one or two of the performers speak their lines at such a pace as to render three parts of them inaudible to the audience.' Yet even he conceded that 'Mr. Ainley reveals to us, with quite wonderful skill, the torment of jealousy that is consuming Leontes' (173). Terry's judgement that Ainley gave a 'wonderful study of the neurasthenic Leontes' (173–4) was paralleled by the critic who found Leontes 'more pathological than poetic, yet ... [giving] an intense, vivid picture of a distraught mind' (*Stage*, 22). What the reviewer meant by 'poetic' was quite likely the Henry Irving tradition of sonorous declamation from which Barker was deliberately breaking.

Henry Irving, whom Barker considered of the 'romantic school of actors' (*Associating with Shakespeare*, 14), was, according to Norman Marshall, 'notoriously slow and deliberate' in his speech. Marshall, writing in 1957, had been 'told by actors who were in the Granville-Barker production the speed was not, according to present-day standards, unduly fast; but it must have seemed a breakneck speed in comparison with the slow and ponderous tread of the Shakespearian actors of that time' (152). Many of the better critics seemed to have little difficulty with the pace of the speaking in Barker's production. Gordon Crosse maintained a high estimation of Irving, whose work had impressed him strongly from his earliest playgoing years; Crosse wrote about himself that he could not be accused of 'undervaluing the excellent elocution of the actors of the older school', but added that such elocution 'was often marred by too great deliberation and too many and too long pauses'. Crosse welcomed the pace of speech in Barker's Savoy productions because 'it was a joy to hear the lines rapidly spoken yet without slurring or gabbling' (*Fifty Years of Shakespearean Playgoing*, 57–8). Elsie Fogerty was particularly discerning. She had founded the Central School of Speech and Drama in 1906, and her voice work, according to John Gielgud, was 'an invaluable help' to the next generation of actors, including Laurence Olivier and Peggy Ashcroft (Gielgud, *An Actor and His Time*, 122). Noting that the pace of speaking in Barker's *The Winter's Tale* was varied, and that 'many of the passages' in the production were 'spoken quite slowly', Elsie Fogerty argued: 'If we are to have the text of Shakespeare in anything like its entirety, if we are to have the music and the variety inherent in his verse and his prose, we must speed up our delivery. It is perfectly possible we shall have to speed up the ears of some of our audience at the same time' (published letter to the press dated 26 September [1912], Harvard Theatre Collection).

Barker 'worked enormously at first on voice, and he had this mania for speed', recalled his Perdita, Cathleen Nesbitt (*Listener*, 13 January 1972, 51). Nesbitt's view was that Barker 'worked *with* his actors and the only thing he ever bullied one about was *speech*, he wanted tremendous speed and clarity, a difficult combination' (*A Little Love and Good Company*, 63).[9] Barker argued that Shakespearean dramatic verse 'must be spoken swiftly': 'My fellow workers acting in *The Winter's Tale* were accused by some people (only by some) of gabbling. I readily take that accusation on myself, and I deny it. Gabbling implies hasty speech, but our ideal was speed, nor was the speed universal, nor, but in a dozen well-defined passages, really so great. Unexpected it was, I don't doubt' (*More Prefaces*, 31–2; from his Preface to *Twelfth Night: An Acting Edition*, 1912).

With refreshing candour, one critic wrote that reviewers

needed more time to write about challenging new work and that it was of 'more importance to the public to have Mr. Granville Barker's own views of what his intentions are than my hasty interpretation of them' (J. T., *Evening News*, 24 September 1912). He cited Barker as saying, in response to criticism of the rapid verse speaking,

> And you notice that the later Leontes takes his speeches in a measured way. I seem to see that indicated in the text. The whole of the first jealous phase of the king is shadowed in the jerky hurried measure of the verse.
> This partly answers your charge that the rhythm of the blank verse is murdered. I am an obstinate heretic. I don't see that the authentic 'slight pause' at the end of each verse is necessary. And anyway, waiving that general question, the nervous, passionate jealousy of Leontes won't allow of that formal treatment.

Barker's judgement about Leontes' early language is reflected in his assessment – rare then and still a minority view today – that the play's tragicomic perspectives are evident even in Acts I to III:

> There is more than one touch in the first half of the play, designed, I believe, to keep the tragedy a little less than tragic. Leontes' jealousy is never, as is Othello's, a strength, even a seeming strength ... it is a nervous weakness, a mere hysteria. He, poor wretch, moreover, even at his most positive, even while he sits in dignity and talks of justice, is conscious of this. (*More Prefaces*, 20)

Ainley's performance seems to have corroborated Barker's views. The critic of the *Westminster Gazette* noted Ainley's departure from romantic tragic acting: 'As a rule Leontes is played so as to make the man seem as dignified as possible – I might say more dignified than is possible.' Instead, Ainley's acting was appropriate to tragicomedy: 'Mr. Henry Ainley avoids the poetical or dignified interpretation.' Ainley's 'displays of physical frenzy are fascinatingly ugly', and the 'effect is powerful, rather horrible, very real, and quite consistent with every word of the part' (*Westminster Gazette*, 23 September 1912, 2). The part, as Barker saw it, was not best expressed by romantic acting: 'If before', in *Othello*, wrote Barker, Shakespeare 'had set out to paint jealousy as a noble passion, and his own genius had defeated the false aim, now he would write a study of jealousy indeed, perverse, ignoble, pitiable' (*More Prefaces*, 21).

Ainley's 'art was the more striking', wrote John Palmer, 'for its contrast in style with the playing of Miss McCarthy [as Hermione]' (*Saturday Review*, 28 September 1912, 391). Lillah McCarthy had distinguished herself by her work in plays by Shaw and Barker, as well as in classical drama, and was from 1906 to 1917 married to Barker (they separated in 1916). Allied with the feminism of her day (Kennedy, *Granville Barker*, 57), she also brought from her experience of the new drama her resistance to falsely inflated acting styles while, in Shaw's view, being 'unrivalled' in her delivery of English verse. 'Lillah McCarthy's secret', wrote Shaw, 'was that she combined the executive art of the grand school with a natural impulse to murder the Victorian womanly woman' (Shaw, 'An Aside', in McCarthy, 8). Writing of her 'quiet dignity', the critic in the *Westminster Gazette*, while praising her for being 'delightfully unstagy', thought if there were any fault 'it is of excessive restraint in the Trial scene'. He also found that 'in the Statue scene she exhibited a comparative coldness. Indeed, Camillo's phrase "She hangs about his neck" was hardly realised in the acting' (23 September 1912, 2). This judgement (echoed by several other critics) probably reflects conflicts within the viewer's horizon of expectations; while receptive to the production, the *Westminster Gazette* critic wanted her to be 'a shade more theatrical' – which may reflect stereotypical expectations of womanly behaviour, of the role, and of older acting styles. But McCarthy avoided such stereotypes and refused to give 'the traditional cry of despair' at the announcement of Mamillius' death (Bartholomeusz, 155).

Responding to critics who found discordances between Ainley's style and Lillah McCarthy's, Barker defended the contrast as appropriate to character and the dramatic moment. When asked by the dramatic critic of the *Evening News* about Hermione's speech at the trial, Barker replied, 'you need the grave, slow measure there' (24 September 1912). Attentive to variation in verse styles, Barker wrote: '*The Winter's Tale*, as I see its writing, is complex, vivid, abundant in the variety of its mood and pace and colour' (*More Prefaces*, 32; from his Preface to *Twelfth Night: An Acting Edition*, 1912). Hugh Hunt recalled that Barker tried 'to persuade his actors of the values of allying rhythm with character' (quoted in Dymkowski, 43).

Barker, who had probed women's issues sympathetically and with keen awareness in his own plays of sexual conflict between men and women (*The Marrying of Ann Leete*, 1901, and *Waste*, 1907, for example), was freer from a stereotypical reading of Hermione's character than many of his critics, who called for greater tenderness in McCarthy's playing of the role. Barker did see in Hermione 'an exquisitely sensitive woman', but by this he implied no sentimentality; he went on to say 'witty too' (*More Prefaces*, 23). For a '"good" woman', wrote Barker in his acting edition, she is 'a remarkably interesting figure'.

> 'Goodness' in drama is too apt to become a merely negative quality ... One can tell that she knows the danger of the man [Leontes], but when the outrageous blow has fallen, even in her utter helplessness, she has perfect courage. Against all the trouble facing her she stands serene; only the cruel side-blow of her son's death fells her. Even then she falls silently, proudly still. (*More Prefaces*, 23)

McCarthy did choose in her final scene to show a 'sudden piercing tenderness' as she embraced Perdita; yet, again, there was no sentimentality. Her measured speech beginning 'You gods look down' (V.iii.121–4) had 'simplicity, largeness, freedom' (*Stage*, 26 September 1912).

Barker's casting and directing supported the strength of the women's parts. Casting Lillah McCarthy as Hermione avoided stereotypes of Victorian womanhood; Barker directed Cathleen Nesbitt, as Perdita, to avoid false poeticism. 'Be *honest*, always. Don't ever listen to yourself sing', Nesbitt remembers him saying to her. 'Be swift, be swift, be not poetical', Barker wrote on opening night in a note placed in her dressing room. During a rehearsal when Nesbitt thought she was 'being very musical' about the 'daffodils, / That come before the swallow dares', Barker intervened – 'You're being too poetical' – and reminded her of Touchstone's dialogue with Audrey (*As You Like It*, III.iii.13–21; see Nesbitt, *A Little Love and Good Company*, 63–5). It is no wonder that Nesbitt's Perdita seems to have been refreshingly free of affectation or set speeches. Critics accustomed to the 'poetical' objected, complaining, for example, that 'as a matter of elocution she did not give full value to some of the lovely lines' (*Westminster Gazette*, 23 September 1912, 2). Demanding 'nobility', some critics combined stock ideas of acting styles with those of social class: 'Indeed, although this gay, dancing Perdita is obviously "the prettiest low-born lass that ever ran on the green sward," Polixenes must have been a regular Sherlock Holmes to find in her something "too noble for this place"' (*Daily Mail*, 23 September 1912). One critic contrasted Nesbitt's portrayal of Perdita 'as a merry country girl, without a trace of anything to indicate noble birth', to Mary Anderson's, whose Perdita he thought a 'Princess in disguise' (*Westminster Gazette*, 23 September 1912, 2). Other critics, however, found Nesbitt's Perdita, with Barker's staging of the sheep-shearing scene, a welcome departure from 'the pretty-pretty shepherds and shepherdesses of Watteau's Arcadia' (unattributed cutting, 23 September 1912; Griffiths Collection, Birmingham Shakespeare Library).

Noting 'the touched-in resemblances between mother and daughter', Barker saw in Perdita 'her mother's courage and self-possession' (*More Prefaces*, 23–4). Similar qualities, in a very different key, characterized Esmé Beringer's Paulina, and critical reception of her acting was largely positive. She 'played her sympathetic part with no little spirit and great conviction' (*Daily Mail*, 23 September 1912). One critic found her 'too prepared and oratorical' as she began her 'great attack on Leontes'; but 'as the speech went on she caught the spirit of that irresistible outburst, and played with fire and intelligence all through' (*Observer*, 22 September 1912). Given Beringer's work in the part, few critics reiterated the stereotype of the shrew; the critic of the *Westminster Gazette* wrote how 'admirably' she played the 'important character of Paulina' (23 September 1912, 2). Paulina's courageous claiming of agency, and her rhetorical power, seemed to have fresh resonance in the production's historical moment; to one reviewer it seemed Paulina would be recognized by the 'young Suffragettes' (*Referee*, 22 September 1912, 3).

Barker emphasized the tragicomic possibilities, as well as the importance, of Paulina's role: 'Was ever a character better contrived to keep the tragi-comic balance than Paulina?' he wrote, adding that the tragic aspect of the scene in which Leontes condemns the baby to exposure (II.iii) 'is yet heavily salted with the comedy of Paulina and Antigonus. At its height it becomes a slanging match' (*More Prefaces*, 20). Furthermore, wrote Barker, even when Leontes repents, 'there is something a little ridiculous in his breathless confession to the surrounding courtiers, his frantic promises to undo what he has done.' In Barker's reading of these moments,

Paulina, too, relaxes from her high-toned scolding to an almost motherly fussiness, and the scene ends in pathos not in tragedy. But is it not this slight touch of the ridiculous which keeps it very human, and holds our sympathy; while the very suddenness of the catastrophe leaves us, paradoxically enough, expectant of some happier solution? Hardened into the finality of tragedy, the whole business would simply be too odious. (*More Prefaces*, 20)

Barker himself risked stereotypes in his words 'scolding' and 'motherly fussiness'. Yet, he wrote, 'I know few things that move me more' than Paulina's lines: 'I, an old turtle, / Will wing me to some wither'd bough and there / My mate, that's never to be found again, / Lament till I am lost' (V.iii.132–5, as quoted in *More Prefaces*, 22–3). His next comment on these lines is in an idiom now almost lost: 'Plucky Paulina; such a good fellow!' Although Barker affirmed Paulina's courage and comradeship, later twentieth-century women directors and actors have given Paulina more complex tones at this moment, and her loss of her husband more weight. Barker saw Paulina and Camillo's proposed marriage as an instance of Renaissance dramatic closure; Audrey Stanley, on the other hand, directing for the Oregon Shakespearean Festival in 1975, saw it as a mutual choice between moral equals. Barker was at the time ahead of most critics in emphasizing the strength of the play's roles for women. But he was interested in Paulina's role especially as it affected the play's tragicomic tonalities. His focus was on the problem of dramatic technique.

Barker's argument for the tragicomic potentialities of *The Winter's Tale*, with its mingled tones and bold yet skilful dramatic technique, was in his time an unusual defence of a play still routinely under attack in the dominant critical tradition. His argument, rooted in his grasp of Elizabethan and Jacobean dramatic conventions, enabled him to take on successfully two of the play's most celebrated dramatic challenges: the presentation of the bear and of Time. 'We had it all, including the bear', began the detailed and largely laudatory review in the *Daily Telegraph* (23 September 1912). Presumably the actor wore the bear's head and full bear-like skin specified in the production's Wardrobe Department list (Account Book). Praising the 'blunt and fiery Antigonus', one reviewer added 'and the bear played his part well, too!' (*Observer*, 22 September 1912, 10). Gordon Crosse, remarking that the bear 'was introduced just at the side in III.iii' (a note confirmed by the Account Book's Scene and

Light Plot), thought the actor performing the bear 'succeeded in being realistic and not ridiculous' (MS Diaries, vol. 5, p. 113, Birmingham Shakespeare Library).

Time's Chorus and the sudden appearance of the bear functioned to create structural shifts, tonal mixtures, and metatheatrical awareness important to the art of tragicomedy. While acknowledging critical questions about the play's sixteen-year 'wide gap' (IV.i.7), Barker argued: 'But in a tragi-comedy, as this is, is it not just some such jar that is needed to break the play from the one mood to the other?' Time, as Chorus? 'The very artifice of the device', Barker continued, 'attunes us to the artifice of the story; saves us, at this dangerous juncture, when Hermione is apparently dead, Antigonus quite certainly eaten by the bear, from the true tragic mood' (*More Prefaces*, 19–20).[10]

Time was an arresting figure of deliberate artifice; Herbert Farjeon found him 'wonderfully grotesque' (*Theatreland*, 11 October 1912). A white spotlight focused on Time (Herbert Hewetson) at his entrance after the production's only interval. He spoke from the platform (apron) in front of the white drop curtain; a photograph (see figure 1) shows one hand in a stylized

1 Act IV, scene i: Herbert Hewetson as Time. Directed by Harley Granville Barker, Savoy Theatre, 1912. By permission of the Shakespeare Birthplace Trust

gesture toward the auditorium, the other hand raised, holding the drop curtain (and possibly, though it is not visible in the photograph, an hourglass, which is listed among Properties in the Account Book). He wore a blue gown (cashmere) with gold waist cord and his cloak (also of cashmere) had leaves of cloth sewn upon it; as is further evident from the Wardrobe Department list in the Account Book, his golden wig had stiffened, twisted strands of hair. His make-up in part resembled a mask. He addressed audiences directly, but not with relaxed informality. He was designed to rivet attention, and to astonish audiences with wonder.

Barker did in part aim to startle audiences, especially out of familiar expectations. Though he wrote of Bohemia as 'pure Warwickshire' (*More Prefaces*, 21), an identification thoughtfully resisted by Desmond MacCarthy (*Eye-Witness*, 3 October 1912, 501), in presenting Bohemia Barker avoided detailed or sentimental pictorialism. One critic objected that there was 'no suggestion of trees, grass, or softness or greenery of any sort' (*Daily Chronicle*, 23 September 1912). Barker instead used bold outlines for the shepherds' cottage, which was perceived to have 'Simple and Austere Line and Clear Surfaces' rather than elaborate realism (*Boston Evening Transcript*, 16 January 1915, 6; see figure 2). Nonrealist, Rothenstein's designs for the costumes, like Wilkinson's for the scenic decoration, countered the dominant picturesque tradition. Costume colours for the pastoral scene were bold and vibrant. Perdita wore a yellow dress with black circular designs; her countrywomen wore skirts together with velveteen bodices of various colours, amongst them green, blue, yellow, and cherry red (Wardrobe Department list, Account Book). Barker accommodated eclecticism of design. For costuming the characters of the 'Bohemian countryside', wrote Barker, 'let us fetter ourselves as little as Shakespeare did' (*More Prefaces*, 24).

'There is an air of improvisation about his [Barker's] work; you feel that he might vary his effects from night to night', wrote A. B. Walkley, commenting on the whole production, especially the pastoral scene. Walkley immediately added, 'If he is now and then a little too freakish, you are ready to forgive him because this queer Shakespeare of his has the sovereign virtue of being alive. In particular, the sheep-shearing revels are not only alive, but kicking.' Noting that only Perdita dances 'featly', Walkley welcomed the country dances as 'none of your "poetry of

2 Act IV, scene iv: H. O. Nicholson as the Old Shepherd, Cathleen Nesbitt as Perdita, Dennis Neilson-Terry as Florizel, Stanley Drewitt as Camillo (with mask). Directed by Harley Granville Barker, Savoy Theatre, 1912. By permission of the Shakespeare Birthplace Trust

motion," but uncouth, rustic bumping and jerking' (*The Times*, 23 September 1912, 7). Even among critics whose traditionalist expectations led them to object that 'the tender sweetness of the idyll [was] replaced by jostle and jerk' (*Daily Chronicle*, 23 September 1912), almost none thought it flagged. Barker only cut approximately eleven lines of the scene (from IV.iv.605–9 and 718–23), if we are to judge by his production's text in the acting edition (pages 92 and 96), yet met one of the play's greatest challenges: he maintained the pastoral scene's momentum and varying energies.

'BE SWIFT. BE ALERT. BE DEXTEROUS. PITCH THE SONGS HIGH. BE SWIFT. BE ALERT.' So wrote Barker on the card he sent for opening night to Arthur Whitby, his Autolycus (Trewin, *Shakespeare on the English Stage*, 53). Walkley found Whitby's performance 'a rich bit of roguery; the philosophic vagabond with just a lurking suggestion of the sinister' (*The Times*, 23 September 1912, 7). Whitby's quick, dry wit helped sustain the scene's diverse energies, as did the vigorous interpretation of the dance of shepherds and shepherdesses. Since he wanted robust, rather than lyrical dancing, Barker got the help of Mary Neal, founder of the Esperance Guild. Dedicated to recovering English country dances, not as in dancing manuals or taught by professional teachers, but as practised and handed down, generation by generation, she brought in a seventy-year-old countryman from Abingdon to rehearse the actors for this dance. Music for the dance was played onstage using tabor and pipe (cf. servant's description, IV.iv.184–5). Gone was the orchestra and its background music characteristic of many productions of the time. 'There was a welcome absence of "incidental music"', wrote Rupert Hyde (*T. P.'s Weekly*, 4 October 1912, 423); music was used when called for by the text. Melodies, arranged by Nellie Chaplin, were said to be based on Elizabethan ones (*Standard*, 21 September 1912). Such Elizabethanism in music and dance was perceived not to be antiquarian but to have 'freshness and spontaneity' (unattributed cutting, Griffiths Collection, Birmingham Shakespeare Library, 23 September 1912; cf. the *Standard*, 23 September 1912, and A. B. Walkley in *The Times*, 23 September 1912, 7).

Barker's pastoral included the Dionysian energies of the satyrs. The 'three carters, three shepherds, three neatherds, three swineherds' who 'have made themselves all men of hair' (IV.iv.319–21), call themselves 'saltiers' (leapers, skilled in jumping). Their dance is signalled by the First Folio stage direction, '*Heere a Dance of twelve Satyres*'. The dance has been cut more often than not, before and since Barker's production, even by Peter Brook; the cut diminishes those stylistic contrasts which make the Bohemian scenes so wide-ranging and varied in their dramatic energies. Both rustic and mythic, Barker's twelve satyrs wore brown and scarlet knee-length britches; with leafage around their waists and necks and wearing wigs of red hue with horns affixed, they bore sticks with stylized masks (Properties Department and Wardrobe Department lists, Account Book). One reviewer found their dance 'too suggestive of a court masque' (*Daily News*, 23 September 1912). His complaint may unwittingly point to a strength in the production, if the play's stylistic mixture is differently understood. The same reviewer thought acting in the pastoral scene lacked restraint, involving a 'realism' quite in contrast to the scenery and 'eccentric' costumes. As Dennis Bartholomeusz put it, the 'idea that the counterpoint between the realism of the acting and the symbolic and mythical suggestiveness of scenery and costumes was deliberate and conscious does not seem to have occurred to him [the reviewer]' (159).

Herbert Farjeon condemned what he called the 'Sabine savagery that is introduced when these twelve performers, with brown, half-naked bodies, suddenly give chase to the screaming country-wenches round about, seize them, and bear them off shoulder-high in a whirl of barbaric passion' (*Theatreland*, 11 October 1912). Not all critics were censorious; even in a rather negative review, the critic of the *Morning Post* thought the 'twelve dancing Satyrs could not have been bettered' (23 September 1912, 8). Critical tastes were shifting; Diaghilev had already brought the Russian ballet to London twice by 1912; Stravinsky, who had composed the music for Diaghilev's *The Firebird* (1910), would bring his own *The Rite of Spring* to Paris in 1913.

Including the satyrs' dance was an important act of reconstruction, helping Barker explore the play's diverse tonal and conceptual range. Even more important was his restoration of a scene often cut from previous productions in its entirety: Act V, scene ii, in which three gentlemen report the news that Perdita has been found. Barker cut not a word of the scene and proved its dramatic viability. His care in casting even small parts with skilled actors is evident in his seeking the experienced Nigel Playfair to play the third of these gentlemen, 'Lady Paulina's steward' (V.ii.26). It is the key role if the scene is to work. The actor must have verbal acumen, wit, energy, and precision, for it is he who evokes at length the woe and wonder of the reunion, in intricately patterned Jacobean prose. Playfair's delivery as the Steward was 'modulated, rendered with cadence', according to one reviewer (*Standard*, 23 September 1912). Critics were virtually unanimous in their praise for his part, which few had ever heard played; in the two previous major London productions – Beerbohm Tree's in 1906, and Mary Anderson's in 1887 – the scene had been cut. 'Mr. Nigel Playfair made something little short of a triumph out of the often omitted Third Gentleman's narrative,' wrote one critic, glad that for 'the first time in over two centuries the whole play is set forth, in its own order of scenes, with only a line or so cut out' (*Daily Chronicle*, 23

September 1912). Playfair was 'a magnificent comedian', according to Cathleen Nesbitt, and 'spurred the other two [gentlemen] on' (*Listener*, 13 January 1972, 51), playing with great 'brio' (*A Little Love and Good Company*, 62).

By all accounts, the dominant tone of V.ii was of high, witty comedy, however serious its import. In his acting edition, Barker implicitly saw the scene as part of the play's tragicomic art, arguing that it strategically prepares the audience for the scene with Hermione as a statue. The final scene 'is so good that hasty naked handling might have spoiled it', wrote Barker. 'But Shakespeare goes about the business with great care. He prepares the audience, through Paulina's steward, almost to the pitch of revelation, saving just so much surprise, and leaving so little, that when they see the statue they may think themselves more in doubt than they really are whether it is Hermione herself or no.' Furthermore, Barker added: 'The [final] scene is elaborately held back by the preceding one, which though but preparation, actually equals it in length, and its poetry is heightened by such contrast with fantastic prose and fun' (*More Prefaces*, 22).

Barker's analysis of the final scene implies that poetry in drama is integral to complex, dynamic dramatic form. From 'the moment the statue is disclosed, every device of changing colour and time, every minor contrast of voice and mood that can give the scene modelling and beauty of form, is brought into easy use' (*More Prefaces*, 22). Barker defined such contrasts, writing that 'the brisk stirring trumpet sentences in Paulina's speech' are soon followed by 'the simplicity' of Leontes' 'let it be an art / Lawful as eating'. Immediately there is 'the swift contrast of the alarmed and sceptical Polixenes and Camillo, then Paulina's happiness breaking almost into chatter' (*More Prefaces*, 22). One might well interpret the tone of particular lines differently from Barker, but still admire his alertness to their variation in 'voice and mood'.

Critical responses to the production's final scene offer praise but little precise detail. A critic (perhaps of romantic tastes) who thought Lillah McCarthy's Hermione 'a little too cold' in earlier scenes, and Ainley's Leontes too forced, thought McCarthy, however, 'absolutely beautiful' and Ainley 'affecting and sympathetic' in the statue scene (*Daily Chronicle*, 23 September 1912). What the critic thought objectionable in earlier scenes may well have been deliberate, part of the director's and actors' exploration of contrasting poetic styles and tonalities.

Barker's staging of the statue scene was unusual in his day and remains so even now. Nineteenth-century common practice was to place the statue of Hermione upstage, the central image in an elaborate built-up set, and framed, of course, by the proscenium. Barker placed the scene downstage, in front of both the proscenium and a drop curtain. The scene was lit non-illusionistically, with white lights on full (Scene and Light Plot, Account Book). Barker's apron staging was especially significant, as Dennis Kennedy has argued, for a scene which could call forth 'tricks of the theatre': 'It is therefore especially significant that Barker was confident enough in his non-illusionist methods to place it ... a few feet from the spectators' eyes' (*Granville Barker*, 126–7). A photograph (see figure 3) suggests the power of Barker's bold presentation which avoided elaborate settings. The drop curtain had stylized patterns, not representational images. Spare yet formal gestures of the carefully grouped actors, and their rapt attention, placed focus upon the statue. Barker saw in the final scene a profound simplicity which can encompass, rather than betray, complexity, implying unstated suffering and grace. 'And then the perfect sufficiency of Hermione's eight lines (oh, how a lesser dramatist might have overdone it with Noble Forgiveness and what not!)', wrote Barker, concluding, 'it all really is a wonderful bit of work' (*More Prefaces*, 22).

Barker's written defence of the tragicomic art that shapes dramatic conventions of *The Winter's Tale* and his production have both contributed to the play's twentieth-century revaluation. In retrospect, it is ironic that the full run of such a significant production was only six weeks (ending 2 November), plus matinées which continued until the end of November even after the opening of his *Twelfth Night* (15 November).[11] Barker's *Twelfth Night* was better received than his *Winter's Tale*; critics had perhaps begun to be accustomed to the mode of his Savoy Shakespeare productions. In method they were virtually the same. Many thought *Twelfth Night* more unified in effect, and more assured. It was certainly the better known and far more critically accepted play; a significant number of objections to Barker's *Winter's Tale* were based on prejudices about the theatrical production or the play itself.[12] About these critical objections Shaw was characteristically blunt: 'What they didn't like was Shakespeare. It will take them ten years to acquire the taste for Shakespeare's later plays' (*Observer*, 29 September 1912, 9).

3 Act V, scene iii: Lillah McCarthy as Hermione, Esmé Beringer as Paulina, Henry Ainley as Leontes, Cathleen Nesbitt as Perdita, Stanley Drewitt as Camillo, Charles Graham as Polixenes, Dennis Neilson-Terry as Florizel. Directed by Harley Granville Barker, Savoy Theatre, 1912. By permission of the Shakespeare Birthplace Trust

Many reviewers of *The Winter's Tale* 'were conservative in their dramatic tastes', writes Dennis Kennedy, 'and should not be completely trusted about challenging innovation'. Artists and others 'of artistic sensibility were not as suspicious'. Kennedy cites the composer Edward Elgar, who 'wrote Barker that "a lot of preposterous nonsense has been written" about the production; he found the entire evening a "great joy"' (British Library Add. MSS 47897; *Granville Barker*, 133). Desmond MacCarthy, while carefully questioning aspects of the production, gave it strong support (*Eye-Witness*, 3 October 1912).

Given the wide divergence in viewers' horizons of expectation, and critical contention between traditionalists and reformers, Barker's production was like a match to a powder keg (cf. Konody, *Observer*, 29 September 1912, 9). It is not surprising that its critical reception was so explosive. Among the more judicious viewers, however, was Gordon Crosse; he wrote (in November 1912) of Barker's *The Winter's Tale*: 'This ought to (but it won't) put an end to the era of "arranged" texts and elaborate changes of scene.' In a later notation (undated) he commented that this prediction had been 'unnecessarily pessimistic. It did' (MS Diaries, vol. 5, pp. 104–5; see also his *Fifty Years of Shakespearean Playgoing*, 59).

Crosse's later notation is an important perception of the impact Barker's *The Winter's Tale* had on twentieth-century Shakespearean production. But no categorical statement can justly sum up the complexity of subsequent twentieth-century practice. Progressive movements existed for a considerable time alongside regressive ones. Though without as much textual rearrangement and elaborate scenic representation as in dominant nineteenth-century practice, new forms of romanticized spectacle, together with heavy cutting, were used in Anthony Quayle's production of *The Winter's Tale* at the Shakespeare Memorial Theatre as late as 1948, for example; compared to it, Peter Brook's 1951 production had more affinities with the spirit of Barker's principles.

Barker's *The Winter's Tale*, progressive as it was, did not achieve its methods or its impact in isolation. Barker's theatrical work had both predecessors and contemporary parallels; it was, however, outstanding among varying reform movements.[13] On the continent, early nineteenth-century Elizabethanist reform movements included Tieck's modified quasi-Elizabethan stage, with permanent sets, for four Elizabethan plays (Bartholomeusz, 132). Max Reinhardt's 'experiments in scene design', as Frederick Tollini defines them, were characterized by 'plasticity of space and the firm rejection of painted illusionist scenery' (Tollini, 85), as is evident in his *Winter's Tale* in 1906 (and *Lear* in 1908) for the Deutsches Theater in Berlin. In these respects Reinhardt's work partially parallels Barker's; William Archer commented upon Reinhardt's 'simple yet impressive decoration', not realistically detailed, for almost all the Sicilian scenes, and his deliberately naive decor for the pastoral scenes (quoted in Carter, 87). In England, Benjamin Webster and J. R. Planché produced *The Taming of the Shrew* at the Haymarket (1844) with screens, curtains, and a semi-permanent set. Curtains or faux tapestries instead of elaborately painted canvas scenery were the most common means by which Elizabethanism was inserted into Edwardian theatre practice. Curtains were used frequently by Charles Fry, by Tree for his *Hamlet* (Mazer, *Shakespeare Refashioned*, 73-4), and of course by William Poel, who had criticized proscenium staging, elaborate sets, and delays between acts and scenes. Poel had eliminated footlights, as had Edward Gordon Craig (1872-1966; see Dymkowski, 25, 39). Both opposed elaborate scenic realism, though often by antithetical means. Poel's Elizabethanism contrasted with Craig's creation of vast stage spaces shaped by light, space, and abstract form. In his *The First Dialogue* (1905), Craig argued such staging should be integral to a unified vision composed of movement, 'rhythm', 'action', 'words', 'line and colour' (repr. in his 1911 *On the Art of the Theatre*, 138). Barker selected elements from opposing camps. Acknowledging his debt to Poel and Craig amid the controversy over his *Winter's Tale*, Barker wrote that Poel 'taught me how swift and passionate a thing, how beautiful in its variety, Elizabethan blank verse might be when tongues were trained to speak and ears acute to hear it'. Craig, he stated, 'destroyed for me once and for all any illusion I may have had as to the necessity of surrounding every performance of a play with the stuffy, fussy, thick-bedaubed canvas which we are accustomed to call stage scenery' (letter to the *Daily Mail*, 26 September 1912, 4). Barker's strength was not so much in sheer innovation as in his power of critical selection and creative synthesis from varied movements in the stagecraft of his time (cf. Mazer, *Shakespeare Refashioned*, 150). Barker newly combined diverse elements, and did so with fresh force.

Rooted, with his eclecticism, in his own historical moment, Barker is the finest exemplar and most articulate advocate of early twentieth-century reforms in Shakespearean production. His work helped certain emergent trends become dominant practices. During and after World War I, there was 'growing acceptance' of Barker's ideas, particularly of less elaborate, not realistically detailed settings, 'speedy playing, continuity of action, reliance on teamwork, and unabridged texts', according to Muriel St Clare Byrne ('Fifty Years of Shakespearian Production: 1898–1948', 10). Barry Jackson used these principles in directing the Birmingham Repertory company (1914–18 and after), as did Bridges-Adams, directing the New Shakespeare Company at Stratford-upon-Avon (1919–34), and Robert Atkins, directing in London at the Old Vic (1920–25).[14] Like Harcourt Williams, whose productions of Shakespeare at the Old Vic from 1929 to 1934 showed Barker's influence, these directors (including former actors) knew Barker and his work firsthand. Their reforms continued to develop in Britain and North America in the work of later theatre practitioners, distinguished as well as lesser known, in national theatres and in regional repertory companies.

The principles underlying Barker's experiments in his Savoy productions circulated even more widely, moreover, because he refined and expanded them in his subsequent lectures, in his well-known *Prefaces to Shakespeare*, and in other published works. His *Prefaces* especially, in which he combines his acumen as director, playwright, actor, and critic, have been cited by a number of directors as the 'most stimulating in the formation' of their 'approach to Shakespeare' (1957 survey cited by Dymkowski, 128). Barker's intellectual influence continued even though he chose to withdraw from full-time theatre production after 1915. After that, he largely devoted himself to writing, though in the next three decades, before his death in 1946, he returned eight times to London to direct or work with other directors (Kennedy, *Granville Barker*, 213–14).

'More than anyone in England or America', according to Dennis Kennedy, 'Barker taught the new century about the power of the open stage, the virtues of swift speaking and restored texts, the force of simple decor and non-representational color and shape.' To these contributions Kennedy adds Barker's emphasis on the actor not as a star but as a craftsperson, devoted to 'the communal experience' of the play (*Granville Barker*, 188). Barker was committed to the repertory principle, articulating, in Kennedy's words, his 'wide awake dream' of a national theatre, though it was not realized in Barker's lifetime. Moreover, concludes Kennedy, Barker's work widely disseminated his 'most consistent principle, that the responsibility of the director is always first to the playwright' (*Granville Barker*, 188).

Barker's published criticism, as Trousdale ('The Question of Harley Granville-Barker and Shakespeare on Stage') and others have argued, is marked by his concerns both as a producer and as a critic of poetic language. As such he gave impetus to subsequent developments in criticism and scholarship concerned with performance (cf. Kennedy, *Granville Barker*, 153). Nearly twenty-five years after Barker had largely given up directing for writing, he agreed, at the special request of John Gielgud and Tyrone Guthrie, to direct for a short time during rehearsals of the 1940 *King Lear* at the Old Vic. Gielgud was in the title role. Lewis Casson was the official director; Barker 'refused to have his name officially announced as director', according to Gielgud (*Stage Directions*, 51). Barker, however, was probably the major shaping force; he consulted before the production in conferences and by letter, and the programme stated that the production was based on his Preface to *King Lear* (though the production and Preface differed in certain respects; see Dymkowski, 177–84).[15] Barker 'had only ten days to work with us on *King Lear*', said Gielgud, 'but they were the fullest in experience that I have ever had in all my years upon the stage'. Barker's 'first concern', Gielgud remembered, 'was certainly for the speaking of the verse and the balance of the voices'. Summarizing Barker's 'high standards', Gielgud wrote: 'Tempo, atmosphere, diction, balance, character – no detail could escape his fastidious ear' (*Stage Directions*, 52–3).

'Gielgud's speech', thought Lewis Casson, 'is a sort of living monument to Barker among English actors' ('Recollections of Harley Granville-Barker').[16] Nearly four decades after Barker's 1912 production of *The Winter's Tale*, strong traces of his ideas about text, verse speaking, acting, and staging lived on in the play's next most significant twentieth-century production. Directed in 1951 by Peter Brook, it had a cast that included Lewis Casson as Antigonus and John Gielgud as Leontes.

CHAPTER II

Postwar renewal: Peter Brook's production at the Phoenix Theatre, 1951

Peter Brook's *The Winter's Tale* in 1951 was the longest-running production of the play in Britain or North America in theatrical record up to that time.[1] Its critical reception expressed the rare consensus that it was the finest production of *The Winter's Tale* most had witnessed. Gordon Crosse, whose manuscript notes include his evaluations of all the major British productions of *The Winter's Tale* he had seen over nearly half a century, judged it 'The best all round performance of this play that I have seen since Granville-Barker's' (Crosse, MS Diaries, vol. 20, p. 73).

In 1957 Brook wrote an ironic response to negative critical judgements still in wide circulation about certain of Shakespeare's plays (including *Titus Andronicus* and *Love's Labour's Lost*) he had recently directed: 'And *The Winter's Tale* – I can remember a review that said, "This is Shakespeare's worst play – preposterous long-winded rubbish"' (repr. in Brook's *The Shifting Point*, 72–3). Reviewers' ideas about *The Winter's Tale* were still very mixed by the time of Brook's 1951 production, though S. L. Bethell (*'The Winter's Tale': A Study*, 1946) and others had already begun the process of its postwar critical retrieval. But almost all reviewers praised Brook's production. Eric Johns noted that while the play was 'little more than a name to the majority of theatregoers', when a Gielgud acts Leontes 'we are left wondering why the play is so rarely performed' (*Theatre World*, August 1951, 7).

When his production opened at London's Phoenix Theatre on 27 June 1951, Peter Brook had recently turned twenty-six years old. He was already a veteran, however, of nearly two dozen productions (David Williams, *Casebook*, xxiii–xxiv) and, Janus-like, looked to both dominant and emergent theatre forms. He had directed five productions of opera at Covent Garden – sometimes with bold innovation. Brook has said his 'first empty space' was a huge white cloth covering the Covent Garden stage for the revolution scene in his *Boris Godunov* in 1948 (*Threads of Time*, 48). His *Salome* (1949) was designed by Salvador Dalí. Earlier, in 1945, he had directed Shaw and Ibsen at the Birmingham Repertory Theatre; but from 1946 onward he was increasingly involved in newer drama, directing plays by Sartre, Anouilh, and John Whiting. Four of his pre-1951 productions were of Shakespeare, three of them at the Shakespeare Memorial Theatre in Stratford-upon-Avon. At the invitation of Barry Jackson, Brook had directed his first Stratford production in 1946 (at the age of twenty-one), a *Love's Labour's Lost* set in an eighteenth-century world based on the paintings of Watteau. Despite the emergence in Brook's work of opposing tendencies, he was still in 1951 committed to theatrical illusionism and its picture-frame stage (see his reflections in his *Threads of Time*, 34–7).

Yet, in contrast to the elaborate pictorialism of Brook's *Love's Labour's Lost*, the restrained design of his *Winter's Tale* five years later, despite elements of pictorial decor, appeared to many reviewers at the time relatively simple, even austere. His iconoclastic 1947 production of *Romeo and Juliet* had disturbed conservative reviewers, but critics open to his experimentation, his range, and his shifts of style realized that they could not stereotype his work. J. C. Trewin wrote that critics, 'fumbling for a label, found that Brook eluded the gum-brush' (*Peter Brook*, 58). Certainly no label could be easily attached to his fine 1950 production of *Measure for Measure* or his 1955 production of *Titus Andronicus*, both at the Shakespeare Memorial Theatre, which, like his production of *The Winter's Tale* at the Phoenix in 1951, challenged earlier critical shibboleths about these plays' supposed defects. Each of these productions was in its time a significant theatrical recovery of a play often neglected or misunderstood in the light of prevailing critical or theatrical norms.

Gielgud, who had played Angelo in Brook's 1950 *Measure*, wrote that it was he who suggested (to the theatrical management, Tennent Productions) that *The Winter's Tale* be produced under Brook's direction during the 1951 Festival of Britain 'largely because of the success of *Measure for Measure* at

Stratford-on-Avon the year before, when the audiences had seemed to find so much interest in one of the lesser-known plays, and I had had the exciting experience of working with Peter Brook as Director for the first time' (*Stage Directions*, 43–4). Gielgud, at the age of forty-seven widely regarded as the finest 'classical' actor in England, and the young Peter Brook drew together for *The Winter's Tale* a cast of extraordinary skill and experience: Flora Robson as Paulina; Diana Wynyard as Hermione (whom Gielgud had admired in the role in the 1948 Stratford production); Lewis Casson, at the age of seventy-five, as Antigonus; George Rose as Autolycus; and Gielgud himself as Leontes. The designer was Sophie Fedorovitch; the playwright Christopher Fry (whose adaptation of Anouilh's *Ring Round the Moon* Brook had directed in 1950) composed the music.

The production was in no way merely a showcase for stellar talent – a 'patriotic' trap into which a postwar festival to assert survival and renewal could fall. Instead, the combined talents at the Phoenix Theatre in 1951 drew upon living tradition and fresh direction for a serious and distinguished exploration of *The Winter's Tale*. The production, wrote one critic (*Evening Standard*, 28 June 1951), 'brought the season as a whole into perspective. In the past few months we have had much banging of the big drum, and some interesting theatrical events; but last night's production is the first and only one to touch greatness.'

One source of the production's strength sprang from Brook's work with the play's structure, which was still under critical attack. His directorial decisions were based on perceptions he later articulated in *The Empty Space* (1968). He perceived the play to be divided 'into three sections':

> Leontes accuses his wife of infidelity. He condemns her to death. The child is put to sea. In the second part the child grows up, and now in a different pastoral key the very same action is repeated. The man falsely accused by Leontes now in turn behaves just as unreasonably. The consequence is the same – the child again takes flight. Her journey takes her back to Leontes' palace and the third part is now in the same place as the first ... Again, Leontes finds himself in similar conditions, in which he could be as violently unreasonable as before. Thus the main action is presented first ferociously; then a second time by charming parody but in a bold major key, for the pastoral of the play is a mirror as well as a straight device. The third movement is in another contrasting key – a key of remorse. (*The Empty Space*, 90)[2]

[64]

Brook's theatrical judgement resembled certain concerns of his contemporaries engaged in practical criticism and new criticism. Brook's interest in the ways diverse elements in the play form complex wholes did not, however, involve a narrow conception of unity; he emphasized that Shakespeare juxtaposes the holy and the rough with a 'conscious mingling of opposites' (*The Empty Space*, 88).

Brook's sense of the play's structure was supported by Sophie Fedorovitch's sets. She created two full-stage settings, with no backcloths, which reflected certain current ideas of elements of 'Elizabethan' staging: balcony levels, a discovery space rear centre on the lower level, entry and exit passageways on either side. Each of the two main fixed sets could be quickly altered by a few properties and hangings; thus, as Bartholomeusz notes, since 'the scenes moved swiftly without disturbing pauses – the Shakespearian principle of continuity established by Barker was very much in play' (180), though Brook did not attempt, as did Barker, to break the proscenium by constructing an apron stage. The fixed set for Sicilia had an arch (with balconies) on either side of the stage and a larger arch in the centre forming a recessed area over which hung, above its balcony, a large crown-like image of royal power. For the accusation scene, II.i, a large arch was added to the centre balcony level, in which a guard appeared; a brazier was added for the baby scene, II.ii; in the return to Sicilia, V.i, the balconies over the side arches, according to Bartholomeusz, 'were hung with funeral wreaths' (178). By contrast, for Bohemia, on either side of the stage were simple two-level timbered structures with a large open space between them, above which hung a great wreath of straw that replaced the Sicilian heraldic crown.

Angus McBean's photographs[3] of the production suggest that good use was made of the spaces and levels these stage structures (not illusionistic 'sets') created. In II.i, for example, Leontes appeared on the stage-left balcony for his dialogue with his lords, which begins 'Was he met there? His train? Camillo with him?' (33). Then, in a striking choice, Leontes remained on the balcony, looking down on the main stage to accuse Hermione of adultery and order that Mamillius be taken from her and she be taken to prison. The photograph of that moment shows a strong diagonal line of vision between Leontes and those on the main stage; this use of two-level staging pointed up Leontes' isolation and near tyrannical use of power. Leontes then exited from the balcony after his line 'He who shall speak for her is afar off guilty – / But that he speaks!' (104–5) and emerged down on the main stage to demand, 'Shall I be heard?' (115; these movements of Leontes are indicated in the Brook production promptbook, 'Act I', pp. 18–20).[4] In a further effective use of the possibilities offered by the stage architecture, another McBean photograph shows that the 'statue' of Hermione in V.iii was presented using the recessed discovery space toward the rear of centre stage.

The court costumes were mainly quasi-Tudor in style. Sophie Fedorovitch's costume designs for the first three acts, in Sicilia, included dark blue for Hermione; burgundy with black velveteen (on the bodice and underneath slit sleeves) for Paulina; and jet-black velveteen with dark burgundy, red, and plum for three court women (designs now at the Theatre Museum, London). One of Fedorovitch's costume designs shows a swatch of deep burgundy velvet for Leontes. John Barber perceived Gielgud as dressed in 'hectic red' (*Daily Express*, 28 June 1951), while Cecil Wilson thought Sicilia was costumed 'in dull, glowing reds to match the smouldering rage of Mr. Gielgud's Leontes' (*Daily Mail*, 18 June 1951). The evidence is uncertain, and only black-and-white photographs are available; but since they show a costume with several layers and a diagonal sash from shoulder to waist for Leontes in his first scene, the costume may well have combined differing fabrics of black, burgundy, and red. By contrast, costumes for country people in Bohemia were light brown, russet, yellow-green, gold, and grey-blue. Perdita wore a blue over-dress in the Bohemia scenes, but the costume design for her in the last act has a note which makes it clear that, when she comes to her father's court, her costume is to be the same as her mother's in the first act (Theatre Museum, London). This design for Perdita's final costume supported the performance of V.i, in which, according to Crosse, Paulina and Leontes conveyed 'astonishment' as they perceived Perdita's resemblance to Hermione (MS Diaries, vol. 20, p. 77). Sprague remembered that, at the end of this scene, Gielgud gazed back in puzzlement at Perdita (Bartholomeusz, 172).

In visual staging, properties were relatively few and usually stipulated by the text (the sword of justice for Acts II and III, for example), or supported by it (a brazier for II.iii, to intensify

Leontes' threat to condemn the baby to the fire). And yet there were still strong traces of the dominant theatrical conventions of the time, as in the tendency to compose stage pictures. The following account of the opening moments of Act I points up just those conventions which Brook was over a decade later to discard: 'As the curtain rises to appropriate music, one sees three doorways with balconies, leading characters standing on these steps, soldiers on the balconies, all standing as rigid as painted characters. The picture is held for a few minutes and then comes to active life with the first spoken words' (*Birmingham News*, 23 June 1951, during a pre-London run at the Coventry Hippodrome).

Looking at photographs and reading contemporary reviews of the production now, one has a double impression: relative to scenically elaborate productions of the time (including Brook's 1946 *Love's Labour's Lost*), his 1951 staging of *The Winter's Tale* appears relatively spare; compared to Brook's 1970 *A Midsummer Night's Dream*, however, the 1951 staging appears markedly pictorial. And there is a further sense in which the production provokes a double impression. On the one hand, it used elements of quasi-Elizabethan staging; on the other, it was very much of the 1950s. Brook himself calls this the 'double image'; since every interpretation – of scholar, actor, director, or designer – is subjective, he argues, it will also be of its time:

> Which means that even if he tries to bridge the ages and say, 'I leave myself and my century behind, and I'm looking at it with the eyes of its own period,' this is impossible. A costume designer tries to interpret one period and at the same time he reflects his own epoch – so he produces a double image. We look at photographs of, say, Granville-Barker's productions – or we look at any production anywhere – and the double image is always there. (*The Shifting Point*, 77)

In the historical moment of its 'double image', the production's design and blocking allowed focus to be concentrated on the actors and their speech. To Eric Johns it seemed that

> Mr. Brook has swept away what Mr. Gielgud calls all the familiar clichés of Shakespearean production. Leontes, as King of Sicilia, has no fanfare or entrance music ... The indoor scenes are without furniture, which means that the audience, instead of being distracted by the elaborate scenery favoured by Charles

Kean and Beerbohm Tree, is left undisturbed to appreciate the full beauty of the words ... Not since the days of Elizabeth has the stage been quite so empty. (*Theatre World*, August 1951, 7–8)

J. C. Trewin judged that 'For years there had not been in London a less ostentatious production of Shakespeare' (*Peter Brook*, 59). Writing of Brook's development at that time, Trewin stated: 'In Shakespeare he was moving from his earliest rash blaze of riot towards a stripped austerity; always he was seeking to probe the dramatist's many-layered thought' (*Peter Brook*, 58).

Brook has said that working with Gielgud brought him back to 'my own interrogation' of plays: 'In *Measure for Measure* at Stratford, then in London with *The Winter's Tale* and again with *Venice Preserved*, I was able to enter a unique and endlessly inventive mind, always open to change' (*Threads of Time*, 91). Gielgud had never before played Leontes and came to the part, he said, 'quite late in my career'; seeing *The Winter's Tale* performed (particularly at Stratford, probably in 1948) attracted him to the role of Leontes (*Shakespeare – Hit or Miss?*, x).[5] Gielgud recalled being drawn to the play, but aware of its difficulties: 'though greatly struck by the beauty of many of its scenes, I thought there was a good deal in it that seemed obscure, and a diversity of action that was difficult to integrate. However, I realized at once that the plot is full of effective theatrical surprises (like *Measure for Measure*)' (*Stage Directions*, 44). Problems in *The Winter's Tale* as well as *Measure for Measure*, Gielgud remembered, lay particularly in some of the speeches: 'I was alarmed to find that so much of the verse was very obscure' (*Shakespeare – Hit or Miss?*, 35). His solution involved a practice he had developed earlier, when acting Antony in *Antony and Cleopatra* – 'to learn about punctuation and breathing. It seemed to me that if you were not quite sure of a very difficult speech in Shakespeare, and you studied the punctuation and got it right, the sense would in some way emerge.' Thus, he later said that, in his work on *The Winter's Tale*, 'I tried to trust to the sweep of every speech, and to mark the commas and full stops and semicolons, and if I observed these correctly, as a bad swimmer begins to trust the water, the text seemed to hold me up' (*Shakespeare – Hit or Miss?*, 34–5).

Comparing his success as Leontes with his failure as Othello (Stratford-upon-Avon, 1961), for which he believed he had 'neither the voice nor the power', Gielgud stated with wit, 'But Leontes' jealousy is so hysterical and paranoid that I somehow found a way to play it.' He continued, 'And in that 1951 production I had Peter Brook's invaluable help. He took the play in his stride, and, as there are not a great many traditions attached to it, we both felt able to work along very straightforward lines' (*Shakespeare – Hit or Miss?*, 83). The term 'straightforward' is, of course, highly relative to particular contexts; and, in his own several brief discussions of this production, Gielgud seems to have had in mind especially the freedom from myriad preconceptions that an opportunity to play a role little known in contemporary memory can give (cf. Flora Robson's similar statement, *Stage*, 9 July 1951). But Gielgud's work on the difficult verse lines was far from simple; it produced rich layers of meaning. His performance seemed to reviewers to draw on both romantic and tragic traditions of acting, to enable him to explore the range and opposite extremes of Leontes' states of mind, and to manage the abrupt transitions the play demands.

Gielgud thought Leontes 'a highly imaginative, poetical tyrant' (*Stage Directions*, 46). Neither Leontes in *The Winter's Tale* nor Angelo in *Measure for Measure*, he thought, was 'a wholly realistic figure': 'Both are presented in comparatively few scenes, and therefore not elaborated with the same detail as are the protagonists of the great tragic plays. The characters are somewhat stylized, symbolic, and tremendously concentrated' (*Stage Directions*, 44). He was quick to point out that, in handling the plays' sudden changes, actors need to avoid melodrama or stock characterization. He observed that even though 'almost without preparation' actors are faced with 'the violent unreasoning hysteria of Leontes', as with the sudden lust of Angelo, 'it is no use trying to act these parts if one imagines them to be melodramatic monsters without a shred of humanity'. Though their earlier 'violent actions are liable to appear unreasonably sudden, and consequently difficult to make convincing', later an actor has the opportunity, he thought, to show complexity of character, since Leontes and Angelo are both given 'scenes of repentance in which they are shamed, humiliated, and at last, forgiven' (*Stage Directions*, 44–5).

Arthur Colby Sprague, who made notes in 1951 on the three performances of *The Winter's Tale* that he saw, later reflected:

'Some great actor of another age, a Macready, say, or a Kean, might have been puzzled by Mr. Gielgud's Hamlet. He would, I am sure, have understood and admired his Leontes' (*Shakespearian Players and Performances*, 165). A critic reviewing Brook's production when it travelled to Edinburgh commented: 'Somewhere between tragedy and romance, Mr. Gielgud sets up his state and there he poises Leontes as a man treading the circle of his own suspicions with the fretful step of the self-deceiver' (T. C. K., *Birmingham Post*, 29 August 1951).

'Somewhere between tragedy and romance': as far as such labels can be of use, this range seems to have been part of Gielgud's response to the mixed genres of *The Winter's Tale*. He was perceived as 'a grave statuesque Leontes' by Gordon Crosse (MS Diaries, vol. 20, p. 73), and by John Barber as one who, 'tortured and rigid ... commands the bare, black stage like a fury' (*Daily Express*, 28 June 1951). His performance was said to exhibit 'the tortuous ways of the diseased mind with an almost clinical certainty' (*Evening Despatch*, 19 June 1951, during the pre-London brief run at the Coventry Hippodrome) and yet to put 'immense romantic fire into the king's mad suspicions and cruel tyrannies' (*The Times*, 28 June 1951). Gielgud gave Leontes tragic dignity; by contrast, Granville Barker had directed Henry Ainley to present a Leontes whose jealousy Barker considered 'ignoble' (*More Prefaces*, 21). The two productions suggest very different ways of understanding the play as tragicomic: Barker even in the first three acts mingled tragic and darkly comic tones, deliberately bringing out what he considered 'less than tragic' (*More Prefaces*, 20). Brook and Gielgud seem in the first three acts to have mingled tragic tones with romantic ones.

In approaching the problem of Leontes' jealousy, Gielgud seems to have entered from the beginning of the play (Brook cut the whole of I.i) with a jealousy that grew in intensity throughout the scene. Critical accounts are difficult to assess and offer somewhat conflicting perceptions of this crucial sequence. Trewin reported Gielgud's Leontes as 'jealous from his opening syllables' (*Going to Shakespeare*, 262; also see Pafford, 181).[6] Other critics write of a subtle process of development (see Frey, 40). Dennis Bartholomeusz is among the latter: 'Showing initially more pain than anger, the jealousy defined as a sickening possibility admitted to himself ... Leontes confronted a private nightmare with regal dignity, almost, but not quite, losing control on "paddling palms and pinching fingers"' (170).

Arthur Colby Sprague, working from notes made at the time of the production, recalled (in a letter to Dennis Bartholomeusz, 29 November 1971) Gielgud's tension on 'Is he won yet?' (I.ii.85; see Bartholomeusz, 170). On the same line in an audio recording for the Shakespeare Recording Society (Caedmon, 1961), Gielgud also increases the tension.[7]

To George Rylands, it appeared that 'when the play opened, John Gielgud was at pains to convey the jealous disposition of a tyrant "with doubts a long time smothering in his stomach" and to follow Shakespeare's original, Robert Greene [*Pandosto*], rather than Shakespeare' (143). But, Rylands argued,

> Leontes is a victim of daemonic possession. He is struck down in a flash of summer lightning, and thenceforward all is dark, dark, dark, beneath the blaze of noon. Had John Gielgud dared an effect of this kind, playing for wonder and sympathy rather than for the suspension of disbelief, he would, in my judgement, have dominated the first movement with greater tragic power. The whole play would have gained in intensity and passion. (144)

Rylands's suggestion that sudden change is not necessarily a defect, but can increase tragic intensity, is a refreshing minority view in 1950s criticism of the play; his subsequent argument, however, may bear traces of a concern to 'motivate' Leontes' jealousy. Noting, as have many editors and critics, that Leontes has no part in the dialogue between Hermione and Polixenes (I.ii.44–85), he asks, 'Is he on the rack – spying on her jealously (as Gielgud played it), or is he absorbed in Mamillius?' Rylands argues that 'the significant words which bring him back into the scene' are Hermione's 'Th'offences we have made you do we'll answer, / If you first sinned with us, and that with us / You did continue fault, and that you slipped not / With any but with us' (I.ii.82–5). Rylands asks: 'Does Leontes overhear these words – and only these? His question "Is he won yet?" with its sequent "At my request he would not" might suggest that the surface is ruffled.' Rylands's argument is similar to that advanced, less cautiously, by Dover Wilson in his edition (with Quiller-Couch) of *The Winter's Tale*, that an actor can motivate Leontes' jealousy if he overhears these words. But the gesture which 'plunges Leontes into the abysm of hell' for Rylands is when Hermione gives her hand to Polixenes as 'friend' (I.ii.107), as once she took Leontes' hand in pledging her love (Rylands, 144–5).

The promptbook for the Brook production does not allow certainty on the issue of whether Gielgud's Leontes overheard Hermione's dialogue with Polixenes, but it seems doubtful that he did. Promptbook annotations (pp. 3–4) suggest that Hermione and Polixenes have been downstage left during the dialogue in question and that Leontes has been upstage right, moving downstage right, not left, just before the speech of Hermione's cited by Rylands and Dover Wilson. But the promptbook (p. 4) does suggest that Brook built tension leading up to the moment Hermione says, referring to Polixenes, 'for some while a friend' (107); when Leontes says, 'Hermione, my dearest, thou never spok'st / To better purpose' (87–8), there is an annotation for a lighting change (p. 4).

In negotiating other performance possibilities of Leontes' first-act speeches, Gielgud at least once used the convention Granville Barker had revived, that of direct address, though Gielgud spoke from within the frame of the Phoenix Theatre's proscenium stage (Sprague, 164). Gielgud addressed the audience during Leontes' speech beginning 'And many a man there is, even at this present, / Now, while I speak this' (I.ii.190–204). One eyewitness remembered Gielgud's 'accelerating into a generalised and refined disgust, on "Sir Smile, his neighbour"' (Dr Peter Naish, quoted in Bartholomeusz, 172).

Critics found through Gielgud's performance that Leontes' jealousy could be very effectively portrayed; likewise, they frequently praised Gielgud's handling of Leontes' repentance. Philip Hope-Wallace found that 'what was unexpected was the strength given to what has often seemed the flimsiest of dramatic schemes. This was partly because John Gielgud at once started Leontes' insane jealousy on so high a note and sustained it so powerfully through the early scenes' (*Manchester Guardian*, 29 June 1951). The critic for the *Observer* wrote, 'one used to write him [Leontes] off as the inhuman peg of a fantastic plot. But here, at the Phoenix Theatre, he emerges as a man, most credible in his flux of folly and immensely moving in his repentance' (1 July 1951). Arthur Colby Sprague's memory of the first moments of Leontes' repentance was that, after the disclosure of the oracle, Gielgud 'seemed at first stunned, then staggered across the stage (the boards sounded), then sank upon the throne' (165). The critic of the *Stage* commented on 'how skilfully he handles the transition to overwhelming grief when

Leontes hears the apparent effects of his insensate ferocity' (5 July 1951). Leontes learns of the effects of his actions not only from the announcement of Mamillius' death but especially, of course, from Paulina. Flora Robson's strong and fine performance of Paulina made viewers rethink preconceptions of the role. Paulina is 'an unexpectedly fine part' wrote Anthony Cookman (*Tatler and Bystander*, 11 July 1951). Despite negative judgements about Paulina's character still to be found in scholarly and critical reception at the time, in the production's theatrical reception theatre reviewers almost without exception found Robson's Paulina admirable: 'She shows us a woman of strong character, not a shrew' (T. C. K., *Birmingham Post*, 29 August 1951). The critic for the *Stage*, despite his opinion of the play's 'absurdities', thought Robson had 'rock-like integrity as an actress' and that her Paulina was 'superbly spirited': 'Every line in the queen's defence is spoken with wholly convincing emphasis' (5 July 1951). Another critic perceived Robson to be an 'angry lioness of a Paulina' (*Evening Standard*, 28 June 1951), while a critic for *The Times* thought she 'holds the stage with every line of the part' (28 June 1951). She was 'always confident and forceful, commanding the scene' (*Birmingham News*, 23 June 1951). In light of the then-dominant view of the play's structure, it is significant that Paulina's role was thought by one critic to connect parts of the play: 'Paulina's unshakable belief in the wisdom of the Oracle, as underlined in this production, creates a thread to link the rather scattered parts of this curious play' (*Stage*, 9 July 1951).

Flora Robson brought her critical sensibility and long experience to work on the role, about which she has written and spoken in interview. In her introduction to the Folio Society edition (1975) of *The Winter's Tale*, she wrote that, after being invited to play Paulina, she 'was immediately taken by the notion, as she [Paulina] is one of the few completely warm and sympathetic mature women characters in Shakespeare' (3). In interview she said that when she first read the part, her perception was of an almost entirely comic role. But 'when we began to play together, I gradually saw it differently': 'I think that however much you feel you understand a part you never do so with any real fullness until you begin to work in the play. At first you see it so entirely through your own eyes it is impossible to relate it properly to the rest of the play' (quoted in *Stage*, 9 July 1951). Her developing interpretation resulted in a performance one critic thought to be 'blending comedy with gravity and emotion' (*Stage*, 9 July 1951).

There is indeed room in Paulina's role for the comic, as the late Peggy Ashcroft, who had seen Robson's performance and who played the role herself at Stratford in 1960, suggested to me in interview (August 1988). Robson has written that she saw comic potentialities in her first scene with Leontes, II.ii, in which she brought the baby to him: 'The juxtaposition of somebody who is being pompous against someone who could not care less for pomposity, is always funny' (8). Robson, with her nuanced verse speaking, also finely negotiated the scene's tragic potentialities. She was, said Arthur Colby Sprague, not 'a scold' (quoted in Bartholomeusz, 173). Rather, with a restrained acting style, deep strength, and focused economy of gesture and movement, she opposed Leontes' misogyny, threats against her life, and orders that she be taken away (see figure 4).

4 Act II, scene iii: John Gielgud as Leontes, Flora Robson as Paulina (kneeling with baby), Lewis Casson as Antigonus (far right). Directed by Peter Brook, Phoenix Theatre, 1951. Angus McBean Photograph. Copyright © Harvard Theatre Collection

Any critic of the play, and any actor in the role of Paulina, must grapple not only with the play's mixture of comic and tragic but also with its mixture of romance with ethical and political issues. In her introduction to the Folio Society edition, Robson wrote that Peter Brook had stated early in rehearsals that the play had the character of a fairy tale (4). While she characterized Paulina as 'Fairy Godmother', she emphasized that Paulina is 'outspoken, down-to-earth', and 'a feminine realist who can hold her own in any surroundings and yet with a heart immediately responsive to the cares of others' (Robson, 4). Robson's statement, while limited from the point of view of later feminist criticism, does oppose what in her day were critical stereotypes of Paulina's part as shrew and answers them in a language Robson's contemporaries very well understood: Paulina, to her, is 'like a monument to sanity and commonsense' (8). A conflict during rehearsals suggests Brook's desire to show Paulina's sane vigour in the second-act scenes. Robson told Dennis Bartholomeusz (2 July 1971) that, during a rehearsal of the prison scene, she addressed the Jailer with the line 'Pray you then, / Conduct me to the Queen' (II.ii.6–7) as Brook wanted it done. She delivered the line, according to Bartholomeusz, 'firmly, sanely – warm with energy and concern' (173–5).

> John Gielgud suggested at the time that the situation demanded a different attack, and that she ought to indicate awe and gloom in her voice. When they rehearsed again accepting his suggestion, she made the words express nervous, hesitant foreboding. She remembered the swiftness of Brook's reaction to the change, his firm statement that a play could not afford two directors, Sir John's gracious apology, and the recovery of the less conventional, earlier reading – all hesitancy banished, the assured, warm light of sense returning. (Bartholomeusz, 175)

To judge from her 1951 account of her rehearsal process, Robson negotiated stereotypes not only of the part but also of female behaviour; although not entirely free of them, she broke through to a crucial point about Paulina's fidelity to the oracle:

> I began to see Paulina as garrulous, but good; tactless, but sincere; and, finally, as the vital character who really does believe in the wisdom of the Oracle. With all her blundering and forcing herself on to people at inappropriate moments, she is deeply concerned for the welfare of Leontes, although even more concerned that the Oracle shall be revered. She is thus able to

nurse and sustain Hermione through those 16 long years in complete faith and strength. (quoted in *Stage*, 9 July 1951)

Later describing how ideas had been generated in the course of rehearsals, Robson wrote that, after Brook and the cast had spent 'a full week working over the text', they discussed an idea that 'became a feature of the production' (introd. Folio Society ed., 5). What they began to explore were 'affinities' between Leontes, Hermione, and Perdita and figures in Queen Elizabeth I's past: 'her towering, jealous, heir-hungry father; Anne Boleyn, the mother she never really knew but whose shadow haunted her whole life; and Elizabeth herself' (5), who, like Perdita, 'was proclaimed illegitimate' (7). Aware of the nearness in time of the writing of *The Winter's Tale* and *Henry VIII*, she noted what seemed to her to be the 'Tudor echoes' in each, comparing aspects of the trial scene of Queen Katharine in *Henry VIII* to that of Hermione in *The Winter's Tale*. Robson also drew partial parallels between the accusations of adultery made against both Anne Boleyn and Hermione. She pointed out, furthermore, concerns common to the reigns of Henry VIII and Elizabeth I that are echoed in *The Winter's Tale*: problems of issue, of illegitimacy, of a kingdom in danger of lacking an heir (5-8).

Robson's suggestion that the play evokes remembered Tudor history is not without its antecedents. Such parallels seem first to have been suggested by Horace Walpole in the second half of the eighteenth century. It was he who thought there were similarities between certain phrases in letters of Anne Boleyn and in the trial scene speeches of Hermione, and he compared Leontes' abuse of power to that of Henry VIII, 'who generally made the law the engine of his boisterous passions' (quoted in Bartholomeusz, 8). Such ideas can be re-examined using methods of contemporary historical and political criticism (see Orgel, ed., 29-31), and without flattening the play, as Bartholomeusz warns (8-9), into a series of quasi-allegorical parallels.

In her Introduction to the Folio Society edition of *The Winter's Tale*, Flora Robson commented that, at the play's ending, Paulina 'finds herself having the tables turned by a rejuvenated, newly-humorous Leontes, and is saddled with a husband' (10). The production promptbook suggests that Brook largely cut references to Leontes' proposed union of Paulina and Camillo; lines from 'This is a match' through 'Come, Camillo, / And take her by the hand, whose worth and honesty / Is richly noted, and here justified / By us, a pair of kings' are omitted (V.iii.137-46; promptbook for 'Act III', p. 18). The promptbook does retain Leontes' lines from the same speech: 'Thou shouldst a husband take by my consent, / As I by thine a wife' (V.iii.136-7; promptbook for 'Act III', p. 18). These lines are marked with a handwritten directive for Paulina to move up centre; but whatever her movement signified, or what may have been her response to Leontes' lines, is unclear. Yet it is unlikely that there was a definite joining of Paulina and Camillo, for the omission of the betrothal was noted by Sprague (Bartholomeusz, 170) as well as Crosse, who stated, 'Her pairing with Camillo was omitted – quite as well' (MS Diaries, vol. 20, p. 77).

Whether any significant omission is 'quite as well' is open to exploration by critics, actors, and directors. Brook did not cut heavily, but he cut considerably more than Granville Barker had done. Additional major cuts indicated in the promptbook for Brook's production included the entire first scene between Archidamus and Camillo, and the whole of IV.ii, the dialogue of Polixenes and Camillo. But what is striking, given the later Peter Brook of *The Empty Space* who writes of Shakespeare's daring combinations and contrasts of the rough and the holy, are two other major cuts: the dance of the satyrs in IV.iv (often cut by other directors as well) and much of III.i, in which Cleomenes and Dion report their encounter with the oracle. If the well-kept promptbook is to be trusted, however, Cleomenes and Dion's dialogue may not have been cut in its entirety, despite what Gordon Crosse states (MS Diaries, vol. 20, p. 73). The promptbook ('Act I', p. 32) shows that Brook cut the first thirteen and a half lines of III.i but added all the rest of that scene (starting with 'Great Apollo / Turn all to th' best!') to the end of the previous scene. After Leontes said 'think upon my bidding' (II.iii.206), two lords remained to speak those last nine lines from the next scene in an almost uninterrupted flow of action.

Though Brook did not use heightened presentation in the report of the oracle, he did so in presenting the bear and Time. He went against the usual placement of an interval after III.iii; instead, the dialogue of Antigonus and the Mariner (III.iii) opened his second act. A snowstorm was created in which the bear rose up and pursued Antigonus; the storm started up again (after the shepherds found Perdita) for the entrance of Time (see promptbook, 'Act II', p. 6; cf. Sprague in 29 November 1971 letter, quoted in Bartholomeusz, 176). Trewin wrote that by 'the simplest of means', Brook and Fedorovitch 'have turned the stage of the Phoenix Theatre to a desolate coast, as eerie a setting as I have known on the stage'. He continued:

> Usually we have to avert our eyes when an actor in a bearskin shambles on to hustle Antigonus towards the wings. Now, for once, I had no desire to laugh while Antigonus, crying 'This is the chase; I am gone for ever,' fled terrified along the angry shore. It was the first time I had ever found that grim direction, 'Exit, pursued by a bear,' properly realized. (*Illustrated London News*, 21 July 1951; see slightly revised version in Trewin's *Peter Brook*, 60)

These effects were selected from the arts of realism, rather than emblematic, as Bartholomeusz points out (176). He is right that Brook emphasized the tragic here; some directors change to the comedic at this moment. Gordon Crosse wrote of the 'obviously human bear' who walked upright ('like a man') across 'the whole width of the stage' (MS Diaries, vol. 20, p. 74). The promptbook ('Act II', pp. 1–3) suggests that the actor portraying the bear, who had lain unseen in darkness (up left of centre), rose up after Antigonus' cry 'A savage clamour! / Well may I get aboard!' (III.iii.55–6). One can further infer from the promptbook that Antigonus' cry 'This is the chase' (56) was evoked by his turning and seeing the bear move towards him, and that hastening to exit (up right) on his 'I am gone for ever!' (57), he was pursued by the rampant bear.

When the snowstorm began again as Time entered, 'the ancient advanced down stage through a dazzling whirl of snow' (Trewin, *Going to Shakespeare*, 264). The snowstorm lasted throughout the opening section of Time's speech, until after 'I turn my glass', at which well-chosen point, according to the promptbook annotation ('Act II', p. 6), the snow was to finish. The actor 'emerges from one of the heaviest snow-storms in stage history to speak impressively for Time', wrote the reviewer in the *Stage* (5 July 1951). An account by Rylands suggests that the stage effects assisted the action's transitions and contrasts: 'The tempest which flap-dragon'd the vessel of Antigonus turned into a whirl of snow through whose flakes Father Time materialized – and melted away. The skies cleared to an open stage dressed with sunburnt rustics in their rye straw hats and all their pastoral "gear and tackle and trim"' (145).

Brook seems to have overcome major challenges that are presented by the play's long fourth act. First, he made its connections with the rest of the play clear. What was 'triumphant', wrote one critic, was to have 'discovered' that 'this pastoral interlude is not after all a different play and that it *is* possible to carry over the mood of the first part and also join it to the last' (*Time and Tide*, 7 July 1951). Second, Brook was apparently able to sustain Act IV's varied dramatic energies, both because of his pacing of the scenes and because he had a superb Autolycus in George Rose. Philip Hope-Wallace commented that 'this vigorous Bohemian episode was probably wisely judged, for it meant that the play did not lose pace, as so often happens, and we were carried on excitedly to the final scenes' (*Manchester Guardian*, 29 June 1951; cf. Wilfred Clark, *Birmingham News*, 23 June 1951). Hope-Wallace found George Rose's Autolycus 'bold'; Rylands found Rose 'pungent as garlic, sharp as vinegar, keen as mustard' (143); the critic for the *Stage* thought Rose did 'the fullest justice to Mr. Fry's music' (*Stage*, 5 July 1951); Gordon Crosse pronounced him the 'best Autolycus' he had seen (MS Diaries, vol. 20, p. 75). One critic suggested that there is 'no better Shakespearian clown on the stage today than he' (Wilfred Clark, *Birmingham News*, 23 June 1951).

A major strength of this production was indeed the quality of the cast, including the actors in supporting roles. Lewis Casson, then seventy-five, seeming to one reviewer to have the 'qualities of a weathered English oak' (*Stage*, 5 July 1951), was widely praised for his performance as Antigonus and was said to have scored a 'triumph' in the scene where he leaves the infant Perdita in Bohemia (W. Clark, *Birmingham News*, 23 June 1951). Gordon Crosse thought the 'strong and dignified' Polixenes of Brewster Mason 'never better done' (MS Diaries, vol. 20, pp. 75–6). Many reviewers commented on the superb work done by the lesser-known actor John Moffatt who, as Paulina's steward (the Third Gentleman) in V.ii, delivered the complex tragicomic Jacobean prose that relates the reunion of Perdita with her father and with Paulina. Moffatt worked skilfully with the language, and critics stressed his artfulness; as one put it, he 'dazzlingly draws a cipher' (*Sunday Telegraph*, 1 July 1951).

Moffatt's work helped validate the complexity of a scene still often drastically cut or delivered as a comic spoof, despite Granville Barker's earlier recuperation of it. Critics as far back as Samuel Johnson have insisted Shakespeare was merely saving himself labour and should have dramatised the reunion of Leontes and Perdita. One reviewer of Brook's production wrote of 'the artistry with which Mr. John Moffatt delivers, towards the end of the play, a long speech into which Shakespeare has crammed the contents of three or four scenes which he simply couldn't be bothered to write' (*Spectator*, 6 June 1951). Trewin, by contrast, wrote, 'It is often held that in employing a form of Messenger speech for the King's recognition of his daughter, Shakespeare avoided a challenge. But he was not a dramatist to avoid anything, and how sure his instinct was, Peter Brook proved in the lively conversation-piece frequently scamped' (*Peter Brook*, 60).

Such effectively reported reunions in V.ii contributed to the power of the dramatized reunions in V.iii. That power also arose from Brook's understanding of changes which occur in Leontes in the final act, and their structural place in what Brook called the 'third movement'; he found in it a 'contrasting key – a key of remorse' (*The Empty Space*, 90). In *The Winter's Tale*, wrote Brook, 'a very subtle construction hinges on the key moment when a statue comes to life.' Pointing out that in the literary estimations of his time, the statue 'is often criticized as a clumsy device, an implausible way of winding up the plot ... usually justified only in terms of romantic fiction', Brook replied: 'In fact, the statue that comes to life is the truth of the play' (*The Empty Space*, 89). That 'truth' for Brook seemed not primarily to reside in the transformation of Hermione but in that of Leontes, who Brook believed had come to a readiness which allowed time, past and future, to be transformed:

> When the young lovers enter Leontes' palace the first and second sections [the earlier Sicilian and Bohemian acts] overlap: both put into question the action that Leontes now can take. If the dramatist's sense of truth forces him to make Leontes vindictive with the children, then the play cannot move out of its particular world, and its end would have to be bitter and tragic: if he can truthfully allow a new equality to enter Leontes' actions, then the whole time pattern of the play is transformed: the past and the future are no longer the same. The level changes, and even if we call it a miracle, the statue has none the less come to life. (*The Empty Space*, 90)

By 'truth', here, Brook did not mean 'plausibility'. Were Sartre (several of whose plays Brook had directed) to have written *The*

Winter's Tale, 'Leontes would be faced with the bleak consequences of his actions', explained Brook. 'Both Shakespeare and Sartre would be fashioning plays according to their sense of truth: one author's inner material contains different intimations from the other's. The mistake would be to take events or episodes from a play and question them in the light of some third outside standard of plausibility – like "reality" or "truth"' (*The Empty Space*, 91). Brook's insistence on 'truth' as established by the world of the play, and expressive of the 'inner material' of the author, contrasts with the appeal to 'realism' by critics who refuse to be disarmed by Shakespeare's own jest that the reunions are 'so like an old tale that the verity of it is in strong suspicion' (V.ii.28–9). Granville Barker had defended the statue scene's stagecraft; Brook defended its congruence with the play's vision. He also based his defence on his experience as a director: 'When working on *The Winter's Tale*', he wrote, 'I discovered that the way to understand this scene is not to discuss it but to play it. In performance this action is strangely satisfying – and so it makes us wonder deeply' (*The Empty Space*, 90). As played, the scene seemed indeed satisfying to viewers, who commented on the combined art of Gielgud, Flora Robson, and Diana Wynyard in evoking the effect of wonder. Commentators agreed that Wynyard's Hermione was, overall, even finer in Brook's production than it had been in Anthony Quayle's 1948 production at Stratford – 'stronger and richer' (Rylands, 143; cf. *Birmingham Mail*, 19 June 1951, and *Birmingham Gazette*, 19 June 1951). Sprague noted that in contrast to the first two performances of Brook's production that he saw early in the run (14 and 24 July), in which Hermione did not appear to have aged in the statue scene, by his third viewing (8 September), Hermione in V.iii had been given white hair (see Bartholomeusz, 173, 175–6). Flora Robson's verse speaking in the scene, wrote one reviewer, created rapt attention 'with its sound and feeling even in its lighter tones' (*Time and Tide*, 7 July 1951). According to the promptbook ('Act III', p. 17), in response to Paulina's 'It is required / You do awake your faith' (V.iii.94–5), Gielgud knelt.

The promptbook suggests that Gielgud remained kneeling until the moment Hermione moved; near the lines 'If this be magic, let it be an art / Lawful as eating' (V.iii.110–11) there is a note in the promptbook ('Act III', p. 17) that suggests he has arisen and embraced Hermione. Muriel Bradbrook's memory, as reported by Bartholomeusz (172), was that, when the statue first moved, Gielgud retreated from it, in a moment which to her seemed utterly convincing. Neither promptbooks nor memories are certain evidence, and productions can change during the course of a long run; yet it is true, as Bartholomeusz points out, that a retreat backward would resemble the moves made by Macready in the nineteenth century and Garrick in the eighteenth (172). If, however, the promptbook for the Brook production and Helen Faucit's written recollections of the earlier Macready production, in which she played Hermione, are correct, there also seems to have been a striking difference in the subsequent moves. Macready, who had been standing as he moved away from the statue, then advanced slowly toward Hermione after Paulina's 'Nay, present your hand' (V.iii.107; see Bartholomeusz, 69). By contrast, in Peter Brook's production Diana Wynyard, as Hermione, advanced slowly toward the kneeling Gielgud. After Paulina's 'Is she become the suitor?' (109), the promptbook notes that when Hermione moved to him he clasped her hands ('Act III', p. 17). When Gielgud at last touched Hermione and discovered 'O, she's warm!', his acting had, for Sprague, an unforgettable depth of sudden awareness (see Bartholomeusz, 172–3). A photograph by Angus McBean (figure 5) suggests that Gielgud carried a sense of repentance into the moments of reunion, so that emphasis was given not to ecstatic joy but to an urgent desire for forgiveness, and to the overwhelming experience of receiving it.

McBean's photograph of the reunion of Hermione and Leontes also suggests a representation of Hermione as an idealized figure of serenity. Her suffering seems occluded, as it was also, apparently, even in the trial scene, in which Bartholomeusz describes her as having 'a statuesque pride and purity' (173). Such a mystique of the feminine stands in sharp contrast to certain productions of the 1990s, such as Fontaine Syer's in 1996 for the Oregon Shakespeare Festival, in which Lise Bruneau as Hermione bore sharply remembered pain in her reunion with Leontes.

'A production is only right at a given moment, and anything that it asserts dogmatically today may well be wrong fifty years from now.' Peter Brook's own 1948 statement that a production belongs to its cultural moment ('Style in Shakespearean Production', 145) suggests an awareness of historical contingency that is in partial

5 Act V, scene iii: Diana Wynyard as Hermione and John Gielgud as Leontes. Directed by Peter Brook, Phoenix Theatre, 1951. Angus McBean Photograph. Copyright © Harvard Theatre Collection

conflict with some of his later ahistorical theory and practice. But this early statement accords with his experimentation and keen ability to rethink his modes of production (as he does in *The Shifting Point*, 1987; *The Open Door*, 1993; and *Threads of Time*, 1998). Even by 1963, in an essay published for the Royal Shakespeare Company volume *The Critical Years*, he argued:

> We must move the productions and the settings away from all that played so vital a part in the postwar Stratford renaissance –

away from romance, away from fantasy, away from decoration. Then they were necessary for shaking the ugliness and the boredom off these well-worn texts. Now we must look beyond an outer liveliness to an inner one. Outer splendor can be exciting but has little relation with modern life: on the inside lie themes and issues, rituals and conflicts which are as valid as ever. Any time the Shakespearean meaning is caught, it is 'real' and so contemporary. (repr. in *The Shifting Point*, 85)

Ideas like Brook's, that the inner life of a play can be represented in ways at once 'Shakespearean' and 'contemporary', have since been contested (see, for example, John Elsom's *Is Shakespeare Still Our Contemporary?*). They remain problematic. But it is important to capture what was at stake for Brook at that moment of the early 1960s, at a turning point for Shakespearean production in England, with Peter Hall having been appointed director of the Shakespeare Memorial Theatre in 1960. Anthony Quayle, who had directed the Memorial Theatre from 1948 to 1956, had produced *The Winter's Tale* in 1948 in a style that exemplified those qualities of the 'postwar renaissance' from which Brook wanted to move away: romantic, picturesque, elaborate stagings. The opening spectacle of Quayle's *The Winter's Tale*, according to Bartholomeusz, 'might have pleased Charles Kean' (203). In response, Brook developed opposing ideas in his call for the 'empty' space.

As others have subsequently pointed out, the seemingly 'empty' stage is not neutral space; it is reflective of an aesthetic with its own cultural assumptions. Yet the ideas Brook developed helped him not only to oppose heavily picturesque Shakespearean production styles, but also to move away from the restrained, residual pictorialism of his 1951 *The Winter's Tale* toward the spare, open playing spaces of his 1970 *A Midsummer Night's Dream*. A year before Brook's *Dream*, ideas of Shakespearean production partly parallel to his in *The Empty Space* shaped a production of *The Winter's Tale* by the man who succeeded Peter Hall as Artistic Director of the Royal Shakespeare Company: Trevor Nunn.

CHAPTER III

Trevor Nunn's production with the Royal Shakespeare Company, 1969–71

At the time ... and in particular in discussion with my closest colleague at the time, Christopher Morley, the principle of the empty space ... was capable of a ritual resonance, a sacred resonance that was, in a very overt and acknowledged way, a theatre space, a place for performance, a place for celebration of text. (Trevor Nunn in interview with the author, 17 July 1988)[1]

Looking back over a wide gap of nearly twenty years since his Royal Shakespeare Company production of *The Winter's Tale* that opened in Stratford-upon-Avon in 1969,[2] Trevor Nunn described his and set designer Christopher Morley's 'permanent design condition' for that season of late plays. His words remind one of a book with impact in the theatre world a year before his production: Peter Brook's *The Empty Space* (1968).

Brook's rethinking his idea of theatre in *The Empty Space* was a major departure from the mode of his own 1951 production of *The Winter's Tale*; the change was reflected, of course, in his landmark production of *A Midsummer Night's Dream*, which opened in August 1970. Nunn's season of late plays had its Stratford run (April to December 1969) the year prior to Brook's *Dream*. Of all productions of *The Winter's Tale*, it is Nunn's (which opened 15 May 1969) that has the greatest affinities with Brook's theoretical reflections in *The Empty Space*. Brook saw Nunn's *The Winter's Tale* and, said Nunn, praised 'the releasing of the imagination that occurred in that space'.[3]

Nunn's phrase 'celebration of text' suggests that he fused his affinities with Brook's idea of 'the empty space' with another, earlier influence: that of F. R. Leavis, who had supervised Nunn at Downing College, and whose formalist criticism, despite Leavis's anti-theatricality, also influenced Nunn's fellow

Cambridge graduates and RSC directors John Barton and Peter Hall (Greenwald, 22; Hall, *Diaries*, 347).[4] In May 1968, Nunn succeeded Hall as Artistic Director of the RSC and 'wanted there to be a season at Stratford which would be recognizably quite separate and different'. Ideas of ritual theatre and of spaces that present themselves as frankly theatrical, and a focus on thematic imagery adapted from formalist criticism were among the currents of thought Nunn selectively used and reshaped as he planned this first season over which he had artistic control and created his production of *The Winter's Tale*.

The aesthetic construct of 'the empty space' was an artistic principle for Nunn but also, he was quick to emphasize in interview, a practical solution: 'the idea of having one shared space' for the whole season was a response to the smaller budget necessitated by the 'very rocky financial state' of the RSC when he assumed its directorship. Pragmatic necessity was made to serve Nunn's aim of finding a new way forward partly in 'reaction against' work 'that had been going on recently in the RSC'. For all his admiration of the work of his immediate RSC predecessors, by the late 1960s Nunn wanted to change the prevailing Stratford production style that he later described in his 1976 newspaper article, 'Back to Stage One':

> For much of the Sixties, there was an identifiable Stratford style, in fact influenced by the Berliner Ensemble, of 'epic' heightened naturalism, densely populated and on a large scale. I remember that when I joined the RSC it was a common thing to have a cast of more than fifty actors in a play; the most overworked department was Wigs and Make-up, and for years it seemed that there were two huge basins in the wings, marked 'Mud' and 'Blood'. (*Sunday Times*, 28 March 1976, 35)

Thus an RSC house style that had been a breakthrough when created by John Bury and Peter Hall for 'The Wars of the Roses' in 1963, which Nunn knew had served the RSC productions of the histories well, did not seem to Nunn in 1969 equally well to serve what he wanted to do in producing the late plays (cf. Beauman, 291–2).[5] 'I knew', Nunn said to me in interview, 'that what we were doing [in the season of late plays] was going to have its antithesis – it was going to have its revolutionary reaction at a later point. But it was vital for that season.' Nunn told me that his purpose in 1969 had involved what he called a 'ritual sense':

I mean that the plays were in some sense going to be looked at in ways other than naturalistically – that they were going to be looked at for their psychological, psychiatric content, their symbological content, and their hieratic content, but not first and foremost their social, realistic content. And we thought, Christopher Morley and I, that was entirely an accurate response to the late plays, whereas it would have been a perverse response to the histories.

Morley's permanent set design for the season Nunn called 'the white box'. Instead of wings, it had 'door scale entrances in the side walls' of the set. With no masking – e.g., no concealment of flies and lights by horizontal strips of curtain (borders) – the walls went so far up into the fly gallery that there was a 'soaring, cathedral-like height to the dimension'. Since, said Nunn, 'it's a terrible contradiction to be doing Shakespeare's plays in a building [like the Royal Shakespeare Theatre, formerly the Shakespeare Memorial Theatre, in Stratford-upon-Avon] that has a solid, heavy brick proscenium with a picture-frame device', Morley also placed white walls 'downstage of the proscenium and piercing through the proscenium'. There was, said Nunn, in the resulting 'overall image something soaring, something optimistic'.

The white box evoked a sense of height, but it also created a chamber setting which 'establishes', said Nunn in an interview with Peter Ansorge, 'that the most important object on the stage is the actor. It has to work within the scale of the individual actor – to make his words, thoughts, fantasies and language seem important' (quoted in *Plays and Players*, September 1970, 17). Speaking a few years later of his 1969 rehearsal process, Nunn again emphasized – like the Brook of *The Empty Space* – the relation between non-illusionist theatrical space, focus on the energies of the actors, and the possibilities of symbolic action: 'Our sense of discovery made us use our theatre in a new way – new to us – a big white void, a free-ranging use of the space defined only by the actors' use of it, a celebration of what was consciously allegoric in the play and not an uncomfortable naturalistically localized series of symbolic nudges' (quoted in Cook, *Director's Theatre*, 117).

Lighting design reinforced Nunn's move away from naturalism. The lighting rig itself, Nunn said, was a 'massive, movable collection of lamps ... a massive white object that could ascend and descend, and simply by doing that could provide completely different intensities and completely different moods'. Nunn commented that it was a 'very pure device to have a bank of lamps at the same intensity and, merely by removing it, totally change the mood and texture and quality of the stage'. He added, 'That cluster of lamps was called "Apollo".' Anecdotal as it may be to know the name that evolved for the lighting rig, Nunn told me, the name is a clue as to how the outlook of the company evolved during rehearsals: 'They understood collectively why the stage was being used in that way, and what was important in that particular season about the plays.'

The season's white-box space with its non-naturalistic lighting was a modernist construction of what Nunn considered 'Elizabethan' levels of storytelling: 'We want the stage to represent earth (as for the Elizabethans) and underneath that stage lies hell, the unknown, the darkly occult. Above it is a canopy, a roof fretted with golden fire, the gods, heaven, Apollo' (quoted by Ansorge in *Plays and Players*, September 1970, 17). Within this cosmic scale, Nunn's emphasis was more on the microcosm of the individual than the macrocosm of society; the white box for this season was a chamber setting for focusing not on the political conflicts of court life but on its domestic conflicts, particularly those within its male protagonist.

On the translucent drop curtain for *Pericles* in the 1969 season of late plays (which also included *Henry VIII* as well as *The Winter's Tale*) was an enlarged image of what Nunn in interview called 'the Leonardo [da Vinci] naked man's expression of perfection locked in the square, locked in the circle of microcosm, that extraordinary Renaissance image'.[6] Nunn's word 'locked' is striking. In the Renaissance, Leonardo's drawing, based in part on Vitruvius' ideas of proportion and referred to as the 'Vitruvian man', was thought to represent ideal measurement of human proportions.[7] By contrast, in its 1969 theatrical representation the drawing is used, as 'locked' suggests, in a modernist version of humanist themes, as a psychological image of an individual's inward disproportions, of a struggle with inner contradictions. Nunn pointed out to me that the drawing suggests 'a universe', within which is both 'a prison of that man and also a setting for that man, and there is a complex contradiction in that drawing'. Nunn went on to explain,

And so we wanted there to be – perhaps in a slightly didactic way, but we were young – we wanted to say (*Pericles* was the opening play of the season), this is what it's all going to be about: that image, the man alone, the man wrestling with his experience, the man trying to find a balance and an equipoise between his animal instincts and his intellect, his instinctual fears and emotions that have taken over, and the power of reason. We wanted those things to be tremendously important in *The Winter's Tale*.

Nunn's focus on a psychological microcosm in Leontes did not exclude a social dimension, but the social was interpersonal rather than specifically political. In his 1970 interview with Ansorge, Nunn commented upon his move away from the political: 'It's being said that the RSC are becoming afraid of throne rooms and courts. I'm sure this is true. In most of our work now we are concerned with the human personalities of a king or queen rather than with their public roles' (*Plays and Players*, September 1970, 16). Nunn's emphasis on inner psychological conflict in Leontes – which minimized other possibilities the play offers for an exploration of the relation of gender roles to political power – was strongly marked by the expressionistic use of stage properties that symbolized Leontes' experience of time, in which dream became nightmare. In an opening to the play which Nunn created, audiences heard (in a voice-over) the first three and a half lines of Time's Chorus – 'I that please some, try all; both joy and terror / Of good and bad, that makes and unfolds error, / Now take upon me, in the name of Time, / To use my wings' (transposed from IV.i). And audiences saw, in flashes of light (seventeen seconds of strobe), a modern transformation of Leonardo's image: a man standing with his limbs outstretched in what seemed a transparent glass box (made of a three-sided perspex cube), revolving as if he were spinning in time. Nunn told me he saw that cube as 'the prison and setting of the Leonardo man who had become Leontes in our production. He was our Renaissance man that we were going to be investigating, all of the contradictions of his life.' Barrie Ingham, who played Leontes, was in the revolving cube; Leontes was, said Nunn, turning in a 'wide gap of time'. The image recurred in a smaller stage property: as he spoke the opening exchange with Archidamus, Camillo played with a small toy cube that contained a similar figure of a man.

The initial image of the man spinning in time was further

developed (IV.i) when Time spoke as Chorus from inside the cube, and even further at the end of the play, when the cube, now containing the statue of Hermione, became a space for transformation. Though Nunn used the term 'allegorical' in defining his approach, his stage images did not stand in a one-to-one relation to traditional meanings, as in medieval or Renaissance allegory, but had fluid correspondences with one another, coalescing with multiple suggestiveness. The cube was, said Nunn, 'multifaceted', a device for presenting Leontes' torment, 'a consciously complex device for the presentation of Time', and 'a device for the staging of a miracle', after which, Nunn pointed out, Leontes speaks of all 'these events having happened in a "wide gap of time"'. Nunn wanted a stage symbol which 'didn't become heavily just one thing, one image, one statement of the designer ... or of the director ... but something that would release a lot of resonance in the play'.

Nunn's psychological approach joined with his formalist attention to connections between iterative imagery and theme. Additionally, his use of verbal images to construct visual stage properties reflected what Hugh Grady (90–103) has defined as a modernist move toward spatial form.[8] Such 'spatialization' of images could be seen when Nunn transposed images from later in the play to earlier scenes, or the reverse, establishing thematic correspondences between them. The verbal image which inspired the symbolic property of the stylized white hobby horse, for example, doesn't appear in the text until I.ii.273, but in the production the adult-sized rocking horse was onstage from the beginning of I.ii, used for the initially playful interaction of Leontes, Hermione, Polixenes, and Mamillius. It then became the target of Leontes' changed, violent mind when he struck the horse as he proclaimed to Camillo, 'My wife's a hobby-horse' (I.ii.273).

Furthermore, the stage image of the rocking horse formed part of a cluster of images suggesting an initial innocent nursery world (figure 6) which was then shattered. Polixenes started a toy top spinning as he told Hermione of the past in which it seemed possible to 'be boy eternal' (I.ii.64). The stage image of the top was derived from Leontes' later ironic assertion that if he is mistaken 'In those foundations which I build upon, / The centre is not big enough to bear / A schoolboy's top' (II.i.101–3). Antigonus' phrase 'Dreams are toys' (III.iii.38) connected both to

6 Act I, scene ii: Barrie Ingham as Leontes, Judi Dench as Hermione, Richard Pasco as Polixenes. Directed by Trevor Nunn, Royal Shakespeare Company, Stratford-upon-Avon, 1969. Thomas F. Holte photograph. Copyright © Shakespeare Birthplace Trust

this earlier image and to Leontes' later ironic line to Hermione, 'Your actions are my dreams' (III.ii.80). Nunn thus used symbolic properties and the non-chronological association of images to express Leontes' subjective relation to time and his inner fantasies, and to establish a central motif: dreams.

That Leontes projected his dreams onto Hermione's actions was suggested by lighting changes at crucial moments in Act I, scene ii, especially, and in Acts II and III until Leontes' repentance, as well as by slow-motion acting used non-naturalistically, even in part expressionistically. To show Leontes' difficulty in distinguishing his dark imaginings from others' reality, Christopher Morley and John Bradley designed lighting shifts that enabled audiences, said Nunn, to 'experience something of the sickness and panic and distress' in Leontes. Of Nunn's use of stroboscopic lighting, Ronald Bryden wrote that in the same season he had seen many productions using 'strobe' light, and it had become 'modish' as a 'trade-mark of avante garde intent'. 'For months I've been waiting for a director who could use it meaningfully, as expressive tool rather than toy', wrote Bryden, 'promising myself to hail him first and most intelligent in his generation. I should have guessed it would be Trevor Nunn' (*Observer*, 18 May 1969).

Creating a visual expression of Leontes' inner nightmare was not only the director's and designers' concept; it also grew from the work of the actors, in improvisation. During the first weeks of rehearsal, scheduling conflicts with *Pericles* rehearsals meant that for work on *The Winter's Tale* only four principal actors were available: Judi Dench, playing Hermione; Barrie Ingham, playing Leontes; Richard Pasco, playing Polixenes; and Nicholas Selby, playing Camillo. Nunn commented a few years later that 'it was really that small group who "found" the play and became very committed to a certain way of expressing it. You can't fake discoveries in this business, and we all knew very early on that a very intractable play was opening up' (quoted in Cook, *Director's Theatre*, 117).

An unusual rehearsal circumstance, at first appearing to be an obstacle, thus turned into an opportunity for experimentation. While working on I.ii, Nunn asked Barrie Ingham at one point, 'I want to know what you are seeing. What are you putting into words in these outbursts? What is actually in your mind?' In improvisation, Ingham began to say what he imagined Polixenes was doing physically to Hermione. The 'terribly disturbing detail', Nunn said, 'was so real to him, and so disturbing to us,' that they felt this work must not be 'a lost ingredient' or 'just be sub-text for the actors' but should be 'released into the play'. Ingham commented to me in interview that improvisations are of most use when 'someone can observe and tell you what effect was created by these improvisations. Otherwise, it's just getting in touch with feelings. The art is called acting, which is a craft, and it is a question of observing what happens when emotions are in play and then reproducing it.' Ingham added that with Nunn guiding 'the results of the improvisations, and then feeding them back into the acting, that can be tremendously valuable'.[9]

The arts of acting and of lighting were the means whereby the company captured for audiences some of Leontes' dark imaginings and revulsion that Ingham had experienced in rehearsal. Nunn said that an additional purpose of the lighting was 'to release the actor playing Leontes from the struggle of having to make believable and credible and naturalistic Leontes' growth of jealousy'. The initial lighting change in I.ii occurred at the moment when Ingham spoke 'Too hot, too hot!' (I.ii.107). Prior to this speech, there had been no sign of disturbance in his Leontes during his first four exchanges with Polixenes (1–27), though Ingham had stressed the word 'tougher' (15) and had spoken very rapidly when replying 'We'll part the time between's then; and in that / I'll no gainsaying' (18–19). His delivery was also swift when asking, 'Is he won yet?' (85). Verbal and behavioural shifts were noticeable on his 'At my request he would not' (86): he spoke sharply, and his earlier playfulness acquired a rough edge as he crossed to Polixenes to shake him in jest, but with his hands on Polixenes' neck. Ingham grew introspective, speaking slowly for the first time, during his speech beginning 'Why, that was when / Three crabbèd months had soured themselves to death' (100–4). These subtle shifts were followed by a much stronger change when Hermione crossed to Polixenes (stage right) and took Polixenes by the hand, naming him 'friend' (107). The light on the three principals slowly changed to become like ultraviolet light, with loss of much other light, making them seem as if they were figures in a dream; in slow-motion mime, Hermione and Polixenes enacted a sequence which alternated four freeze positions with movements, including a moment in which Hermione whispered in Polixenes' ear. Ingham crossed down to centre forestage, a tightly focused spotlight on him as he spoke his aside beginning 'Too hot, too hot!' (107) as if he were astounded, appalled, at what his mind was now presenting to him. In changed light, Polixenes and Hermione performed a surreal visual evocation – not a 'literal' enactment – of Leontes' inner dark imaginings. Altered light lasted through the whole of Leontes' speech (107–18), which Ingham took as an almost whispered aside; the light did not return to normal until the word 'brows' (118), at which point he addressed Mamillius.

That in his diseased 'Affection' (137) Leontes 'Communicat'st with dreams' (139) was heightened by the second major lighting shift, on the word 'collop' (136), and was sustained throughout Leontes' speech, until Polixenes put his hand on Leontes' shoulder, saying 'What cheer? How is't with you, best brother?' (147). This line in the Folio (and in the Signet classic edition Nunn was using for the promptbook) is given to Leontes; in giving this line to Polixenes, Nunn follows not only many editors (e.g., Pafford in the Arden edition) but also his own vision of a Leontes so caught up in his own imaginings that he needs to be taken back into the world of others.

That Leontes was still in his world of dark dreams before Polixenes touched him and spoke was communicated not only by visual means but by a striking vocal change. Judi Dench greatly elongated the word 'unsettled' in her comment about Leontes: 'He something seems unsettled' (146). She offered the audience the word as if they could hear it inside Leontes' mind, hear his blurring the lines between his dream and others' reality. As she pointed out in interview with me, 'It's as if he hears the voice' through ears as 'distorted' as his eyes.[10]

The most disturbing visual enactment suggesting Leontes' distorted images of Polixenes and Hermione occurred during the third lighting change (I.ii), which began as Leontes said, 'I am angling now, / Though you perceive me not how I give line' (178–9), and continued as he imagined 'How she holds up the neb, the bill to him! / And arms her with the boldness of a wife / To her allowing husband' (181–3). In the changed light, a slow-motion enactment of intimacies occurred – Polixenes seeming to caress Hermione's breasts and pregnant belly, and to kiss her neck as she leaned back to expose it. Audiences were offered not a crudely reductive visual attempt to mime Leontes' every word but a surreal evocation of Leontes' inner vision.

At crucial points in Act II, lighting changes further intensified the presentation of Leontes' inner experience. Leontes was upstage in tightly focused light, with light reduced on the overall acting area, from the beginning of his speech (taken as an aside), 'How blest am I / In my just censure, in my true opinion!' through to its conclusion, 'I / Remain a pinched thing, yea, a very trick / For them to play at will' (II.i.36–52). He had 'drunk, and seen the spider' (45); the non-naturalistic lighting emphasized the isolation of one with poison raging in his mind.

A stunning change of lights at the end of Act II, scene iii sharpened the viewers' sense of irony at Leontes' megalomaniacal certainty that the oracle would justify him, and at his tyrannical announcement of a 'just and open trial' (II.iii.204). At that pronouncement by Leontes, a black cone-shaped device, in which was a bank of lights, descended slowly, focusing an ever-narrowing pool of light on Leontes. As he said 'My heart will be a burden to me' (205), the lighting defined his growing mental isolation, and Barrie Ingham delivered Leontes' final line in the scene – 'And think upon my bidding' – with unusual volume and emphasis, stressing the word 'my'. At once there was a sudden blackout. The contrast to the next moment was maximal: as Cleomenes and Dion began to speak of the oracle at Delphi, the bank of lights Nunn and Morley called 'Apollo' changed the stage lighting to a brilliant white – a quality of light not seen again until, in Bohemia, the lost Perdita was found.

Lighting changes also supported actors in the difficult, rapid transitions and contrasts toward the end of the trial scene, as Leontes began to repent. At the announcement of Mamillius' death, a change of light, initially stroboscopic, focused attention on a slow-motion faint of Hermione. 'As Hermione fell', said Nunn, 'the perception of everything that had gone on to date was happening to Leontes. Through that slow motion we were returning to reality.' Hermione's collapse triggered a 'massive psychological crisis, climax for Leontes', said Nunn: 'Only by wreaking that much destruction on everything and everybody could he be released from it. It was his own infernal machine.' What Nunn called Leontes' 'terrifying brainstorm climax' was emphasized, Ingham told me in interview, by his own idea to give physical form to Leontes' inner state. He appeared to have experienced a stroke; when he got up, he had a limp, his arm seemed withered, his speech was altered. 'We tried', said Nunn, 'not to make it just a sort of medical syndrome; we tried to be imprecise about it; but at that moment he was horribly and dreadfully damaged. It was self-induced.' Ingham told me that his Leontes was healed physically only when Hermione, in the statue scene, touched him.

It is Paulina, of course, who attempts to heal Leontes before he wreaks the damage which, in his Act III, scene ii repentance, he begins to face. To be 'physician' and 'counsellor' (II.iii.54–5) to Leontes, Paulina uses both deed and word, and her speeches offer a wide range of comic and serious possibilities. Very different parts of this range were used by each of the two gifted actors who performed Paulina in Nunn's production: Brenda Bruce, in the opening season at Stratford-upon-Avon in 1969, and Elizabeth Spriggs, when the production transferred to London at the Aldwych Theatre for the 1970–71 season. Their work brought critics' attention to the 'originality and complexity of Paulina's role', as Roger Warren put it (13).

Brenda Bruce brought out the comic possibilities of the part to a degree unusual when compared to her predecessors in the role, without abandoning its seriousness. When confronting Leontes with the baby Perdita (II.iii), she was 'playing but not milking Paulina for laughs', wrote Peter Roberts, making an important distinction (*Plays and Players*, 30). The 'perkiness' of Brenda Bruce, thought Neville Miller (*South Wales Evening Argus*, 19 May 1969), 'serves Paulina outstandingly well and at the first night was rewarded with applause as she made her exit from the scene involving the baby'. Furthermore, although the old idea that Paulina is a nag dies hard, critics saw there was more to the part. Bryden found Brenda Bruce 'clear and good-natured behind her nagging' (*Observer*, 18 May 1969), and J. W. Lambert wrote that she 'radiates behind all the nagging a priestess-like embrace which makes it no surprise that – a subtly piercing touch of Mr. Nunn's, far deeper than his showier diversions – it is to her, his principal scourge, that Leontes turns in his agony of heart and mind' (*Sunday Times*, 18 May 1969). For Gareth Lloyd Evans, the performance illuminated the significance of the role: 'Brenda Bruce grips Paulina's sturdy honesty and intuition firmly and, for me, explained for the first time why the character is so important – she is Leontes' confessor: through her he talks out his own sickness' (*Manchester Guardian Weekly*, 22 May 1969).

The quality of spiritual guide was also striking, in my experience, in the performances of Elizabeth Spriggs, whose playing of the role was less overtly comic in her earlier scenes, though subtly witty. Both actors used impressive anger in the trial scene; Bruce was more visceral, Spriggs more commanding. Ingham commented in interview, 'No one is big enough' to stop Leontes, 'apart from Paulina', who 'smashes the hell out of him'. It was in Act V, scene i that the priestess role deepened in Elizabeth Spriggs's performance. Ingham found that Elizabeth Spriggs 'gets in touch with something almost cosmic', saying with wit, 'I get the feeling that Elizabeth would probably have been in touch with Apollo about this.'

Paulina's roles of 'priestess' and 'psychiatrist', as Roger Warren puts it (writing of Brenda Bruce's acting), were supported by the staging, especially of Act V, scene i. Leontes was 'kneeling in prayer, with Paulina standing over him with outstretched arms. The point was instantly made that she had been in charge of his psychological and spiritual development in the intervening period' (12–13). Such transformation by the first scene of Act V is not simply a given in the script; other actors have emphasized darker tones in the beginning of the scene. As Patrick Stewart played Leontes in the RSC production of 1981–83, Leontes in V.i was still locked in a winter of near despair. Equally moving was Ingham's very different approach. Ingham remarked that for him it was necessary to show 'a slow process of healing through love' in order 'to prepare' for the final scene, so that Paulina could see that 'when he is ready, she can bring them [Leontes and Hermione] together – not for his sake, but for love's sake', knowing, as she does, of Hermione's suffering.

Ingham had, indeed, underscored Leontes' newfound commitment to change earlier, at the end of the trial scene, in the way he spoke his lines: 'Once a day I'll visit / The chapel where they lie, and tears shed there / Shall be my recreation' (III.ii.236–8). It was his idea to pronounce the final word with an emphasis on its first two letters, as 're-creation', and to make the 'e' in 're' a long vowel (as is clear in the recording made during one of the last performances at the Aldwych, 27 January 1971, for the National Sound Archive). For Ingham, one clue assisting his choice to emphasize Leontes' process of repentance and renewal was the rhythm of the line, in which it is possible for 're' to receive relatively heavy stress. Reflecting on his approach to verse speaking, which shares aspects of formalism also present in the work of John Barton and Trevor Nunn, Ingham commented that if you follow Shakespeare's 'stresses on words' and 'follow his timing', it is like 'reading a musical score'. If you 'soar with him', Ingham said, 'he'll give you spiritual joy you can find in very few authors'.

The final moments of the trial scene pose another decision for actors and directors: to what degree are Leontes and Paulina at this stage reconciled? Promptbook notations for both 1969 and 1970–71 suggest a Paulina not only more in sorrow than in anger by the final lines of the scene but compassionate. Saying that Leontes' visit to the chapel would be his (spiritual) exercise – 'I daily vow to use it' – Ingham rose from his kneeling position, holding his hand toward Paulina, who took his hand to lead him.

Major turning points in the trial scene were followed by a series of transitional scenes facilitated by Nunn's non-illusionist methods. Stroboscopic lighting greatly assisted the notoriously difficult transition '*Exit pursued by a bear*'. The 'bear' structure was 9 feet, 9 inches in height, 'made of goatskin with expanded polythene on a bamboo frame', requiring an actor inside the frame 'to wear special eight-inch high boots', according to the *Birmingham Post* (16 May 1969). The stroboscopic lighting used during the sequence when the bear struck Antigonus (four times), and then enveloped him, made the bear seem twice its literal size, a 'looming shadow', at which no one laughed, according to Trewin (*Birmingham Post*, 17 May 1969). For Milton Shulman, the 'cinematic' strobe lighting on the bear created a 'moment of chilling horror' ('Cinematic techniques catch up with the Bard', *Evening Standard*, 16 May 1969). Amid Antigonus' screams and the sounds of thunder, the stroboscopic light created a nightmare image that stayed in the mind during the five seconds of silence that followed the exit. To these 'things dying' there followed a total contrast: brilliantly intense light, and 'things newborn' – the thin wail of a baby's cry.

Contrasts of light began and ended the presentation of Time as Chorus at the opening of the second half. A blackout of house and set lights was followed by light on the large cube, which in the invented opening prior to I.i had contained Leontes and now contained the spinning figure of Time. The connection was verbal as well as visual: the rich, deep voice of Alton Kumalo, the African actor playing Time, had in the show's beginning been heard speaking a few lines from Time's Chorus. Nunn's symbolic presentation of the Chorus of Time in this mirrored cube suggested a thematic construction of time, in Dennis Bartholomeusz' words, as 'both within and outside the self'. Bartholomeusz suggests that, in later using the cube for the statue scene, Nunn also wanted 'to show the centrality of Hermione in the play' (214). Bartholomeusz reports that one of his own students wrote to Nunn in 1970 to suggest that 'as the mirrored case was used both by Time and Hermione, the thematic connection between them, now focused so sharply, showed that the resurrection of Hermione was the final culmination of the process and progress of time which has distorted and revealed so much throughout the play'. Bartholomeusz quotes Nunn's response: 'it was almost uncanny for me to read what sounded like sections of my first talk to the company about the play' (214).

Nunn's reasons both for doubling the parts of Hermione and Perdita and for his multiple uses of the cube resemble formalist emphases on thematic parallels and on unity. His decision to have Hermione and Perdita played by the same actress, he told me, was taken before he knew of the one previous time in theatre history such doubling had been done, by Mary Anderson at the Lyceum in 1887. The chief reason for Anderson's doubling seems to have been to heighten her prominence as a star; by contrast, the primary reason for Nunn's choice was both symbolic and structural. 'In one sense, Hermione does not die,' he said in interview. 'Hermione's child is called Perdita, that which is lost, and Hermione is that which is lost to Leontes.' Gerald Jacobs reports that Nunn, in approaching Judi Dench about the possibility of doubling the parts, said: 'I just now have a vision of the play where, were you to play both Hermione and Perdita, the ironies between the central, pastoral section of the play and the very cruel, tragic first part would become much more pronounced, much more painful and the play would become much more coherent' (quoted in Jacobs, 74–5). Nunn's decision brought losses, especially in the final scene, as well as gains, but the rich range of Judi Dench's work enabled her to perform both parts superbly, without minimizing the distinct differences between them.

To choose an actor so relatively young as Judi Dench was (age thirty-three in 1969) to play Hermione was to move from traditional conceptions of the role. 'What, mothers' parts already?', Jacobs reports Dench as saying laughingly when Nunn offered her the role (quoted in Jacobs, 74). Few actors could have done both mother and daughter, but, as Barbara Leigh-Hunt put it, Dench's work as an actor shows how splendidly she 'bridged the gap between being a juvenile actress, in the old commercial jargon, and more mature roles' (quoted in Jacobs, 177). Furthermore, in casting *The Winter's Tale*, Nunn continued his break from tradition by casting a relatively young Leontes in Barrie Ingham; the role had typically gone previously to older actors – Gielgud, of course, in 1951, and Eric Porter (directed by Peter Wood) at Stratford-upon-Avon in 1960 (cf. Warren, 11). Richard Pasco, whom Nunn cast as Polixenes, had experience – at the Bristol Old Vic, for example – but was in his first season with the RSC. As Roger Warren has pointed out, Nunn's casting 'broke the mould so effectively that most productions since then have presented the three protagonists as young people' (11).

Dench brought a freshness to the role of Hermione that was

widely noted by reviewers. Trewin named what seemed to him new in the unaffected integrity of her work:

> I have not known anybody play Hermione better than Judi Dench does now (and I have seen a good many productions of *The Winter's Tale*). You have only to listen to her, to note the phrasing, and to observe how thought and speech are allied ... She is an actress with a clear purity of her own, not one of the sheet-armour Hermiones but a woman deeply wronged and in no mood to boom about it like a 21-gun salute. (*Birmingham Post*, 24 May 1969)

As Dench played the Hermione of the first court scene, she was witty, playful, generous. She entered running, playing a game of tag with Polixenes, Leontes, Mamillius, and Camillo; she was full both of pregnant life and of laughter. Her initial spontaneity established an innocence – not naivety – in her Hermione which, she told me in interview, gave her a 'journey', that of a 'younger, more childlike woman who grows up as the play goes on'.

Terry Hands, years later, remembered these qualities and advantages of her performance. Re-rehearsing his 1986 RSC production of the play for its 1987 transfer to London, he spoke to his cast in the Barbican rehearsal room about what he considered Dench's breakthrough performance as Hermione, stating that her avoidance of stereotyped, rather grand 'dignity' in I.ii enabled her to present a much greater authentic dignity in the trial scene.[11] Hermione is 'very different by the trial scene', Judi Dench told me in interview; she spoke also of the 'passion' and 'fire' which comes from Hermione, adding that her 'courage is extraordinary'.

Judi Dench commented that she kept her Hermione and her Perdita 'in separate compartments' of her awareness as a performer. The two roles were rehearsed in separate blocks of time – Hermione in the first weeks, Perdita in the next weeks – until the two roles were both worked on in later phases of rehearsal. One reviewer found that she 'differentiates the parts so well' that 'she reduces the thematic relevance of one actress playing both parts' (Gordon Parsons, *Morning Star*, 16 May 1969). But in my view this very differentiation reduced the danger of a heavy underscoring of thematic parallels while at the same time suggesting the resonances between Dench's playful Hermione of I.ii and her vitality as Perdita.

Dench also avoided the traps into which those playing Perdita can fall. Trewin noted that her gaiety and gentleness were 'without a hint of skittishness' (*Birmingham Post*, 24 May 1969). Granville Barker, one imagines, would have applauded her barefooted, swift, vigorous movement ('be not poetical' had been his note to his barefoot Perdita, Cathleen Nesbitt). Dench's performance was earthy, warm, direct, strong and, like Pennie Downie's nearly a decade later (RSC 1986–87), sensual. She suggested Perdita's country upbringing by adapting certain aspects of a Yorkshire accent that she used, noticeably but not heavily, in the role. Born in York, Judi Dench had lived there until going to London to study at the Central School of Speech and Drama (where her voice tutor was Cicely Berry, by 1969 director of voice work at the RSC). Dench's use of a Yorkshire accent was in no way forced in her performance of it. At the National Sound Archive, in the audio recording of the entire performance at the Aldwych on 27 January 1971, towards the end of the run, one can hear, for example, her pronunciation of certain short vowels: in 'pranked up' (IV.iv.10), 'blush' (12), and 'summer's' (80), the 'u' was sounded like a double 'o' in the Standard English pronunciation of 'look'. At one point Florizel playfully imitated these sounds, delighting in his guise as a 'hu[oo]mble swain' (30). There was no affectation or caricature of Perdita's country nurture in Dench's vocal work; rather, in its contemporary British context, the accent evoked differences in location and class from urban upper-class or aristocratic accents even as it added to the vigour of her acting.

Dench's Perdita was consonant with a pastoral scene that avoided the conventional 'idyll'; Nunn eschewed nostalgia. Costumes, music, and movement which drew selectively from the popular culture of the 1960s, with its rock music, hippie trends, and liberation of instinctual energies, were especially useful for Autolycus and for the satyrs' dance. The cultural transposition gave Derek Smith's Autolycus a strong connection to the contemporary audience (particularly its younger members); his amplified songs became like numbers sung to the audience at a rock musical. The lyrics were largely those given to Autolycus in the text, but composer Guy Woolfenden and production assistant Buzz Goodbody made some emendations, adding, for example, to Autolycus' first song – 'When Daffodils Begin to Peer' – the refrain, 'Forget tomorrow and live today'. Allusions to the culture of hippies found their best (though partial) parallel in Autolycus since, like them, he is not native to the pastoral world. However, of course, hippies were urban voluntary dropouts, whereas Autolycus, by his own account, is in involuntary exile from the court and connives to return to its favour, though he seizes the day and much else his fingers light upon.

The rock elements in the music and dance were also a contemporary effort to express the sexual energy of the satyrs. Nunn is among the creative minority of directors in the twentieth century to have included their dance, but he transposed its position, putting it just before the dance of the shepherds and shepherdesses. Five of the actors who had danced as satyrs, remaining in the same hippie gear, became the shepherds (joined by Florizel, to make six male dancers with six female dancers, including Perdita). This merger – rather than contrast – of satyrs and shepherds, the close sequence of the dances (the First Folio order separates them by approximately 176 lines), and the earthy vitality of John Broome's choreography for the dance of shepherds and shepherdesses: all created an impression of vital sensuality. Sensuality was strongly, as well as sensitively, embodied in Judi Dench's acting with David Bailie's Florizel (see figure 7).

7 Act IV, scene iv: David Bailie as Florizel and Judi Dench as Perdita. Directed by Trevor Nunn, Royal Shakespeare Company, Royal Shakespeare Theatre, Stratford-upon-Avon, 1969. Thomas F. Holte photograph. Copyright © Shakespeare Birthplace Trust

The music for the dance of shepherds and shepherdesses was not rock music, but based on lighter syncopated rhythms. The music, movement, and costuming for Nunn's pastoral scene should not be merely reduced to the catchwords 'hippie' and 'pop', though some reviewers did so. Gareth Lloyd Evans refused to paint with such a broad brush:

> Shocked academics have been heard to cry 'out, harrow' at an Autolycus who sings apparent 'pop', at dancers who 'twist' their way through a sheep-shearing ceremony. In fact, it is not simply 'pop' – within the brash sounds there are subtle dying falls; neither is the dancing entirely 'twist' – it has some movement-phrases of great grace, in one of which Perdita looks exquisitely Botticelli-like. ('Interpretation or Experience?': Shakespeare at Stratford', 134)

Indeed so; Guy Woolfenden's music made sophisticated use of the contemporary cultural trends upon which he drew, as in the sitar cascade he composed, for example, for the production's beginning. Occasional critical comparisons between Nunn's production and *Hair* were grossly misleading, despite superficial similarities such as the relatively bare stages and the use of rock music and hippie culture. *Hair* had opened in New York on 7 October 1967, produced by the New York Shakespeare Festival, but Nunn has set the record straight about any influence: 'For what it is worth I saw the London production of *Hair* some two or three months after my production of *The Winter's Tale* opened in Stratford, and I was deeply surprised when critical comparison was made between the two' (Bartholomeusz, 218, citing Nunn's letter to him of 13 March 1970). Yet given the historical moment – despite the very different cultural context of the musical, with its urban characters and political protest – some audience members found an amusing reverberation in the servant's line that the carters, shepherds, neatherds, and swineherds who have come to offer a dance 'have made themselves all men of hair' (IV.iv.319–21).

Nunn's pastoral scenes evoked a mixed reception from reviewers, though Judi Dench's performance as Perdita was strongly praised. Critical debate, however, focused on the effects in the final scene (V.iii) of doubling the parts of Hermione and Perdita, since they are of course both required to be present simultaneously. Nunn attempted to solve the problem in the following way. When Judi Dench entered as Perdita at the beginning of the scene, she saw in the centre-stage perspex cube the 'statue' of Hermione (an actor doubling Hermione); Dench gave Perdita's first speech, which ends 'Dear Queen, that ended when I but began, / Give me that hand of yours to kiss' (42–6; Perdita's only other words in the scene, 84–5, were cut). Paulina, responding, 'O, patience –', touched the cube containing the statue of Hermione, and the cube began to revolve. Judi Dench, as Perdita, followed around the turning cube as though not to lose sight of her mother's statue. Just after the actor who had represented Hermione's statue exited unseen, Dench, also out of view and now in a costume visually identical to that of the Hermione double, entered the cube before it continued its revolution. When the cube had come full circle, Dench was in her role as Hermione, standing as a statue. While this was happening, another actor, costumed as Dench had been for Perdita, came downstage (right) as though coming from behind the cube, following its revolution to seek her mother's image. Judi Dench has reflected on the challenges she experienced in doubling her roles at these moments:

> It is difficult for me to know whether it looked all right from the front, but it did not work for me. Even when it did work well, it left the audience wondering how on earth it had happened, instead of feeling the emotion of what was happening between the characters. I didn't feel so much moved as breathless, by the time I had swapped with the double who played Perdita and rushed round to take the statue's place in the perspex box at the back of the stage, but I did feel as though I was another actress, which is a very strange sensation. (Dench, 'A Career in Shakespeare', 205–6)

For some critics, too, these moves necessitated by doubling the roles of Hermione and Perdita in this scene proved distracting. Roger Warren, who praises what he calls the mould-breaking strengths of the production, nonetheless found problems with a doubling which required 'an elaborate technical contrivance' in the statue scene (12). R. P. Draper was mixed in his evaluation of 'the clever execution of the trick', which he judged was in some degree distracting (61). But Nunn's device was effective for other critics, including Ronald Bryden (*Observer*, 18 May 1969); Milton Shulman (*Evening Standard*, 16 May 1969); John Barber, who found it 'ingeniously staged' (*Daily Telegraph*, 16 May 1969); and John Shorter, who believed 'the ending in its wonderful theatricality is most moving' (*Daily Telegraph*, 3 July 1970).

Apart from problems raised by the doubling of parts, the statue scene gained from Nunn's heightened, symbolic visual presentation. Since the cube containing Hermione was the same visual space as the cube for the Chorus of Time, those in the audience were invited to connect Time's 'joy and terror' (IV.i.1) to their past memory of the destroyer in Leontes (spinning as he stood in Time's cube) as well as to their present wonder at the recreation of Hermione (with myriad reflections of her white-robed figure created by white lighting on that same cube). Visual presentation was strengthened by ritual action, which was especially marked toward the end of the scene. After Judi Dench, having moved from the cube to embrace Leontes, spoke Hermione's first words in the scene, to Perdita – 'I, / Knowing by Paulina that the oracle / Gave hope thou wast in being, have preserved / Myself to see the issue' (125–8) – the word 'issue' became the cue to the ensuing ritual enactment: Hermione kissed the kneeling Perdita on the head, and then turned to kiss Leontes; Florizel moved and knelt downstage of Hermione, kissing her hand and then taking Leontes' hand. All turned to Leontes, who kissed Hermione and put his hand on Perdita's head in a gesture of blessing. There followed a moment rarely seen in production – Polixenes extended his hand to Perdita's head and, by so doing, blessed what he had formerly cursed, implicitly accepting his coming role as her father-in-law. The bonds connecting Hermione, Leontes, Perdita, Polixenes, and Florizel that had been so violently broken were now made whole, and their hands were joined; the grouping held for several moments. Irving Wardle remarked on the effectiveness of this 'spectacle' of 'a silent circle of reunion' (*The Times*, 16 May 1969).

In my own experience of the production in some dozen performances over the course of its long run (1969 into 1971), I found I could simultaneously be aware of the theatrical artifice Nunn used for the statue scene as well as of the scene's moving human encounters. Indeed, the experience of Nunn's entire production remains strongly etched on my mind. Engaging in revaluation of it in light of current critical perspectives, I am aware in new ways of its cultural moment, and of what it did and did not realize of the play's possibilities.

An examination of some of Nunn's textual cuts helps to focus on three aspects of the play not fully explored in his production, the first and third of which involve problems in the social construction of gender and power. First, though the production gained in symbolic and thematic awareness of time, it lost fuller sight of the cost of time, particularly for Hermione. Second, though it achieved an ecstatic final reunion, it lost a darker, tragicomic mingling of tones. Third, cuts in Paulina's lines reduced nuances of gender-charged social roles and issues of authority which characterize Paulina and Leontes' relationship.

By doubling Hermione and Perdita, Nunn emphasized Hermione's statue as symbol of that which was lost. However, he erased a crucial sign of Hermione's particular experience of loss by cutting eight lines (V.iii.27–34), beginning with Leontes' words 'But yet, Paulina, / Hermione was not so much wrinkled, nothing / So agèd as this seems.' Leontes' speech thus moved from his remembrance of Hermione's 'infancy and grace' (27) and his exclamation, 'O, thus she stood, / Even with such life of majesty – warm life', to facing the pain of the present – 'As now it coldly stands' (34–6) – with no recognition of the loss and passage of time for Hermione. Nunn's cut thus diminished the cost to Hermione and emphasized instead a brief reverie of an innocent time past in which Hermione was seen through Leontes' gaze.

To cut reference to Hermione's wrinkles is also to lose the inclusion, in the fundamentally non-naturalistic style of this scene, of contrasting perspectives. If the play were, strictly speaking, allegorical, its mode would consistently emphasize abstract personification; but its remarkable range includes an art rooted in concrete particulars drawn from everyday experience. Leontes' line 'If this be magic, let it be an art / Lawful as eating' (110–11) was cut, and with it also a social, even political, nuance, as the word 'Lawful' can also imply Leontes' validation of Paulina's and Hermione's 'magic' and art. The line signals that he no longer accuses Paulina of witchcraft or Hermione of wrongful deception. The cut is thus a loss, and part of a pattern of losses the cuts reveal, despite the fine visual effect substituted for the line: a silent moment, after Hermione moved toward Leontes, as their hands met, reflected in the cube of Time.

Nunn's treatment of this moment is characteristic of his view of the play as 'allegorical', as well as his emphasis on the ecstatic potentialities of the scene rather than on its tragicomic undertones of remembered pain. He saw the ending, to cite his description of his set, as 'something soaring, something optimistic'. He cut the lines in which Leontes laments that Hermione's image evokes so strong an awareness of what might have been that it is 'Now piercing to my soul' (34). He also cut one of the final moments of remembered pain (though it can be mingled with new joy) when Leontes remembers he severed bonds between Hermione and Polixenes: 'What! Look upon my brother. Both your pardons / That e'er I put between your holy looks / My ill suspicion' (147–9). The next lines (149–51), when Florizel is introduced as 'troth-plight to your daughter', were also cut, thus losing a last moment of discovery for Hermione. This cut, too, was replaced by visual action – the silent ritual of reunion, in slow visual mime, after Hermione's line to Perdita that she has 'preserved' herself 'to see the issue' (127–8). Cutting the lines about Florizel that Leontes speaks as he introduces Florizel for the first time to Hermione – 'This your son-in-law, / And son unto the King' (149–50) – not only loses a moment of discovery for Hermione, it loses social and political nuances concerning union and future lineage for a kingdom, issues relevant both to the play and to its Jacobean audiences.

A more pervasive loss of social nuances in the final scene involves the subtle issue of authority between Paulina and Leontes. Paulina has had the extraordinary courage to name and to protest against Leontes' tyrannical behaviour earlier in the play (II.iii and, especially, III.ii), speaking her truth to his power in scenes that are charged with gender-based conflicts between Paulina, Leontes, and his male courtiers. Leontes has even given her the political power to choose for him – should the time seem right to her – a wife, thus putting in her hands the future succession in his kingdom (V.i). The opening lines of the final scene, however, show that the relationship between Paulina and Leontes has changed following the discovery of Florizel and Perdita, who will indeed inherit the kingdom. Paulina now greets Leontes with an awareness of royal lineage and social class, in lines that Nunn cut:

         all my services
You have paid home. But that you have vouchsafed,
With your crowned brother and these your contracted
Heirs of your kingdoms, my poor house to visit,
It is a surplus of your grace which never
My life may last to answer. (V.iii.3–8)

Paulina's lines are easy to dismiss as conventional, and it could be in keeping with Nunn's desire to move away from naturalism that these lines seemed expendable to him. But in this scene Shakespeare mingles a highly selective representation of social reality, as he constructs it, with symbolic stagecraft. What is lost in cutting these opening lines by Paulina is their setting up of the expected relationship between a gentlewoman and her sovereign against which we can register departures from that relationship as Paulina, at many moments in the scene, takes command of Leontes. Nunn cut (there being no curtain on the cube containing the statue) both Leontes' command 'Do not draw the curtain' (59) and Paulina's reply: 'No longer shall you gaze on't, lest your fancy / May think anon it moves' (60–1). Leontes' next command, 'Let be, let be' (61), became, in this visually oriented production, 'Let's see, let's see!' Because of a subsequent cut – of Leontes' 'Proceed. / No foot shall stir' (97–8) – the audience lost an opportunity to see Leontes supporting Paulina in her command: 'Then all stand still – / Or those that think it is unlawful business / I am about, let them depart' (95–7).

Thus particular social nuances of gender and power were minimized in Nunn's directorial decisions for this scene, as was Hermione's particular experience of the cost of time. Ironically, in a production that helped critics recognize the magnitude of Paulina's part, her political role was not explored, though her political importance would not have had to eclipse her spiritual significance. The vigour of Brenda Bruce's Paulina (1969), the intelligence of Elizabeth Spriggs's Paulina (1970–71), and the vital, generous range of Judi Dench's Hermione and Perdita counterbalanced the erasure of important textual details. But the cuts and emphases of Nunn's production ran the risk of seeing the women primarily in relation to Leontes' psyche – in particular, Hermione and Perdita as symbols of 'that which is lost' represented chiefly what was lost to Leontes. Indeed, Leontes' journey was given emphasis by a number of the brilliant inventions of the production: his spinning in Time's cube, the nursery-world properties, and an expressionistic use of lighting changes to show Hermione and Polixenes (in I.ii) enacting not their reality but Leontes' nightmare.

Nunn's production richly deserves its place in theatre history as a breakthrough in production styles for *The Winter's Tale* and a rethinking of its principal roles. The production realized core motifs in the play with extraordinary freshness, effectiveness, and impact for its contemporary audience. But Shakespearean production belongs to time; we do Nunn's achievement no honour, nor do we learn as much from it, if we do not see that it is of that time, of that place, when the very strengths of his approach to symbol and image ran the risk of losing touch with the particulars of gender and political relations which inform the conflicts of even so non-naturalistic a play as *The Winter's Tale*.

CHAPTER IV

Audrey Stanley's production with the Oregon Shakespearean Festival, 1975

The first woman to direct a production of Shakespeare at the Oregon Shakespearean Festival was Audrey Stanley – in 1975, when the Festival was observing its fortieth anniversary. *The Winter's Tale* she directed remains one of the play's most important productions not only in Ashland[1] but in the United States. Stanley's orchestration of all aspects of the production to build towards the extraordinary performance of the play's final scene has earned high critical praise (see, for example, Alan Dessen, 'The Oregon Shakespearean Festival, 1975'). Furthermore, the production had affinities with feminist thought emergent in the United States during the early 1970s.

Close, intensive exploration of language, a hallmark of Audrey Stanley's work, added to the strengths of this production, as did her knowledge of classical and Renaissance staging; both spring in part from her training and remarkable combination of active theatre practice and scholarly work. Among the first graduates of the newly instituted joint-honours degree programme in Drama at the University of Bristol, she took her BA in English Literature, French, and Drama in 1950, having studied with H. D. F. Kitto and Glynne Wyckham. After subsequent study at the Bristol Old Vic Theatre School, she founded the University of Bristol Dramatic Society Touring Company and also worked with the London Artists Theatre Company. For her PhD thesis (1970) in Dramatic Art from the University of California, Berkeley, she researched ancient Greek theatre sites. When she directed at Ashland in 1975, she was on leave from full-time teaching at the University of California, Santa Cruz. In 1982, she brought together people from the University, professional theatre, and the community to found Shakespeare/Santa Cruz.

Now nationally and internationally known, their annual productions emphasize – as hers did in Ashland – detailed voice and text work, bringing together the academy and the theatre.

In part because of her familiarity with production of Greek drama, Audrey Stanley directs Shakespeare with acute awareness of heightened moments involving references to the gods. Such consciousness informed her handling of *The Winter's Tale*'s final scene: the entire production 'has been conceived in the light of this ending' (Director's Comments, Festival Program, 14), she wrote in 1975. As she later put it, 'Every single thing worked towards the artistic expression of that final reconciliation – set, costumes, lighting, music, sound effects, casting, acting' (lecture at Vanderbilt University, 1990).[2] The result was a significant contribution to stage history.

The pervasive, subtle alertness to issues involving women that distinguished the production was also present in Stanley's own reflections. She 'believed in the strengths of women characters in Shakespeare', she told me in interview, and thought they 'had not been given their due' in Shakespeare productions she had seen. Stanley wrote in 1975 that the play 'shows fathers within the intimacy of their family relationships treating wives and children as objects or as stone, and only through considerable agony can a new depth of feeling and a different relationship take place' (Stanley, quoted in Laing, 44).[3] In interviews with me[4] Stanley analysed the ways Hermione is treated as an object in the early court scenes. In Leontes' distorted view, she is a decorative trophy won by Bohemia (Polixenes), worn 'like her medal, hanging / About his neck' (I.ii.304–5). When he accuses her of adultery, one of Leontes' misogynist epithets for Hermione is 'O thou thing' (II.i.82). Opposing such objectification, Stanley's production emphasized Hermione's spiritual and moral agency in the statue scene. Paulina was also presented as a serious moral agent; her interventions were not comic. Stanley saw the danger to Paulina but also her courage as she confronted Leontes and the male courtiers in Act II, scene iii and dared to engage in a 'power struggle' with the Lords in Act V, scene i. Paulina became, furthermore, a spiritual guide to Leontes. Perdita was likewise directed by Stanley to stand up for herself strongly, as seen in her dialogue with Polixenes concerning the grafting of flowers, and in her assertion that the 'selfsame sun that shines upon his court / Hides not his visage from our cottage, but / Looks on alike' (IV.iv.441–3).

Representation of the feminine in the production was partly indebted to Jungian psychology, as was some feminist Shakespearean criticism in the 1970s and the critical work of C. L. Barber, Stanley's colleague at the University of California, Santa Cruz. For Stanley, *The Winter's Tale* suggested the need for a Jungian balancing of opposites – the contrasting yet complementary values not only of court and country, but of yin and yang. James Edmondson told me in interview that he saw in his role of Leontes the eternal boy, the Jungian *puer aeternus*: 'Leontes is a man who never grew up, and was forced to grow up'; he 'must get his spiritual life together'.[5] To the role of Hermione, Le Clanché du Rand brought a consciousness of feminist concerns which coincided with her interests in Jungian thought (including the work of Esther Harding and Marie-Louise von Franz). Exploring the psychological implications of the play as a tale, she perceived mythic resonances. As she later wrote to me, Hermione's initial youthful, total trust in Leontes changes through darker knowledge: 'Like Persephone she is "raped" into consciousness.' She 'never dreams that he could regard her the way he actually does until it is made brutally clear'. The reunion of mother and daughter in the final scene was, she thought, like 'Demeter / Hermione after the loss of Persephone [/ Perdita]'. She added: 'The reunion with Perdita was a reunion with my and Leontes' past selves but with the wisdom of our present selves there to love her as well as we could.'[6]

While most directors and leading actors, like many critics, have understood the play's action primarily as Leontes' journey, this production equally emphasized the centrality of Hermione's choices in making transformation possible. Furthermore, as the final scene developed, it became the ceremony of a community, encompassing the separation and reunion of two families. The play is 'not Leontes' story, necessarily', said Edmondson; it 'is not [about] one character. It is a wonderful ensemble ... And the gods watch all.'

To express a sense that 'powers divine / Behold our human actions' (III.ii.27–8) and to move towards her sense of an ending, Stanley used the resources of the indoor Angus Bowmer Theatre fully. Unlike the productions by Granville Barker, Brook, and Nunn, hers was in a theatre built expressly to enable non-proscenium staging. The Bowmer, which opened in 1970, seats approximately six hundred; it was designed by Richard L. Hay to be a highly flexible space and its forestage, movable via hydraulic lifts, can change to simulate a thrust stage. Bartholomeusz calls Hay 'one of the great set designers of our time' (191). For *The Winter's Tale* in 1975, Hay created a permanent abstract set with a thrusting yoke platform shaped like a great inverted 'Y', spreading wide at its front, bounded by three semicircular levels, or steps, going down to the auditorium floor. This thrusting forefront and its curving steps provided opportunities for direct address and close relations between actors and audience. The non-illusionist set, changing before the spectators' eyes, supported continuity, rapid juxtapositions, symbolic presentational figures (Time and the bear), and spectacle. The set was 'not at any time a static background', according to Bartholomeusz (192). Its great arch, which spanned the width of the stage, had two movable halves that were divided in varying ways throughout the action, then came together only in the statue scene. At the very end of that scene the arches swung completely open to either side of the stage, 'as if in response to the generous impulse and great warmth with which the final scene was played' (Bartholomeusz, 192).

Staging, lighting, and costume design reflected Audrey Stanley's view that the play had 'three worlds' in two main parts: the first part was a 'tragedy of sexual jealousy' in the court world, culminating in Antigonus' death; the second part encompassed both the world of Bohemia with its 'strong rural comedy' and the changed world of Sicilia in Act V. Writing in 1975 at a time when the play's 'unity' was still a dominant critical problem, Stanley argued:

> Here are three worlds which exist powerfully in their own right. And yet the play creates its own world and its own values so strongly that it seems inevitable the tragic Winter world would give rise to the final reconciliation through a rebirth of feeling in the summer countryside. The desire to show the inherent unity of the play together with the forward thrust of the action has affected the way the director and designers conceived this production. (Stanley, quoted in Laing, 42-3)

Stanley emphasized in her lecture at Vanderbilt that 'the set should not be realistic, but symbolize the mood and movement of the play'. Contrasting worlds of Sicilia and Bohemia were to come together at the end in 'harmony and a revelatory opening out, to include the audience'. Stanley 'wanted all this with only one set to emphasize the cohesion' of the play's three worlds. The vast arch of Hay's design, on which were sun and flame motifs, was split at the centre, remaining out of kilter until the final scene. In the first three acts, said Stanley, the arch halves pointed 'in different directions to show the world of Sicilia in disjunction'. As in expressionist technique, 'vertical lines' at the back of the set 'were leaning to one side to suggest the state of imbalance in the mind of Leontes'. For Bohemia, despite shifts to soft, round shapes in lighting, and to mingled colours of spring, summer, and autumn, the set was 'still very much askew'. Each of the arch halves 'opened out in the opposite angle, and the platform shape moved some 90%'. In the statue scene, Sicilia changed: each half of the arch 'centred to form a complete arch and the platform also centred to form a symmetrical and harmonious set for the first time' (Vanderbilt lecture). When Hermione turned to see her daughter, part of the platform at the rear of the stage raised up, lifting 'to its highest point when Leontes asked forgiveness of Hermione and Polixenes' (interview). In the final moments, each great half of the centre arch 'opened right out' in a wide span 'as if over the audience'. Not a classical arch with its keystone in place, this final configuration was open; it suggested, Stanley told me in interview, not closure but 'new possibilities'.

Concepts governing the production's stage design were also expressed in the costume designs of Jeannie Davidson; the costumes, as Audrey Stanley pointed out, deliberately suggested a court world of 'display', 'stiffness, and a lack of reality and truth' (interview). A 'harsh asymmetry' characterized the court costumes, which were of 'dark jewel-like winter velvets', with 'rich intricate root-like patterning' (Stanley, quoted in Laing, 43). Leontes' costume was a burgundy so deep it suggested thickened blood (cf. I.ii.169); his crown had shapes symbolizing flames (of his passion, jealousy), as did the stylized motif at the base of his gown. In her Vanderbilt lecture Stanley said that she had wanted the 'idea of winter' expressed in early court scenes; costumes and lighting were 'to reflect the sharp colors and splintered light of northern cathedrals and their stained glass windows' in winter light. In strong contrast to this court world, Davidson used rough textures in colours expressing what Stanley said was symbolic 'spring, summer and autumn' in the country: light green (for Perdita's dress and Florizel's shirt); blue-green (Florizel's jacket); deeper green, blue, yellow, gold, dark orange, beige, tan, and brown for others in Bohemia. For the final scene, in which the lighting was clear and grew in intensity, the costumes, in flowing lines, were in shades of white, from pale grey to the whitest of whites for Hermione.

The same desire to build toward the final scene that shaped the production's design decisions also governed Audrey Stanley's choice of Le Clanché du Rand to play Hermione and James Edmondson to play Leontes. Stanley knew the depth of their previous theatre work and had previously directed du Rand in her award-winning performance as Hedda in Ibsen's *Hedda Gabler* (University of California, Berkeley, Alumni Repertory Theatre, 1967). Le Clanché du Rand had played Hermione in 1972, in one of her four seasons at the Colorado Shakespeare Festival, where she had met Edmondson. She told me in interview that she also drew as an actor on her experience of Balinese theatre: 'Acting had always been a spiritual experience for me, and Balinese dance and theatre confirmed and deepened this perception'.

Stanley knew that Edmondson could emphasize tragic intensity in the first three acts. 'My power zone as an actor', Edmondson told me, 'lies in pain'. As Stanley put it in her Vanderbilt lecture, 'Depth in the first part helped to lead the audience toward the conclusion.' To have Leontes jealous before the play begins or to have him 'making far too much of Hermione's friendship and social attention to Polixenes so that his jealousy is seen as absurd' would 'undercut the extreme physical agony of Leontes' jealousy'. Edmondson was able acutely to project that agony through what Stanley calls the 'physicality' of acting. The 'large physical jolt' he registered when he felt sexual betrayal enabled him, she said, 'to explore a wider spectrum of emotions, so that his repentance when disaster (or Apollo) strikes can likewise be huge, and drive him physically to the ground'. Edmondson's intensity as an actor enabled him in the statue scene to achieve a spectrum of emotion from deep pain to extreme joy. As Leontes in 1975 and as director of *The Winter's Tale* for the Utah Shakespearean Festival in 1996, he explored what he calls 'verticality' – the heights and depths of human experience, and human connection 'with the gods or God'.

Edmondson and du Rand shared with Stanley a grounding in close textual work, using Folio and quarto texts to wrestle with decisions involving punctuation and versification. They understood such decisions to be interpretive; they did not claim to have found the one correct reading inherent in an immutable text with fixed meanings. Their performances and their interview discussions of the crucial opening sequence of Act I, scene ii, before Leontes' 'Too hot, too hot!' (107), gave detailed examples of what they perceived the text to offer.[7]

The scene began with a strong gesture: Leontes entered with his arm around Polixenes (played by Peter Silbert); the two toasted with goblets, arms intertwined and lifted upward like the twin branches of one tree. Stanley was working from the image in Camillo's speech in the previous scene: 'there rooted betwixt them then such an affection which cannot choose but branch now' (I.i.22–3). The initial stage image in I.ii created a vivid but fleeting impression of the kings' friendship; seeing them celebrate their relationship from time past, audiences could feel more keenly what they soon began to sense was being lost in time present.

When Hermione came up to the men a moment later, they interrupted their toasting. The interruption suggested the disequilibrium Stanley perceived in the triangular situation: they were dealing with the effect of marriage on a close male friendship rooted in childhood. The men had separated to marry and to assume responsibilities of kingship; when, as Stanley put it, Polixenes returns after many years to visit his friend, and Hermione is there, 'it is an entirely different relationship'. Costuming emphasized Hermione's fertile womanhood; great with child, she appeared very near the end of her nine months.

As Stanley and Edmondson read the verse, they perceived tension in the initial dramatic situation in I.ii. Tension arose, said Stanley, from the contrast between the 'smoothness of the speeches of Polixenes and the curtness, the abruptness, and the disturbed rhythms' of Leontes' language. Polixenes' language, she explained, is 'flowery, and his cadences roll'; his opening, ornate speech contrasts with Leontes' 'crisp, monosyllabic, half-sentences'. Of Leontes' first six short utterances, four, she perceived, are commands (9–10, 17, 18–19, 27). Four pick up the half-line of the speaker before him (9, 15, 27, 33); Edmondson cut in swiftly with these lines, suggesting a Leontes who does, as Polixenes says, 'press' him (19). Stanley spoke of 'explosive' consonants in Leontes' opening lines – 't', 'p' (9–10, 18); 't', 'b', 'p' (15–16); 't', 'd', 'k' (27) – and Edmondson commented on their staccato quality. Leontes' first three lines to Hermione are even shorter than all but one of Leontes' first four short speeches to Polixenes. Leontes' speeches, said Edmondson, 'are not graciously formed thoughts. "Tongue-tied, our queen? Speak you." It is biting, piercing.' Taking his cue from his reading of the language, Edmondson entered the scene not overtly jealous like Kean, or smouldering like Gielgud, but unsettled, his disturbance as yet undefined. He carefully made each of Leontes' initial four exchanges with Polixenes a bit more rapid and emphatic than the one before. He suggested slight impatience on Leontes' first line; his next two lines were swifter, and he stressed the word 'tougher'. He cut in quickly with 'One sev'night longer', making it a command. Edmondson built tension to an initial climax on Leontes' fourth speech, speeding up and emphasizing 'I'll no gainsaying.' On this line he was so insistent that Polixenes began to back away.

Responding to Leontes' 'Tongue-tied, our queen? Speak you' by saying 'I had thought, sir, to have held my peace until / You had drawn oaths from him not to stay' (I.ii.28–9), Hermione came between Leontes and Polixenes during this speech and her next (I.ii.34–44). In Audrey Stanley's words, 'I had her coming between them so as to try to emphasize, symbolically, that this is what her marriage to him has done.' For Le Clanché du Rand, Leontes' initial brief responses to Polixenes showed the truth of 'You, sir, / Charge him too coldly' (I.ii.29–30). She responded to the growing tension, she said, 'with lightness of spirit, thereby hoping to lift his, and by trying hard to have Polixenes stay, as I surmise it is Polixenes' imminent departure that is upsetting Leontes'.

Leontes' response to this three-way tension was to turn in relief to Mamillius. He crossed upstage right toward Mamillius, partially distracted by playing with the boy, intermittently half-hearing Hermione and Polixenes during their long dialogue that followed (I.ii.44–85). He did not hear Polixenes' consent to stay. Leontes turned his back on Hermione and Polixenes – he could not bear to look at them – but turned round just when he could make a slight misinterpretation, as Polixenes kissed Hermione's hand. Audiences could question Leontes' tension, for Hermione and Polixenes were doing everything in view of other members of the court, not in secret. Polixenes and Hermione crossed farther down left after Polixenes' 'Your guest, then, madam' (I.ii.55). Leontes began to move downstage on Hermione's 'Grace to boot! / Of this

8 Act I, scene ii: Le Clanché du Rand as Hermione, clasping hands with Peter Silbert as Polixenes (front); Todd Reichenbach as Mamillius, held by James Edmondson as Leontes (back). Directed by Audrey Stanley, Oregon Shakespearean Festival, 1975.
Hank Kranzler photograph

make no conclusion, lest you say / Your queen and I are devils' (I.ii.79–81). It is a conclusion about Hermione that Leontes soon made (see figure 8). He came behind Polixenes and Hermione just in time to overhear her say, 'If you first sinned with us, and that with us / You did continue fault, and that you slipped not / With any but with us' (I.ii.83–5). Audrey Stanley commented to me that what Leontes overhears 'without the context, is sufficiently questionable that he says, "Is he won yet?" in four crisp monosyllables'. She added that when told by Hermione that Polixenes will stay, Leontes feels 'it's not as if his wife had been that close to Polixenes, unless something else has happened.' Leontes' reply – 'At my request he would not' (I.ii.86) – implied fear that faith has been broken between himself and Polixenes. Such interaction among three strong principal actors suggested double disturbance in Leontes: he feared losing his bond to Polixenes as well as his bond to Hermione.

Thus Leontes was moved to say that Hermione never spoke to 'better purpose' – 'Never but once' (I.ii.88). 'The tension between them has been so strong', said Stanley, 'that Hermione knows what he is referring to' – her consent to marry Leontes. Le Clanché du Rand, who said she had been 'relieved and joyful' to have made Polixenes stay for Leontes' sake, tried with light teasing on 'What, have I twice said well?' (I.ii.89) to 'bring Leontes to a personal level of emotion'. Her speech, said Stanley, was 'deliberately extravagant, full of sensuous richness, of voluptuous imagery, together with a spiritual desire that he name her consent to marry him a deed of "Grace"' (I.ii.98). 'She's asking for this moment', said Stanley, 'and he is just cutting her down with his language.' Leontes 'shuts me out', said du Rand, with what Edmondson called Leontes' 'terrible speech':

> Why, that was when
> Three crabbèd months had soured themselves to death
> Ere I could make thee open thy white hand
> And clap thyself my love; then didst thou utter
> 'I am yours for ever.' (I.ii.100–4)

'A strange remembrance of the courtship', said Edmondson. 'It is not a gracious remembrance.' His judgement parallels Derek Traversi's that 'past memories of untarnished happiness are being imperceptibly sullied, turned to present disillusionment' (*Shakespeare: The Last Phase*, 114).

Stanley pointed out that Edmondson put a 'sense of possession' on Leontes' remembrance of Hermione's gift – '"I am yours for ever."' Expressing keen sensitivity to the implications of

Leontes' speech, du Rand made her reply – '"Tis grace indeed' – 'a very serious moment', said Stanley: 'You sense the great abyss that is in front of all of them.' Le Clanché du Rand said she tried 'to anchor' Leontes 'with pure feeling and groundedness' in '"Tis grace indeed.' On her 'for ever earned a royal husband', she offered her hand to Leontes, but he could not bear to be touched, so turned aside. She next tried to join Polixenes' and Leontes' hands, wanting to bring the two men together; she was, said Stanley, 'again rejected in the action'. Hermione then gave her hand to Polixenes, who took it, just before Leontes said 'Too hot, too hot!' She moved away from Leontes with Polixenes because, in Stanley's words, 'Leontes in that language of "crabbèd months", "soured", "death", has shattered her, and she needs to recover.' That du Rand was able subtly to suggest the pain that prompted her move 'helps a Leontes', Stanley commented: 'If you have got that, then the buildup for "Too hot, too hot!" is already there. You see, it is not just how Leontes gets there, but it is how the whole scene gets there.'

Edmondson said he 'spit out' the words 'Too hot, too hot!' He explored the physical impact of jealousy in his body, as if experiencing heart palpitations, on 'I have *tremor cordis* on me' (I.ii.109). Stanley pointed out the 'physicality of his acting' in these moments: his hands were trembling, beating, as if he were burning. Stage front and centre for this first aside, he at times glanced at Polixenes and Hermione (stage left) and at times expressed his feelings directly to the audience. Early in the production's run, several reviewers thought Edmondson had, as Phillip Johnson put it, 'perhaps a bit too much fire' (*National Observer*, quoted in the *Mail Tribune*, 14 March 1975, 18). Four months later, according to C. Turlock, Edmondson's performance had matured and other actors had 'refined' and 'clarified' their roles in a production Turlock now found 'masterful'; Edmondson eliminated any excess, so that 'his Leontes is now a genuine tragic figure' (*Willamette Valley Observer*, July 1975). Alan Dessen wrote that in Edmondson's Leontes, 'the unmotivated jealousy was never a problem. With fine facial and body control, Edmondson built slowly, keying on hints and phrases (e.g., Hermione's comment to Polixenes "if you first sinned with us ..."), moving gradually but inexorably to the near madness in his naming of Bohemia to Camillo' ('The Oregon Shakespearean Festival, 1975', 92).

Dessen's account, Bartholomeusz' and Turlock's perceptions of Edmondson's Leontes as a tragic figure, and discussions offered by Stanley and Edmondson all suggest this production's affinities with Peter Brook's. Though Stanley (who saw Brook's 1951 production) remembered Gielgud showing jealousy earlier than she directed Edmondson to do, in both productions Leontes built tension from the beginning of I.ii to his first aside. Gielgud and Edmondson both suggested that Leontes overheard, and misunderstood, in Hermione's dialogue with Polixenes, such words as 'sinned' and 'slipped' (83–4). Moreover, in both productions, as distinct from Granville Barker's, Leontes was a fully tragic figure in the first three acts.

For Edmondson, Leontes' jealousy 'had to be enormous'; many know what it is to be jealous, he told me, but most 'do not know what it is to be jealous and to be a monarch'. Tyrant-like, he became so violent with Antigonus (II.iii) that audiences often applauded Paulina (Randi Douglas) for confronting Leontes (Dessen, 'The Oregon Shakespearean Festival, 1975', 91). A sense of danger, not of comedy, provoked such audience response. Seizing the baby, Leontes tried to put it into the flames of the brazier (downstage front) over which he had earlier brooded.

Yet Edmondson's Leontes did not alienate audiences; his range was wide and humane. Edmondson early began to build what he called 'a tender side' to Leontes. In his first scene he turned frequently to Mamillius for comfort; he showed pain when suddenly wondering if the baby Paulina brought him might be his and when confessing, 'I am a feather for each wind that blows' (II.iii.153). Such moments were, said Edmondson, 'the threads' of connection to his ability at last to say, 'Apollo, pardon'.

During the trial scene (III.ii) that led up to Leontes' repentance, the offstage audience, as much as the onstage audience, was the public to whom Hermione made her case. Her hair down, wearing a simple shift, she showed how recently she had given birth, yet du Rand was a 'figure of great stature and dignity', wrote Alan Dessen, and she 'dominated the stage with voice control and little movement' ('The Oregon Shakespearean Festival, 1975', 92). She stood in a dock (stage left of centre), moving from it only once, as she explained to me in interview, in 'a last desperate attempt to connect with him'. Edmondson had come from the throne, accusing her: 'You knew of his [Polixenes'] departure, as you know / What you have underta'en to do in's absence.' In response, Hermione came from the dock toward Leontes saying 'Sir / You speak a language that I understand not' (III.ii.76–8). She stretched out her hand toward him; he barely began to reach out, then refused. The possibility of contact was shattered by his reply, 'Your actions are my dreams. / You had a bastard by Polixenes, / And I but dreamed it' (80–2). Edmondson spoke this last line as a question. They were 'pleading with each other for help', said Edmondson, 'and the world just disappeared'. Yet in the middle of the same line (82) he returned to the throne, changing to his public voice: 'As you were past all shame... Look for no less than death' (82–9).

Leontes' violence culminated in what Edmondson called 'the ultimate paranoia, the ultimate human pride: the gods are wrong'. At the announcement of Mamillius' death, however, his Leontes 'perceives the gods are right – that she is innocent': 'Though beyond immediate comprehension, there is something that pierces the room. So there is a little bit of limbo, and then, "Apollo, pardon". Then, as great as the blindness is, as great the revelation. It is as if the gods give him one moment of clarity before they crush him entirely ... He has to have clear vision before he is told that she [Hermione] is dead.' Edmondson went down on the stage floor by the circular, translucent orb that had contained the oracle's words. When Paulina entered, 'she really laid on the stripes', said Edmondson, 'so that she was sure I really understood'. Finally, gently, she helped him rise and they exited – not apart, as in some productions, but together.

In keeping with Stanley's emphasis upon the tragic, as distinct from tragicomic, tones of the first three acts, the bear was a towering nightmare figure. As Stanley pointed out, with 'a symbolic set and a spiritual journey, a realistic bear would be anticlimactic in my production. So I had the shadow of a bear rear up some 20 feet tall.' Lighting designer Steven Maze and set designer Richard L. Hay skilfully used a light source projected onto a rear stage scrim from behind it. Behind the scrim stood an actor in a bear suit, his silhouette enlarged by means of lighting from behind his feet. Audiences saw a dark bear shadow grow to huge proportions. It 'makes audiences gasp' said one reviewer (Bertrand Evans, *Los Angeles Times*, 17 August 1975, 44); for Alan Dessen, it was 'an ominous and convincing end to the winter section of the play' ('The Oregon Shakespearean Festival, 1975', 91).

To suggest symbolic resonances of the storm in which the bear appeared, thunder sounded at particular moments earlier in the production. Distant thunder echoed during the latter part of Leontes' wild accusations to Camillo (I.ii), in the accusation scene when Leontes sent Hermione to prison (II.i.125), and when Leontes ordered the baby taken to some place 'Where chance may nurse or end it' and Antigonus took it up (II.iii.182–4). Storm sounds intensified when Leontes denied the oracle and again when Hermione was borne out by Paulina and the women (III.ii.138, 150–1). Symbolic light and sound effects also helped the transition between the nightmare in which Antigonus lost his life and the daybreak in which the Old Shepherd discovered the baby. During a flash and sudden blackout, the expanding bear shadow vanished, replaced by a projected image of the sun. In the calm after the storm, audiences heard the singing of a bird.

The sun, heralding the pastoral scenes, was also central to the production's overall design motif as a symbol of Apollo. Time's costume bore a stylized circular sunburst crest (on a dark-blue silk tabard worn over a long, light grey robe). Time was thus connected to light-bringer Apollo, to the oracle, and to the idea that truth is the daughter of time ('*Temporis filia veritas*', the title page motto of the play's source, *Pandosto*). There was nothing heavy-handed about the use of symbolic images in this production; they suggested ideas and images and were given just the right weight in varied contexts. Like Time in Granville Barker's production, the figure of Time here was not the traditional Father Time but a teller of tales that aroused wonder. Time's 'glass' (IV.i.16) was a translucent crystalline rod. He entered (from rear stage) immediately after the only interval; when he had finished speaking, as he exited into the stage-right vomitorium (vom), passing the first rows of seats, audiences could simultaneously see, on the stage, the new present in Bohemia beginning to unfold.

Strong rural comedy presented the 'freshest things now reigning' (IV.i.13). Such comedy, according to Stanley, evoked 'Jacobean England'. Her ideas had affinities with those of her colleague and friend C. L. Barber, whose *Shakespeare's Festive Comedy* (1959) connected Shakespeare's early and middle comedies to holiday practices and folk ritual in rural England. For the '*dance of Shepherds and Shepherdesses*' (IV.iv.167), Stanley's choreographer (Joanna G. Harris) and composer (Maggi Payne) created a maypole dance. Moving round the maypole, in and out of each other's paths, holding coloured streamers, the dancers intertwined. Lighting projected onto the 'sky' of the set's arches and onto the stage floor gave the effect of dappled sunlight on leaves. This Bohemia was a green world in which Mark D. Murphey's captivating Autolycus was a trickster without a dark edge; emphasis was on festive renewal. Yet the end of the maypole dance was full of wilder, more Dionysian, energies. These helped trigger Polixenes' disturbance, and his outburst broke the celebratory spirit. Again a father's destructive rage threatened bonds of love and hope of future generation.

For Leontes, passionately intense repentance followed his earlier destructiveness; the fifth act opened in darkness, with sounds of Leontes lashing himself. Lights then revealed Leontes fallen, his shirt off, a whip in his hand. Fresh garments were put on him, but he felt no newness of life. He sat weak, in corpselike make-up, a figure of death in life during the sharp conflict between Paulina and the lords who wanted, through his remarriage, to secure royal succession. 'I made it a real power struggle between Paulina and the nobles,' said Stanley. She thus brought out the scene's political dimensions, though the production's emphasis was primarily psychological and spiritual. Leontes, still largely bound to the past, was almost oblivious to the argument with the lords; his dialogue with Paulina sprang from his inner pain. Only at the announcement of Polixenes' name did his attention change. He breathed with new energy; the pace of his language, with its questions, reflected his emerging engagement in present action.

A moment later, Florizel, in a gold robe, and Perdita, in a gold satin gown, entered through an upstage curved arch edged with sun-flames (in Hay's designs termed the 'Apollo Arch'). Though none onstage knew the oracle was being fulfilled, Edmondson marked Leontes' wonder on seeing Perdita by a long pause before uttering 'goddess!' (V.i.130). Such staging and acting heightened the mythic resonances of Leontes' 'Welcome hither, / As is the spring to th'earth' (V.i.150-1). Leontes' quickened spirit was evident in his decision to persuade Polixenes to accept Florizel and Perdita's betrothal; as Edmondson put it, Leontes for the first time placed 'his sovereignty in the service of others'.

Mythic overtones in the staging gained power by Stanley's

strong use of ritual. In the statue scene, an incense urn, Grecian in style, was borne in by servants just prior to the entry (from rear stage) of the court members dressed in white and gold; they processed down the curving stage onto which they put the incense holders and lighted candles they carried. The urn, its smoke rising, had been placed downstage centre. Then, at that very place, a white-curtained, cylindrical structure began to arise from under the stage, to music from a harp, the urn crowning the structure as it rose to its full height. When Paulina drew open the white curtains, Hermione's statue seemed a column of light. Smoke from the burning incense moved upward, seen in beams of light projected up from the base of the structure in which Hermione stood.

The music to awaken her was Canon in D by Johann Pachelbel (1653–1706) – played by stringed instruments in slow, yet rising cadences. In Pachelbel's piece, the canon form leads back to the beginning of the melodic line repeatedly, creating a sense of circularity, of an infinity of connected endings and beginnings. Movement, speech, and sound were 'choreographed' together in this scene, said Stanley, adding, 'Every cadence had to be right.'

To guide the timing and phrasing of Paulina's speech (V.iii,98–103) to Hermione's 'statue', the actors worked with First Folio punctuation:

> 'Tis time: descend: be Stone no more: approach:
> Strike all that looke upon with mervaile: Come:
> Ile fill your Grave up: stirre: nay, come away:
> Bequeath to Death your numnesse: (for from him,
> Deare Life redeemes you) you perceive she stirres:

The Folio has ten colons in the four lines beginning "'Tis time: descend:' before Paulina says 'you perceive she stirres:'. In Stanley's view, these colons offer pauses in which an actor might breathe more deeply than on commas, yet carry the thought forward to the next phrase more than if there were full stops. Using these pauses, Randi Douglas made Paulina's phrasing and timing imply risk for both herself and Hermione. In the gravity of these moments, everything hung in the balance. Hermione might or might not move toward transformation; Paulina could invite it, but not command it.

Le Clanché du Rand's Hermione descended neither by magic

nor by Paulina's manipulation but by her own courageous choice. As Stanley put it, only when Hermione 'feels that the King is repentant, but not until then, will she step down'. Stanley suggested that Hermione decides to come down because she has witnessed Leontes' confession: 'I am ashamed. Does not the stone rebuke me / For being more stone than it? O royal piece! / There's magic in thy majesty, which has / My evils conjured to remembrance' (V.iii.37–40). Hermione has seen Leontes so 'wrought' (58) that Camillo and Polixenes have tried to ease his grief (49–56), which Edmondson portrayed with intense anguish.

Hermione was at the scene's centre, toward the forestage, near to the audience. Such placement was possible because of du Rand's extraordinary stillness. For the full twelve minutes that Hermione was onstage without moving, du Rand held complete focus, achieved in part by extensive preparation before each performance, including meditation. Court members stood on either side of the stage, and Paulina, initially near the edge of the forestage, her back to the audience, moved gradually up toward the statue as she urged Hermione to choose life. Technically, Paulina's movement put a greater focus on the statue, but it also suggested tension in Paulina. Her speech to the statue was a dangerous moment for her and for all onstage, said Stanley, because Paulina 'is not just simply a stage manager', which 'makes Paulina in command of the scene – and I did not want that':

> I wanted Hermione to be the one in command of the scene, so the spiritual values that are emphasized in why she comes down become apparent, and it is not just a magic trick. If it is Paulina who is pulling everybody's strings, then the play is a bit reduced to the level of this woman who has been wonderful, but is also slightly a figure of fun, in that she is a virago ... So if you allow that person to manipulate the end of the play, you are missing the whole spiritual level.

Stanley did not present Paulina as a priestess, though the scene was highly ritualistic. To give Hermione choice meant, as Stanley put it, that not Paulina but, rather, 'the statue has the power'.

'When Paulina finished her plea for the descent', wrote Alan Dessen, 'Hermione delayed, leaving the viewer in suspense for a telling moment' ('The Oregon Shakespearean Festival, 1975', 92).

Having stood in deep stillness, du Rand let Hermione's new breath be glimpsed for the first time on Paulina's word 'redeems': 'Bequeath to Death your numbness, for from him / Dear life redeems you' (V.iii.102–3). 'I played the first movement of the statue and it also played me,' wrote du Rand. Her phrasing suggests a complex interaction of her choices with that which was beyond herself: 'It was pure grace, as if there were a meeting between heaven and earth. It was pure *numinosity*; there was a power and energy that contained all of us in that scene, and also the audience.'

As it took courage for Hermione to descend, so it took courage for Leontes to take her by the hand, said Stanley; when the 'statue' moved, everyone onstage drew back in fear, not only Leontes. Edmondson's move backward in amazement came from his own response to the performance moment, not from an awareness that previous actors – Macready, Kean, Gielgud, for example – had made similar choices. Unlike Gielgud, Edmondson was not kneeling when Hermione presented her hand to him. Having drawn back, Edmondson stretched out his arm at full length to meet the hand of Hermione, whose arm was also outstretched (see figure 9). The moment was extended, explained Stanley, 'like a phrase in music where you are waiting and waiting for the note to fall'; it was 'drawn out as long as those actors could take an audience'. When their hands touched, Hermione and Leontes each arched backward. Leontes' 'O, she's warm!' was a discovery, in the midst of remembered pain, which brought ecstasy.

'We were bathed in pain remembered', wrote Le Clanché du Rand, 'and loss which was not repressed. *By allowing the pain* and the loss, it opened a door. It allowed the transformation into joy which is indescribable.' When she saw Peter Hall's 1988 production at the National Theatre, with its troubled meeting of Leontes and Hermione in its final scene, she wrote to Hall that, in her experience of the role, forgiveness was at the heart of the scene. For her, such forgiveness was complex: it worked to integrate, rather than repress, the dark side of experience. She did not attempt to erase the cost of time, even in its outward signs – her wrinkles, greyed hair, and gravity of movement. She saw reunion with Leontes not as simple or complete but as a 'powerful beginning': 'Because of what we had been through we were two different people from Act I; in effect we are reborn into two

9 Act V, scene iii: Le Clanché du Rand as Hermione, Randi Douglas as Paulina, James Edmondson as Leontes. Directed by Audrey Stanley, Oregon Shakespearean Festival, 1975. Hank Kranzler photograph

conscious, separate beings who are bonded by the miracle of a second chance into the unknown with each other.'

'The reunion with Leontes is the fulcrum of the scene's other reunions,' du Rand has said. For her, 'In the decision to descend, Perdita weighs *almost* equally with Leontes.' In the text, Hermione does not speak until she turns to Perdita. For neither du Rand nor Stanley did this mean, as it did for Peter Hall in his 1988 production, that Hermione's reunion with Leontes was tentative; its silence the more showed off its wonder. Hermione turned in place to Perdita, they joined hands and, looking upward, raised their arms to the gods in a wide gesture (see figure 10). Hermione's reunion with Perdita was 'the moment in which the oracle of Apollo comes to fruition', Stanley told me, noting Hermione's first words:

> Not 'my husband', not 'my daughter', but it is 'You gods look down.' Then Hermione becomes more domestic: 'Tell me, mine own, / Where hast thou been preserved, where lived'. Greek drama teaches you that you acknowledge the gods and you ask their blessing. The way Le Clanché dealt with that lifted the whole thing beyond the reunion with a daughter, and took it up into the world of the gods. (interview)

To show Hermione coming back into 'the living community', in Stanley's phrase, the actors gave each encounter distinct focus. If performers or readers hurry over Leontes' final speech, they blur or diminish each of its implied discoveries and reunions. Alan Dessen pointed out how skilfully 'the subsequent revelations' were 'controlled by Edmondson through face, voice, and gesture' ('The Oregon Shakespearean Festival, 1975', 92). He and the director gave weight, for example, to Paulina's irrecoverable loss of Antigonus before Leontes urged Camillo to 'take her by the hand'. In many productions the moment is awkward or comic. Edmondson said 'O peace, Paulina' neither to silence her, nor in lamentation; he spoke the line as a blessing. Audrey Stanley did not want the proposed betrothal of Camillo and Paulina to be laughable or awkward, but a recognition of Paulina's 'worth and honesty' (V.iii.144). Laughter was averted by taking these moments slowly. And Camillo took 'a step forward towards Paulina before he was named by Leontes, so that he made his own decision, and was not puppet-like in responding to the King's request', according to Stanley. 'Because directly you introduce laughter' here, she said, 'you have reduced the level.'

The actors sustained a serious tone in the next encounters.

10 Act V, scene iii: Carmi Boushey as Perdita, Le Clanché du Rand as Hermione, James Edmondson as Leontes. Directed by Audrey Stanley, Oregon Shakespearean Festival, 1975.
Hank Kranzler photograph

When Hermione saw Polixenes, 'The look Le Clanché was able to give Polixenes was so profound, so moving, that [it heightened] another moment that often is missed,' said Stanley. She added that the moment is 'a discordant one that has to be turned into a dominant [key]' (interview). The turn to concord came when Leontes asked, 'Both your pardons / That e'er I put between your holy looks / My ill suspicion' (V.iii.147–9). When Hermione, reunited to Polixenes, was presented to Florizel, each of Leontes' phrases occasioned Hermione's fresh discoveries, despite her sorrow evoked by the word 'son'; there was hope of new generation where lineage had seemed lost: 'This your son-in-law, / And son unto the King, whom heavens directing, / Is troth-plight to your daughter' (V.iii.149–51). Leontes' phrase 'heavens directing' suggested to Audrey Stanley that the man who earlier had dismissed Apollo was now much more deeply 'aware of the gods' (interview). Such was the larger recognition toward which the entire production had been moving.

Continuing Pachelbel's music through to the very end of the play helped to sustain tones of wonder. So did the visual motif of joining hands that was part of each reunion and new meeting. This motif, Dessen noted, helped also 'to fulfill a visual pattern Stanley had developed throughout the play' ('The Oregon Shakespearean Festival, 1975', 92). In their first court scene, the two kings had toasted with intertwined arms. Leontes had refused to accept Hermione's hand, however, which she extended while saying 'for ever earned a royal husband'; had refused again when she tried to join his and Polixenes' hands; and had erupted when Hermione gave her hand to Polixenes, 'for some while a friend' (I.ii.107). In the trial scene, Hermione had offered her extended hand; Leontes had started to take it, then drew his hand back. But in the final scene, Leontes met Hermione's outstretched hand with his. Later he joined Hermione's and Polixenes' hands together and theirs to his.

The final recognition was between actors and audience. The cast moved to the forestage and raised their joined hands, their gesture to the audience forming a wide arc of celebration. The actors moved into the audience (through the voms) to exit. Many times audience members found it difficult to leave the theatre until they had begun to absorb the impact of the performance; indeed, accounts of this production often focus on its final scene. As Alan Dessen put it, 'The heart of this play lies in the final scene, and here superb acting by Edmondson and du Rand, along with directorial control of blocking and detail, produced one of the most moving moments I have experienced in the theater.' Dessen pointed out the cumulative power of such artistry: 'All the details here (and in the scenes building up to this moment) were carefully orchestrated to produce the maximum effect' ('The Oregon Shakespearean Festival, 1975', 92–3).

Though this production was very important to Audrey Stanley's work, she has said (in a seminar I led for the Shakespeare Association of America in 1989 and at greater length in her 1990 lecture at Vanderbilt University) that she would not attempt to direct *The Winter's Tale* in the same way in changed historical circumstances. In her Vanderbilt lecture, she proposed and illustrated scenarios for a possible production of *The Winter's Tale* in each of the three previous decades (1960s, 1970s, 1980s). The brief scenarios, each played by a different pair of actors, were designed to provoke experimentation by actors and discussion of performance decisions in their cultural contexts, but not to offer a detailed analysis of historical contingencies. Working with the last two speeches of the play (by Paulina and Leontes), she explored the possible match between Paulina and Camillo. She termed the l960s version 'festive' (using the key term from C. L. Barber's *Shakespeare's Festive Comedy*). This version would emphasize comedy throughout; to find Paulina a husband in this version, suggested Stanley, 'would be a totally happy act. Laughter would be the appropriate expression.' The 1970s version, like her own, she said, sought to 'treat the play as a spiritual journey'. Owing to his moral integrity and loyalty, Camillo would be the 'only fitting person to marry Leontes' spiritual guide Paulina. The joining of these two very special people is a sacred act, and should not get laughter.' The 1980s version, reflecting intensified feminist critique and concerns over gender and power, explored the possibility that Paulina might not agree to the proposed marriage. One interpretation, said Stanley, would have Paulina 'refusing because of her fresh grief on hearing about her husband's terrifying death'.

Stanley noted in her Vanderbilt lecture that First Folio punctuation could support any of these three interpretations. Paulina could refuse, for example, to take Camillo's proffered hand in any of the pauses marked by the Folio's colons in Leontes' prompting or by the full stop after 'kings':

> Come Camillo,
> And take her by the hand: whose worth, and honesty
> Is richly noted: and here justified
> By us, a pair of kings. Let's from this place.

Could a refusal by Paulina motivate Leontes' 'Let's from this place'? Stanley is right that the text leaves open the possibility of Paulina's refusal, and Stanley's perception of this is an exception to the rule. Philip McGuire argued in 1994 that the absence in theatrical and critical history of recognizing 'even the *possibility* that the marriage Leontes calls for does not happen demonstrates the gap between what the playtext allows and what theatrical and critical practice have long authorized' (*The Jacobean Plays*, 173). Paulina's and Camillo's silences in the play's closing moments are an instance of what McGuire calls 'open silences' in a play's text (see his *Speechless Dialect: Shakespeare's Open Silences*). Stanley's critical reflectiveness as a director, and her perspective on her own work, affirm how vast is the play's spectrum of possibilities.

'Beyond joy', Edmondson said of the ending; 'it goes beyond, anyway, modern psychology.' He referred to 'another dimension' of consciousness. To be in ecstasy is by definition to be placed outside ordinary awareness (Greek *ek*, out, + *histanai*, to place). Edmondson and du Rand could suggest remembered pain without reducing ecstasy. Was the reunion totally completed? 'I did not think we had arrived; I thought we had potential,' said Edmondson. When his Leontes spoke of 'this wide gap of time since first / We were dissevered' (V.iii.154–5), he simultaneously called for time past to be made known, registered its losses, and suggested new possibilities opening into time future. 'I could not make the word "wide" wide enough,' said Edmondson. 'Wide. With all the longing.' The ending is not 'tidy', he stressed; 'it is not resolved totally', nor have they 'returned to who they were' sixteen years before. 'They are different people' who 'now have this extraordinary potential'. Such growth as is possible is 'really our job, I think. To wake up and to get bigger. To achieve grace.'

CHAPTER V

Jane Howell's television production for the British Broadcasting Corporation, 1980

In all my work I do attempt to be rigourously honest and *clear* – of course it is only my view of the play that you see – but the nature of the television medium forces directors to make choices – to stake their understanding – it is a hard medium – every shot has to relate to the text, to the specifics of the actor's performance and to the vision of the play the director wishes to offer up. (Jane Howell, letter to Mary Maher, 1988)[1]

Television is a challenging medium indeed for the director using it to present *The Winter's Tale*. Shakespeare's transformation of one genre into another – of romance narrative into drama – involves virtuoso stagecraft that dares to play with its theatrical artifice. The *coup de théâtre* signalled by the First Folio stage direction that Antigonus is to '*Exit pursued by a Beare*', the direct address of the Chorus of Time as it breaks and makes theatrical convention, the symbolic presentation of Hermione as a statue: such stagecraft moves the play far from that naturalism or realism of representation for which television is most often used. As David Self has put it, 'Television is certainly happier with the intimate than with the epic. It conveys realism more easily than the symbolic or impressionistic' (10). Yet it is important to point out, as has Raymond Williams, that television's tendencies toward naturalism have been a historical result of its adapting dominant naturalistic theatrical conventions: 'Indeed these emphases could be seen as internal properties of the medium itself, when in fact they were a selection of some of its properties according to the dominant structure of feeling' (*Television*, 56).

Jane Howell, who directed *The Winter's Tale* in 1980 for the British Broadcasting Corporation's 'BBC TV Shakespeare' series, might agree with Williams that naturalism is not an inevitable or inherent property of the television medium. 'I don't think television is realistic – I don't think it needs to be,' she has said. 'What needs to be – what has got to be real – is the actor's performance, but what's around that need not be realistic at all' (quoted in Fenwick, 18). Though she considered directing *The Winter's Tale* in a naturalistic style, she chose instead to use the camera and studio settings in ways frequently analogous to theatrical non-illusionism; as she has explained, 'I am interested in breaking away from naturalism – whatever that word means!' (quoted in Fenwick, 19).[2] Howell's work marked a sharp departure from the BBC TV Shakespeare series 'house style' in the era (1978–80) of its first producer, Cedric Messina, who urged that Shakespeare on television must be produced *'naturalistically'* (Bulman, 'BBC Shakespeare', 51–2). In her adaptation of frank theatrical artifice to the television medium, Howell also departed from the rich visual pictorialism, with its allusions to Renaissance painting, that characterized productions by Jonathan Miller, who was acting in 1980–81 as overall producer for the BBC series when she directed *The Winter's Tale*.

Jane Howell was a director of at least seventeen years' experience in theatre at the time Miller invited her to direct *The Winter's Tale* (taped 9–15 April 1980). Howell, who had earlier directed the play twice in the theatre (Fenwick, 18), created a television production of *The Winter's Tale* for which she judiciously and selectively used non-realist techniques. Her first production for television, it is especially characterized by what Susan Willis calls (in all Howell's television work) 'abstraction, image, and ensemble' (107), even more than are her five subsequent critically acclaimed television productions for the BBC Shakespeare series – the tetralogy of the three parts of *Henry VI* (1981–82) and *Richard III* (1982), plus *Titus Andronicus* (1985).

Given the distinctive theatrical artifice of *The Winter's Tale*, Howell's use of considerable stylization seems wise. Her production style selectively incorporates naturalistic aspects – e.g., in certain instances close-up shots emphasize psychological interiority; a live baby represents the infant Perdita; and partial illusionism is used for the dark quasi-interior court scenes of the restless Leontes (II.iii), the return to Sicilia (V.i), and the statue scene (V.iii). But overall, particularly in set design, Howell makes a striking break from naturalistic conventions. Michèle

Willems divides the BBC TV Shakespeare productions into three kinds: 'naturalistic, pictorial, and stylized' ('Verbal-Visual', 96), praising Howell's stylization. Series policy was to use as 'unmodified' a text as possible; Willems points out the problematic consequence that 'the play text would have to serve as film [i.e., television] script' (94), arguing that in these circumstances 'an approach where the visual element is used as functional or suggestive', like Howell's, 'is preferable to one in which it is referential [representing supposedly verisimilar reality] or decorative' ('Verbal-Visual', 100).

Graham Holderness, interviewing Jonathan Miller, contrasts Howell's break from illusionism with Miller's pictorialism:

> But there are stage sets designed to give the impression that when the characters walk off-stage they are entering another area of a real world; and there are stage sets so provocatively abstract as to fracture that kind of illusion. When Jane Howell directed *The Winter's Tale* for the BBC series, she used a set so abstract as to make it unimaginable that the actors could be entering from or exiting to a real world. (*The Shakespeare Myth*, 197)

To 'fracture' naturalistic illusion, Howell made use of an austere set forming one unit around an open playing space. As in all her BBC productions, Howell's unit set was designed 'for suggestivity and flexibility' (Willis, 292); the set was especially abstract for *The Winter's Tale* (Taylor, 106). Its designer, Don Homfray (winner of a design award for the series), explained that the set was intended to be '*not real*, not illusionistic. You were always in the same space, which wasn't a real landscape and wasn't an interior, just a space with shapes' (quoted in Fenwick, 21).

Through changes of lighting and a few properties, the space was modified selectively while remaining largely non-illusionistic. The principal set was a wide, flat main playing area surrounded by a background of large wedge shapes on either side of a rear-centre triangular corridor (which, narrowing at its end, was used for exits and entrances). This set was white for Sicilia in Acts I and II.i; for Cleomenes and Dion, III.i; and for the trial, III.ii – with the addition, in that scene, of a black guard rail, a red carpet, and an elevated dais with throne, all suggesting Leontes' show of authority. For the pastoral scene, in contrast, the light on the set's backdrop (a cyclorama) was yellow, on the wedge shapes a blend of rose and gold, and soft green on the playing space floor. Harvest sheaves of grain were either side of the exit-and-entrance corridor; the bare tree used in selected Sicilian scenes in Acts I–III now had autumnal russet and red-gold leaves. The final scene began as if in a dark interior, with candlelight and the lit rim of the chapel's entry arch surrounded by blossoms; at the scene's end, the characters exited into a brightly lit space on the white set in which the play began, its surfaces now subtly lit with shades of green. 'We were using light like a paintbrush,' explained Homfray (quoted in Fenwick, 21), reflecting on his work with the production's lighting designer, Sam Barclay. Colour, often created by lighting and used symbolically rather than naturalistically, suggested for the early Sicilia scenes metaphoric winter; for Act IV, scene iv, harvest; and gradually, by the end of the final scene, spring. Governing these lighting changes was Jane Howell's vision of the play: 'The seasonal sense was very important, for me, in *The Winter's Tale*, the sense of rebirth.' The 'returning of spring' is 'fundamental to the play, as well as the second chance'. Howell added: 'My centre for *The Winter's Tale* was that everyone can have a second chance' (quoted in Willems, 'Entretien', 84).

Howell's use of a unit set creatively adapted to television what she considered to be one of 'the original rules of theatre, which is that you have a space and it can be anything' (interview with Mary Maher, 14 March 1988).[3] But looking back on her 1980 production, Howell had reservations about the set: 'It's too harsh, unaccountably harsh' (quoted in Willems, 'Entretien', 84). Moreover, Howell's reflection to Susan Willis about the set – 'It looked wonderful in the studio' – implied, Willis thought, 'that the effect may not have fully transferred to the television screen' (167). As Willis put it, 'This geometric abstraction may have taped a bit coldly' (169). The set's limitations, however, should not eclipse the importance – and, often, the effectiveness – of Howell's break from illusionism. The costumes, like the set, avoided detailed representation of one specific period. Costume designer John Peacock emphasized that while he drew in large part from the 'early 1600s', period references 'went backwards and forwards quite a bit'. Botticelli's paintings, for example, inspired Perdita's costume, Bruegel the costumes of the country people (quoted in Fenwick, 22). Peacock thus honoured both in the observance and in the breach the original, potentially stifling guideline mandated by the United States financial underwriters, that the 'plays were to be set in Shakespeare's own time or in the historical period of the events' (Willis, 11).

Relative freedom from illusionism and naturalistic detail may have helped Howell and the actors work with the challenge of using the television medium to present one of the play's celebrated cruxes – the inception of Leontes' jealousy. Naturalism could set up a viewer's expectation that his 'motivation' would be delineated, yet the text leaves any question of 'explanations' for the jealousy remarkably open. Any director and any actor playing Leontes must face the question of whether Leontes gives any sign – clear or deliberately ambiguous – of suspicion or even tension before he begins to voice it overtly at 'Too hot, too hot!' (I.ii.107). During the long preceding dialogue between Hermione and Polixenes (45–85), for example, during which Leontes does not speak, what does he do? Does he overhear or watch any of Hermione and Polixenes' dialogue? Whereas theatre audiences can, potentially, see all the scene's characters onstage simultaneously – though theatre directors use visual as well as verbal means to focus audience attention – television viewers are guided even more closely by the director's use of the camera.

Howell established separate spaces for Leontes, seen at a distance in the rear acting area, and Hermione and Polixenes, seen in the foreground during their dialogue (I.ii.45–85); the viewer is thus uncertain whether or not Leontes has overheard any part of Hermione and Polixenes' interchange before Leontes asks, 'Is he won yet?' (85). A viewer used to scanning the visual signals of a stage production could be disconcerted by the absence of opportunity to observe Leontes carefully in this televised scene. It is important to remember, however, that in a number of stage productions as well Leontes' performance is ambiguous or shows no sign of disturbance until he voices it explicitly. The play's text does not mandate a step-by-step build to a moment of disclosure, though it can be performed so; disclosure may happen by sudden juxtapositions, as it does in Howell's production when Leontes (played by Jeremy Kemp) directs his response 'At my request he would not' (86) into the camera as an aside to the viewer, a close-up of his head and shoulders filling much of the frame. The viewer's first awareness of Leontes' jealousy is precisely on that line. 'I do believe', Howell said, 'that the way to handle the jealousy is just to take it off one moment' (interview with Maher). To do so, her production takes the theatrical convention of directly addressing an audience and adapts that convention to television by non-illusionist use of the camera.

At other times, however, Howell uses the camera to reinforce psychological subtleties in the acting. Just before Hermione's 'But once before I spoke to th' purpose? When?' (99) there is a cut to a close-up (head and shoulders) of Leontes; uneasy, embarrassed, he looks aside as if in pain at speaking private memories in public. When he looks at Hermione as he speaks of what has become in his mind their courtship's 'Three crabbèd months' (101), a close-up captures the moment when Kemp's voice shifts almost to a whisper as he recalls her '"I am yours for ever"' (104). These close-ups intensify the viewer's awareness of implied emotion and create nuance by focusing on small but highly significant facial and vocal changes. Such techniques imply Leontes' tension in the segment (86–107) before Kemp explores it in his first long aside, 'Too hot, too hot!' (107–18).

Through close-up presentation of facial expression, television gains one kind of intimacy while inescapably losing another – that simultaneous interaction of an actor with a live theatre audience that is possible using the convention of direct address. Watching a television play, a viewer knows the actors' performances have been filmed in the past; a viewer cannot, in one strict and crucial sense, interact with the performers in a shared present. In performing Leontes' asides, Jeremy Kemp conveys mounting anxiety but cannot, simultaneously, interact with a live theatre audience while trying to persuade them to see Hermione and Polixenes as he sees them and to agree that there are cuckolds among the audience 'even at this present, / Now, while I speak this' (I.ii.190–1).

Stanley Wells raises a further point about the challenge of filming a Shakespeare play in a television studio with the presence of cameras nearby: the problem of scale, especially for rhetorical effects. His perception was that some performers

> have shown the strain of trying to find a way of reducing the scale to an acceptable level while not altogether denying the dramatist's style. So in *The Winter's Tale*, it seemed to me that Jeremy Kemp as Leontes used understatement in a way that removed the obvious danger of embarrassing emotionalism at the expense of depriving us of an appreciation of the character's anguish. ('Television Shakespeare', 274)

Wells's assessment was similar to Kenneth Rothwell's, who found Kemp's Leontes too consistently 'understated' (401). Critical reception, however, also included the opposite response: Anthony Masters praised Kemp's 'effectively underplayed Leontes' (*The Times*, 9 February 1981, 8); Joseph McLellan thought Kemp 'makes the madness of Leontes believable' (*Washington Post*, 8 June 1981); John J. O'Connor thought the 'language emerges brilliantly' (*New York Times*, 8 June 1981).

The problem of scale arises in part, of course, from one of television's characteristics: its relatively small screen. However, as Sheldon Zitner points out, 'this limitation does have some advantages. Television puts a tighter frame around language' (6). Howell used this potentiality; finely tuned to her actors, she gave priority to the verbal life of the drama. Furthermore, tight-frame close-ups, as Ann Jennalie Cook has argued, 'are particularly effective in pulling the spectator into the jealous obsession of Leontes'. For Cook the 'intimacy of the camera' creates a 'sense of closed space almost claustrophobic at times' which is, far from a failure of scale, 'precisely the point'; such an atmosphere 'is the confined incubator that hatches and nurtures suspicion, admitting no access to its dark, secret space from a wider world where things look quite different' (37). Particular shots emphasize Leontes' increasing isolation; the camera, as Donald Wineke has pointed out, becomes Leontes' 'closest confidant' and, after Camillo's departure, 'his *only* confidant' (5). Leontes' pain is not communicated in this production by rhetorical volume or largeness of scale but in the 'steadily quickening pace of Kemp's deliveries' of his asides, 'by the tension in his body and his fixed stare into the camera, a stare that does not seem focused on the audience so much as on the images that his puritanical and chauvinistic notions about women generate' (Wineke, 6).

Camera work in I.ii compels a close experience of Leontes' limited, distorted perspective, showing his mind in motion. When direct address to the camera is used by Leontes, it intensifies communication of his darkened perception. When other characters in Acts I and II use direct address, however, it can be to counter Leontes' view. After Leontes accuses Hermione of adultery, for example, and refuses his lords' counsel, he orders the lords to follow him: 'We are to speak in public, for this business / Will raise us all.' Antigonus turns to the camera, with sharp comic effect, to say, 'To laughter, as I take it, / If the good truth were known' (II.i.197–9). Vowing to confront Leontes, Paulina confides directly to the camera 'If I prove honey-mouthed, let my tongue blister, / And never to my red-looked anger be / The trumpet any more' (II.ii.32–4). Antigonus' and Paulina's instances of direct address to the camera use the television medium to create tragicomic perspectives. Such asides to the camera provide sudden changes of perspective and mingled tones which are vital to the play's tragicomic art.

Close-up camera work is also used in Howell's presentation of the trial scene (III.ii), but the scene – a notably public one – presents challenges for television because of its relatively large scale. In the BBC production, certain speeches are intimate in scale that some critics thought would have had more power had their scale been public. At times the trial becomes more a defence of Hermione's private integrity than of her public honour. Hermione's last speech (117–21) is presented in a quiet, confidential aside to the camera; of this decision Stanley Wells asks, 'Why should only we learn that the Emperor of Russia is her father?' (*Times Literary Supplement*, 20 February 1981, 197). But Howell effectively uses close-ups to register the reserved but intense strength of Hermione and her clear argumentation, even under great pressure. Furthermore, though close-up camera work at the turning points in Leontes' repentance makes its significance more individual than cosmic or social, close-ups support a quiet, convincing presentation of it. At other moments, using wide shots, Howell creates an equivalent for television viewers of a theatre audience's access to multiple awareness of all characters present in a large public scene.

The opening of Howell's trial scene departs imaginatively from the stage direction given in the text used for the production, which specifies at the top of the scene: '*Enter* LEONTES, LORDS, *and* OFFICERS.' That text's entrance for Hermione after line 9 reads, '*Enter* HERMIONE, *as to her trial*, PAULINA, *and* LADIES.' It is printed after the Officer has requested Hermione's appearance and before his call for 'Silence!' (III.ii.10).[4] Instead of following those stage directions, Howell confronts viewers with a blank white frame for three seconds as the scene opens, while they listen to the insistent, loud tapping of the court being called to order. A close-up of Hermione (played by Anna Calder-Marshall) is gradually brought into focus; her eyes closed, she is listening to Leontes' initial speech, presented in harsh tones. There is slow disclosure by the use of an unusually sustained shot: the camera is gradually pulled back to a medium shot (from the waist up) of Hermione; the camera continues to pull back and upward, making an arc to the viewer's left until it rests at a high-angle shot of the whole court. This wide shot from above offers viewers a perspective looking down on the entire public scene.

Leontes sits at a distance from Hermione, his throne (under a formal red canopy) raised on a platform several steps above the level on which she stands, their positions reinforcing the contrast between her lack of political power and Leontes' tyrannous use of it. More silence follows the reading of the indictment: it is ten seconds before the camera cuts to a mid-shot of Hermione, reacting, again in silence. When she at last speaks, with clarity, consciousness, and courage, in a space designed to dramatize her disempowerment, each of her words is the more important. Furthermore, camera shots and cuts support her words exactly. Thus, despite the visual image of Hermione's outwardly vulnerable position and condition, viewers are offered an intimate sense of her inner strength, what Howell senses in Calder-Marshall to be a backbone of 'steel' (quoted in Fenwick, 24). Calder-Marshall's subtle performance portrays finely tuned anger, an inner capacity to endure suffering, and a willingness to speak truth to power.

Camera work effectively intensifies the viewer's sense of conflict by cutting back and forth between Leontes' irrational accusations and Hermione's reasoned arguments. A low-angle camera cut to Leontes on his 'I ne'er heard yet / That any of these bolder vices wanted / Less impudence to gainsay what they did / Than to perform it first' (III.ii.53–6) augments a visual impression of his dominance as he looks down at Hermione while attempting to discredit her. Cutting swiftly to Hermione on her reply – 'That's true enough, / Though 'tis a saying, sir, not due to me' (56–7) – emphasizes her quick verbal strength. A rapid cut to Leontes' 'You will not own it' (58) underscores his impatient retort, which is immediately countered by a close-up shot of Hermione giving her clearly reasoned reply: 'More than mistress of / Which comes to me in name of fault I must not / At all acknowledge' (58–60). The shot is sustained as Hermione pauses; there is no reply from Leontes. It is as if Hermione's argument has halted, for just an instant, the crossfire between them.

Thus far, Hermione and Leontes have remained relatively still, using subtle facial and body movement. After a cut to Leontes on 'Your actions are my dreams' (80), however, Leontes rises, descends, and moves toward Hermione; a subsequent sequence of shots effectively suggests conflicts of gender and power. A camera angle near Leontes' shoulder as he looks down on Hermione presents his profile in the right side of the frame, enlarging the image of his furred hat and collar so that he seems almost bestial as he attempts to dominate her. On Leontes' phrase 'Which to deny' (84), a camera cross-cut over Hermione's shoulder presents the moment from her point of view, as she looks up toward Leontes' head and shoulders. The deliberate visual disproportion between them suggests Leontes' misuse of power and his violence towards the feminine and the child: 'Thy brat hath been cast out, like to itself, / No father owning it' (85–6).

Partly because Howell relates camera shots and cuts so clearly to the text and to the details of the actors' performances, the turning point of the scene, when Leontes learns of Mamillius' death, works remarkably well. That is no mean feat; as Jeremy Kemp remarked, Leontes' sudden emergence from his diseased passion 'perhaps is a greater problem for an actor than getting into it' (quoted in Fenwick, 25). If the timing, tone, and physicality of Leontes' repentance are not handled well, there is a danger – even in the scale of a theatre – of melodrama. Howell's camera work and editing enable her to use the potential intimacy of the medium to support Kemp's restrained performance; thus Leontes' repentance becomes an intense inner experience. A shot over his shoulder shows him listening to the messenger's report of Mamillius' death; the camera cuts to a medium close-up of Leontes as Kemp says, in a hushed tone, 'How? Gone?' (143). After a pause, in a strong whisper to the servant-messenger and to himself, he slowly forms the words, 'Apollo's angry, and the heavens themselves / Do strike at my injustice' (144–5). Speaking quietly to the camera, with pain, he confesses, 'I have too much believed mine own suspicion' (149). It is a line made private, as is Kemp's restrained plea for forgiveness, as he looks upward: 'Apollo, pardon / My great profaneness 'gainst thine oracle' (151–2). The camera then captures the public nature of what has become, in effect, Leontes' own trial: Kemp delivers Leontes' next lines, from 'I'll reconcile me to Polixenes' through 'No richer than his honour' (153–68) as a public confession to his court. Cutting from private to public speech in this scene does run the danger of what Stanley Wells calls 'too explicit a distinction between private and public utterance' (*Times Literary Supplement*, 20 February 1981, 197); but camera work supports the actor in making the sudden repentance of Leontes both credible and clear.

Close-ups rather than largeness of scale, speech directly to the camera rather than direct address to a theatre audience: these differences between the capacities of television and those of Shakespearean theatre also affected Howell's presentation of the bear and of Time. Her use of stylization rather than naturalism served her well in attempting a television performance of these highly theatrical figures, though she was quick to admit problems in the presentation of the bear, especially. 'I don't think it really worked,' she has said of the scene. 'It's hard enough in the theatre ... but it's even worse on television' (interview with Maher).

Certain stage productions, taking advantage of the large scale possible in a theatre, have used an enlarged, stylized bear shape in the background (e.g., with the addition of special lighting effects, both Nunn, 1969–71, and Stanley, 1975). In her television production, Howell does the opposite: she gains visual impact by bringing images of a stylized dark bear into the screen's extreme foreground. The viewer sees Antigonus neither exiting nor being pursued; rather, it is the viewer who is confronted by the bear – and led to imagine Antigonus likewise confronted. After Antigonus' line, 'This is the chase' (III.iii.56), a full-frame bear head moves closer to the foreground, as if seen through Antigonus' eyes, until the screen goes entirely dark. The non-naturalistic technique breaks viewers' expectations and is an attempt to create tragicomic surprise.

Dark then yields to light in a sequence of images that accomplishes the transition demanded by the play's turning point. The 'blackness' which suggests Antigonus' death 'mixes through into the same set', as Howell put it, but the viewer is presented with 'much gentler colours and the shepherd is sitting there, and the play as it were turns over and starts coming up the other way' (quoted in Fenwick, 23). A non-illusionist image follows the exit of the Old Shepherd with the baby: a blank white screen, over which are heard the first words of Time's speech. Holding a large hourglass, Time appears and gradually comes into focus, beginning on his words, 'try all' (IV.i.1). Time (played by Harold Goldblatt) directly addresses the camera during his entire speech, combining a non-naturalistic technique with a confidential tone. A slow-tracking camera brings the actor increasingly nearer the viewer until Time's head fills the screen during the end of his speech (IV.i.29–32); his face then moves out of the frame's right side, leaving a blank screen. This presentation of Time's speech is a workable adaptation of the theatrical convention of direct address, though it inevitably loses the full effect of the theatrical artifice with which Time wittily persuades a live audience to accept his and the playwright's 'argument' (29) with its 'wide gap' (7). Shakespeare creates a three-way pact between himself, the actor, and the audience that is very difficult, in the absence of live interaction, to create on screen.

Equally difficult to recreate for television is the large-scale visual spectacle of the statue scene; this is because of the size of the television screen, the visual selectivity of camera shots that favour sequential rather than simultaneous awareness of an entire scene, and a tendency to emphasize individual responses rather than ritual action. In addition, the medium has a different relation to time; in watching a television production we do not inhabit the same moments of time as do the actors. For all these reasons, it is not surprising that some viewers have found that, in watching the BBC statue scene, they, like Stanley Wells, miss 'the thrill of ritual participation' (Wells, 'Television Shakespeare', 271–2).

Viewers of Howell's production may lose a sense of participating in live ritual; however, they need not lose awareness of community. Howell fosters such awareness partly through deep-space composition encompassing the gathered characters (though not all these characters and the statue appear in any one frame simultaneously), and partly through sensitive reaction shots. Viewers do lose the continuous visual presence of the statue as a primary source of wonder. Elizabeth Otten perceives a diminished representation of Hermione in the scene: 'Hermione is on camera exactly half the scene's playing time, most of that as a small piece of the background; her image clearly dominates only five of its thirty-eight shots' (5). But Howell offers viewers a different source of wonder: detailed awareness of the statue's impact on the beholders, registered in their moment-by-moment responses to each distinct movement toward restoration.

Howell's gains are achieved in part by extraordinarily clear storytelling, work with the actors, sensitive camera work, and skilful continuity editing to create a sense of flow from shot to shot. The first section of the statue scene opens with a long sustained sequence that establishes a community gathered for a ceremony of remembrance. In a second major section, close-ups emphasize the interplay between characters, particularly between Polixenes and Leontes, which builds to Paulina's assurance of Leontes' readiness for restoration. In a third and final sustained sequence, framing and distance guide viewers' perception to the crucial moments as each major relationship in this small community is renewed.

Communal aspects of this reunion scene are highlighted from the beginning of the first section, in its long shot that establishes the setting. What the viewer first sees evokes the atmosphere of a chapel: against a dark background, used for almost the entire scene, is an arch entwined with blossoms, its rim outlined with light; on either side in front of the arch are two lighted candles on large, standing candlesticks. Lighting and properties in this establishing shot frame the communal procession as each character comes through the arch toward the viewer. The first main characters to come through the arch are Perdita and Florizel (led in by two Gentlemen on either side of them, bearing candles), as if Howell is initially emphasizing the metaphoric springtime of the couple, rather than – as in a number of productions (e.g., RSC 1976, RSC 1981, National Theatre 1988) – the continued winter of Leontes' suffering. When Polixenes enters, he renews trust with his son, taking Florizel's hand. The final entrant is Paulina, after Leontes; Howell then uses a wide depth of field to show a ceremonial grouping. In the background, nearest the entry arch, are Paulina and Leontes; standing at either side of the entryway are Polixenes and Camillo with Gentlemen; in the foreground, their backs to the viewer, are Florizel and Perdita. This long shot of the opening *mise-en-scène*, accompanied by the music of a single wind instrument, creates a ceremony and establishes a sense of community. As the sequence continues, the sight lines of this community begin to turn toward the place of the as-yet-unseen statue. On Paulina's 'Behold' (V.iii.20), the tracking camera comes to rest in a long shot of the curtained place of the statue; then viewers momentarily share the characters' lines of vision, in a shot from the characters' points of view.

Just after the curtains part, viewers get their first sight of Hermione standing like a statue.

It is the impact upon members of this community that now becomes the primary emphasis of the scene's second major section. Reaction shots sensitively register the differing responses of individuals, but not as isolates; seldom is a character – excepting Hermione – alone in a frame.[5] Howell's use of camera cuts, artfully joined in classical continuity style, tells the story with clear attention to each visual response and verbal exchange. Visual thus supports verbal in a sequence in which camera cuts create impact and emphasis as well as building tension.

A cut, for example, creates force when, after Paulina's 'Behold', a close-up of Leontes' face (together with a marked silence) registers the impact upon him of his first sight of the statue. Emphasis is further created by the director's cutting back and forth between Paulina and Leontes, building tension in their dialogue. One camera shot, for example, captures Leontes' wonder at Hermione's 'natural posture' (23); another pinpoints his painful reply to Paulina's suggestion that Hermione looks as if 'she lived now' (32). Kemp as Leontes replies with subtle emphasis on the verbs in 'As now she *might have done*' (32; italics mine). Paulina, aware that sight of the statue has 'wrought' Leontes (58), states that he shall no longer 'gaze on't, lest your fancy / May think anon it moves' (60–1); a sudden cut to a reaction shot of Leontes on his quick 'Let be, let be' captures his mounting agitation.

Effective as such camera work is, and though there is always more than one of the gathered characters in the frame, the tendency to foreground individual responses through shots and cuts to close-ups does have limitations which are at times difficult to evaluate. A key instance is the cut from Leontes, using an over-the-shoulder shot to Paulina, as she says directly to him, 'It is required / You do awake your faith' (94–5). Though this line has also been spoken directly to Leontes in some theatrical productions, a close-up two-shot on television does result in a loss of viewers' simultaneous awareness of the response of other characters to this moment.

The third and final section of the statue scene (V.iii.98–155) is filmed using a sustained sequence of shots, with skilful control of framing and distance. Camera tracking brings Hermione's image closer and closer to us until, for the first and only time in the entire scene, only one character appears in the frame. Just after Paulina's 'Strike all that look upon with marvel' (100), the focus of viewers is on Hermione as they hear each of Paulina's additional distinct promptings to her: 'come, / I'll fill your grave up. Stir – nay, come away, / Bequeath to Death your numbness, for from him / Dear life redeems you' (100–3). Viewers' attention, then, is drawn to the moment after Paulina's 'You perceive she stirs' (103), when Calder-Marshall as Hermione extends her hand. The camera pulls back, still with Hermione alone in the frame, as she reaches out and moves downward and forward. After Paulina's 'my spell is lawful' (105), other characters, including Leontes, appear in the frame. Slowly, as Paulina prompts him, 'Is she become the suitor?' (109), Leontes extends his hand to meet Hermione's. The camera moves closer to Leontes' face during his intake of breath on 'O', and his release of breath, 'she's warm!' (109).

Since Howell's final scene does not primarily concentrate attention on the statue but, rather, on the re-entry of Hermione into her community, an important function of this final, remarkable sequence is to sustain wonder at each distinct succeeding moment of renewed relationship. The camera moves in to a shot of Hermione's reunion with Perdita just before Hermione speaks for the first time ('You gods look down,' 121), her hands in a gesture of blessing on Perdita's head. The camera pulls back to show Paulina as Camillo walks toward her to 'take her by the hand' (144); control of timing and of vocal tone avoids evoking any inappropriate comic response to this moment. Camera work continues to call attention to the repeated motif of hands extended and rejoined. After Leontes' 'Let's from this place' (146), Polixenes extends his hand as if to help escort Hermione. She demurs; Leontes, realizing why Hermione looks down, joins Polixenes' and Hermione's hands, asking for 'Both your pardons' (147). The camera then shows Hermione's response to each subsequent moment of renewal: she learns she is to have a son-in-law, and then that it is the son of Polixenes who is troth-plight to her daughter.

The final grouping offers a strong sense of the effects of renewed bonds and future promise in this small community. As Leontes speaks his final lines (151–5), framing includes the rest of the court in a depth-of-field composition. On Leontes' request to Paulina to 'Hastily lead away' (155), she enters into view. As Paulina leads them out, the characters do not exit through the arch of the darkened chapel in the background. Instead, a camera cut, deliberately breaking the continuity of the *mise-en-scène*, shows the characters exiting along a path between the wedge shapes of the main set, now brightly lit. The final visual composition is a fine contrast to the 'ill suspicion' (149) a royal husband had put between his wife and friend in the first court scene; in this ending, Hermione exits with Polixenes on her left side, Leontes on her right, taking each by the hand.

Clarity through exact timing of camera shots and cuts, plus artful continuity editing, are major strengths not only of the statue scene but of the overall production. Howell uses the visual to support the verbal: camera selectivity supports the spoken word. Her emphasis, in directing Shakespeare on television as well as in the theatre, is on the language. As she put it, 'The dramatic energy is in the words – *not* in the scenery, *not* in the costumes, *not* in the cups and the daggers and the benches and the furs; it's *not there*. It's in the words, *that* is where it all takes place' (quoted in Fenwick, 27). Howell's commitment to the language is suggested, too, by her relatively few textual omissions. Like many modern directors, she omitted the satyrs' dance (IV.iv), but she cut only approximately 38 lines. The production gives viewers an opportunity to experience a very lightly cut version of the play.

Critical reception of Howell's BBC production of *The Winter's Tale* was mixed; Rothwell and Hedrick alike found it, as Hedrick put it, 'too tame' (4). Jane Howell herself has said she is not fully happy about her BBC production of *The Winter's Tale*, despite her strong response to the play. She has written that 'the values of the shepherd and his son are *so* important – Leontes has thrown his child out – they find a child and accept it – joyfully. It is this acceptance – this generosity of spirit – which turns the play – which makes the process of regeneration possible. It is this compassion which lies at the centre of a seemingly dark world which makes it possible to go on' (Howell, letter to Maher). But she finds her own production 'a bit stark, a bit lacking in salt and pepper, in flamboyance'; she also has said 'I think it was over-tightly directed and I think I wouldn't do it like that now' (interview with Maher, 14 March 1988). Howell's own reservations about her BBC *Winter's Tale* apply also to its need for greater varieties of tone and changes of pace. The pace often seems slow. Yet as John Wilders points out, television has the capacity to allow performance at a rapid pace (13). Howell's subsequent BBC productions of the *Henry VI* plays and *Titus Andronicus* reveal more consistently skilled, varied, dynamic, and complex uses of the television medium. Nevertheless, Jane Howell's BBC production of *The Winter's Tale* is a substantial achievement. First of all, especially in visual design and presentation, it makes a remarkable break from the then-dominant naturalistic mode of the BBC Shakespeare plays series through its use of stylization. Second, it makes important use of intensifying techniques, notably in non-illusionist direct address to the camera. Third, a number of actors deliver strong performances: Margaret Tyzack is an impressive Paulina, with commanding precision of speech; Rikki Fulton as Autolycus works well with the camera to play up Autolycus' self-reflexive awareness of his multiple roles and con artistry; Jeremy Kemp as Leontes, Anna Calder-Marshall as Hermione, and David Burke as Camillo all give nuanced performances that contribute significantly to the clarity of the production – as evidenced, for example, in the presentation of Leontes' jealousy and in the trial and statue scenes. While the problems of the production often involve the difficulties of creating a television production from a theatrical text of the nature of *The Winter's Tale* – with its bold presentational styles, its heightened symbolic stagecraft, its metatheatrical reflexiveness – even critics who have major reservations about the production have responded to what Hedrick calls its 'elegance and clarity' (4).

CHAPTER VI

Peter Hall's production at the National Theatre, 1988

They [the late plays] are so contradictory in their texture, so extreme in their colours. So utterly therefore un-simple. Because any statement that is made is contradicted, any solution that is proffered is questioned. And I think the only honest way to do them is to try to embrace that complexity and show just how rich it is. It is certainly contradictory. (Peter Hall, interview with the author, 11 August 1988)

Speaking of his 1988 season of Shakespeare's three late plays – *The Winter's Tale*, *Cymbeline*, and *The Tempest* – Peter Hall made clear that his last project as Artistic Director of the National Theatre (later the Royal National Theatre), particularly his *Tempest*, was not a farewell to his art; he regarded it, rather, as 'a call to arms' (South Bank Show, 1988). This statement was his gauntlet thrown down to the Arts Council after years of struggle with certain of their policies; it was his protest against a romantic view of *The Tempest* as Shakespeare's farewell to the stage; and it reflected his view that these late plays, much darker than usually thought, are 'hard-edged, sharp' (opening talk to the company, December 1987). The plays, continued Hall, show us 'dark forces' that 'well up in us' and present 'extremes of experience'.[1]

Hall's view of the late plays as dark, contradictory, and extreme is the first of several major ways his season of late plays differed from that presented by the RSC in 1969–71 during Trevor Nunn's Artistic Directorship. Nunn, like Derek Traversi and many leading literary critics of the time, thought the plays offered an ultimately affirmative vision. Nearly two decades later, Hall's view was in some respects the opposite; like Stephen Orgel in his Oxford edition of *The Tempest* (1996) and other critics, Hall perceived the plays to be primarily disturbing or problematic. Second, Nunn and Hall included different plays in their seasons: Nunn presented *Pericles* and *Henry VIII* as well as *The Winter's Tale*; Hall chose *Cymbeline* instead of *Henry VIII* and, changing his initial plan, decided to present *The Tempest* instead of *Pericles*. Though many factors, including pragmatic ones, entered into these decisions, Hall's selection supported his exploration of what is 'contradictory' in the late plays. Third, at the National, one director and one company of actors and designers produced all three plays; at the RSC, though the whitebox set and certain over-arching concepts connected three productions, each was designed and directed independently. Fourth, Nunn's season was marked by his youthful, exuberant sense of breaking with prior theatrical production styles as he constructed a seemingly 'empty' space; Hall's was marked by a desire to re-explore his characteristic use of production styles with seemingly 'Renaissance' visual references. In 1988 he pointed out that only one of his approximately twenty-five Shakespearean productions to date had had no suggestion of Renaissance location (in interview with Ralph Berry, 209).

Nunn's 1969–71 production of *The Winter's Tale* reflected the then-current critical interest in myth and symbol; by contrast, Hall's 1988 production, though it was not strongly political, did, like some Shakespearean criticism, particularly since the mid-1970s, give more attention to political issues. Chief among these, an issue debated during the reign of James I when the play was written, is the danger of political absolutism. The Caroline period (especially its mid-1620s to 1640s), which was the basis for Alison Chitty's costume designs, was, as Roger Warren has pointed out, a historical moment when 'absolute monarchy was at its height' (23). Design for Hall's *Winter's Tale* thus reinforced the extent – limited but important – to which the production explored the dangers of political absolutism suggested by Leontes' tyrannical behaviour.

Leontes' abuse of power is at once political as well as personal, destructive to court and kingdom as well as to himself and those nearest him. The psychological and domestic consequences of tyranny had great impact in the intimate Cottesloe (seating capacity up to four hundred) in which the production opened 18 May 1988 for an initial week before its tour – together with *Cymbeline* and *The Tempest* – to the Moscow Art Theatre (27 May to 4 June), the Rustaveli Drama Theatre in Tbilisi, Georgia (9–12

June), and the Tokyo Globe Theatre (18–24 June). The three plays returned for the whole of July at the Cottesloe before transferring to the larger, open-stage Olivier (seating capacity approximately 1160), where *The Winter's Tale* premiered on 13 August. Hall compared his experiment of playing in both the Cottesloe and the Olivier to Shakespeare's company's use, at the time of the late plays, of both a chamber setting at the Blackfriars and the larger spaces of the Globe. Witnessing the plays in both venues at the National, one could to a certain extent test the view held by many scholars that the plays flourish equally well, if differently, in both kinds of theatre space. *The Winter's Tale* is a play that uses both intimate and wider scales. The force of psychological conflict in Leontes' asides and in the trial scene was especially memorable in the Cottesloe; the play's political implications, and the cosmological aspects of Alison Chitty's set – its movable disk with a Copernican image of the 'heavens', for example – were especially memorable in the Olivier, despite mechanical problems in adapting to the new space (see Wardle, *The Times*, 1 October 1988). Yet the greater size of the Olivier did not preclude an intense realization of intimate conflict. Roger Warren, during a performance late in the run at the Olivier (in November 1988), found the experience was 'in many respects *more* intimate than it had been in the smaller Cottesloe'. The performance caught precisely what he believed the company sought – 'lightness of touch, lucid clarity, truth to the extremes of human feeling' (156). To him this suggested the possibility that 'the Globe, likewise, could seem intimate when required, and that *The Winter's Tale* had as great an impact there, where Simon Forman saw it, as at the Blackfriars' (157).

In both the Cottesloe and the Olivier, changes in lighting and colour palette were effective: hot red for Sicilia, because of sexuality and jealousy, said Hall; strong greens to evoke pastoral Bohemia; darkly lit off-white spaces for the return to Sicilia. The company learned, however, during their unforgettable seven performances in Tbilisi, Georgia (then part of the Soviet Union), when transportation problems left them with neither set nor costumes, that the art of the plays is the art of the actor. Michael Billington found that *The Winter's Tale* (performed in rehearsal clothes and staged in the Rustaveli's smaller house, seating three hundred) 'emerged with startling clarity and power': 'The result was a staggering demonstration of what theatre is about: the primacy of acting and language over spectacle and design' (*Guardian*, 15 June 1988; cf. John Higgins, *The Times*, 15 June 1988, 18). Billington also perceptively named a major contribution that Hall's productions of the late plays made to theatre history. 'Hall has stripped the plays of their romantic Tennysonian aura', he wrote, 'and showed that re-generation is both precarious and difficult' (*Guardian*, 31 May 1988). Hall wrote that forces of 'betrayal, jealousy, sexual insecurity and lust for power' are 'purged' – 'but only in part, by integrity, fidelity, penitence, and reconciliation' (*Daily Telegraph*, 19 January 1988, 12). Hall's phrase 'only in part' is crucial to his *Winter's Tale*, in which purgatorial processes were seen to be incomplete. 'Far from offering consoling images of reconciliation', wrote Irving Wardle, 'these are violently unreconciled works' (*The Times*, 23 May 1988).

Representing more time's terror than its potential joy, Hall's production seems, from extant theatre records, to be the first in England to present *The Winter's Tale* with an ending so strongly marked by pain and disturbing ambiguity. Sally Dexter's Hermione, in the beginning full of sensual warmth and delight, was in the end distant from Leontes, only beginning to emerge from frozen grief. Tim Pigott-Smith explored a wide range in Leontes with great distinction, notably the role's most disturbing passions; Eileen Atkins's acutely perceptive Paulina was fierce, in her ministry a scourge. The figure of Time (played by Michael Carter) did not engage audiences with a tale of wonder; he was an inexorable, enigmatic force, reminding us that intertwined with life is death. And in Hall's Bohemia, the Arcadian met the Bacchic in a Dionysian satyrs' dance, thus releasing the Bohemia scenes' darker sexual energies – often lost when the satyrs are omitted. Ken Stott's Autolycus had not only a touch of the satyr but also a strong dose of the cynic. Hall spoke of the Bohemia scenes as in part an 'idyll', to which Autolycus provided an extreme contrast.

Not only its dark energies but also the artistic virtuosity of *The Winter's Tale*, particularly of its language, strongly engaged Hall's attention. He was acutely aware of the play's extraordinary stylistic range, from what he called 'the coruscating soliloquies of Leontes', often 'harsh and strange', to 'the stand-up comic routines of Autolycus' (December 1987 workshop with the company). Directing three late plays during the same time period with one acting and design company, he created a five-month rehearsal period (December 1987 until the season's opening on 18 May with *The Winter's Tale*) that enabled the actors to work for the first weeks on text, starting with an extended workshop on verse speaking.

Hall used a typescript of a specially prepared, conservatively edited text from which he had largely removed modern editorial punctuation and stage directions. Frequent reference in rehearsals was made to a facsimile of the First Folio as well as to the one-volume Oxford *Complete Works* (eds Stanley Wells, Gary Taylor, John Jowett, and William Montgomery, 1986) and its *Textual Companion*. Given Hall's emphasis on verse and prose structures as the basis for actors' work, an approach he explicitly opposed to what he called 'post-Stanislavsky' approaches (December 1987 workshop), his principle was to cut as little as possible. He made minimal cuts to *The Winter's Tale* – approximately sixty lines (mainly from dialogues of the Clown and Autolycus in IV.iii and IV.iv) – and Hall made these with regret. Even with such a relatively full text, playing time was just three hours (not counting a fifteen-minute interval). Emphasizing, as Granville Barker had done, speed of speech, Hall said (December 1987 workshop): the 'overriding thing about Shakespeare's writing' is that 'it is like quicksilver'.

If Hall in part reaches back to Granville Barker, Hall's verse work also, of course, is grounded in his early work with the Royal Shakespeare Company and has strong affinities with textual and voice practices of former colleagues such as John Barton (e.g., in *Playing Shakespeare*). He shares with Barton certain formalist assumptions about texts; furthermore, Hall, like Nunn, was a student of F. R. Leavis at Cambridge. Subsequent critical theory and textual scholarship that emphasize linguistic indeterminacy and material vagaries of textual transmission would pose questions about Hall's view that 'Shakespeare tells the actor very clearly what to do, how to phrase, when to go fast, when to go slow, what rhythm, what line to emphasize, what word to emphasize. You can work all that out; there are very clear clues' (South Bank Show). But without denying what is questionable in Hall's statement – its implied emphasis on authorized, inherent meanings, for example – it is important to understand his practice.

The issue is complex partly because Hall has himself recognized a danger: 'If you're very keen on the text, and the shape of the text, you can end up with a lot of talking heads stiffly moving around. So you have to have that freedom of physical and emotional life against the form of the text' (South Bank Show). Hall insisted in rehearsal on certain guidelines – observing line endings, antitheses, inversions, alliteration, and assonance; carrying through energy until the end of the line; breathing on the end of a line or caesura; connecting in pulse and tone a verse line divided between more than one speaker; and taking care to scan lines with an alertness to variations in stress as well as to metrical pulse. But he also pointed out that 'once you've established the shape [of the verse lines], there are an almost infinite number of acting choices.' Saying Shakespeare 'supports the actor but also restricts', he added, 'Shakespeare gives so much freedom' (December 1987 workshop).

Hall's approach elicits important theoretical questions about textual authority; post-structuralist approaches to text, voice, and verse can also (in ways different from Hall's) make exploration of a play's language central in theatrical practice. A practical result of Hall's giving actors so much time to work on language was that audiences were given verse speaking with extraordinary nuance and range, especially from Pigott-Smith as Leontes, Eileen Atkins as Paulina, and Tony Church as Antigonus. Critical reception singled out the actors' speech for high praise, despite particular reservations. Perceiving occasionally constricted physical movement in *The Winter's Tale*, one critic nonetheless commented, 'The architecture, argument and imagery of Shakespearean speech certainly emerge with unusual clarity throughout the trio of late plays' (Michael Ratcliffe, *Observer*, 22 May 1988). Another found that 'the productions offer a rare chance to hear every single word uttered with skill and intelligence' (Michael Coveney, *Financial Times*, 23 May 1988). Charles Osborne noted, 'A fine balance is maintained between sound and sense, often by the simple expedient of pausing ever so slightly to acknowledge the line endings' (*Daily Telegraph*, 20 May 1998). Several critics (e.g., John Peter, *Sunday Times*, 22 May 1988) were nonetheless troubled by occasional over-emphasis on line endings, as was Stanley Wells, though he praised the company's work on language. Referring to *The Winter's Tale* in particular, he wrote: 'I was struck by the actors' full comprehension of every nuance of meaning, along with their sensitive attention to the poetic and musical qualities of their lines. But occasionally (as also in *Cymbeline*) the effects of Sir Peter's coaching were over-apparent in pauses at line-endings held a fraction too long, unnaturally interrupting the sense' ('Shakespeare Performances in England, 1987–88', 143).

Among those actors who most notably showed what Wells calls 'full comprehension of every nuance of meaning' was Tim Pigott-Smith, speaking with what for Gerald Werson was 'exemplary clarity' (*Stage*, 26 May 1998). The 'metaphors of a schoolboy's top, a spider in the cup and wives being sluiced like ponds' were 'isolated with such care' by Pigott-Smith, wrote Michael Coveney, 'that they cannot escape our attention' (*Observer*, 22 May 1988). Delivering Leontes' tortured, compressed language with such clarity was part of Pigott-Smith's ability to portray what Michael Billington termed 'demented logic': 'He almost reasons his way into madness.' Billington continued: 'What makes his Leontes memorably disquieting is not so much its violence (at one point he stabs Antigonus' hand with a dagger) as its quiet clinical accuracy' (*Guardian*, 20 May 1988). Such seeming 'quiet' concealed its opposite – inner violent passion – in Pigott-Smith's Leontes.

'Shakespeare not only doesn't prepare you for the outburst to jealousy', Tim Pigott-Smith told me in interview, 'he does exactly the opposite. He prepares you for a world of idyllic brotherly love, motherhood, children, boyhood friends.' Like Ernest Schanzer (introd. New Penguin edition, 22), Pigott-Smith believed that, up to Leontes' first aside, audiences are presented with a paradisaical world. Similarly, Hall believed that, in watching these exchanges, 'somebody seeing *The Winter's Tale* for the first time should think they are seeing a domestic comedy' (South Bank Show).

Unlike Audrey Stanley and James Edmondson in the 1975 Oregon Shakespearean Festival production, neither Hall nor Pigott-Smith perceived the verse to be under pressure in the opening exchanges (I.ii.1–107) of Leontes, Polixenes, and Hermione. Pigott-Smith's relative ease in this initial dialogue was established early in rehearsals and largely governed his performances. During the run of the production, however, he subtly changed his performance to reflect what he had come to feel were, for Leontes, 'two moments of insecurity' (interview).

One was 'at my request he would not' (86), which he covered with heartiness, jesting with Polixenes. The second, more noticeable moment of insecurity came in his slower speed and darker vowels on 'Why, that was when / Three crabbèd months had soured themselves to death' (100–1). He did not play Leontes as *conscious* of jealousy or even suspicion on those words, emphasizing in interview that it is 'only a moment, a one-line hint'. 'Certainly I go for "crabbèd" and "soured." But I never play it psychologically', to indicate jealousy; 'that's reserved for the next moment, on "Too hot, too hot!"' The two moments of insecurity were fleeting, ambiguous; apart from them, there was no suggestion earlier even of disturbance on Leontes' part; he was genial, playful. Boyhood innocence was evoked in a rare and poignant gesture: when Polixenes (played by Peter Woodward) recalled that he and his playfellow 'knew not / The doctrine of ill-doing, nor dreamed / That any did' (68–70), Pigott-Smith momentarily took Woodward's hand. Seconds later, on Hermione's witty retort to Polixenes 'that you slipped not / With any but with us' (84–5), Pigott-Smith laughed lightly.

Fully present for the dialogue of Polixenes and Hermione (38–85), Pigott-Smith listened to it all and saw it all. Noting that there is no stage direction in the First Folio that Leontes '*draws apart*' (part of a stage direction interpolated by Quiller-Couch and Dover Wilson, Cambridge ed., I.ii.44, as well as other editors), Pigott-Smith asked, 'Why should he not be part of it? If you draw apart, it doesn't matter what you do or how you do it, the audience knows you're suspicious.' He wanted audiences to see 'Polixenes and Leontes together, as the innocents that they were' and thus to register the terrible loss when Leontes destroys bonds rooted in boyhood.

Pigott-Smith's Leontes came with maximum suddenness to his first aside. Ian McKellen, in John Barton and Trevor Nunn's 1975–76 RSC production, also came to this first aside unexpectedly, but during the prior sequence had been more restrained and intense than Pigott-Smith, who was robust in wit and seemed at ease before his mind's darkening. The previous 'high comedy' of the opening 'hospitality game' in Hall's production, wrote Irving Wardle, 'with any amount of inventive business between the three loving friends', had the effect of 'making you wonder if the blow is ever going to fall and hugely strengthening the shock when, finally, it does' (*The Times*, 20 May 1988).

'The basis of the change is on a half line', said Hall, of this crucial moment. Hall was convinced that for Leontes to begin 'Too hot, too hot!' with maximum force, the half line immediately before it – Hermione's 'for some while a friend' – has to be 'fed' to Leontes with great energy, provoking him to want her to 'shut up' her 'too hot' speech and behaviour. Working with Hall's idea that the half line should be picked up quickly by the speaker completing that verse line, Pigott-Smith swiftly flamed into rage and spoke his first aside with bitter irony. Hall commented: 'I think it's the most shocking thing in drama' if it happens that abruptly (South Bank Show).

'Up to that point', said Hall, Leontes 'has worn a mask of total geniality, charm, warmth, and adjustment. Suddenly he rips the mask off' (South Bank Show). Hall's image of the mask fits his view that 'the jealousy has been there for months' (quoted in Warren, 104); Warren points out, however, that he found it difficult to fit Hall's idea to Pigott-Smith's playing of Leontes' sudden '*tremor cordis*' (Warren, 104–5). When I probed this disparity in interview, Hall implied he did not mean that the audience, or even Leontes, was conscious such a mask was being worn, but that dark forces, of which Leontes has been unconscious, now erupt. It could remain ambiguous both for Leontes and the audience whether, in retrospect, the jealousy has been latent or has just struck; the effect of suddenness would be the same. What was crucial to Hall in either case was that Leontes must not be seen to be jealous from the start. Leontes' jealousy must be a surprise to audiences, Hall stressed in an early rehearsal read-through (December 1987), or one will 'remove the wonder of Shakespeare's technique'.

The argument made by Hall and Pigott-Smith for presenting Leontes' jealousy with maximum suddenness has affinities with the argument of Stephen Orgel, though Orgel's is differently based. Orgel negotiates points of contact between Renaissance texts and psychoanalytic ideas. Citing Emilia's definition of jealousy as lacking 'cause' ('It is a monster / Begot upon itself', *Othello*, III.iv.156–7), Orgel comments that 'Leontes' psychology in the opening acts' seems 'strikingly modern in its dramatic recognition of the compulsiveness of paranoid behaviour, and more generally, of the self-generating and autonomous nature of consciousness itself' (Oxford ed., 19).

Leontes' consciousness is rendered in his asides by verse techniques of highly compressed syntax, irregular rhythms, and startlingly unusual diction, which suggest that his mind is under extraordinary pressure. Such mental disturbance is implied in the Renaissance term *'tremor cordis'* (palpitations of the heart); Roger Warren's research helped Tim Pigott-Smith to explore connections between this physical symptom and sudden disease that affects the mind. To their understanding of *'tremor cordis'* they added symptoms of another heart disease, myocarditis, which Warren explains as an 'inflammation of the heart muscle' resulting 'in a racing pulse, breathlessness, and feelings of intense weakness'. He pointed out that Pigott-Smith used these details to present Leontes' 'mental state in a precise and specific way, and to avoid the dangers of rant and generalization' as Leontes' jealousy grows: 'As he first mentioned it [*tremor cordis*] he clasped his heart, as if he had experienced a sudden spasm. He repeated this gesture at "Affection, thy intention stabs the centre" (1.2.140); at "This sessions ... / Even pushes 'gainst our heart" as he opened the trial (3.2.1–2); and at "Apollo's angry" (3.2.145) as the delusions finally left him' (Warren, 105).

Leontes' delusions have political consequences. Though Hall's production did not explore the play's political potentialities as much as it might have done, it gave a more detailed representation of social power relations, particularly in its first three acts, than had productions by Nunn, Stanley, and Ronald Eyre (RSC, 1981–83), which emphasized the play's mythic and/or psychological potentialities. Pigott-Smith emphasized that when the King, subject to irrationality, becomes a tyrant, he is extremely dangerous politically. 'That is why I reject absolutely, categorically, any attempt at comedy,' Tim Pigott-Smith said in interview, thinking of the scenes (II.iii and III.ii) in which Leontes is in conflict with Antigonus and Paulina. 'Leontes, a jealous tyrant': Pigott-Smith, citing these words of the oracle, stressed the word 'tyrant'. 'The first three soliloquies' develop Leontes' disease and 'are to do with jealousy', he said, 'and from then on it seems to me to have much more to do with tyranny.' When, for example, he entered to speak 'Nor night nor day no rest' (II.iii.1), Pigott-Smith held not only a large candlestick but also a sword, as if a sword of state; as he thought of 'revenges' on Polixenes but resolved to take 'present vengeance' on Hermione, he seemed to merge a speech out of revenge tragedy with what Paulina calls, as she then enters, his 'tyrannous passion' (28).

When the revenger is a king, there is peril for the whole realm. As Pigott-Smith saw it, 'if Leontes is a ridiculous figure, then everybody would be able to stop him. He shouldn't be ridiculous, he should be dangerous, which is why I opt for cutting Tony's hand' (interview). Tony Church's Antigonus, warning Leontes that his 'justice' might prove 'violence' (II.i.127–8), continued to try to reason with him. Leontes, proclaiming that his senses could detect adultery, said sharply, 'I do see't and feel't, / As you feel doing thus' (152–3). The textually opaque 'thus' has occasioned a wide variety of business in stage history (see also Orgel's summary of editors' suggestions, Orgel, ed., p. 126, n. 153). Frequently in productions, as Pigott-Smith noted, Leontes pulls Antigonus' beard in that moment after 'thus', often with semi-comic effect. There was no trace of the comic as Pigott-Smith took out his sword and cut Antigonus' right hand; this action was like that of a dictator using violence as deterrence. As Pigott-Smith explained in interview, Leontes was attempting to intimidate not only Antigonus but also the other courtiers.

Church's Antigonus faced Pigott-Smith's Leontes with powerful opposition. Every bit a match for Leontes in quick, sharp wit, this Antigonus was utterly serious, both dignified in his anger and penetrating in his severity. He was strongly supportive of Paulina, with no effort to restrain her, however he might fear for her. To Leontes' misogynist effort to silence Paulina by mocking Antigonus for lacking mastery of her, Church replied with a firm counter-statement, articulating the rhetorical antitheses in Antigonus' speech with great clarity. He emphasized 'run' in 'I let her run' and paused before the next line: 'But she'll not stumble' (II.iii.51–2). In some productions of the play, when Leontes accuses Antigonus of failing to 'stay' his wife's 'tongue', Antigonus' reply – 'Hang all the husbands / That cannot do that feat, you'll leave yourself / Hardly one subject' (109–11) – can invite uncritical laughter which colludes with the line's possible residual misogyny. Church avoided such laughter by delivering the line with anger and sharp irony. The King's threat to put Antigonus' hand in the fire of the onstage candlestick had an edge of real danger as Leontes commanded him to 'Take it [the baby] up' (182). Moments later Leontes held the sword of state over the baby; Antigonus reached forward to prevent him from killing it. Such performance of these exchanges between Leontes and Antigonus helped audiences to see the fusion of domestic and political issues.

Paulina's confrontation with Leontes is, likewise, both personal and political. Leontes attempts to silence Paulina by accusing her and all his male courtiers of being 'A nest of traitors!'; Tony Church spoke Antigonus' reply, 'I am none' (II.iii.81–2) with fierce indignation. Eileen Atkins delivered Paulina's rejoinder 'Nor I, nor any / But one that's here, and that's himself' forcefully, clearly implying the King was a traitor, stressing 'himself' so pointedly that Leontes was startled. Speaking with knife-edge precision, choosing her words strategically, Atkins made Paulina's daring disclaimer, 'I'll not call you tyrant', evoke the danger she goes on to name: that his 'most cruel usage of your Queen ... something savours / Of tyranny' (II.iii.115–19). Church and Atkins matched each other in seriousness, clarity, power, and precision of verse speaking; they were perhaps the strongest combination in their roles since Brook's 1951 production with Lewis Casson and Flora Robson, who likewise avoided the wrong kinds of comic playing, which can become tinged with the very stereotypes (henpecked husband and shrew) of which Leontes accuses them.

Leontes' dangerous absolutist use of royal power for his own will was signalled when he entered (from rear centre) to begin his staging of Hermione's trial, holding aloft the sword of state. Giving his command, 'Produce the prisoner', he crossed down centre, placed the sword on a stand, and took up an unusual position: his back was to the theatre audience. His throne was on a gangway built from the forestage into the auditorium. As Pigott-Smith used this staging, it intensified the impact of certain striking decisions later in the scene to face the offstage audience and address them directly. When his Leontes, for example, replied to Hermione's first great speech at trial, he attempted to persuade the offstage audience to assent to the bitter wit of his dismissive reply: 'I ne'er heard yet / That any of these bolder vices wanted / Less impudence to gainsay what they did / Than to perform it first' (III.ii.53–6). And he turned to face the offstage audience for his rash pronouncement, 'There is no truth at all i'th' oracle' (III.ii.138). Leontes' and Hermione's speeches were, in this staging, entirely public, though at a few critical moments their eyes also met. They made eye contact when she delivered a line directly to him and when Leontes rose to give force to an accusation (e.g., on 'You knew of his departure'), crossing to her for a sharp exchange which prompted her response: 'Sir, spare your threats' (76–89).

The staging of the trial scene, furthermore, was an innovative way to give strong focus to Hermione. Her costume for the trial was also an unusual means of heightening our sense of her dignity. Rather than wearing clothing which reminded audiences of her ordeal in prison (as had Goldie Semple's torn dress in the moving scene in Stratford, Ontario, 1986, or Gemma Jones's simple shift in the RSC 1981 production), Sally Dexter wore a courtly red garment, more muted in tone than her red dress in I.ii, but deliberately like it in style. Lost was the impact of Hermione's extreme suffering, but gained was a heightened political awareness that this was the trial of a queen. She stood as if in a dock, by a plinth on a centre-stage pedestal, her bearing statue-like; there was little movement of her body, even of her face, which was pale, ravaged. In extreme contrast to her vivid, buoyant movement in her first scene, her formal bearing now suggested a growing inner numbness later to be presented fully in the statue scene.

Leontes' sudden reversal in the trial scene was played on the gangway bridging the forestage and the auditorium, thus giving audiences (particularly in the small Cottesloe) an opportunity to experience Leontes' repentance up close, in full force. No overreliance on special effects covered the moment, as can happen when directors and actors fear the swift change. Pigott-Smith came down the gangway, facing the audience, to hear the messenger's announcement of Mamillius' death. His anguish on 'Apollo's angry' had physical impact in his body, which he gripped in pain; going to his knees on 'Apollo, pardon', he was face down by the end of his long speech (III.ii.151–70). When he heard Paulina cry 'Woe', he shook his head as if to deny what he sensed was coming; hearing the Queen was 'dead' (199), he raised his head in a silent scream.

Paulina's subsequent encounter with Leontes likewise gained impact by being acted on the gangway between forestage and audience. Eileen Atkins's Paulina excoriated him with clear, focused intensity. Hall's rehearsal directive to Atkins, she said in interview, was 'You've got to put him through it.' Leontes is 'saying "I'm sorry, I'm sorry, I'm sorry" and you're saying, "That won't do, Mister; what you've done is much worse than that"'. Atkins's approach sprang also from her decision that, though Hermione had seemed dead, her Paulina knew to the contrary before re-entering. The opposite decision – that Paulina believes

Hermione to be dead – was made by (among others) Susan Wright (Stratford, Ontario, 1986) and Tamu Gray (Oregon Shakespeare Festival, 1996). Their cries for justice came out of deep grief and thus enlarged – by showing its cost – their change to compassion for Leontes. As both Wright and Gray pointed out in interviews,[2] Paulina's major act of forgiveness, not solely Leontes' repentance, is a crucial turning point. Wright, prostrate with grief, extended her arm toward Leontes (also prone), slowly meeting his hand. Tamu Gray, seated on the ground, holding Leontes, wrestling with her own great losses, drew on immense spiritual strength to make her request for forgiveness a costly act of giving it.

Hall and Atkins emphasized not Paulina's compassion but her cleansing harshness. Atkins's outrage, though it did not exclude compassion or grief, sprang mainly from her desire to make Leontes face his appalling destructiveness. When reprimanded by a lord that 'you have made fault / I'th' boldness of your speech', Atkins did not pause, as some actors do, or silently acknowledge fault (as did Joy Richardson at the Globe, 1997), but picked up his half line very quickly, giving Paulina's reply – 'I am sorry for't' – an assertive edge. Her next words, 'All faults I make, when I shall come to know them, / I do repent' (III.ii.217–18), were not an apology. As Atkins paraphrased the words in interview, they meant 'All faults I make, when I come to know that this is a fault, I shall be sorry for it; but until I know it's wrong, I won't be sorry for it.' Roger Warren suggested additionally (in conversation with me)[3] that Atkins's reply was designed to teach Leontes (see figure 11). She turned from fury to tenderness on her 'good my liege', taking Leontes' head in her lap; she asked forgiveness not for her supposed excess, but because she could now believe Leontes' sorrow to be genuine. As she led Leontes out to begin their long journey, that the process was to be purgatorial was clear in Tim Pigott-Smith's emphasis: 'tears shed there / Shall be my *re*creation' (italics mine).

Despite his repentance, the destructive consequences of Leontes' actions, of course, continue, as Antigonus meets his death. Peter Hall stated in rehearsal (December 1987) that the bear should suggest rough, raw, rude nature; he wanted it to be grotesque and as much like a live bear as possible. He stressed that audiences must not expect the bear to appear – it must be a surprise. The execution was not as powerful as the conception.

11 Act III, scene ii: Eileen Atkins as Paulina and Tim Pigott-Smith as Leontes. Directed by Peter Hall, National Theatre, London, 1988. John Haynes photograph

A bear costume with an enlarged head added a foot to the size of the actor inside for a total of seven feet, and the scene worked passably well. What was extremely effective, however, was the decision made by Tony Church as Antigonus: seeing the bear move toward the baby, he intervened, protecting Perdita at the cost of his own life. A striking choice (paralleled, for example, in the Oregon Shakespearean Festival production of 1954), it reduced the scene's danger of provoking a wrong kind of comic effect.

The presentation of Time was more haunting and effective than that of the bear. The actor representing Time carried traditional Renaissance emblems of scythe and hourglass; unusually, however, he was so stark in movement and voice that he was more the grim reaper than witness to the 'freshest things now reigning' (IV.i.13). The set's great circular Copernican background disk with emblems of the heavens, now in gold light, descended to an almost vertical position behind Time, rising up again at the end of his speech. The cosmic emblem evoked awe, yet Time hinted more at 'terror' than at 'joy' (IV.i.1). He was not a storyteller engaging the audience; a ghostly figure, he stared straight ahead, moving from rear centre stage down the gangway and out the centre aisle, in a formal march. Taking half steps, with pauses in between timed with pauses in his highly stylized verse speaking, he moved as if to a metronome, slowly, inexorably.

This conception of Time as an enigmatic force connected not only to the darkened tones of this production's ending but also to the death of Antigonus. Time's Chorus was not separated from Antigonus' death by the usual interval after the baby is found. Instead, at the Cottesloe, Hall placed the one interval at the end of the trial scene (III.ii), opening part two with Antigonus and the baby; at the Olivier, he changed the interval, placing it after both the Chorus of Time and Polixenes and Camillo's dialogue in IV.ii. Time's sombre presentation was echoed in their treatment of this dialogue to emphasize time's losses and the continued pain of remembrance: Camillo's sense of ageing and of exile and Polixenes' sharply resurgent grief on hearing of 'that fatal country Sicilia'. Furthermore, as Roger Warren points out, Basil Henson as Camillo and Peter Woodward as Polixenes skilfully played 'two experienced politicians testing one another for confirmation of their own sources of information', so that the scene 'seemed much more than the mere narrative transition that it has seemed in other productions' (131).

In the Bohemia scenes, Ken Stott's Autolycus did not sound a contrasting light note; rather, dark tones emerged from his harsh strumming on a mandolin, and he 'glared at the audience and made them wait for his opening song' (Warren, 132); at the end of his first scene, he deliberately played against the text's 'merrily hent the stile-a' by sticking his tongue out at the audience. He portrayed much of the wolf; for sheep's clothing he had little use, preferring his con act to have 'a lot of cruelty' (Stott, in interview). This fallen courtier on the make, striving to get back to court, was, Stott said, 'looking out for number one'. He had the style and tone of a streetwise, highly cynical opportunist and was 'urban, scruffy', said Hall, who perceived a sharp contrast between Autolycus and the pastoral 'idyll' (December 1987 rehearsal). Hall and Stott admirably strove to 'pull Autolycus within the play as opposed to allowing him to be a comic relief and a diversion', said Stott. Hall sensed they had 'discovered the function of Autolycus': he seemed to be 'an inversion almost of Leontes, an unruly spirit in another apparently peaceful place' (Hall, in interview). Autolycus' repentance – in this production clearly another con job – was parodic of Leontes' own. After the pastoral, Stott's Autolycus continued to disrupt the potential harmony, giving a mocking laugh when he heard the gentleman's report that Antigonus had been eaten by a bear (V.ii.62).

Though the caustic wit of Stott's Autolycus rightly removed all traces of false, generalized merriment, he did not engage the audience as successfully as Joe Ziegler at Stratford, Ontario (1986), who also had a dark edge, though not as extreme. As Roger Warren suggests, Stott's approach 'froze audience response', and 'the part is simply too long to maintain attention in an audience which has been alienated' (132). Thus the production, like many, flagged in the long, changing sequence of episodes in Bohemia. To release the varying energies of these scenes, there needs to be not only an Autolycus who is extremely skilful at connecting with the audience but also a very strong Florizel, a vital Perdita, and a highly skilled comic actor in the role of the Young Shepherd; the actors in these roles were competent but did not come up to the level of Michael Bryant's Old Shepherd, who was, in Roger Warren's phrase, 'the epitome of stubborn integrity and courtesy in the role' (133). Hall believed the pastoral scenes were not fully successful in previous productions he had experienced and knew how difficult it is to make them work; they were the weakest parts of this production.

Stanley Wells's programme note, written independently of the production, does not go so far as Hall and Stott in thinking Autolycus is evil, but, like the production, usefully points out the darker side of the pastoral: the 'innocent beauty of Bohemia', wrote Wells, 'is astringently laced with the amorality of the cashiered courtier turned tinker, Autolycus, and violently disrupted by the self-regarding passion of Polixenes' anger at being excluded from his son's wedding plans'. Polixenes' rage was performed by Peter Woodward with such sudden, explosive force that its echoes of Leontes' violence and irrationality were clear; moreover, the production offered a strong trigger for that rage – the sexual energies of the satyrs' dance.

This bacchic dance, so often cut, helped give vitality to these problematic Bohemia scenes. Hall included it because it seemed, he said in interview, to do a number of things: 'It moves us from a sylvan pastoral to something which is completely earthy and passionate. And it completes the journey of Perdita. If she is to love and she is to give herself, this is part of it. And it seems to me that if you remove it, the transition to Polixenes' outburst and the terribly difficult situation that Florizel and Perdita find themselves in is much harder to get into.' Hall's view was effectively borne out in performance. The anarchic, bawdy energies of the satyrs (showing bare bottoms and sporting large artificial phalluses) provided a sharp antithesis – which Roger Warren rightly termed a 'grotesque anti-masque' (135) – to the measured dance of Florizel and Perdita. In *The Winter's Tale*, however, the 'anti-masque' elements are reversed from their traditional position in the masque: they occur not before the harmonious dance but after it. One implication of this can be – as Hall implied in interview – that the satyrs are not to be banished so that an ideal vision can follow but are part of an inclusive vision of eros, both light and dark. Retaining the satyrs' dance also intensified Polixenes' anxiety over what in Florizel and Perdita's relationship seemed an anarchic threat to his patrilineal order, spurring his 'Is it not too far gone? 'Tis time to part them' (IV.iv.339).

These pastoral sequences, to use Hall's characterization of the late plays cited in the epigraph to this chapter, were indeed 'contradictory in their texture' and 'extreme in their colours'. In the statue scene, however, he emphasized the extremity of sorrow, but not of joy, preferring to place the 'solution that is proffered' (interview) under great pressure. Remembrance of

things past, not restoration, governed the dynamics of the scene.
  Hall's staging of the statue scene was as unusual as his staging of the trial scene, but somewhat in reverse. As judge in the trial, Leontes had his back to the audience, and the focus was on Hermione's still figure, standing in a dock; conversely, Hermione's back was to the audience when she was standing *'like a Statue'* (First Folio) in the final scene. In Peter Hall's view, 'The important focus is not on the statue coming to life, it's on Leontes.' Terry Hands, in the Royal Shakespeare Company production of 1986 (Stratford-upon-Avon) and 1987 (Barbican), also placed focus on Leontes in the statue scene, positioning Hermione downstage of centre with her back to the audience. The view that the play is primarily about Leontes' journey, which has long dominated criticism but which has not been characteristic of women directors, was in both productions strongly emphasized.
  Hall also thought that 'it's easier to believe a statue if you don't see it. It's easier to believe what the words say. But it's tricky' (interview). To Stanley Wells, the placement of the statue with its back to us was 'surely a mistake': 'Admittedly, it enabled us to focus on Leontes' reactions, but we, as well as he, need to marvel at Hermione's appearance; and we should hold our breaths ... expecting against expectation that the impossible will happen, the stone will become flesh, art will be transformed into nature' ('Shakespeare Performances in England, 1987–88', 144). Hall's emphasis, however, was not on wonder but on remembered pain.
  The face of Sally Dexter (Hermione) was frozen in grief in the trial scene when, learning that Mamillius was 'gone', she descended from the pedestal on which she had stood. As she descended in the statue scene, her face was similarly immobile; she had barely begun to bequeath to death her numbness. As Peter Hall said in interview, 'She's still frozen, she's still a statue.' Her embrace of Leontes was stately, reserved. That 'formal feeling' Emily Dickinson said comes after 'great pain'[4] still dominated her expression and slow movement even in her final exchange with Leontes, after the others had exited and the two were left alone onstage. She allowed a very brief meeting of eyes with him, but no further deepening of warmth; turning, she exited first down the centre walkway from the stage (towards the

auditorium). Leontes followed, his face showing great concern, hers staring ahead in pain.

This ending, darker than in any previous major English twentieth-century production, was challenged by some critics. With energetic engagement in rethinking, Pigott-Smith said in interview with me almost three months after the 18 May opening of the production that he had found it very constructive to exchange ideas with a particular scholar who had disagreed about the ending and 'we're working on the ending now'. During the subsequent run, without losing gravity, ambiguity, and disturbing silences, the exchanges between Hermione and Leontes, still very restrained, suggested a greater possibility of future renewal. It had already become clearer by the reopening in the Olivier (13 August 1988) that though Leontes longed for greater response from Hermione, her restraint was in no way cold or unforgiving, but expressed her sense of extreme loss. At the end of that evening's performance, when Leontes was alone with Hermione, she reached up with her hand and slowly touched his cheek, in an echo of the gesture she had used with Perdita earlier; he put his arm briefly, tentatively, round her shoulder before they separated to exit. The subtle interaction between Hermione and Leontes in these last moments in the final performance of late November 1988 suggested a fine tension between potential reconciliation and the presence of past pain. 'It would be marvellous', said Pigott-Smith in an early rehearsal, 'if in performance we could get some of the fragility of that final balance.' In some performances, they did.

Peter Hall's ending to *The Winter's Tale* was not as radically inconclusive as Ingmar Bergman's seven years later (1995–96), but he saw in it considerable ambiguity. 'It is unresolved', Hall said to me in interview, pointing out that 'It doesn't end with a couplet.' Earlier in the statue scene, Paulina comments to the assembled court, 'I like your silence; it the more shows off / Your wonder' (V.iii.21–2). But Hall did not apply these possibilities to Hermione's silence in the scene; on the contrary, to Hall her silence implied darker feelings. Moreover, he said, the possibility of reconciliation is 'also so complex, you couldn't express it', adding with deliberate paradox, 'Hermione's silence is extremely eloquent.'

Hermione's silence is followed, Hall suggested in interview, by Leontes' 'uneasy attempts at union': 'the introduction of the son-in-law to be, the idea of Paulina marrying Camillo, the introduction of Polixenes'. For Hall, Leontes is 'trying to get Hermione to melt. I don't say she's completely rejecting him; I just think if she's been waiting for sixteen years, after what he did to her, it would be fairly incredible in human behaviour to wind it up with an easy happy ending.' Hall's understanding of behaviour, with his appeal to psychological realism, can be seen in a fascinating exchange during a rehearsal (a moment captured on film in the South Bank Show). Eileen Atkins was concerned that the ending was so troubled; Hall responded: 'I think they [the audience] will think in human terms that it is impossible to re-meet your husband who killed your son and put you in prison after sixteen years without a great deal of anguish and difficulty.' Tim Pigott-Smith agreed that a happier ending would make the 'darkness which has always been there' disappear. Turning to Eileen Atkins, Hall said, 'The one thing she [Paulina] does not deal with is the growing together of these two again. Because she can't. Only time can do that.' But time in this production had not conclusively emerged a healer.

Only time may also test the match between Paulina and Camillo that Leontes attempts to arrange. Basil Henson as Camillo did follow Leontes' directive to 'take her by the hand' (V.iii.144); he crossed to Paulina and, taking her hand, kissed it. But Hall took pains not to turn the moment into a conventional happy ending. He said that in rehearsal he felt the actors were overplaying reconciliation, so that it became sentimental; it became darker as they explored Hermione's not speaking and why she didn't speak. One consequence of her silence, as Hall saw it, was that it prompted Leontes' effort to join Paulina and Camillo, which is otherwise, said Hall, 'like a parody of the tying up of the bows at the end of the comedies unless it relates to Hermione and Leontes'.

> I mean, he [Leontes] is looking there at a man who has been exiled from his country for sixteen years because of what Leontes did, and he's looking at a woman whose husband has been killed because of what he did. They are two old people now. He wants to give them happiness and union and the completion of marriage. But I think he's also using it as a prompt to Hermione. If they marry, perhaps she would remarry. I think that's all in that moment. It stops it suddenly being a kind of flip moment; it is a very tender fragile moment. Also a dangerous moment for them. (Hall, in interview)

What we are presented with at the end of *The Winter's Tale*, Hall said, are 'seeds' of reconciliation; it is impossible that it should happen quickly (interview). When I told Hall that Tim Pigott-Smith had said (in interview) that he wanted to suggest reconciliation will occur, but that it will take time and involve costly pain, Hall said, 'I totally agree; it will occur.' But, he added, 'If you go through an experience as horrific as this has obviously been for two people, they cannot and will not and should not return to where they were. That is impossible. They will resume their lives together in some other position.' Stanley Wells's programme note similarly departs from the celebratory tone characteristic of productions of the 1960s and 1970s; he emphasizes not restoration of past bonds but what is lost, unresolved, and precarious:

> There is sobriety as Leontes in his closing words suggests how each may heal the wounds 'Performed in this wide gap of time / Since first we were dissevered'. We are more conscious of the older generation than of the young lovers. Antigonus is dead, Leontes – though he is now rewarded – has 'in vain said many / A prayer' upon Hermione's grave, and he needs pardon from both Polixenes and Hermione. The individuals must salvage what they can.

At least one critic had reservations about the presentation of the ending. Perceiving that Leontes and Hermione were left 'looking at one another with some unease', Stephen Wall wrote: 'The implication is that the old incompatibilities are not yet laid to rest. Psychologically there may be something to be said for this, but it mutes the mythic power of the play's conclusion and makes it seem a smaller work' (*Times Literary Supplement*, 16 June 1988, 649). Critical reception in the main, however, found Hall's astringent emphasis on the darker tones of the play an admirable departure from stereotyped views of 'romance' – a label given in the later nineteenth century by Edward Dowden, which Hall discarded (Hall, *Daily Telegraph*, 19 January 1988; see also Michael Billington, *Guardian*, 31 May 1988; John Peter, *Sunday Times*, 22 May 1988; Irving Wardle, *The Times*, 23 May 1988). Hall is 'having none of the serene, full-barns-and-plenty view' of the late plays, wrote Christopher Edwards, noting that 'tragicomedy can provide a most severe and testing world. Here there is no orderly path to prosperity and forgiveness' (*Spectator*, 28 May 1988).

Between these poles of critical reception is the particularly nuanced view of Roger Warren. Fully crediting Hall's important insistence on the play's darker forces, Warren nonetheless felt that the 'radiance' of the ending in David William's production (Stratford, Ontario, 1986) 'was a truer response to the potential of the text than Hall's', which 'seemed to me to miss those very extremes for which he was striving':

> He [Hall] achieved the extreme of mental disturbance and its consequences superlatively; but because he deliberately avoided the opposite extreme of complete healing and reconciliation, the second half seemed something of an anticlimax, first because of the insecure Bohemia scenes and then because of this muted ending. In this interpretation, Leontes' spiritual journey, and Hermione's, were incomplete at the end of the play. For Hall, expanding a suggestion made by Stephen Orgel in his edition of *The Tempest*, this ending typified the sense of 'unfinished business' in these late plays. (Warren, 153–4; reference is to Orgel, ed., *The Tempest*, 55)

Hall's production came at a cultural moment when dominant twentieth-century critical and theatrical views of *The Winter's Tale* were beginning to be contested by emphasis on what is unresolved in the play. Though published eight years after Hall's production, Stephen Orgel's introduction to his single-volume edition of *The Winter's Tale* (1996) would in many respects resonate as much with this production as his earlier edition of *The Tempest* (1987) had with Hall's view of that play. Orgel's emphasis on what is problematic in *The Winter's Tale* is part of his challenge 'to abandon the fiction of Shakespeare ... producing a drama of wisdom, reconciliation and harmony' (Orgel, ed., 6). Hall's production implied that while a purgatorial process will continue, healing not only will be hard won but will be only partial. The ending bore the seeds of a new beginning, yet it was still a metaphoric winter. For Ingmar Bergman, six years later (1994–95), time and the possibilities of healing were even more tentative and enigmatic.

CHAPTER VII

Reinvention and cultural translation: Ingmar Bergman's production with the Royal Dramatic Theatre of Sweden, 1994–95

Time, a silver-haired elegant older woman in a long black dress, moved slowly onto the stage from the audience; she placed on the forestage a large alarm clock, its hands at five minutes to midnight. Proceeding slowly upstage and through the rear centre exit, she held behind her (flowing down nearly as long as the stage was deep) a black cloth lined in red. This was the last movement of an actor in Ingmar Bergman's 1994–95 production, in Swedish, of *The Winter's Tale* (*Vintersagan*).[1] Her stage in life suggested the wisdom of the crone; with the blood-red lining of her black train, she was a figure of life and of death, and therefore of time in both its cyclical and linear aspects. After her exit, the audience was left with a final image – the clock, ticking.

Those who know Bergman's film work will recognize in the ticking clock one of the devices which bears Bergman's signature. A mantelpiece clock helped to frame the beginning and ending of *Fanny and Alexander* (1981–82), for example, the film with which his production of *The Winter's Tale* had the most affinities. Bergman's inventive handling of the play's Chorus of Time was one of many instances of his shaping of the script, as were his striking additions and cuts. He cut slightly over half the lines from the text he was using, based on J. H. P. Pafford's edition (Arden Shakespeare, 1963), from which a careful translation into Swedish was done for the production by Britt G. Halqvist and Claes Schaar. Bergman's work stands in contrast to Granville Barker's reclamation of a virtually full text of *The*

[174]

Winter's Tale for his 1912 production, and to Peter Hall's approach to text work for his 1988 production. All productions of Shakespeare are mediated in a particular cultural moment, and all are therefore, in a sense, re-visions; but to a degree rare among directors of *The Winter's Tale* in the twentieth century, Bergman saw the play's text as 'raw material' for reinventing Shakespeare.

The phrase for theatrical texts, 'raw material', is Bergman's; he argued that 'absolute word fidelity is trumpery in the theater. The text is not a prescription but raw material, a frequently hidden path into the writer's consciousness' (quoted in Marker and Marker, 101).[2] As Roger W. Oliver wrote of Bergman,

> When he directs a play, he shapes the text as a writer would, cutting and rearranging material, sometimes in a radical way. Although the plays he chooses to direct do not have the same biographical and personal identification as much of his film making and writing, they still reflect many of the themes, both psychological and mythic, found in his work in those media. (Oliver, xii)

Oliver gave an example: 'It is doubtful that Bergman's richly textured production of *The Winter's Tale* would have been possible if he had not created *Fanny and Alexander* first' (xii). His view resonates with that of Donya Feuer, Bergman's long-time choreographer: '*The Winter's Tale* is a long play with complex language. Ingmar edited it and cut it as if it had been a film, creating a rhythm' (quoted in *Dramat*, 15).

It is as a film director that Bergman is typically best known outside of Sweden and continental Europe, but his long and distinguished work as a theatre director deserves to be equally well known. His work began to draw extensive public attention in Sweden after his appointment in 1944 (when he was twenty-six) as artistic director of the Hälsingborg City Theatre; and he attracted international attention in the 1950s when he directed for Sweden's Malmö City Theatre (Marker and Marker, 34). Bergman first directed for the Royal Dramatic Theatre of Sweden (Kungliga Dramatiska Teatern, popularly known as Dramaten) in 1951; after his return to Dramaten in 1961, he directed there with frequency. Bergman was Dramaten's artistic director and managing director for three years (1963–66); he subsequently continued as its most famous stage director. His growing international renown as a theatre director led (especially after his first production outside of Sweden, in 1967) to international tours of his productions and to periods as a guest director at many European theatres (see Marker and Marker, 1–2, 291–307). For a considerable time, particularly since having to cancel a production of it originally planned for 1989, he had wanted to produce *The Winter's Tale* at Dramaten. Prior to the time his *Winter's Tale* opened in 1994, he had directed approximately twenty-eight productions for Dramaten (*Dramat*, 43). He told its Artistic and Managing Director, Lars Löfgren, 'My blood is forever connected with the veins of this theatre' (quoted in *Dramat*, 4).

Bergman's production reflects Dennis Kennedy's view that 'some of the most innovative and exciting productions of Shakespeare' in the last quarter of the twentieth century were in languages other than English, and where (in Europe and Asia, for example) there was greater 'freedom from an accustomed linguistic approach': 'These productions often made it their business to register the cultural differences between the original texts and the target audiences' (*Foreign Shakespeare*, 14–15). Furthermore, Kennedy points out that all non-Anglophone productions, even if they do not set out deliberately to play upon cultural difference, inevitably involve more than verbal equivalence and 'require not only linguistic translation but also cultural adaptation' (*Foreign Shakespeare*, 2). As Kennedy suggests about other directors, Bergman's revisions may help us to remember that, since we can never have access to an unmediated 'original', all productions are in a sense cultural translations.

Where Bergman was most innovative in his *Winter's Tale*, he often drew most inventively on aspects of Swedish artistic and social culture as well as on motifs from his film work. The metatheatrical frame action he created for the production strongly reflected this, drawing as it did on the work of one of Sweden's most important nineteenth-century writers and musicians, Carl Jonas Love Almqvist. The sets for the production were built to resemble the Royal Dramatic Theatre in Stockholm, the very place in which Swedish audiences experienced the performances. The choreography made fresh use of a Swedish nineteenth-century theatrical tradition of '*figuranter*', adding non-speaking actors whose subtle, highly trained movement was closely related to the action. Act IV, scene iv of *The*

Winter's Tale, in which the action in 'Bohemia' partly alludes to English sheep-shearing festivals, drew, in Bergman's production, upon Swedish midsummer festivals. Bergman's *The Winter's Tale* was also shaped by concerns recurrent in his film work: the child as witness to, and victim of, parental violence; profound ambivalence toward inherited religious traditions, yet a strong sense of spiritual quest; intense exploration of inner torment – psychological, sexual, and spiritual.

While Bergman's vision was the shaping force of his inventive cultural adaptation of *The Winter's Tale*, it was brought into being as he worked with a team built up over years of association: Leontes was played by Börje Ahlstedt (who had played the title role in Bergman's stage production of *Peer Gynt*, 1991, and Claudius in *Hamlet*, 1986, both at Dramaten); Paulina was played by Bibi Andersson (whose work with Bergman began at least as early as 1955 in his film *Smiles of a Summer Night*); and Hermione was played by Pernilla [Östergren] August (Maj in *Fanny and Alexander*, 1982; and at Dramaten, Ophelia in Bergman's *Hamlet*, 1986, and Nora in his *Doll's House*, 1989). His choreographer for *The Winter's Tale* was Donya Feuer, and his designer was Lennart Mörk, both of whom had worked with Bergman since the 1960s.

Lennart Mörk's set immediately held the mirror up to theatre for Swedish audiences, who found themselves entering an auditorium in which the stage set resembled the place where they had just been, the Marble Foyer of the Royal Dramatic Theatre itself. Bergman said that he and Mörk imagined the 'theater space merging into the audience space, which in its turn becomes the Marble Foyer'.[3] This setting accorded with Bergman's idea that 'theatrical creation must always remind the audience that it is watching a performance' (quoted in Marker and Marker, 32). Actors in nineteenth-century dress had been assembling onstage while audience members were arriving. The performance had thus begun even before audiences were told by a narrator's voice-over that the actors were here to celebrate the nineteenth birthday of a 'Miss Ulricke Sofia' at a 'hunting lodge deep in the Swedish forest', for which her 'relatives and friends' would perform *The Winter's Tale*. While house lights were still up, and a piano (in the orchestra pit area, stage left) was being played, a voice-over told audiences the name of the pianist: 'Mr Almqvist'.

Music throughout the production drew upon the work of

C. J. L. Almqvist (1793–1866), using both his *Improvisations for the Pianoforte (Fria fantasier för piano-forte)* and especially a number of his poetic musical compositions called *Songes*. Almqvist's music was crucial to Bergman's decision at last to produce *The Winter's Tale*. Twice before he had abandoned plans to do so: once, as a master of his craft, in 1989, and once as a boy of fourteen, in 1932, when he longed to produce it (as well as *The Magic Flute*) in his puppet theatre. The medium of puppetry posed problems for the young Bergman: 'I realized early on that my Hermione puppet was utterly incapable of being resurrected. The puppet remained a puppet.' Bergman explained: 'I gave up mainly because, to my way of thinking, the conclusion was the most beautiful, the most moving and the most magnificent that I had come across in my as yet rather limited experience. I still think so today, sixty-three years later', he said in 1995, reflecting on his experience of directing the 1994–95 production of *The Winter's Tale*:

> I am never profoundly moved by anything that I have a professional or creative hand in. In the case of *The Winter's Tale*, this principle has broken down. Already when mapping out the stage instructions (the walking, standing, where am I/you going to say what?), already at that point my emotions were in great turmoil ... After that, at every rehearsal, every repeat, every piddling little detail, my feelings have been in an unprofessional upheaval, difficult to suppress. It has been a peculiar experience, unique in my professional life. (Bergman, quoted in Salander, 12)

The catalyst for Bergman, at the age of seventy-six, to produce *The Winter's Tale* in 1994, though five years earlier he had cancelled a planned production of it, was his experience of Almqvist's music:

> One afternoon on Fårö [the Baltic island where Bergman made his home], I was sitting in a chair in my study looking at the light over the sea ... I was listening to music: Jonas Love Almqvist's *Songes* sung by Irene Lindh ... Her interpretation of this complicated music was crystal clear, fervent, moving, perfect. Through the songs – darkly glowing, sweetly smiling, full of pain, mysteriously pleading – I could suddenly see *The Winter's Tale*. (Bergman, quoted in Salander, 12)

The art of Almqvist, who greatly admired Shakespeare's work, was evoked by Bergman's adaptation not only of his music but also of Almqvist's metafictional framing device – guests gathered at a hunting lodge, entertaining each other with stories and performances, particularly on dark autumn and winter nights, as they do in Almqvist's multi-volume *The Book of the Wild Rose* (*Törnrosens bok*, sometimes translated *The Book of the Thornrose*), a work richly composed of diverse genres that contains fifty of those musical poems he entitled '*Songes*' (see Romberg, 58, 67, 190).[4] Almqvist's word '*songes*' means more than the English term 'songs', and is often translated 'dreams'. He thought of them 'as little stage plays, *tableaux vivants*, full of movement and sound' (Romberg, 72).

In the Swedish programme for *The Winter's Tale*, there is a piece entitled 'Theatre Evenings at the Hunting Lodge'; its preface states that 'In Almqvist's *Songes* the brothers Henrik and Frans Löwenstierna speak about their father Hugo's planned theatre project for the great and famous parlour at the Hunting Lodge.' The subsequent programme citations – taken from Almqvist's *Book of the Wild Rose* – show a self-reflexive aspect that seems to have resonated with Bergman. Frans explains: 'My father plans to call this invention [his theatrical representations] dreams [*drömmar*]; he is planning to set up theatrical pieces that he will call *Songes*.'[5] Frans continues: 'The dreamlike performances that my father intends to arrange are of course in the nature of short stage plays' (Romberg, 73).[6] Bergman adapted Almqvist's framing device to his own metatheatrical use. 'Where is *The Winter's Tale* set?' he asked himself when listening to Almqvist's music. 'In the yellow salon. In the manor house. In Almqvist's *Book of the Wild Rose* ... A parlour game taking place between the wintry afternoon sunset and the moonlight supper of the evening. Seamless transition between the play and the play within the play' (quoted in Salander, 12).

The wit of Bergman's invention would have been clear to most theatregoers in Sweden, where Almqvist's work is widely known and his writings have long been studied in schools.[7] In addition, audiences in Sweden found in their programmes a seeming reproduction of a nineteenth-century playbill. It announced the performance of *The Winter's Tale* as part of the Löwenstierna family celebration for Miss Ulricke Sofia during Christmastide (28 December) at the 'Hunting Lodge'. The programme also contained a letter (dated 1925) purporting to be by a German Professor Emeritus at the University of Halle, one Hugo Wallenstrahl, concerning his supposed discovery of this playbill, in which Almqvist – whom one of his colleagues declares 'equal to A. Strindberg' – is listed as playing the part of Dion. Many in the audience must have suspected that Bergman was the author of the playbill and letter which, in a clever parody of scholarly factoids, purported to explain the frame action.[8] As John Lahr, who saw a performance in Sweden, put it, in this production, 'the play begins with the program' (*New Yorker*, 3 October 1994, 105).

Bergman's use of Almqvist, mixing wit with seriousness, was more in earnest than in jest, however. Dramaturg Ulla Åberg described the sound of Almqvist's songs to me in interview as 'very clear', 'aesthetically spiritual'. Bergman seemed to use the pure tones of Irene Lindh singing Almqvist to evoke moments of spiritual vision, even while keeping such moments at a distance, in his frame story. Perhaps this approach – to treat the spiritual as the aesthetic – enabled him at last to attempt the final scene of the play.

The first of the solo songs sung by Irene Lindh came at the end of the initial frame action and just before the language of *The Winter's Tale* began (I.i). She stood toward the forestage, silent, while behind her, actors playing members of the Löwenstierna family and friends changed into 'characters' from *The Winter's Tale* before the audience's eyes: Börje Ahlstedt put on his deep blue robe to present Leontes; Pernilla August (in a red dress, and not visibly pregnant until II.i) put on her red stole to present Hermione. They were joined by Krister Henriksson as Polixenes, and the three actors sat on a wrought-iron bench; the platform which held the bench was pulled slowly forward by a young girl, who had put on a mask of tragedy, and a young boy, who had put on a mask of comedy. The rest of the cast surrounded them.

As the actors held this visual composition, audiences heard the crystalline tones of Irene Lindh singing Almqvist's 'Heart's flower' ('*Hjärtats blomma*', *Songe* XV), with its image of the 'Wild Rose' standing 'in the heart's abode'.[9] As the image develops, it tells of suffering: 'Thorns of the Wild Rose / wound the heart and blood spurts out.' Almqvist, while warning against allegorical interpretation of his symbols, wrote of the Nordic wild rose that it symbolized 'wild grace and chastity' (Romberg, 112). Those qualities could suggest Hermione, but the exact use of the image in the song poses problems if one tries to press the analogy, because, in the play, wounding comes from Leontes, though he may think the thorns are Hermione's. Since Bergman's technique in theatre, as in film, however, is to suggest rather than to define, the relation of this song to *The Winter's Tale* is not that of one-to-one equivalence; rather, it is oblique, evocative.

Bergman also drew on Almqvist's *Songes* to express a wide range of human experience at other points. Except for two of Almqvist's songs used within Act IV, scene iv, his songs were used before or after scenes, assisting transitions in the action. 'My galleon' (*'Min gälar'*, *Songe* XXVII), for example, was used at the beginning of II.i; the song's image of the sail 'full of foulest storm and gale' suggested Leontes' passions and their effect on Hermione. After Leontes asked to be brought 'To the dead bodies of my Queen and son' (III.ii.233), Almqvist's song 'The Grave' (*'Graven'*, *Songe* XXV) echoed Leontes' situation: 'Ring bell, in the tower! / Now they are carrying my last flowers to the grave: / My wife's grave!'

Even more closely integrated into the moment-to-moment action than Almqvist's songs was the choreographed use of *figuranter*, which grew out of Bergman's close collaboration with choreographer Donya Feuer (with whom he had worked since 1964). *Figuranter*, in this context, were those actors skilled in singing, movement, and dance who did not speak but whose presence onstage, by their positioning and movement, expressed and gave form to what Feuer called the 'spirit of the text' (in a post-performance discussion at the Brooklyn Academy of Music, 2 June 1995). In this, she made innovative use of a nineteenth-century theatrical tradition made known by the distinguished Swedish theatre critic Herbert Grevenius. Like Grevenius, Feuer insisted that *figuranter* need not be mere 'extras' but actors whose movement is integral to the action. In an interview with me, Feuer explained that *figuranter* 'do not simply move, they play a role'.[10] Her approach, she said, had been influenced in part by her experience in Japan of the disciplined movement of actors in the Noh drama. She saw it as her task 'to heighten and to make visible' Bergman's intentions regarding movement (*Dramat*, 38), as well as to find and express what she calls 'the choreographic rhythm of the text'. One could say of the sixteen *figuranter* she used in *The Winter's Tale* what one critic said of the actors she choreographed in Bergman's production of Yukio Mishima's *Madame de Sade*: 'They move as if to the measures of an inaudible music' (Ingmar Björkstén in *Svenska Dagbladet*, quoted in Marker and Marker, 257). Integration of movement with the action at a given moment was Feuer's primary aim. One aspect of *The Winter's Tale* she wished to suggest, by 'changing the pulse' of the movement, 'quickening and slowing it down', was what she saw in Shakespeare's late verse as the 'broken' rhythms and elliptical structures which often (particularly in Leontes' language) express the 'irrational'. In Act I, scene ii, for example, the *figuranter* remained throughout the entire scene, playing the role of members of the court, sometimes in the background engaged in stately court dances, sometimes, in alert stillness or in subtle movement, expressing what they sensed as they witnessed the main action. According to Feuer, Bergman said the *figuranter* 'hear what's going on'; Feuer added that the *figuranter* wonder at times 'if it is something happening only in Leontes' head'. During Leontes' dark imaginings, 'Inch-thick, knee-deep' (I.ii.184), the *figuranter*, in three slanting parallel lines facing downstage toward Leontes, moved very subtly. When Leontes asked if Camillo did not perceive 'My wife' (and here Börje Ahlstedt paused, putting his hand over his mouth) 'is slippery?', a slight gasp went up from the *figuranter*.

The *figuranter* in these instances gave shape and density to the life onstage, becoming part of its changing pulse. As Feuer put it, they play 'a role in the life of the actors, who are playing the roles of Leontes [and other characters]'. The *figuranter* could also change at times into other roles, as in a night-walking scene Bergman invented and inserted between the second and third scenes of Act II. They became ordinary people of the city, peasants, an organ grinder, a blind person, a lame person; Leontes wandered among them, just before giving voice to his anxiety: 'Nor night nor day no rest' (II.iii.1). In the trial scene (III.ii), the *figuranter* became a crowd of soldiers and peasants watching in the background. In the next scene, clothed in brown, they helped to suggest the impact of the storm on trees and persons, in a deliberately *faux naif* enactment which suggested the 'amateur' stagings, similar to the *tableaux vivants* that Almqvist had envisaged for his *Songes*, to be performed in the yellow parlour of the hunting lodge. And when, in the same scene, a nineteenth-century-style theatrical wind machine was operated in full view of the audience, the shade of Almqvist met a moment of postmodern staging.

Feuer's use of *figuranter* heightened Bergman's strong sense of visual composition and movement. His equally great gift for control of pausing and timing, especially in presenting inner torment, was strongly evident in the production, particularly in Börje Ahlstedt's Leontes. Not surprisingly, in light of Bergman's other work, the strength of this production was the exploration of Leontes' psycho-sexual conflicts. To augment this exploration as well as to heighten audience perception of the impact of Leontes' violence on others, Bergman made significant additions both to Leontes' role and to that of Mamillius.

Violence suppressed, then suddenly emerging from beneath an elegant façade: this Bergman motif is strongly present in his films like *Cries and Whispers* and *Fanny and Alexander*, for example, and in certain of his stage productions, including *Hamlet* and, especially, Yukio Mishima's *Madame de Sade*. The motif was realized in detail by Ahlstedt's Leontes, and helped him successfully to negotiate the dramatic crux of the eruption of Leontes' jealousy.

Ahlstedt's Leontes gave early suggestions of covert suspicion held in check; with sudden intrusive moves while Polixenes and Hermione were speaking, he built Leontes' suspicion to the point when it was overtly voiced ('Too hot', I.ii.107). Leontes, having left Hermione and Polixenes on the bench (centre stage), moved upstage but turned to see Hermione win Polixenes: 'Not your jailer, then, / But your kind hostess' (58–9). There was a long pause; all onstage went still; Hermione, troubled by what she sensed in herself, pulled away from Polixenes. Pernilla August, playing Hermione, told me in interview[11] that Bergman directed this move to indicate that Hermione senses a new tone to her interaction with Polixenes without being certain what it is or why. August believed that audiences were not meant to think Polixenes and Hermione have had an affair, but that what was 'in their minds and hearts' was indeterminate; she said that Bergman's view in rehearsal discussions was that the relationship was ambiguous.

When Hermione and Polixenes' dialogue returned to a lighter tone ('Come, I'll question you', I.ii.59), other actors onstage began to move again. But the tension tightened a second time just before Hermione's 'By this we gather / You have tripped since' (I.ii.74–5): Ahlstedt came forward, bent down, and hid behind the bench on which Hermione and Polixenes sat; he

[183]

suddenly rose up, in seeming jest, just as Hermione said 'slipped not / With any but with us' (84–5). After Hermione replied to Leontes, 'He'll stay, my Lord', Bergman directed a long pause before Leontes' 'At my request he would not' (86). At Hermione's 'What, have I twice said well?' (89), Leontes jumped onto the bench, facing Hermione, who put her long red stole about Leontes' neck and drew him toward herself, sensuously. She was trying, Pernilla August told me, to 'reach him', because she sensed his jealousy from his behaviour. After Hermione said she had earned 'for some while a friend' (107), giving her hand to Polixenes and rising with him to move upstage, a discordant sound echoed in the theatre. The *figuranter* stopped their slow movement, and there followed an unusually long pause (approximately ten seconds) before Leontes, sitting alone on the bench and staring out into the audience, began to voice his inner terror: 'Too hot' (107).

Even in those parts of Leontes' asides often performed as direct address to the audience, Ahlstedt's focus was inward. 'Gone already!' (183), for example, was spoken to himself, in low tones, slowly. His statement that many a man's wife 'has been sluiced in's absence' (192) expressed Leontes' individual fear, rather than being a satiric observation about cuckoldry; as he said the line, he picked up Hermione's red stole and, in an ironic echo of her earlier gesture to him, drew it very slowly around his neck. At times he suggested by altering his vowel tones and by changing tempo that he was caught in a nightmare, as in his speech about 'Affection': 'Thou dost make possible things not so held, / Communicat'st with dreams' (137–45). On Hermione's 'Are you moved, my lord?' (149), Leontes gave a slight start and then ceased to use his altered tone and speed.

That Bergman's direction of timing was acute all reviewers agreed; but there was less agreement about some of his additions to Leontes' acts of violence. After Leontes' line to Camillo to 'Make that thy question, and go rot!' (I.ii.321), Bergman did not follow the First Folio exit marked for Leontes, but kept him onstage. Bergman directed a pause of nearly twenty seconds; in the invented sequence that followed, as *figuranter* formed three circles of dancers, Hermione and Polixenes re-entered and joined one of these circles (upstage left). Leontes strode into that circle, removed Polixenes, staggered slightly, then danced with Hermione in the centre of the circle, appearing affectionate but, putting his face to her neck, suddenly caused her to break from his grasp; she paused to stare back at him and quickly exited. Pernilla August told me in interview that Leontes had called her 'whore'; but audiences could not hear what he said, so the sudden reversal remained puzzling. Bergman might have thought it was dramatically functional ambiguity. Leontes then crossed to Polixenes, kissed him roughly, ran down into the first row of the auditorium where the actors representing guests at the hunting lodge were seated, seized a young gentlewoman, took her onstage, forced her to the ground, and tried to rape her, having to be pulled off by two courtiers. John Lahr thought it 'a beautifully staged and awful moment' (*New Yorker*, 3 October 1994, 106). The action was an arresting expression of Leontes' psycho-sexual turmoil, and perhaps it could be argued, in terms of the fictive frame, that an 'amateur' actor playing Leontes could have a moment when his own unconscious was so stirred by the part he was playing that he would break from his role, mixing the play world with his 'reality'. But the attempted rape seemed to me to raise difficult questions about the relation of *The Winter's Tale* to Bergman's frame action.

Subsequent directorial decisions emphasized the danger in Leontes' rage with greater clarity. When Paulina brought Leontes the baby, Börje Ahlstedt, having said 'This brat is none of mine' (II.iii.92), attempted to crush the baby, putting his foot in its cradle (which had been laid on the centre stage). Bibi Andersson, as Paulina, quickly intervened, kneeling to put her body on top of the cradle. The impact of Leontes' rage was deadly, however, in its impact on Mamillius, and here the violence he did to his child was psychological. Bergman extended the role of Mamillius as witness to his father's violence, and audiences saw more fully Mamillius' brief, tragic journey from childhood playfulness to terror. For this extended role, Bergman chose an accomplished young, petite woman actor, twenty-four-year-old Anna Björk. At the beginning of Act I, scene ii, Mamillius, playing near Leontes, Hermione, and Polixenes, held a toy theatre; like Alexander's toy in *Fanny and Alexander*, it was a miniature of the Royal Dramatic Theatre of Sweden. Bergman not only had Mamillius sense Leontes' disturbance to a degree uncommon in productions but he also cut the conventional exit for Mamillius (in Rowe's edition, not in the Folio) at 'Go play, Mamillius; thou'rt an honest man' (I.ii.208). Instead,

Mamillius withdrew, but returned, listening from afar, when Camillo told Polixenes that Leontes 'swears ... that you have touched his Queen / Forbiddenly' (409–12); on that line, Mamillius ran out. Later, Mamillius saw his father accuse his mother directly (II.i). In many productions, Mamillius is taken offstage by one or more of Hermione's gentlewomen when Leontes charges that it is 'Polixenes / Has made thee swell thus' (II.i.61–2), but there is no stage direction in the First Folio for this exit. Bergman had Mamillius listen and watch from behind three screens at the rear of the acting area representing Hermione's bedchamber, unseen by those onstage. Mamillius looked out, anxiously, from behind the screen as his mother was accused by his father of being 'a traitor' (II.i.89) and, on Leontes' order that she be taken away to prison (103), watched as two men clapped manacles on his mother's wrists. Frozen in fear, Mamillius witnessed his father in rage thrust Antigonus to the ground. When, for the prison scene, the screens were removed, Mamillius went downstage left, his hands over his ears, and then leant his head against his shoulder, numbed.

Just as Bergman's genius for suggesting psychological conflict was a great strength of the production, so was his fascination with theatricality. His interest in the relation of theatrical illusion and reality, together with his creation of the frame action, enabled him to negotiate the play's sudden shifts and *coups de théâtre*. Bergman effectively presented, for example, Shakespeare's abrupt end to the nightmare world of Leontes and its consequences in the appearance of the bear and of Time.

In presenting the bear, Bergman doubled the stakes: he used two bears and, as in other parts of the production, exposed theatrical artifice to the audience's view. The effect was comic, but not broadly comic, since a sophisticated breaking of dramatic illusion, via exposure of the mechanism of performance, underlay the seemingly naive 'amateur' dramatics. The first bear – an actor in a white polar bear suit – emerged from behind a storm cloth (being held and moved in view of the audience by the 'friends and family' presenting *The Winter's Tale*). After roaring, the actor took a long pause, as if an amateur waiting for audience response; he then pursued his quarry. Just after Antigonus' final words, the bear (standing) placed his foreleg on Antigonus' head and gently pushed him toward his exit. To add to the comic effect, after shots of a hunt rang out (the frame tale was taking place, after all, in a hunting lodge), a small brown bear ran out on all fours and took its theatrical moment: it paused downstage centre and reared up on its back legs before making an exit. Just after the Young and Old Shepherds left the stage, the audience was told by a serving woman that 'Dinner is served'. The hunting lodge guests seated within the theatre audience rose and went onto the stage before exiting, thus signalling the coming interval. Adding to the metatheatricality of this exit procession was a reappearance of the actor who had played the polar bear, now with his white bear's head in his hand; an actor in a small brown bear suit followed soon after, as did dancers and the two children who had earlier donned masks of tragedy and comedy when the action of *The Winter's Tale* began.

Bergman's strategies for breaking illusionism were also strongly in evidence in the unusual and expanded use he made of the figure of Time – as a woman (played by Kristina Adolphson).[12] After the one interval, audiences saw a woman with silver hair, wearing a long black dress, arise from her chair in the first row centre of the auditorium, come up the steps onto the stage, and sit downstage centre to address them. A long red cloth lined in black cascaded from the front of her waist (a reversal of the black cloth that would flow behind her in the final moments of the play), its blood-red length draped over her lap, the forestage, and the steps down into the auditorium. Then, in sudden contrast to her striking solemnity, just before she began to speak she took out a large brass alarm clock and held it in her lap. The deliberate anachronism and clash of styles were part of the wit of Bergman's presentation of Time, as was the idea that the clock was such a prop as might be to hand for houseguests presenting the play. On her words 'I turn my glass', Time turned the clock toward herself, and the alarm rang. 'Fa!' she exclaimed, as she tried to turn it off.

Having deliberately provoked awareness of his own theatrical jest, Bergman had prepared the audience for non-naturalistic storytelling. As Time said their names (IV.i.22–4), Florizel and Perdita entered (Perdita in a dress whose red echoed Hermione's from Act I). Part of their dialogue was transposed from Act IV, scene iv, lines 1–14 to follow Time's speech (see figure 12). Florizel was disguised not as a shepherd but as an aspiring painter, for this was not a sheep-shearing festival but a midsum-

12 Act IV, scene i: Kristina Törnqvist as Perdita, Kristina Adolphson as Time, Jakob Eklund as Florizel. Directed by Ingmar Bergman, the Royal Dramatic Theatre of Sweden, Stockholm, 1994. Bengt Wanselius photograph

mer one. Florizel's language (IV.iv.2–4) was therefore changed.[13] He praised Perdita as Flora appearing not in 'April's front' but 'in summer's front', and it was not for a 'sheep-shearing' that they were costumed but for a 'midsummer feast'.

As Florizel and Perdita exited, Time went down into the auditorium to sit (centre front), hunting lodge guests either side of her, to observe the action. Before the festivities began, Camillo and Polixenes entered for their dialogue, dressed as hunters. Following them, Autolycus entered with a duck dangling from his hand, as if he had poached their quarry. His story of himself was updated; he said he had become a tax collector and had then dabbled in fishy deals. His role was given in the Swedish programme as a petty swindler (*småsvindlare*). The Shakespearean text certainly offers the possibility that he is an improviser, even if he speaks no more lines than are set down for him; but this Autolycus, in a contemporary version of what may have been possible in the popular theatre of Shakespeare's time, coined new lines directly to the audience: 'I am freelancing', he said. Trying to hide the dead, limp stolen duck, he quipped to audiences at the Brooklyn Academy of Music: 'He's a bit tired from his long flight from Sweden.' But the improvised jokes were sometimes outdated or fell flat, despite the zany dark energies of this cross-dressing Autolycus who, for his pedlar's disguise, wore a corset and bra, then added a skirt.

The strength of Bergman's Act IV, scene iv was its cultural translation into a Swedish midsummer festival. A large cross, entwined with green leaves, was raised just stage right of centre, similar to crosses erected in Sweden for midsummer celebrations, as dancers and singers helped to set up the festivities. Two Almqvist songs gave a Swedish local habitation to Act IV. 'Away all sorrow / take up fiddle and bow' ('World's end', '*Världens slut*', *Songe* L) was sung by a chorus after part of Florizel and Perdita's opening dialogue. Some of the song's lines set the tone for Autolycus and the Young Shepherd: 'Let every clown make trouble, let every fool make double.' Other lines in the song suggested potential for renewal: 'Forget all sorrow / O my mother and father ... there's a cure ... for the spirit's torments too.' Also sung chorally by singers and dancers (as the IV.iv festivities were set up) was Almqvist's 'Why have you come to the meadow?' ('*Varför kom du på ängen?*', *Songe* XXIV), which suggested the love games of a midsummer's night:

> Why have you come this evening, say?
> I've come to meet you.
> Will you again tonight go away?
> No, never will I leave you.
> Will you stay all night with me?
> Tonight I'll spend with you.

Despite the energies of music and of dance, and despite Bergman's cutting over half of Act IV, scene iv (approximately 488 lines cut), the verbal and performative energies of the scene were not sustained, and it was not until Bergman could again focus on psychological conflict that the production regained its dramatic tension.

Bergman's vision of what happens after the pastoral sequences of Act IV, scene iv is suggested in his description of how he came to see the structural movements of *The Winter's Tale*. Its first half, he said, 'has the severity of a Beethoven symphony':

> The second half is more like *The People from Värmland* [Swedish opera by Andreas Randel, 1806–1864, that includes some Swedish folk music]. Suddenly Beethoven's angry sounds pierce

the idyll. Then right away a noisy scherzo and finally a chorale to the Sacredness of Man and endurance of Love. This mixtum compositum no longer seemed the least bit strange. I couldn't understand what it was that had presented such obstacles before' [in Bergman's earlier plans to produce *The Winter's Tale*]. (Bergman, quoted in Salander, 12)

Bergman's acute alertness to music is clear here, as is his interest in the sudden contrasts of a 'mixtum [mixed] compositum'. But to judge by his cutting, obstacles must have seemed to him to remain, and his cuts have particularly striking consequences in Act V.[14]

In cutting over half of the last act, Bergman excised the political conflicts of the play that are part of Leontes' dialogue with his courtiers and Paulina in V.i. The role of Paulina was played with great skill by Bibi Andersson; but the extensive cuts to the script here, as in her earlier exchanges with Leontes in II.iii and III.ii, left little opportunity for her to explore the political potential of her role in this scene, in which Paulina wins from Leontes the power to choose him a wife. Bergman's cuts also radically changed the religious language and ideas in the play. Almost all references to the gods and to the oracle were cut. Earlier, the entire scene of Cleomenes and Dion's report about the oracle (III.i) was cut; and the words of the oracle, when read at the trial, were taken out of the tip end of a cane (not out of a sacred object, as in many productions). In V.iii, Bergman cut Hermione's first spoken lines, to Perdita – 'You gods look down, / And from your sacred vials pour your graces / Upon my daughter's head!' (121–3) – as well as her lines, in the same speech, concerning the oracle (125–8).

Alteration of the play's religious language, with its subtle and complex blend of classical and Christian references, particularly affected Act V. The setting for the opening of Act V suggested a convent, with Leontes as flagellant. Leontes knelt centre stage, his back to the audience, his shirt stained with his blood, in front of a statue of the Madonna with a cross in her arms; two nuns stood on either side of the statue. To the rear of the stage, in movement too similar to pantomime to have anything but an uncertain, partly comic effect, a rapid procession of nuns seemed to be casting out a devil. Then an Abbess standing near Leontes spoke in serious tones – an Abbess whose role Bergman created, giving her his revised version of Cleomenes' opening lines (V.i.1): 'You have done enough, my son.' Leontes was helped to his feet, a fresh garment slipped over his head, and the flagellant's whip taken gently from him.

Setting the first scene of Act V in a convent rather than at court, Bergman intensified his focus on Leontes' inner state but cut the crucial debate about the political state: in a patriarchal, hereditary monarchy, who will rule if Leontes remains childless? Shakespeare, in a striking departure from patriarchal power, has Leontes, over the objections of his courtiers, give his promise to Paulina to let her choose him a wife. In the Shakespearean text, sixty-four lines (20–84) are given to the debate; Bergman cut them all. These cuts resulted in a sharp, almost cinematic juxtaposition of Leontes' speech of remorse that begins 'She I killed?' (17–20) to the announcement of Florizel's arrival (85).

The reported reunion of Perdita and Leontes in V.ii was given a broadly comic treatment, far from the subtler elements of parody interwoven with the witty tragicomic Jacobean prose. Renaissance comic satire has some affinities, however, with an invention used in the scene: Autolycus, disguised as a friar, picking the pockets of the Old and Young Shepherds, added: 'The Lord be with you.' But opportunities offered by the scene's rare mixture of wit and seriousness were undercut by stage business. Women scurried quickly in the background during the report of the reunions. Four men bearing candelabra entered to get a chair, hopping out with it just before the report that 'attentiveness wounded' Perdita (85) as she learned the cause of her mother's death.

Bergman's mastery of his production's tone, timing, and visual composition, however, began to reassert itself in the final scene. In a striking departure from dominant stage tradition, Hermione was not presented standing like a statue; instead, she was borne in, reclining on a catafalque (placed downstage centre). A silken, silver-grey cloth covered her body; when Paulina unveiled the 'statue', we saw Hermione lying in a red dress, the colour reminiscent of her first court dress. Bibi Andersson performed Paulina's 'It is required / You do awake your faith' (V.iii.94–5) with fine movement and timing: just before speaking it, she moved silently in a semicircle, turned in a three-quarter view towards the theatre audience, then spoke the line, addressing both the onstage and offstage audiences; she took a moment's pause, and moved again. All principal onstage witnesses to her actions took hands. After Paulina said 'Music; awake her' (98), Hermione's movement was not accompanied by instrumental music, nor by one of Almqvist's *Songes*, but by the sound, from actors in the scene, of human voices humming. This moving choice echoed Bergman's autobiographical statement: 'I believe a human being carries his or her own holiness, which lies within the realm of the earth; there are no otherworldly explanations' (*Images*, 238).

The final reunions were at least as tentative as those in Peter Hall's 1988 production, and were more muted in tone. Hermione did not 'descend' or 'approach' (these words were cut); but on 'be stone no more' (99), her fingers moved and she slowly rose to a sitting position, facing the audience, her gaze intense with the weight of time and loss even as it registered, subtly and with gravity, moments of new life. At Paulina's 'present your hand' (107), Börje Ahlstedt sat on the bench-like catafalque beside Hermione and slowly, gently touched her hand before saying 'O, she's warm!' (109). Perdita put her head on her mother's lap. Hermione did not rise to embrace Leontes, nor did she hang about his neck (lines 111–15 were cut); instead, Bergman substituted a subtle movement. Leontes had rested his head on Hermione's back; she leaned slightly backward toward him, her head brushing his shoulder. John Lahr wrote of this moment that it was 'an immense gesture', 'a miracle of the heart' (*New Yorker*, 3 October 1994, 108).

These carefully measured, precise gestures contributed to the muted, autumnal quality created in the scene. This was not an ecstatic reunion but a slow awakening. Bergman directed Hermione to speak very softly, and he cut her references to the gods and the oracle in her speech to Perdita, leaving only: 'Tell me, mine own, / Where hast thou been preserved, where lived, how found / Thy father's court?' (123–5). Facing the audience, Hermione kept her enigmatic gaze; to adapt a remark of Jean-Luc Godard on Bergman's early film work, 'the past and present play[ed] hide-and-seek in the face' (38). The muting of Hermione's response was, indeed, so strong that it might have been more effective in the close-up of a Bergman film. But to a degree unusual even among contemporary productions, this ambiguity and restraint valuably unsettled traditional expectations of restoration in the play's final scene and etched on the mind an unforgettable instance of a tentative and precarious renewal.

Hermione did not rise until the beginning of Leontes' final speech. Tentatively she took Leontes' hand, then released it after she arose. On 'Hastily lead away' (155) – rendered in the voice-over translation as 'Come away' – there was a very slow tempo; Leontes once again reached his hand toward Hermione and then helped Perdita to rise. As the three, together with Paulina, turned upstage to exit, there was a moment's pause: it was Perdita who assisted the reunion; after giving her mother her hand, she gently guided her mother's hand towards her father's. Hermione's and Leontes' reunion had begun, yet it hung in the balance, its fulfilment not a certainty.

With Bergman's rescripting, the play did not end with an exit after Leontes' final line. In John Lahr's apt phrase for the next moment of action, 'Life's banquet goes on' (*New Yorker*, 3 October 1994, 108). The frame story reasserted itself; an older serving woman entered and said to the audience, 'Excuse me, but supper has been on the table a long time.' But in sharp contrast to this earthy reminder, and in tension with the tentativeness of the reunion, were the clear, soaring tones of Irene Lindh singing the final song, Almqvist's 'The Listening Mary' ('*Den Lyssnande Maria*', *Songe* I). The last words audiences heard were 'O Lord, how lovely / To die in music and in song'.

Enactment did not end there; Bergman presented audiences with the more disturbing image of Time, who had risen from our shared auditorium space to go onto the stage, the long, red-lined black cloth she held trailing behind her as she processed upstage. After Time's procession across the stage and her exit, audiences were confronted by the final image – witty, enigmatic, and haunting: the large alarm clock she had left behind on the forestage, ticking. The previous stage action bidding the guests to a banquet suggested that the feast of life goes on; the last song suggested that music can ease the prospect even of death; the final image, however, suggested a vision of time that was under the aspect not of eternity but of mortality.

CHAPTER VIII

Declan Donnellan's production with the Maly Drama Theatre, St Petersburg, 1997

Reflection on translation confirms a fact well known to theatre semioticians: the text is only one of the elements of performance and, in the context of the activity of *translating*, the text is much more than a series of words: grafted on to it are ideological, ethnological, and cultural dimensions. (Patrice Pavis, 'Problems of Translation for the Stage: Interculturalism and Post-modern Theatre', 41)

Declan's sober and non-romantic approach to directing makes this interpretation of this tale very unique ... It is always useful to meet a director with different concepts, a different approach to the play. Especially of a different national background. It makes you aware of new possibilities. It makes you look at things from a new angle (Lev Dodin, in interview by Naum Pinkhasik, 3 October 2004).[1]

The Winter's Tale as performed in Russian by the ensemble of the Maly Drama Theatre of St Petersburg presents what Dennis Kennedy calls a 'complicated theatrical internationalism', a 'postmodern condition of nearly borderless theatre' (*Foreign Shakespeare*, 15–16). A team of noted British theatre artists, director Declan Donnellan and designer Nick Ormerod, collaborated with the distinguished Maly ensemble for a production of *The Winter's Tale* that premiered in St Petersburg on 30 October 1997. After its performance in Moscow in April 1999, it was awarded Russia's Golden Mask (equal to Britain's Olivier Award) for Best Production – the first production by a non-Russian director to receive that distinction – and was further honoured by Golden Mask nominations of Pyotr Semak (Leontes) for Best Actor and Declan Donnellan for Best Director. Performances of *The Winter's Tale* occurred not only in Russia but also in

England: touring six English cities, 27 April – 4 June 1999, it was performed in Russian with English surtitles.

Internationally acclaimed for its cohesive, permanent ensemble; its intensive, continuous training of actors; dynamic working methods; and socially engaged productions, the Maly Drama Theatre was awarded by the Union of European Theatres, in September 1998, the title of 'Théâtre de l'Europe'. It is a distinction held by only a few other theatres; the first to receive it was the Odéon in Paris, the second, Strehler's Piccolo Teatro di Milano.[2] After Lev Dodin became Artistic Director of the Maly in 1983, he built on the work of his predecessor Efim Padve and developed the Maly into a world-renowned company (of over sixty actors, in an enlarged auditorium holding approximately 460 people) that Peter Brook has called 'the finest ensemble theatre in Europe' (*Time Out*, 13–20 April 1994). Since the Maly's first performance in the West in 1988, it has taken productions by Dodin to Britain, Canada, France, the United States, Germany, Greece, Italy, Yugoslavia, and Japan, among other countries. 'We have travelled half the world', Dodin has said; we 'have realised that our spectators live in different parts of the world ... In this sense I consider [the Maly] a European theatre' (interview with Arkady Ostrovsky, *Financial Times*, 5 June 1999).

International crosscurrents making the 1997 Maly production of *The Winter's Tale* possible had been developing for over a decade. Donnellan met Dodin in 1986 in Helsinki, where each, separately, was directing a Finnish production; they grew to admire each other's work over years of international theatre festivals (Shevstova, *Dodin*, 31–2). The Maly's extraordinary commitment to ensemble acting influenced Donnellan and Ormerod after they founded their own company, Cheek by Jowl, in 1981. Subsequently the company brought several of their Shakespeare productions (in English) to the Maly Drama Theatre: *Measure for Measure* (1994), a revival of their all-male *As You Like It* (1994), and *Othello* (2004).

The Maly Drama Theatre ensemble had never acted with a British director until Donnellan was invited to guest direct in 1997.[3] In the Maly ensemble 'there was a tremendous hunger to do Shakespeare', Donnellan has said. 'I chose a play I wanted to do anyway, but which is about being people looking back – it's about forgiveness and redemption after a long period of estrangement. It isn't explicitly about the Russian condition but obviously we drew on the actors' experience' (quoted in *Metro*, London, 25 May 1999).

One result of drawing on the experience of the Maly company in its historical contexts was that the play's political critique, so often given minimal attention in criticism and production, was given prominence and located in Russian cultural moments. Early seventeenth-century English concerns about the dangers of Jacobean absolutism, exposed in Leontes' tyranny, were at moments re-imagined to carry resonances of twentieth-century Russia. Donnellan avoided a heavy-handed 'concept' or imposing a message: 'We are not saying that this is a didactic comment on Russia. These are just the references that we use to tell the story. Russia is just very rich in strong, resonant references' (quoted in *Financial Times*, 25 April 1999). Yet, as Pavis has noted, telling the story in any theatrical production, especially one rendered into another language, is inevitably to have 'grafted on to it' other 'cultural dimensions' (Pavis, 41).

Enculturation encompasses far more than a text; nonetheless, particulars of a linguistic translation being used and the production text prepared from that translation are critical factors. The Russian translation used in the Maly production of *The Winter's Tale* was by Pyotr Gnedich (1855–1925), first published in 1904 (by Brokhaus-Efron) in a fourth volume of Shakespeare's complete works. Used in the 1903 production of *The Winter's Tale* at the Alexandrinsky Theatre in St Petersburg, where Gnedich – playwright, producer, art historian, and translator – had been head of the company since 1901, the translation seems for its time partially to have moved away from high romantic styles. The Russian critic Leonid Popov thought that the Maly 'selected the not-so-new translation of Pyotr Gnedich specifically because it is farthest from romantic, elevated language: Shakespeare is a bit rough in this translation – and thus, possibly, maximally adequate in comparison to the original' (*Evening Petersburg*, 31 October 1997).

Not all scholars would agree with Popov's word 'rough', but the translation (at least in the production script), if not always 'farthest from' elevated language, does at times sharpen the colloquial force of parts of the Shakespearean text. Most Russian reviewers found that Gnedich's translation, though it dates from the reign of Nicholas II (1868–1918), was still effective and clear to contemporary audiences. One reviewer qualified her response: 'In spite of the archaism of Gnedich's translation, the play sounds contemporary' (Olga Bobrova, *Petersburg Gazette*, 7 November 1997, 5). Lev Dodin, to judge from his assessment of Gnedich's translation, would agree that the translation can seem 'contemporary' but would challenge the term 'archaism'. For him, Gnedich's translation 'has two important ingredients. First, it is very stylish and classical ... meaning it reflects the time in which it was created.' Second, he adds: 'At the same time, the language is simple enough to be relevant for a modern audience. I'm really against using translations that are, how to put it, archaic.' For Dodin, when 'old-fashioned language overpowers and muddies' the 'original', it 'becomes more a museum manuscript'. But he is also 'suspicious of translations that are too modernized' because they 'kill the poetic quality' of the text. For Lev Dodin, Gnedich's work avoids both extremes: 'So this combination of classical high style with its patina of time and absolutely modern simplicity is characteristic of Gnedich's style and differentiates him from the extremes of other translators' (interview).

Working from the Maly production script based on Gnedich's translation, Olga Kuskova noted significant differences between it and the English Shakespearean text.[4] Considerable cutting – approximately eight hundred lines – was done for the production script. Apart from cutting, among the most important linguistic differences were that certain Russian words had an even sharper colloquial edge than was suggested by their equivalents in the Shakespearean text, and that other words were intensified – some subtly, some strongly. For example, when Leontes demands of his lords, 'Will you not push her out?' (II.iii.73), his strikingly harsh colloquial Russian rhetoric, according to Olga Kuskova, 'is what one would use to order a stray dog or a mouse to be chased out' and 'suggests both a dehumanizing and a perpetual process' – that this creature not only be chased out of his chamber at once, but out of existence for ever. In Hermione's line, 'innocence shall make / False accusation blush' (III.ii.29–30), the word 'false' was translated '*podliy*' – an extremely strong insult which can mean 'deceitful, dishonourable, conniving, inhuman, treacherous, [characteristic of] worthless low-life. It is one of the strongest insults in the Russian language' (Olga Kuskova). The translation thus sharpens Hermione's critique: not only do the charges dishonour her, but Leontes, in making them, has grossly debased himself. When Hermione continues 'and tyranny / Tremble at patience' (30–1), the Russian can be translated 'and the tyrant shall tremble before the victim' – for in this kind of trial, as Olga Kuskova put it, 'the defendant is nothing more than a victim'. In Hermione's phrase 'if I shall be condemned / Upon surmises' (109–10) the word 'if' is translated 'when' in Russian, thereby augmenting her critique of the 'rigour' (cruelty) which is 'not law' (112). These linguistic differences result in an even more steely protest by Hermione than is emphasized by an English Shakespearean text of the play. In Gnedich's translation, furthermore, Hermione seems even more certain that the outcome of the trial is a foregone conclusion. In certain aspects of this trial scene, then, Gnedich's translation enabled a political critique that was particularly trenchant, especially given the cultural resonances of the production's design decisions.

Court costumes in the Act I court scenes recalled the reign of the last of the tsars, Nicholas II, who, like his courtiers, often wore a naval officer's dress uniform. Leontes and Polixenes wore virtually identical naval dress uniforms, Leontes with a red sash, Polixenes with a blue one. Sailor-suited Mamillius reminded reviewers in both England and Russia of Nicholas II's son, the Tsarevich, who, as numerous photographs record, was often seen in a sailor suit. Costume designs provided resonances, however, rather than strictly imitating a fixed time period. Military uniforms 'were the best way to accentuate the aristocratic nature' of the court characters, according to the production's Assistant Director, Natalia Kolotova (interview).[5] Boundaries of one era crossed those of another; costumes for the officers in the trial scene, made by a former Soviet Navy uniform cutter, recalled for some reviewers the Stalinist era (1924–53), though one must be careful not to make a simple identification of styles from the Soviet years with Stalinist ideology. Hermione's Chanel-like tailored suit and the women's trial scene clothes (some of which were retrieved from the Maly's storage) were from the 1940s and 1950s. Such cultural resonances, from early and middle parts of the century, spanning two world wars and beyond, suggested to reviewers partial comparisons to regimes rooted in such differing historical contexts, ideologies, and practices as Jacobean absolutism, the autocratic rule of the tsars, fascism, and Stalin's totalitarianism. Though crucially diverse, the eras to differing degrees involved the dangers of tyranny. Because no one period was represented in naturalistic detail in the Maly production, audiences could see, when Leontes degenerated into tyrannical behaviour, dangers of authoritarian leadership in other times and places, both past and all too familiar in more recent times. Thus design reflected what Dennis Kennedy calls a 'postmodern delight in eclectic transtemporality' (*Foreign Shakespeare*, 15).

Transformations of the play's figure of Time, its suffering and hope, were played by the same actor in two guises: a babushka (an older Russian woman, especially an elderly grandmother) and a young woman. The dual persona was meant to suggest Time is 'ageless', said Natalia Kolotova: 'She can be both this and that' (interview). An invented visual prologue at the production's beginning presented a freeze-frame tableau of Leontes' court, in the midst of which Hermione and Mamillius were posed as if about to dance with each other. One figure was in motion, a kind of Grandmother Time – the babushka, with head covering, shawl, and a besom (broom made of twigs tied together), sweeping the stage as if, wrote Paul Taylor, members of this court were 'already objects in the museum of memory. Then the first chime sounds.' Called by Assistant Director Natalia Kolotova (in interview) the toll of a 'watch bell', this chiming sound at later strategic moments, according to Paul Taylor, also 'punctuates the action, either freeze-framing it or startling it into life' (*Independent*, 6 May 1999). Time as a babushka appeared again at the end of the first three acts, initiating the only interval as she swept the stage. At the beginning of Act IV, when Time re-entered, sweeping, she was at first bent as if old; then, having reached centre stage, she removed her head covering and appeared transformed, as a young woman with golden hair. Speaking of the promises of new life, she introduced Perdita and the Old Shepherd (stage right), Polixenes and Florizel (stage left), and Leontes (centre stage). Later, at the end of Act V, she made a final, surprising appearance. In yet another directorial invention, Mamillius had entered after his parents' reunion; Time then appeared (still in her younger persona), a silent reminder that he could not remain. Opening her arms to him, with compassion and firmness, Time took Mamillius away.

'Spare and open' design by Ormerod, which freed the audience from expectations of naturalism, consisted of a wooden floor and back wall panels, with 'four palace chairs for the Sicilian court of King Leontes, four benches [configured as two long benches] and a table for the Bohemian sheepshearing' (Jeremy Kingston, *The Times*, 7 May 1999), to which were added, as needed in various scenes, simple properties. At the beginning of the final act, Leontes knelt in grief by an austere memorial (with a vase on it) and presented Mamillius' toy train, together with red roses for Hermione. In the final scene, Hermione sat, as if a statue, on a chair placed on a short, raised platform. Minimalist design heightened visual groupings of actors, as in the freeze-frame tableaux. Partially 'unlocalized' staging easily allowed the unscripted appearances of Time at the production's beginning, before the interval, and in the final scene, as well as Time's scripted Act IV, scene i monologue. That 'less is more', in a phrase often attributed to Mies van der Rohe, was proved in the impact on audiences' imagination of the unseen bear, produced by noises offstage. Surrounded by terrific storm sounds, the figure of Antigonus stood with his flashlight amid thick darkness. Then audiences heard growls, roaring; Antigonus' flashlight having been extinguished, spectators stared into blacked-out space.

Ormerod's design supported Donnellan's clear direction, which Jeremy Kingston found 'precise and elegant, creating, through a general stillness from which violence erupts, the portrait of a dangerously polite society never far from chaos' (*The Times*, 7 May 1999). Writing of the 'tragic psychological split that so quickly opens up within Leontes', Alastair Macaulay, who travelled to St Petersburg in 1997 to see the production early in its run, thought Pyotr Semak, as Leontes, 'perfectly grasps the nettle' of presenting Leontes' sudden jealousy: 'His Leontes is poised, taut, from the start, and remains so. The ramrod spine, the impeccable diction, the absolute dignity and hauteur: these seldom falter. The change in his nature from generous chivalry to icy rage comes from his constant containment' (*Financial Times*, 6 November 1997, 23).

'When Pyotr Semak's Leontes' started 'suspecting his wife, his face became set in the rictus grin of a corpse', wrote Lyn Gardner (*Guardian*, 8 May 1999, 5). After Leontes' words, 'Too hot' (I.ii.107), his torment mounting during this first explicit extended voicing of his jealousy, other actors onstage froze, thereby directing audience attention to a Leontes caught in the toils of his inner imaginings, as he stared at Polixenes and Hermione motionlessly clasping hands. Selected actors freezing as Leontes delivers his asides has become common in productions of *The Winter's Tale* since Nunn's daring (and partially different) use of the technique in 1969; but, as Charles Spencer observed, though at times 'overused', the 'device is highly effective here' (*Daily Telegraph*, 10 May 1999, 19). A sense of 'something hard and unyielding, that will only break, not bend, provides a fine foil to the feverish emotions' of the play, thought Lyn Gardner: the production 'is like a piece of music in which discipline and emotion constantly tug at each other. You wonder if this was ever a really happy marriage. Leontes' jealous rage – a kind of illness or fever – is not so unexpected after all' (*Guardian*, 8 May 1999, 5).

Leontes' jealousy may to some seem unexpected, but to Donnellan it does not need to be explained. 'We all get jealous without a reason', he believes, adding, 'We have no idea why we are jealous, because we do not know ourselves. We suddenly can feel abandoned, lonely and enraged for apparently no reason but the reasons are locked in our heads' (quoted in *St Petersburg Times*, 24–30 November 1997). Prior to his first extended voicing of jealousy (I.ii.107–19), Leontes 'did not act as though he had suspected something or was disturbed by something', said Assistant Director Natalia Kolotova: 'Jealousy pierces him like an arrow' (interview).

After Leontes' jealousy broke forth in I.ii, it was allied with intense pride, expressed with explosive yet precise, incisive verbal energy by Pyotr Semak. Leontes, wrote John Peter, 'drives forward and deeper into crime, justifying himself in half-waking horror, like Raskolnikov before the deed' (*Sunday Times*, 16 May 1999). 'Decidedly frightening, rather than, as so often with this story, fantastical', was the response of the reviewer Simon Fanshawe, who found Leontes a 'simmeringly violent father' whose 'bitter and paranoid asides' were 'delivered to his young son' (*Sunday Times*, 25 April 1999). Leontes 'cuffs' (strikes) Mamillius (Ian Shuttleworth, *Financial Times*, 7 May 1999, 19), directing 'the bulk of his anger' onto him, 'hauling him back from attempts to escape and subjecting him to brutal interrogation' (Paul Taylor, *Independent*, 6 May 1999). Leontes then 'brutally casts aside' the son he first 'confides in' (Charles Spencer, *Daily Telegraph*, 10 May 1999, 19).

Mamillius, in turn, violently attacked Hermione in Act II, scene i, as if, wrote John Peter, 'subconsciously, he sensed what his father was accusing her of' – an action John Peter found psychologically a 'Dostoevskian moment', but problematic: 'it disrupts the scene', causing Leontes' 'terrible entry' to be 'less effective' (*Sunday Times*, 16 May 1999). Yet Semak's accusation of Hermione so portrayed autocratic behaviour that it made disturbingly intelligible Leontes' leap from charges that 'She's an adultress' to 'More, she's a traitor' (II.i.88–9, which was translated into Russian to mean 'she's guilty of government betrayal'). Alluding in Russian ('*Gosudarstvo eto ya*') to the phrase often attributed (rightly or wrongly) to Louis XIV, 'L'état, c'est moi', Leonid Popov wrote: 'In the royal household, a wife's betrayal is equivalent to a government betrayal – "the government is me"' (*Independent Gazette*, 2 December 1997).

Pyotr Semak's Leontes thus managed to connect the personal to the political. His performance, supported by stark sets with formal groupings of the court in naval officers' uniforms, made Sicilia seem sternly militaristic to more than one British reviewer: 'When Hermione is accused and led away to jail for treason, the courtiers line up with their backs to the audience like a firing squad' (Lyn Gardner, *Guardian*, 8 May 1999). Hermione, wrote the Russian reviewer Nikolai Pesochinsky, was 'led off in handcuffs' by an officer 'in the uniform of the Soviet navy' (*Chas pik*, No. 167, 12 November 1997, 15). Since the courtiers 'stand slavishly at attention around their tyrant king, the criticisms they finally manage to utter intensify their distress; and the trial of Hermione, played with a most affecting dignity by Natalia Akimova', wrote Jeremy Kingston, 'is a sinister reminder of totalitarian show trials' (*The Times*, 7 May 1999; see also Paul Taylor, *Independent*, 6 May 1999).

While taking care to cite Donnellan's remark that the production was not heavily didactic, John O'Mahony found Hermione's trial to be 'laced with visual allusions to Stalinist show trials of the 1930s' (*Financial Times*, 28 April 1999, 22). Professor Maria Shevstova (Goldsmiths College, University of London) found resemblances to 'a Stalinist show trial' a 'brilliant stroke' which 'inspired immediate recognition, as did Pyotr Semak's dictatorial Leontes' (*Dodin*, 32). Semak delivered what Simon Fanshawe called 'the portrayal of a paranoid dictator and its overtones of Stalin' (*Sunday Times*, 25 April 1999).

Among Stalin's numerous trials of those he accused of being enemies of the state, the most notorious held for the appearance of legitimacy were three large, public Moscow show trials of 1936–38, which claimed the lives of all but a few of seventy so-called 'conspirators' (Knappman, 232–3). Reviewers did not claim that the production's trial scene suggested the huge scale or precise nature of Stalinist show trials. Nor would reviewers think the Maly production suggested that Leontes' destructiveness was parallel to Stalin's massive 'Great Terror' (approximately 1934–41), during which, according to Sergo Mikoyan's report of the unpublished memoirs of his Politburo father (Anastas Mikoyan), between 1 January 1935 and 22 June 1941 nearly twenty million people were arrested and seven million died (see Conquest, 487). To draw a close parallel to the immense suffering under Stalin would of course be a naive failure to acknowledge both the enormity of that tragedy and the historical and ideological differences between it and the dangers of Jacobean absolutism probed by *The Winter's Tale*. Assistant Director Natalia Kolotova emphasized that 'Stalinist Russia was thousands of times more terrible than absolutist regimes of Shakespearean drama' and thought the play's power conflicts offered, instead, recurrent 'archetypal situations and behavioural examples' true for differing cultures and times (interview). Director Declan Donnellan did not set out to give a detailed depiction of a specific historical period, yet traces of the tragic travesty of justice represented by the show trials, which remained in the historical memory of the production's audiences, had a potent echo.

Critical reception of the production in Russia as well as England showed response both to its evocation of the Stalinist era and to the transtemporal recurrence in history of tyrannical rule. Yelena Alekseyevna's analysis was that Donnellan's

> choice of the space of Russia and the Stalinist epoch is not accidental. The despot king, painfully cruel and suspicious, is a figure that we understand better than anyone else. Both in deep history and in our century, there have been plenty of tyrants. The director does not look for literal associations; the actors, too, are interested in moral-psychological parallels, rather than in painting portraits of historical figures. (*Russkaya mysl*, No. 201, 11–17 December 1997, 10)

Nikolai Pesochinsky found that the production 'provokes political associations', depicting 'tyranny, borders, refugees, dissidents, sentences, jails'. Playing on a famous line of Pushkin's – 'There is Russian spirit here, it smells of Russia here' – Pesochinsky wrote: 'There is Russian spirit here, it smells of Soviet Russia here' (*Chas pik*, 12 November 1997).

Though focused on accusations brought against only one person, the trial scene in *The Winter's Tale* offers a sharp lens through which to understand that violations of due process – including maltreatment, imprisonment without evidence or access to counsel, and persons 'condemned / Upon surmises' (III.ii.109–10) – are recurring dangers of autocratic rule. 'Führer Leontes' was the Russian reviewer Leonid Popov's epithet (*Independent Gazette*, 2 December 1997). Already having judged Hermione guilty of 'high treason' and of conspiracy, Leontes stages her trial in order to clear himself of suspicion: 'Let us be cleared / Of being tyrannous, since we so openly / Proceed in justice' (III.ii.4–6). Hermione, in World War II clothes, was made to respond to charges against her by speaking into a microphone. Facing the offstage audience, she stood on a centre stage platform; officers in military garb stood in the background (see figure 13). House lights were up, making the audience more fully part of the tense spectacle. Leontes applauded his wife with derision as she spoke in her defence. Natalia Akimova as Hermione conveyed an awareness that the proceedings were corrupt and that she fully expected the death sentence to be administered. That Leontes observes the formality of allowing the oracle to be read, wrote Leonid Popov, is only 'a refined form of tyranny'; when the oracle declares Hermione's innocence, 'everyone is shocked not by that news, but by the fact that Leontes is stunned by that news and the sentence is not carried out.' With further irony, Popov added: 'The king acknowledged his mistake!' (*Independent Gazette*, 2 December 1997).

Until Leontes' repentance, Charles Spencer noted, the tragedy seemed 'even more savage and painful than usual'. In juxtaposition, there was 'a gentle humour in the Bohemian party scenes (the men are too shy to dance with the ladies) and a beautiful tenderness in the Old Shepherd's discovery of the infant Perdita that beautifully contrasts with the icy hate of the first half of the play' (*Daily Telegraph*, 10 May 1999, 19). The grown Perdita was 'pranked up' (IV.iv.10) with a wreath of flowers in her hair; she

13 Act III, scene ii: Natalia Akimova as Hermione, and members of the court. Directed by Declan Donnellan, the Maly Drama Theatre, St Petersburg, Russia, 1997. Victor Vasilyev photograph

wore a white blouse over which was a dress modelled on the traditional Russian *sarafan*. Her costume recalled nineteenth-century Russian peasant clothing, as did that of Florizel, who was disguised in a white peasant shirt, with a cord around his waist hanging down over black pants tucked into high black peasant boots. Only Florizel and Perdita wore such traditional clothing of the peasantry. Some of the shepherds wore quilted jackets and hats with earpieces; additional characters in the scene wore twentieth-century clothing characteristic of many working Russian country folk.

The Bohemian country folk spoke with a dialect partially styled after the speech of Belarus (a republic to the south-west of Russia that declared independence from the USSR in August 1991, some months before the collapse of the USSR in December 1991). Belarusian, an East Slavic language that connects Russian and Ukrainian languages, has a standard dialect characteristic of the Belarus capital of Minsk, and has many words borrowed from Polish. Belarusian is thought by some Russians to include among its speakers good-hearted country farming people who might, if they too readily trust in rulers, be easily deceived and manipulated. The production's quasi-Belarusian accent was deliberately stylized and not exact; it was used, explained Assistant Director Natalia Kolotova, not at all satirically, but 'simply because for the Russian ear it is the most amusing sounding accent' (interview). And to judge from reviews, that is how it was received, especially in Russia, where the dialect met with immediate and delighted recognition.

Cultural resonances evoked by the Bohemia scenes were not limited to Belarus. Donnellan, thought one reviewer, turned the Bohemia scenes 'into a Russian – or, rather, slightly touched by Sovietism – country village':

> *A la russe* outfits exist side by side with inexpensive costumes from the village shop [*'selpo'*], and in the celebration scenes, lonely girls invite each other to dance and, taking small steps, begin to dance. Everyone is familiar in this village – the simple Old Shepherd of Nikolai Lavrov, and the vagrant Autolycus of Sergei Vlasov peddling imported goods, and Sergei Behterev's Young Shepherd (the unsuccessful secretary of the party organization). Even the final transformation of the villagers into courtiers is reminiscent of the transformation of rural [*'selsky'*] inhabitants into city officials. (Marina Davidova, *Moscow News*, 16 November 1997)

While these aspects of the Bohemia scene blended amusement with gentle irony, other aspects provoked the laughter of strong critical irony. The 'brave new Russia of pirate capitalism', wrote John Peter, was one target of this production's Act IV, scene iv witty critique:

> The young try to look blasé and wear clothes they think are smart. Autolycus half belongs to this world and half invades it: with his smart-tatty trench coat, dark glasses, ghetto blaster and cheap videos, he brings the villagers the promises and curses of phoney prosperity. This is a completely Russian picture but also an entirely Shakespearian perception, as is the moment when Autolycus rounds on the two Shepherds like a brutish official, the type who has battened on people since the time of Potemkin. (*Sunday Times*, 16 May 1999)

Autolycus arrived listening to rock music (also audible to the audience) on his large headphones. He seemed the kind of con artist 'increasingly familiar in the new Russia', according to Ian Shuttleworth (*Financial Times*, 7 May 1999, 19). Repeatedly trying to snatch the Young Shepherd's waist pack, clapping his headphones on the young man's ears as a distraction, the better to pickpocket him, Autolycus eventually resorted to donning a fake sign with the Russian word for 'Invalid'. A familiar con act in much of the world, this stratagem recalled for some Russians a widely known children's book, *The Golden Key, or the Adventures of Buratino*, by Alexei Tolstoy (a variation on the Pinocchio story); in Tolstoy's tale the cat Bazilio wears a board on his chest with 'Invalid' written on it.

In his final costume in Bohemia, toward the scene's end, Autolycus appeared not as a Renaissance counterfeit courtier, but as an officious twentieth-century bureaucrat, demanding of the Old and Young Shepherds their passports – clearly made to look like the required internal Russian passports – and then exacting payment as his condition for giving the passports back. From audiences in the Maly this scene aroused the laughter of recognition. 'Technically in present-day Russia a Russian citizen can live anywhere in the country – that is the law. But in Moscow and St Petersburg the Soviet-era policy that one must be "registered" in a particular habitation has continued to be enforced' (Professor Karen Fox, email message to the author, 23 June 2007). Thus the operative reality is that, if you dwell in either one of these major Russian cities, 'you must have permission to reside there' and must carry the requisite documentation 'in your internal passport to that effect' (Professor Karen Fox, letter to the author, 22 July 2001).[6] Autolycus' disguises were satiric echoes of contemporary social types in the Russia of Boris Yeltsin (President 1991–99), types Maria Shevstova calls 'crass, wheeler-dealer New Russians, as this breed emerged after perestroika' ('Resistance and Resilience', 316).

Successfully given a Russian local habitation, the pastoral scenes were, however, heavily cut. Approximately 360 lines were omitted from IV.iv (out of a total of 835 in the Orgel edition), most noticeably lines 113–228 and 257–327, including Florizel and Perdita's lyrical dialogue, the dance of shepherds and shepherdesses, Autolycus' pedlar's songs and trio with Mopsa and Dorcas, and (a far more common cut) the dance of satyrs. Rather than fine knick-knacks for Renaissance ladies, this Autolycus flogged imported goods, and the community disappeared to watch erotic videos sold by him before Polixenes decided it was time to part Florizel from Perdita.

'It is a play in which fathers also turn brutally against their children', as Jeremy Kingston observed (*The Times*, 7 May 1999), yet learn to see better. In the midst of tragic loss largely of his own making, when Leontes is given the gift of new possibilities with the arrival of Florizel and the disguised Perdita (V.i), Pyotr Semak rendered the scene's tragicomic contrasts, changes, and tonal complexities with passion and daring. Still in mourning, 'sad and ageing', wrote John Peter, suddenly 'he embraces the newly arrived Prince Florizel, Polixenes' runaway son, and whirls him around, as if he were his own lost son, in an explosion of incredulous joy' (*Sunday Times*, 16 May 1999). A moment later, seeing Florizel's 'fair princess – goddess! O! Alas' (V.i.130), Semak's 'haunted Leontes', wrote Kingston, 'stares in a kind of horror at the girl he will [later] discover to be his long-lost child' (*The Times*, 7 May 1999).

Semak's complex intensity gave his Leontes a 'saint-like sorrow' (V.i.2) indeed. His depth and range in the final scenes prompted Charles Spencer to contrast Semak's acting to Antony Sher's Leontes in the 1999 RSC production. Sher specified initial triggers to Leontes' jealousy, and 'charted its terrible course with more precision and power' than Semak, wrote Spencer. But where 'the Russian comes magnificently into his own is in Leontes' tragic realisation of guilt, and in his extraordinary mixture of grief, happiness and physical frailty at the end. It is a performance that pierces the heart' (*Daily Telegraph*, 10 May 1999, 19). Semak's detailed work in the final scene, when Leontes, as predicted by Hermione, comes 'to clearer knowledge' (II.i.97), has affinities with Donnellan's own emphases in speaking of Leontes' journey: 'Time changes us', he has said. 'We can't change who we are, but over time we can see who we are. And sanity is about seeing who you are. This is a play about becoming sane. It is a play that holds out the hope of salvation, of redemption' (quoted in Simon Fanshawe, *Sunday Times*, 25 April 1999, 23).

Potential for redemption was intertwined with a profound sense of loss in an 'inspired rethinking' (*Independent*, 14 May 1999) of the last scene. Lyn Gardner found the 'final, devastating scene' the most 'fresh' and 'visually symbolic' aspect of the production (*Guardian*, 8 May 1999). Staging was elegantly simple. Members of the court were led in to see the 'statue' of Hermione, walking as though exhibits were to be seen; according to Assistant Director Natalia Kolotova, it was as if they were 'in a museum. When they all stand with their backs to the audience and to the plinth in the centre, Hermione enters and sits in a chair on the plinth. Then the court stands apart and sees her' (interview). Hermione's left arm was extended; her back to the theatre audience, she faced the onstage audience. Theatre audiences could thus see the responses on the faces of all in the court as they looked at Hermione. Seeing the 'statue' of her mother, Perdita clung to her surrogate father, the Old Shepherd. For music to awake Hermione, Leontes tried to sing, brokenly, a waltz theme heard in the first court scene and woven with variations throughout the production; slowly all onstage joined in creating the music. After Paulina's prompting her to new life, Hermione rose slowly, as if in a dream. Slowly turning toward the theatre audience, she moved forward. Earlier in this scene Leontes had gone down to the floor in grief; now Polixenes and Camillo supported Leontes physically until he walked forward, having been encouraged by Paulina to 'Give her your hand. In the days / Of blooming spring, she gave you / Her hand, now give her yours.' Gnedich's Russian translation (even as here rendered into English) was culturally layered, drawing on associations of a frequently used Russian expression, 'in the days of blooming spring' (as if to say 'in better times'), in order to capture this moment's complexity. Such remembrance of things past also evoked present consciousness of loss.

When Leontes touched Hermione's hand, amazed it was warm, she turned toward him, looking deeply at him for the first time; she took his hand, rather than embracing him. After Hermione then moved a few steps further downstage centre, theatre audiences could register clearly that she, like Leontes, had aged markedly; years of pain were etched on their faces. That the cost of Hermione's suffering was so marked in her countenance brought about 'a climax of crunching emotional force' (Carole Woddis, *Herald*, 10 May 1999). Leontes went down on his knees to her. Perdita knelt and bowed deeply, her face touching the hem of her mother's deep purple garment. The last words spoken in the production were from Hermione's speech to Perdita (cut to two lines, given here in a translation of the Russian): 'You gods, lower your gaze towards us / And cover my daughter with blessings!' Visibly 'worn by pain and time', wrote Maria Shevstova, Hermione and Leontes 'bend with grief before their daughter' (*Dodin*, 33). Their action now stilled, in a silent tableau, Hermione's visage remained dreamlike, in a 'rapture that is also grief' (Jeremy Kingston, *The Times*, 7 May 1999).

Cutting both Paulina's and Leontes' final speeches, Donnellan substituted a last visual sequence. Exact details vary in diverse accounts of the scene's performance, which may be due not only to inevitable differences in viewers' perceptions but also to changes in the dynamic life of theatrical performances over time. Mamillius entered, led by Time (according to the production script, Assistant Director Kolotova in interview, and some reviewers); he then slowly circled the stage, looking at each person surrounding the stilled figures of his mother, father, and the sister he never knew. Moving towards his family, he looked at Leontes and, in reports of some performances, knelt in front of his father. Standing, Mamillius then placed his hand on his father, in a gesture perceived by viewers in multiple ways, among them as longing for love, or as benediction and/or forgiveness. Whether Mamillius put his hand on Leontes' shoulder (as seen in a relatively early Maly photograph and in added typed stage directions in the Maly production script) or 'lightly touches the hands, shoulders, hair of his family' (Alyona Zlobina, 'The Truth of the Tale', *Znamya*, No. 10, 1999) or, as most reviewers and Assistant Director Kolotova (interview) report, put his hand on Leontes' head, the gesture was richly expressive. To Charles Spencer, Mamillius seemed even 'to bestow absolution on his father' (*Daily Telegraph*, 10 May 1999, 19). But tonalities were at the same time sombre. Mamillius was not restored to ongoing life with his family; Time took him away. 'Time beckons to Mamillius with a gesture', according to the Maly production script, giving him (according to one account) a loving but deeply regretful shake of the head. Time held out her arms to Mamillius, took his hand, and exited with him, as the lights went down, into the darkness.

Though most reviewers found these final moments unforgettably effective, John Peter raised probing questions about this extra-textual invention:

> The revival of Hermione is brilliantly staged; but then follows a moment of breathtaking sentimentality. The ghost of little Mamillius trots in, places his hand forgivingly on the heads of his repentant elders. Are they aware of this? If not, who is being cheered up? Ghosts are never comforting presences in Shakespeare: he knew that what's done cannot be undone. His great

reconciliations are always deeply felt but hard-nosed moral accounting jobs: hope is bought at a vast expense of spirit in a waste of guilt and shame, and it is the knowledge of this that makes the waste bearable and gives happiness a sense of maturity. Mimsy little ghosts suggest that you do not really believe in the ending and need a cup of sweet tea to cheer you up. (*Sunday Times*, 16 May 1999)

In contrast to John Peter's view of the 'sentimentality' of Mamillius' appearance at the play's ending, Lev Dodin cites this directorial invention as an example of 'Declan's ability to find the fine touch that gives the play its tragic intensity and meaning' (interview). Mamillius' gesture was 'free from the taint of false consolation', wrote Paul Taylor, 'since we recognize that it can only be achieved in just such a wistful, out-of-time moment' (*Independent*, 6 May 1999). Similarly, Charles Spencer found Mamillius' gesture 'almost unbearable in its poignancy, suggesting both forgiveness and a sense of irrecoverable loss' (*Daily Telegraph*, 10 May 1999, 19).

'Both' is the key word; John Peter's questions rightly warn about possible dangers of a return of Mamillius' ghost at the end, but most reviewers thought even this part of the ending mingled effectively with the darker tones of the production's final scene. Mamillius 'will remain forever as the ghost between his parents', wrote Lyn Gardner (*Guardian*, 8 May 1999). For Maria Shevstova, 'This closing moment is shot through with an unbearable feeling of waste – of joys that can never be retrieved, of broken lives that can never really be mended. So intensely powerful was the scene that audiences choked with emotion, knowing, moreover, that the road to salvation, if feasible, was taken at an inestimable cost' (*Dodin*, 33). Forgiveness, yet inestimable cost: Shakespeare requires actor and viewer, in Donnellan's words, to be open 'to ambiguity, ambivalence and, very, very importantly, to conflicting action . . . *The Winter's Tale* starts with the stakes impossibly high . . . and you have to keep the stakes there and at that level of energy so that people are torn in two directions, in equal conflicts in their souls' (Donnellan, London, 30 December 1998, quoted in Shevstova, *Dodin*, 33). This 'Shakespeare of torn directions', Shevstova adds, 'which start with an unresolved conflict in Leontes that drives his jealousy and finally leads to an amazing but dreadful grace, is the Shakespeare discovered by the Maly through Donnellan' (*Dodin*, 33).

Tonal ranges in the final scene and Semak's ability to present inner conflict, including Leontes' awareness both of the enormous destruction he has caused and of the possibilities of new life, reflect Donnellan's sense of what Shevstova calls the ending's 'amazing but dreadful grace'. Leontes and his spiritual journey toward redemption were at the centre of Donnellan's focus, more than the restoration of a community or kingdom. In *The Winter's Tale* as in other late plays, Donnellan has said, 'characters who are potentially tragic like Macbeth and Othello are given the chance to see ... Leontes is given the chance to see.' He added: 'At the end of *The Winter's Tale* there is redemption and there is love. Independent, mysterious, confusing love, a love that will save us whether we like it or not, a love that will save us on its own terms and not on ours. A love we run from because it annihilates us' (from the bilingual Russian/English programme available at the Maly Drama Theatre, St Petersburg). As this statement by Donnellan suggests, his major emphases were more on the personal, interpersonal, and psychological aspects of the play than on its political conflicts. Yet critical reception of the Maly production in Russia and in England has borne witness to the production's enculturation with what Donnellan, while avoiding 'didactic comment', called its Russian cultural and political 'references' (quoted in *Financial Times*, 25 April 1999).

Political resonances in the Maly production were the more remarkable because Russian and Soviet critics had often deemed *The Winter's Tale* a 'fairy-tale.' According to Artistic Director Lev Dodin, 'If you read the essays by Anikst [Aleksandr Abramovich Anikst, 1910–88] – one of Russia's foremost specialists on Shakespeare – on "The Winter's Tale", you constantly come across the epithets "fairy-tale" or "fabulous".' Furthermore, frequently 'Russian – Soviet – theatre nurtured an overbearingly respectful attitude towards Shakespeare and even in the best productions romanticized him out of measure,' said Dodin (quoted in *St Petersburg Times*, 24–30 November 1997). Supported by Ormerod's stark set and costume designs and Donnellan's relatively anti-romantic conception and direction of the production, the Maly actors, drawing on their own historical experience, broke from romantic assumptions which not only in Russia, but also in British and North American criticism and production, have often obscured the play's potent political critique.

CHAPTER IX

'A world ransomed, or one destroyed': English *Tale*s at the millennium

by Carol Chillington Rutter

Reviewing Nicholas Hytner's *The Winter's Tale* at the National Theatre, London, in May 2001, Susannah Clapp noticed that productions of this theatrically rather neglected play were suddenly thick on the ground. Hytner's was 'the fifth' *Tale* she'd 'seen in four years'. Were directors sensing something in the wind, some national mood that needed addressing? Perhaps. *The Winter's Tale*, once considered 'a "problem play"', was being mobilized, it seemed to Clapp, to do cultural repair work, to tell a redemptive story of 'a world ransomed', and she suggested that it was 'Consciousness of the millennium' that was giving 'lustre to this account of a new golden era being bred out of a frozen past' (*Observer*, 27 May 2001). How very different was the play Michael Schmidt had reviewed a decade earlier, directed by Simon Usher at the Leicester Haymarket: a dark *Tale* that told of 'a world ... destroyed'. Schmidt wrote in the *Daily Telegraph*: 'I used to think' that *The Winter's Tale* 'was a glorious redemptive romance'. Not any more. Usher's bleakly 'problematic production' spoke to him of decadence, human self-destructiveness, history's end: apt preoccupations for a century staggering toward its own uncertain end. Usher had shown him that *The Winter's Tale* was very definitely 'a "problem play"' (24 January 1991).[1] Of course, both plays – of ransom and ruin, of the frozen and the flourishing, of winter's secret, whispered tale-tellings and summer's rowdy sheep-shearings – are comprehended in the double design, in the twin experiences that *The Winter's Tale* explores throughout. 'Thou metst with things dying,' says the Old Shepherd to the Clown, his son, who's just watched a bear munch his way through a Sicilian courtier, 'I with things newborn': the old man is holding in his bearish arms the lost one, baby Perdita, his 'findings'. Depending on which way a production tilts the *Tale* (and by how many degrees), the play speaks with optimism of things new-born, of 'Dear life' redeeming time; or, despairing, it remembers time lost, love avoided, lives wasted, things dying. Productions of *The Winter's Tale* in England over the past twenty-five years have played between these two poles, occasionally offering spectators upbeat 'millennial Shakespeare'. But then again, 'Shakespeare *fin de siècle, fin du globe*': *Tale*s that have set Sicilia 'away' and 'ago' in St Petersburg, Chicago, or Narnia – but have simultaneously fixed on 'here' and 'now' to probe the heart of Englishness. This final chapter looks at some of this work on the English stage, ranging across eight productions (at the National, the Leicester Haymarket, and by the RSC, Complicité, and Propeller) to consider the choices they made, shaping the world of their *Winter's Tale* as one 'ransomed, or one destroyed'.[2]

First beginners

Each of these productions opened with bold stage images, images that announced the productions' interests, their visual regime, and a performance vocabulary for thinking and working their way through the text. On the RSC's main stage in 1999 in a production directed by Gregory Doran, Sicilia was put in tsarist Russia, circa 1900. Cued perhaps originally by Hermione's line 'The Emperor of Russia was my father', this setting located the play (with accruing significance) in an opulent, autocratic, and orthodox culture where the ruler ruled absolutely – but where the material power of the divine might enter human life awesomely. The opening was a formal state occasion staged in a state apartment, a long, wood-panelled gallery under (after Magritte) a billowing, silk-swagged canopy of clouds giving out (evidently) onto a balcony far upstage overlooking a public square. Leontes (Antony Sher), Hermione (Alexandra Gilbreath) and Polixenes (Ken Bones), swathed in ermine and velvet, a gem-studded Romanoff crown on Sicilia's sleekly oiled head and a full Prince Albert beard on his chin, first made a ceremonial entrance the full length of the stage, flanked by courtiers, then retired to wave at a distantly cheering crowd before tugging off the regalia – duty done – leaving the men to stand in frock coats knocking back vodka as they argued – manly 'brothers' – about leave-taking. On the Olivier stage at the National Theatre in 2001, in a production directed by Nicholas Hytner, the 'royals' were thoroughly modern figures that could have stepped off the society (or gossip) pages of that month's *Hello!* magazine: figures to evoke England's very own dysfunctional royal family and the anxieties – or rage – they provoke. Hytner put the opening in Sicilia's private apartments, an ultra chic minimalist glass-and-steel penthouse overlooking a London skyline where Leontes (Alex Jennings) wore chinos and a sweater and Hermione (Claire Skinner) kicked off shoes to perch herself on the arm of a leather sofa while the 'brother' kings – still kids at heart, still childishly competitive – tossed a rugby ball as they niggled each other with 'must go', 'must stay'. At the Leicester Haymarket (1991) Simon Usher situated his *Tale* in the 1930s in a world that observed the patriarchal rules of engagement grounding Shakespeare's text, a testosterone-fuelled culture of unquestioned family loyalty, vendetta, and honour killing. His royals were Sicilian Mafiosi relaxing under a sweltering sun – hot white light was directed blisteringly onto the stage – at an *al fresco* dinner, smoking, conversing, guarded by men in fedoras patrolling with snub-nosed machine guns. Matthew Warchus (RSC at the Roundhouse, 2002), too, saw the 'family' as gangsters, but a branch that had cut its ties with the old county (and its precisely observed old world courtesies) and was now living in 1930s Chicago – or perhaps New Orleans – where they congregated in dim speak-easies, wore evening dress like a second skin, spoke in a strange mix of accents drawn from North Carolina, Appalachia, and West Texas, and played, for real, scenarios out of Edward G. Robinson films. Leontes (Douglas Hodge) was a bald, bullet-headed thug in a dinner jacket; 'one of those strong, ostentatiously macho men whose swagger hides a rankling insecurity', wrote John Peter (*Sunday Times*, 21 April 2002). Hermione (Anastasia Hille) was a trophy wife to a boorish upstart: high cheek-boned, sculpted, delicate (or perhaps brittle), jewelled, her blonde hair in a Grace Kelly French roll, her sea-grey satin empire dress held up by diamanté straps, her soft southern accent making her the cultural superior of her husband.

All of these openings played across crowds and bustling activity, but they worked effectively to isolate Leontes' single self-consciousness, to frame the perspective from which he would watch and interpret the scene's next moves. And all of them were edgy, troubled by something not quite right between king and subject, father and child – or father *as* child. Sher's court was a whispering gallery, the place vibrating with his courtiers' low-buzzing gossip; Jennings's, a place of arrested boyhood, the table cluttered with executive toys, the wall papered with a more-than-life-sized prep school photograph of himself and Polixenes as kids in muddy sports kit. (By contrast, Sher's Mamillius (Emily Bruni, cross-cast to double Perdita) was a crippled kid in a *faux*-military uniform and a wheelchair – and sidelined.) In Usher, Mamillius (Oliver Payne) was a boy who played with snakes – and offered one to his mother, dangling it from a stick; in Warchus, he was a pint-sized magician in top hat and tails (Toby Parkes) who precociously 'performed' for the adults: his 'turn' was the 'dead woman in the box' routine, staged with a 'Glam Assistant' (as the promptbook called her). He sealed her in a coffin, made her disappear, then, to the screaming accompaniment of trad-jazz horns, brought her back to life, the coffin opening, the lady rising from the dead, the kid beating the Big Sleep. This was child's play that would haunt Mamillius' own future.

Other *Tale*s began by marking time – literally, figuratively. They opened with parties, liminal moments, in a Sicilia that had so much to celebrate – but a Sicilia where, did they but know it, clocks were running down and a world was about to vanish for ever, taking with it an age of innocence and expectancy, of children's games and play whose trace memories would linger, would later be remembered nostalgically in objects that would somehow survive the impending wreck. At the Lyric Hammersmith (and later, on tour) in 1992, Theatre de Complicité's Sicilia exploded from a huge wardrobe, a fairy tale erupting from Narnia into the funky acoustic world of a Diana Ross hit single, a royal court on holiday bringing with them fireworks, red balloons, a Christmas tree; popping champagne corks and playing blind man's bluff. This was a scene of 'intoxicated frenzy' (wrote Michael Billington, *Guardian*, 4 April 1992) that, for theatre spectators, suddenly sobered up when Leontes (Simon McBurney) appeared on top of the wardrobe, 'gazing miserably down' as 'his heart' was 'gnawed' by the infection worming its way into him (Charles Spencer, *Daily Telegraph*, 10 April 1992).

In the Swan production (RSC, 2006) directed by Dominic Cooke in a promenade space dressed for a high-spirited 1940s high society 'do', the adults were celebrating New Year – Mamillius (Jonathan Clowes) clearly having been allowed to stay up past bedtime. A clock chimed, the dance music died, a raucous countdown to midnight began, 'happy new year!' rang out, everyone – promenaders included – joined hands to sing *Auld Lang Syne*. Then, as the crowds dispersed, groups breaking into pairs, hugs, handshakes and congratulations exchanged, two champagne-drinking courtiers appeared on a balcony, surveying the happy scene, to comment on a friendship between Sicilia and Bohemia that, 'rooted' in 'their childhoods', could not 'choose but branch now': 'there is not in the world either malice or matter to alter it.' In 1992, in a production directed by Adrian Noble on the RSC's main stage, the party the adults had organized was for Mamillius – a birthday party for an Edwardian seven-year old. Dressed in a brand new blue sailor suit (his first long trousers?), Mamillius (Marc Elliott) sat alone, far downstage in the dark before the lights came up, the only child attending this party, playing with a snow scene in a glass globe which instantly evoked the opening of *Citizen Kane*, the lost childhood remembered in 'Rosebud', and the film's dissolve into a snow-bound history contained in a glass. Shaking his little world, holding it high above his head to catch the light as he watched the snow settle, Mamillius at play seemed to be summoning up parallel play, another scene from another closed-in world: behind him the lights came up on a white gauze box, reaching up into the flies. Inside was his parents' court – twenty adults in formal dinner clothes sat conversing and laughing, their gilt chairs tied with red, blue, yellow balloons.

Again, all of these openings were troubled: Complicité's by the sweating, twitching surveillance of Leontes; Cooke's by the distance, in that heaving sea of guests, that had opened up between the wire-rim spectacled Leontes (Anton Lesser), who looked more like an accountant than a king, and his sumptuous, full-bodied Queen (Kate Fleetwood); Noble's by the weird, hallucinatory feel of the action seen through the gauze that distorted innocent gestures into actions somehow lewd, Hermione (Samantha Bond) bending forward to catch what Polixenes was saying – or perhaps thrusting herself into his hungry face. Here, the multiple, queasy, clean-but-dirty meanings of 'Go play, boy, play – thy mother plays, and I / Play too' were anticipated.

Propeller's *Winter's Tale* (directed by Edward Hall, Newbury Watermill Theatre, 2005, then on tour) came after Hytner, and after Warchus. It came, that is, after a couple of hijacked planes slamming into the twin towers of New York's World Trade Center exploded in the smug face of western capitalist democracies whatever 'millennial consciousness' of a new golden age they'd so far entertained. But after, too, what Russia considered its own national version of 9/11: the Beslan school siege in September 2004 that ended with 334 hostages dead, 186 of them children. And after, in the UK, the Soham schoolgirl murders, which played out across British television screens night after night in the summer of 2003, the killing of children in the house of their favourite teacher by her partner, the school caretaker. In England, where terrorism and IRA bombing campaigns were recent history, a terrible national prep-course (had we but known it) for a post-9/11 world, it was Soham that stopped middle England's heart, Soham that particularized the fears 9/11 put on general release. The stunning terrorist attacks in New York (attacks the world shared; attacks the world watched on television as moment by moment they unfolded) produced, even for spectators struck by the complicated politics of the attacks, an overwhelming global sense of the fragility of human life. But it was the localized, domestic attacks on the school and the household that brought the realization home: we were living in a world where we could not save our children. And we were living in a world where children were not just the victims of abuse by adults, of (mass, domestic) atrocity; they were as likely to be atrocity's perpetrators. This, post-Soham, was the terrible burden of Martin McDonagh's dystopian (but very English) *The Pillowman*, with its *fin du globe* fairy tales of child killing and child suicide, which played at the National Theatre then toured the UK throughout 2004.

Performed by Edward Hall's all-male company and visibly bearing the weight of current anxieties about the cultural valuation of childhood – the precious child versus the throw-away child – Propeller's *Winter's Tale* turned the optical instrument of Shakespeare's playtext around, to begin by looking not at the mind of Leontes in the making but at the mind of the *next* Leontes in the making. This production opened with a single figure, a child, a boy in striped pyjamas, Mamillius (Tam

Williams) alone on a cold, blue-lit stage, himself held in a circle of golden light, playing with android-shaped dolls. Into his toy wagon from above fell a stream of sand, as though spilling from some cracked cosmic hourglass. This wordless play scene, a kind of 'time out', ended when the adults burst in and their play took over – and Mamillius retreated to the edge of that 'grown up' world to gaze on 'with a haunted horrified look', as though 'the whole thing' were 'a midwinter night's dream, in which the latent anxieties of a boy' about what would 'be expected of him as a man' were 'feverishly played out' (Dominic Cavendish, *Daily Telegraph*, 1 February 2005). This was a *Winter's Tale* that extended the work of earlier directors who had foregrounded the role of Mamillius: Declan Donnellan with the Maly Theatre Company in 1997 (see Chapter VIII); Warchus, 2002; and Hytner, 2001, where Mamillius was another pint-sized hot-housed 'performer', this one (Thomas Brown-Lowe) kitted out like a Lilliputian Father Time, complete with scythe and wings, who served as a prologue, reciting for the grown-ups Shakespeare's Sonnet 12 ('When I do count the clock that tells the time') before retreating upstage to play Schubert on a grand piano. Edward Hall took things further. His was a *Winter's Tale* that would be seen through the eyes of the child, a story all about a boy.

'Infection'

What trips Leontes' mind into the spasm that erupts in his 'Too hot, too hot!'? For McBurney's Leontes (Complicité, 1992), paranoia was chronic, brought on with his first entrance; for John Nettles's Leontes (directed by Noble, 1992), it was unanticipated, the sudden flipping of a cranial switch (cued by a dramatic change of lighting). Usher's Leontes, Kevin Costello (Leicester Haymarket, 1991), gave away nothing physically: he faced squarely downstage, calm, erect. (His insanity revealed itself later, as, dangerously, sexually, he caressed Camillo's face, urging him to murder.) For Propeller's Richard Clothier (2005), it wasn't so much a trip as a slow slide. The Watermill's stage is a postage stamp, and the 150 spectators the theatre can hold are pushed right up against the stage on three sides, less an audience than collaborators complicit in imagining the story they're making happen. This stage was furnished to look like a gentlemen's snug (complete with upright piano and bearskin rug) in an oak-panelled Jacobean hall that had been renovated from something much older: bits of Greek masonry, no longer structural, were worked into the architecture, the white marble somehow 'remembering', distantly, a time when oracles were consulted and believed. Clothier's courtiers were men in suits who smoked cigars, drank brandy; Hermione (Simon Scardifield) was a dignified, gracious presence in a simple floor-length dress, her head covered, her pregnancy beginning to show. (Propeller's men make no attempt to impersonate the women they're playing; the actors are role-players, their costume signifying role, simply, directly.) To begin with, this scene of elegantly formal farewells, whose warmth contrasted to the chilly blue-wash ambience, was full of love: spectators were privy to a beautiful house party and a friendship that radiated good will. Only imperceptibly did Leontes segue into the absurd conclusions his male fantasy provoked him to. (When it slammed into Hermione in II.i, his violence was appalling: as she sprawled on her knees, floored by a blow to the face, he kicked her in the belly. Mamillius, lunging toward his mother, had to be restrained as courtiers pulled Leontes away and Paulina struggled to protect the assaulted Queen.)

By contrast, in Sher's performance (RSC, 1999), spectators could observe, precise step by precise step, 'the infection' of the 'brains' that finally felled him spreading along the synapses of Leontes' nervous system. The germ was there, somehow, already, waiting. In that first processional entrance, conducted in near dark, almost like sleepwalking, Sher's Leontes experienced his court as an echo chamber. Its ambient 'white noise' was court gossip hissing *him*, 'rattling around', wrote Benedict Nightingale, 'his paranoid brainbox' (*The Times*, 8 January 1999), silenced only when the full lights came up, the nightmare ended, and the royals were shown surrounded by adoring courtiers. Gilbreath's splendidly waddling Hermione, in dove-grey silk, the image of one of Queen Victoria's elegant Russian cousins, couldn't get her workaholic husband's attention when, his regalia shed, he occupied himself at a desk with state papers, peering through gold pince-nez, scribbling busily. Shrugging indulgently, she motioned Polixenes to sit beside her, then to dance to music from a wind-up Victrola as he told her of the golden boyhood he'd shared with her husband. On 'Is he won yet?' Leontes rose briskly, then nearly strangled on his own squawk of indignation: 'At *my* request he would not!' When Hermione playfully invited him to 'cram's with praise, and make's / As fat as tame things', and pressed his hand meaningfully against her bulge, Leontes began a smile, but it froze, then soured as she turned to smile at Polixenes – and spectators saw him suddenly caught, as John Peter wrote, at a moment when something happened inside him, 'like a blood clot forming from its own substance in his vein' (*Sunday Times*, 10 January 1999). Reminding her of their courtship, that it took him 'Three crabbèd months' of wooing before she would 'clap thyself my love' and 'utter / "I am yours for ever"', he stood rigid, his face taut, terrible, the recollection unexpectedly dangerous. His hands laced in hers made a playful motion that turned into painful grinding: the memory was a test that she failed when, acknowledging her 'for ever' 'royal husband', she turned to extend a gracious hand to a 'some while ... friend'. Across her 'turned' body, Leontes saw his truth: 'Too hot, too hot!' As John Peter observed, as the scene went on, this was a performance that portrayed 'the side of Leontes that Leontes does not know'. He 'knows that jealousy is terrible to feel but not that it is undignified to see'. Sher played 'its ridiculous aspect: the tetchy, irascible little man scavenging for clues in Hermione's handbag', who, looking for comfort in the 'fact' that cuckoldry is the common destiny of man, strode downstage to peer primly into the front rows of the audience, pointing to 'a man there' who 'holds his wife by th'arm', never thinking she's been 'sluiced in's absence' by 'Sir Smile, his neighbour' – a finger flick indicating a fellow sitting one row back. This was a man who looked for betrayal, expected betrayal, found betrayal, sweated betrayal from every pore. The slicked-back hair cork-screwed, as though twisted by betrayal. Scene by scene, his gestures epilepsied, as though the actions that betrayal produced were the absurd disjointed moves of a wind-up toy. More and more shrill under pressure of his incredulous courtiers in II.i, Leontes was finally felled by betrayal: he keeled over backward, dropped like an oak. News of Hermione's death felled him again. He knelt, sobbing, heaving his grief through a shuddering frame, clutching at a heart that was breaking, then reached out arms to Paulina to lead him, childlike, away. Sixteen years later, he would be found in this same state of collapse, knees hunched up, sitting on the floor, back against the wall of his empty state apartment, eyes staring past the little book hanging listlessly from his hand.

'Good Queen, I say good Queen'

Compared to Leontes and Polixenes with their shared history of prelapsarian childhood, their 'boy eternal', Hermione has no back-story – except what she reveals at her trial of her just-lost present ('your favour', the 'crown and comfort of my life', 'lost, for I do feel it gone, / But know not how it went') and, breathtakingly, fleetingly, of her own childhood, 'The Emperor of Russia was my father'. Rather than containing a past, the role is about the future. It's about imminence. The ripening female body that publicly proclaims its active sexuality ('mutual entertainment' that, as *Measure for Measure* puts it, is 'writ' upon the woman) flaunts, too, the triumph of that female body. Almost at term, her pregnancy splendidly demonstrates the consort's fulfilment of her duty to the royal bed. For Gilbreath (RSC, 1999), Hermione's pregnancy was key to her sensual unselfconsciousness, her frank openness: her gravid heaviness made her sit with legs splayed, made her lean into Polixenes' support. For Hille, too (RSC, 2002), though a cooler queen, the pregnant body licensed itself. When Hille's Hermione felt the baby kick, she grabbed the hands of Leontes *and* Polixenes and planted them *both* on her belly. Gently teasing, touching, moving between men, her hands eloquent, Simon Scardifield's Hermione (Propeller, 2005) was entirely dignified – and entirely at ease: a devoted wife, an adoring mother to a Mamillius who looked to her for prompts, for approval. (In the opening scene, all of these Hermiones were queens first, mothers second: Hille observed her precocious show-off son indulgently from a distance; Gilbreath vaguely noticed her crippled son, parked in a corner, where he kept his head down, hunched over his drawing. Neither was, like Judi Dench at the RSC in 1969, a mother who grabbed her boy as he flew past and tucked his shirt-tail in.)

For Hermione, almost totally oblivious to the cross-currents of male meaning running like a rip tide between husband and friend, the opening scene is literally gracious: 'grace indeed'. That changes in her next scene, set in a 'woman's room' where (typically in these productions) 'women's work' is performed – laundry is folded or embroidery is stitched – while 'women's chat' – the old wives' tale – circulates. Setting up female space and female government, II.i then stages their violation. The child whom Hermione wants her women to 'Take … to you' – 'he so troubles me / 'Tis past enduring' – is soon enough recalled – 'Come, sir, now / I am for you again' – and invited to 'sit you by us / And tell's a tale'. But while Hermione and Mamillius settle into intimacy, the boy whispering his big-eyed, goblin-filled tale of 'a man' who 'Dwelt by a churchyard' into his mother's ear, another scene is superimposed upon that one, Leontes raging about the runaways, Camillo and Polixenes, before stepping in to the women's space to snatch Mamillius: 'Give me the boy.' When Bond's Hermione (RSC, 1992) protested, 'What is this? Sport?', Nettles's Leontes sent her sprawling with a backhander across the face, then as she crouched on all fours, heaving to recover her breath, he grabbed her from behind, groped her, playing upon her body his lewd fantasies: 'adultress'; 'bed-swerver'; 'let her sport herself / With that she's big with'. Found by her husband in the palace games room, Skinner's Hermione (NT, 2001) played the scene across a ping-pong table, so that 'sport', here, figured as an ironic joke while the place itself tacitly offered 'game' as a monstrous pun, both its innocent self and its obscene double, and a refashioning of 'go play, boy, play'. No such ugly wittiness operated for Hille's Hermione (RSC, 2002). She was simply, physically, brutalized: grabbed by the throat, her body, still in evening dress, twisted and bent, her head shoved down onto the surface of one of the cocktail tables, pinioned there one-handed while Leontes ranted. Scardifield's Hermione (Propeller, 2005) stood dry-eyed, immovable as stone, cut to the heart by the accusations. The evenness of her voice, leaving her husband for prison, spoke her determination to endure: 'I never wished to see you sorry; now / I trust I shall.' Significantly, Propeller's production put Paulina in II.i to witness Leontes striking his wife and kicking her unprotected belly, shocking witness that would direct her protection of the Queen for the next sixteen years.

On trial, Bond's Hermione (RSC, 1992) stood in the rain, the court under black umbrellas: a public spectacle exposed to the public gaze, she was required 'To prate and talk for life and honour fore / Who please to come and hear'. But in her long, black velvet coat, with her red-gold hair hanging plaited down her back and her face bearing not the slightest mark of her ordeal in prison, she was every inch the queen and loving wife, not least when she reached out a hand to hush her husband's insane raving, to protect him by pushing his mad accusations back into his mouth. Kate Fleetwood's formal Hermione (RSC, 2006) (in gloves, a fitted suit) stood on a raised wooden platform, marooned in space opposite Anton Lesser's Leontes, seated (composed, in suit and tie) on another platform, an unbridgeable gulf between them packed with promenaders who turned from defendant to appellant as if they were watching centre court at Wimbledon. Jennings's Leontes (NT, 2001) had set up a show trial in an interrogation room furnished as if according to some military instruction manual: a baize-covered table, a carafe, a single piece of equipment – a microphone – which Skinner's Hermione turned contemptuously aside, refusing to speak any way but directly to her accuser. When Hille's Hermione (RSC, 2002) appeared in court, her transformation was painful. Shoved into the centre of a circle, harsh light thrown into her eyes, she stood there blinking, dazed, wrecked, her feet clumpy in prison lace-ups, her body coarsened in a long, grey prison smock. Shockingly, she was tethered to the floor, chained by her ankle, but not so much a bear tied to a stake as 'a deer to warm up the dogs' (*Independent Review*, 17 April 2002), observed by a Leontes who lounged against a wall, as senseless as the bricks. Sher's Leontes (RSC, 1999) came to court in full royal kit: the dazzling crown, the three-pile ermine, the absurdly high-rise throne. But he fumbled to find his notes in his pocket, then again his spectacles; and he stumbled as he read the indictment, excursions into the buffoonish that began to register this trial a joke – until spectators were pulled up sharp by Gilbreath's Hermione. The Queen who entered was a ruin. Her hair was prison-cropped, matted; her face, grey, hollow-eyed. She was in a coarse smock, filthy, dark with sweat stains around the neck: her birth labour in prison had been awful. Brought to the bar, she stood there, fists clenched, swaying but refusing to faint, listening intently as the arraignment was read – and Leontes silently mouthed words he had evidently written. Her answer did with words what her self-control was doing with her body: holding things together, gripping reality by hanging on to history. Speaking slowly, measuring her words, never permitting the voice to pitch into hysteria, but registering the puniness of her husband's threats against the 'flatness of my misery', this Hermione conducted an anatomy of her present condition that brought her to the rhetorical question her accuser could not answer: 'what blessings' have I 'here alive,' she asked her husband, 'That I should fear to die!' It was a relief to Sicilia's suffering court when Hermione finally descended the bar, shuffling forward several paces to include the gaping crowd in her appeal to the oracle – 'Apollo be my judge' – but when she turned, spectators gasped: her gown was streaked with stains of birth fluid and dried blood.

This is a performance Paulina is required to watch. Deborah Findlay (NT, 2001) stood hatchet-faced. She was a cross between Aeschylus' Clytemnestra and *The Archers'* Linda Snell, in twinset and pearls, a bosom like the bulkhead on a battleship, and, like a battleship, formidable. Delivering his newborn baby to Leontes in what looked like the cabinet office in II.iii, she harangued him as he took refuge behind his mandarin-sized desk – then thrust the wailing bundle into his arms before smartly exiting, leaving him staring, stunned, at the baby who'd hushed the moment he took her. In Usher (Leicester Haymarket, 1991), Judy Liebert's dead-calm Paulina deposited the baby on a settee beside the father who sat, knees up under his chin, clutching his ankles, rocking manically back and forth as he shrieked at his courtiers. (Sixteen years later, she would nurse him, topping up his sickroom beaker as he sat slumped in a chair like the village idiot, slurping tea.) Myra Lucretia Taylor's sturdy Paulina (RSC, 2002) met Leontes over a pool table – his cure for insomnia. Squaring up to the thug, speaking in a Jamaican voice, she seemed to have a whole history of black (feminist) reaction to white (patriarchal) oppression to unleash against the tyrant. In Complicité (1992), a tiny fury of a Paulina in Kathryn Hunter's performance was like a terrier savaging Leontes, and all the more poignant in the report of Mamillius' death – since she doubled the parts. This Paulina, then, reacted to her own lost child. (Later, Hunter would double the Old Shepherd and Time, making her now the bringer of change and redemption.) In Doran (RSC, 1999), Estelle Kohler's feisty Paulina – an elegant 'mankind witch' in Russian furs whose tongue stung like a nest of scorpions – produced the baby magically out from under her shawl and shamelessly worked the crowd of enchanted courtiers, making them gather tight around her to see – 'eye, nose, lip', the 'copy of the father' – what even Leontes, caught, bent forward to discover in the tiny face. When she suddenly dumped the bundle into his arms – ''tis yours ... farewell, we are gone' – Leontes silently held his baby, a long pause, deciding

14 Act I, scene ii: Alexandra Gilbreath as Hermione, Antony Sher as Leontes, Geoffrey Freshwater as Camillo, Ken Bones as Polixenes, Emily Bruni as Mamillius (wheelchair), and members of the court. Directed by Gregory Doran, Royal Shakespeare Company, Royal Shakespeare Theatre, Stratford-upon-Avon, 1999. Malcolm Davies photograph. Copyright © Shakespeare Birthplace Trust

15 Act I, scene i: Stephen Rashbrook as Cleomenes, Steven Elliott as Dion, Joe Dixon as Camillo, Nick Sampson as Archidamus, and members of the court offer competitive hospitality. Directed by Nicholas Hytner, National Theatre, London, 2001. Philip Carter photograph. Copyright © Philip Carter

16 Act I, Prologue: Tam Williams as Mamillius plays alone with his toys before the grown-ups arrive. Directed by Edward Hall, Propeller, Watermill Theatre, Newbury, 2005.
Robert Day photograph. Copyright © Robert Day

17 Act IV, scene iv: Richard McCabe as Autolycus, descending by balloon transport, entertains Bohemians at the sheep-shearing. Directed by Adrian Noble, Royal Shakespeare Company, Royal Shakespeare Theatre, Stratford-upon-Avon, 1992. Malcolm Davies photograph. Copyright © Shakespeare Birthplace Trust

something, then groaned, roared 'traitor', and thrust out the 'bastard', arms-length, to his courtiers who scattered. At Hermione's trial, this Paulina listened stony-faced, like the Queen, dry-eyed, while tears silently slid down the faces of the other women. When Mamillius' death was announced, when Hermione collapsed, Kohler's Paulina broke through the barricade of men to tend the Queen, then brought news of her death in a voice so terrible, with accusations so relentless, that Leontes quailed before her, a harpy, an avenging angel of doom, who finally gathered up the weeping King and led him away, custodian of his 'recreation' and his 'sorrows'.

Enter ... Exit ... Exit ... Enter ... Enter ... Exeunt ... Enter ... Exit ... Enter ... Exeunt ... Enter ... Exit

As if to counter the appalling headlong, headstrong rush of the play's first three acts, as if to capture Leontes in the suspended animation of 'sorrows' he must daily contemplate across the 'wide gap of time' that will be his next sixteen years, Shakespeare writes a whole series of transitions in the middle of *The Winter's Tale* – of

18 Act IV, scene iii: James Tucker as Young Shepherd reads out his sister's shopping list surrounded by baffled sheep. Directed by Edward Hall, Propeller, Watermill Theatre, Newbury, 2005.
Christopher Kennedy photograph.
Copyright © Christopher Kennedy

place, time, mood, verbal and visual style – shifts that force the play through a pain barrier into a world where 're-creation' may be possible. First, Antigonus, the good servant sworn to do bad service, arrives on the coast of Bohemia in a black storm, instructed by Hermione in a dream to leave the baby she names 'Perdita' in the kingdom where, Antigonus (mistakenly) concludes, the child's true father reigns. Complicité (1992) staged the voyage to Bohemia: spectators 'saw' the journey as a ship's captain in oilskins carried a model galleon across a billowing cloth while downstage Antigonus recounted his dream-tale. At the National (2001), Geoffrey Beevers's Antigonus appeared in a vast, empty space, gripping the pathetically tiny Moses basket. The baby 'blossom' it contained was condemned to 'loss, and what may follow', but he found it hard to leave her, delaying the moment by finding her bottle, testing its temperature, nursing her one last time. Ben Onwukwe's Antigonus (RSC, 2006) left the baby sheltered under his umbrella; Andrew Jarvis's Antigonus (RSC, 1992) turned to go – but then turned back, bent over the child again, tucked blankets in more tightly against the storm. That's when he felt a hot breath on his neck, heard, above the storm, a 'savage clamour' – and turned to face a monster.

Antigonus' departure in the Folio may stand as the most famous stage direction in Shakespeare: *'Exit pursued by a Beare.'* But as Greg Doran ruefully observes, for a director trying to stage this play, 'the challenge isn't "Exit pursued ...". It's "Enter bear".' His bear, he admitted, didn't work. It was meant to emerge out of the darkened landscape, a monstrous form taking shape (helped by a metal frame, pushed forward from upstage) out of the billowing silk-swag storm clouds that fell from Sicilia's heavens when Hermione died. But more often than not, the effect looked less like a bear than a landslide. Complicité's bear worked better (1992). Played by Dhobi Oparei, this bear was truly terrifying, bursting snarling out from under the mariners' turbulent cloth, making itself *out of the cloth*, transforming crashing ocean into wild beast, disaster at sea into fatality on land – and bowling over bawling mariners like so many comically scattering ninepins.

The bear, that is to say, along with the terror, brings on *laughter*. He's the next of Shakespeare's calculated transitions. With him, as if coming out of hibernation, the play shifts certain degrees closer to summer, to comedy. How so? The bear makes us laugh ironically: in the bear, poor Antigonus, his desires appallingly materialized, finds the foster-parent he fondly wished for the banished baby in II.iii. The bear makes us laugh sarcastically: mankind is the real brute in the play; here, in the uncanny meeting of man and animal, Antigonus (Leontes' scapegoat) gets what man's nature deserves. We laugh like children frightening themselves in the dark with tall tales of 'once upon a time'. (But who would have expected a *bear?*) We laugh with relief. (The killer bear is so much kinder than the killer father. The bear goes for the courtier, not the child. The miracle baby survives!) Propeller's bear (2005) was self-consciously theatrical, giving a goofy, self-knowing nod to the pleasures of performance and the switch the play was making from pain. Man and beast didn't meet – the audience, instead, imagined the meeting. Antigonus exited. Mamillius, understood to be dead, still in pyjamas, still lingering in the background, performed Antigonus' death, acting the sinking of a toy ship and holding up his teddy bear to attack an android Antigonus-proxy. Then 'Bear' entered. He was the bear skin rug from the opening scene animated, flung over the back of an actor who made 'rah, rah' sounds – 'I am bear' – and menacing motions with his 'paws' before exiting in Antigonus' direction. Noble's bear (RSC, 1992) was altogether more realistic – and fearsome. As Andrew Jarvis's Antigonus fussed over the baby, far downstage, on a wide, empty stage where the light was thick with the storm's gloom, spectators became aware of a shape moving into vision far upstage, shuffling, shaggy, shambling. Antigonus nursed the baby. The bear, huge head swinging, approached, stood behind him, breathed hot breath down his collar. The man leaped up. The bear stopped, eyed him, eyed the bundle on the ground. What happened next was pure Marx brothers. Antigonus ran, froze in mid-flight, reversed course, leaped to save the baby, froze again, then flew again. The perplexed bear closed in on the bundle, stood straddling it, considering. Then two things happened. A 'wraith'-figure of Hermione appeared in the heavens as if returned from Antigonus' dream. And the baby cried – a tiny wail. The big bear gently swung its head, nosed the bundle as if kissing her farewell, then turned on Antigonus. In the theatre could be heard the sound of an entire audience exhaling.

With the bear, off, entertained by the courtier, Perdita's case is more desperate than ever. Abandoned, bereft, cast away to strangeness on a wasteland shore, the baby is lost in space, lost in name, lost in story. In 1992 and 1999, Noble and Doran intensified the lonely agony, directing a long, silent pause before the next entrance. When their Old Shepherds appeared (Jeffery Dench in 1992, James Hayes in 1999) they looked like bears, padded up in thick sheepskin coats and hats and furry boots. A look-alike bear, *like* the bear, the Old Shepherd turns the play another few degrees toward comedy. He transforms the play's acoustic. Since I.ii *The Winter's Tale* has been speaking in verse – and in a kind of verse whose surface slipperiness, sliding from this to that, from beautiful memories to rancid fantasies, from true things to their ugly 'mockeries', has produced the persistent effects of psychic pain. Now, the Old Shepherd's demotic prose – 'I would there were no age between ten and three-and-twenty, or that youth would sleep out the rest; for there is nothing in the between but getting wenches with child, wronging the ancientry, stealing, fighting' (III.iii.58–62) – stunningly introduces a new way for the play to talk, not least when, as Hayes played it, crouching over the bundle he had noticed when it started grizzling, 'what have we here? Mercy on 's, a bairn!', was pure wonder. At court, the baby was trash for the fire. Here, she was precious 'findings'. If 'A BAIRN!' cracks the ice of the play, the Young Clown's account of the 'two such sights' he has just seen on land and sea finishes the thaw. In 1992, Graham Turner (RSC) was a great, galumphing, gormless and totally endearing simpleton in miniature bowler hat, over-size boots and bib-overalls whose interpolated shout of 'Father, father', coming from offstage just as Dench's Old Shepherd moved to pick up the child, had the magical effect of ventriloquizing the baby, constructing for Perdita a whole new foster family. Equally magically, Turner's physical performance of the storm, and the wreck, and the bear, and the bear's human lunch was a *tour de force* that 'did' all the disasters in a clod-hopping ballet that, by playing into the rhythms Shakespeare writes ('sometimes ... now ... anon ... then ... to make an end ... he's at it now'), translated disaster into hilarity.

Productions of *The Winter's Tale* regularly put the interval at the end of III.iii, on the Old Shepherd's upbeat exit line, "Tis a lucky day, boy, and we'll do good deeds on't'. That means that Time, the Chorus opening IV.i, conducts spectators into the second half, sliding 'O'er sixteen years', filling the 'wide gap' with story, told across sixteen rhyming couplets – one for each year. 'I turn my glass', says Time – and turns the play several more degrees toward summer. In 2001, however, Hytner (at the National Theatre) withheld the interval, tinkered with the shepherds, and replaced Time's account (cutting thirty-two lines to four) with performance: little Mamillius, dead and captured now for eternity in that costume from the opening scene's sonnet recital that turned him prematurely into Father Time, entered, stood over his abandoned baby sister's Moses basket, put fingers to his lips gesturing 'Shssssh', then watched as Florizel entered, caught sight of a sixteen-year-old Perdita who had just appeared, and, love-struck, followed her off. Thereupon, the ghost of Mamillius gently carried away the baby's basket. Warchus the following year appeared to be quoting Hytner – staging, pre-interval, the same tableau of the lovers' first encounter; then, hard on the heels of an alarmingly realistic bear that only just turned out to be fake, he achieved the same uncanniness of Hytner's ghost effect by putting a real animal on stage. In this production the (textually remembered) occasion of Florizel's stumbling upon the shepherd's cottage was played out. A real falcon was released to swoop gracefully across the wide open air space of the Roundhouse auditorium – but, while the moment was dazzling, it was also, it has to be said, gratuitously imposed and merely distracting, one more 'Flash Harry' effect laid on, complained John Peter in the *Sunday Times*, by a director determined to turn Shakespeare's plays 'into big-time showbiz playgrounds' (21 April 2002).

By contrast, in 2005 Propeller's inventiveness grew organically: having acted the shipwreck and the bear, summoning histories out of toys, Tam Williams's Mamillius (perhaps quoting Hytner) returned after the interval to play Time. The depopulated court of Leontes stood frozen while the boy passed among them, whitening beards, making 'stale / The glistering of this present' even as he promised a new world of 'freshest things', 'now grown in grace / Equal with wond'ring'. In 1992 at the RSC (directed by Noble) it wasn't so much wonder that Time performed as delicious daftness. Across the interval Paul Jesson's Polixenes and Benjamin Whitrow's Camillo sat in wicker chairs set on the forestage against a heat-shimmering screen, the one dozing, a copy of the 'Bohemia Times' shading his upturned faced, the other finishing the crossword. Sicilia had been a place of chilly blue light, heavy velvet, coats buttoned up to the throat. Bohemia was sun-drenched; the only 'formal' wear under its hot sun was the linen suit, the panama hat. The scene was motionless – except for the concentrated flicks of Camillo's pencil. But then spectators became aware of something slowly (oddly) dropping in from – heaven? – a rolled-up paper, tied to the string of, absurdly, a red balloon (which 'remembered' the party balloons of the opening scene). Holding the string in one hand, so that the child's toy bobbed and swayed ludicrously over his geriatric head, Camillo unrolled the scroll with the other and read out Time's message. Finishing, but none the wiser, he peered dubiously up at the sky, perplexed; then shrugged, removed his tie pin, popped the balloon with a BANG – and woke Polixenes, who launched straight back into the argument he had evidently been half-way through when he dozed off.

Shakespeare offers one final transition to mark the play's final shift from winter to summer, from 'fond jealousies ... grieving' to 'grace' grown 'Equal with wond'ring'. It's the entrance of Autolycus at IV.iii. In Noble (RSC, 1992) spectators had the bizarre sense of suddenly dropping with Alice down a rabbit hole into a place where time and objects stretched – or shrank – or swung back into sight as distorted versions of themselves. When Camillo and Polixenes exited, the white screen flew out. Behind was a vast blue cyclorama dotted with clouds. Descending gently into view, repeating what spectators had just seen, the child-sized red balloon returned, but now it was magnified, multiplied, transformed into a giant bouquet of green balloons, an airship captained by Autolycus, floating down from the sky and singing raucously off-key. This Autolycus (Richard McCabe) was a down-at-heels 'city con man in battered Bud Flanagan boater and joke overcoat', a green plaid so eye-wateringly loud that it made spectators reach for their sunglasses (Michael Billington, *Guardian*, 3 July 1992). And he was dangerous. His 'wicked gobstopper eyes rolling and bulging subversively' under eyebrows that moved like exclamation marks (Paul Taylor, *Independent*, 3 July 1992), and his smile fixing into a lip-drawn snarl, he delivered a CV – ' I am out of service'; 'beating and hanging are terrors to me' – which he illustrated by producing a newspaper whose banner headline screamed 'Servant Guilty!' even as he pulled from around his neck a grubby scarf, exposing an ugly mottled bruise. This Autolycus, wrote Taylor, was 'a shrewdly controlled identity crisis' who could 'slip in and out of impostures as nippily' as he slipped 'in and out of other people's pockets'. Ian Hughes at the RSC in 1999 played an altogether more genial 'snapper-up of unconsidered trifles', appearing out from under the production's signature billowing silk – now no longer storm clouds or bear but evidently 'white sheet bleaching on the hedge' – pumping a little squeeze box and singing lustily as, one after the other, some of those 'doxies' he had encountered 'over the dale' untangled themselves from his dalliance and appeared out from under his rustic bed. He had once worn 'three-pile' but now wore only his long-johns, his skull cap, and his inventiveness: when the Young Clown appeared on the horizon, Autolycus 'magicked' from out of nowhere a dickey-collar and transformed himself into Welsh chapel minister. In Usher at the Leicester Haymarket in 1991, Robert Langdon Lloyd's Autolycus was distinctly nasty, a venomous son of

Mercury who, out of service, was the kind of masterless man who worried early modern magistrates – and who blights urban centres today. A guy who pissed on trees, drew a knife on the Clown, and made thieving cynical work, he was a threatening Autolycus who had no music in him. These performances took spectators deeper into their productions' illusions. Marcello Magni's for Complicité (1992) went the other way, putting 'performance' squarely into the lap of the audience. When his Autolycus came on, the house lights came up. This outrageous Zeppo Marx-style con man in shapeless coat and baggy trousers spoke in a furious-paced Italian that he then translated into broken-backed English as, astonishingly inventive in his physical performance, he accosted some hapless woman in the front row, chatted her up with hilariously suggestive gestures – then made off with her handbag. After Magni's Autolycus appeared on stage, Complicité's *Winter's Tale* was going to be a story that turned its full face to the sun.

Shearing sheep, fleecing shepherds, borrowing flaunts

Reviewers might complain of 'Flash Harry' directors who turn Shakespeare's plays 'into big-time showbiz playgrounds', but the sheep-shearing sequence in IV.iii – an astonishing sweep of 835 lines whose kaleidoscopically cross-cutting action zooms in and out of close focus on five separate but interdependent stories – is surely just the kind of bravura production number that begs for showbiz treatment. It is the kind of production number that Shakespeare, never shy of theatrical razzmatazz, was a master at staging: at Capulet's ball in *Romeo and Juliet*, on Pompey's (drunken) galley in *Antony and Cleopatra*; at the masked dance in *Much Ado About Nothing*; in the caterwauling midnight kitchen in *Twelfth Night*; on the carousing nightwatch in *Othello*. The challenge for the sheep-shearing scene is to find a theatrical language to ground its deeply felt pastoral ritual (ostensibly set in Bohemia but actually all about Shakespeare's Warwickshire) in a cultural space that makes sense of its complex references, its welter of tonally distinct voices. Here, Whitsun pastoral meets Ovid's *Metamorphoses*. Here, Proserpina and Dis debate horticulture over an English florilegium. Here, old men and lads who might have stepped out of the Wakefield *Second Shepherd's Play* tot up the fleeces they have sold, reckon their wealth, lay in provisions ('sugar, ... currants, rice – ... rice?'), and throw a party – where they are fleeced by a quick-fingered fox in sheep's clothing, one littered under Mercury, perhaps, but certainly great-grandson to the sheep-stealing Mak. This scene is thick with guisings and disguisings, with opportunistic people wearing other people's clothes, with dissemblers dressing up and dressing down: a daughter conning her dad (who himself is conning his child – just like the other dad in the scene); a prince conning a king; a servant, his master; a clownish Jack, his two rival Jills; and a con man, a genuine con man, conning the lot. The wonder-full and farcical go cheek-by-jowl in this scene; the sacred with the sluttish, 'country matters' with holy vows, festival with carnival: here a 'queen of curds and cream' is crowned – and authority, *uncrowned*.

In 2001, Hytner at the National Theatre staged the scene as a mock Glastonbury Festival, England's annual summer solstice mud-and-music homage to its (recent) hippie and (more distant) Druid past: Glastonbury's famous pyramid stage is built over the Glastonbury–Stonehenge ley line, and festival-goers pitch tents on farmland transformed into something resembling a medieval encampment-cum-trade-fair. Hytner reproduced the 'right-on' feel of a 1970s festival while importing into it various topical political concerns agitating today's rainbow warriors. The austere grey-toned high-rise of his production's first half gave way to a full-colour jamboree in the second, backed by a stylized panorama of a 'rural retreat' Somerset, where yellow haystacks (straight out of Thomas Hardy) decorated the horizon of an impossibly blue sky (this was England in *June*, remember). In the middle distance there were ridge tents and benders, a dilapidated car seat someone had dragged in for furniture, banners proclaiming 'Stop animal torture', a herbalist's pitch offering 'crystal therapy', piles of leaflets ('CO_2 emissions'; 'Kyoto Conference'), and a crowd of superannuated designer hippies in tie-dyes, dreadlocks, and standard-issue love-beads. While eco-warriors gave disguised Polixenes a hard time about his notions for improving stock by grafting plants (Perdita silently handing him a flyer on 'GM Crops'), gangs of tiny-tot flower children, faces painted like animals, dashed around the site. Phil Daniels's Autolycus was an electric-guitar-banging rap star in red and white shell suit who flogged CDs instead of ballads and, instead of 'Whither? O whither?', performed with Dorcas and Mopsa the 'Bohemia Rap', a

Shakespeare medley composed of one-liners (among them, 'out vile jelly' and 'oh for a muse of fire'). But while this sheep-shearing achieved a 'look' – designer grunge – and traded on knowing gags – Perdita's 'unusual weeds' were spliffs – it lacked soul. Actors were playing at parts, not inhabiting them.

Even less happy was the sheep-shearing at the Roundhouse in 2002. Ironically, a real falcon conducted spectators to a Bohemia that felt totally fake, set somewhere in Appalachia (viz., Daisy Mae and Li'l Abner) or Oklahoma (viz., 'the farmer and the cowman should be friends') or maybe Disneyland. The costumes were 1930s – and 1950s. The multiracial casting made no sense in either time-frame. The 'shepherds' appeared to be an extended family clan of Coen brothers characters. Felix Dexter's black minstrel Autolycus was apparently Jim Crow staging his revenge on the local poor white trash – in the historical context gestured at, a political absurdity. Blue jeans and neck scarves, shirtwaists and tulle petticoats underneath poodle skirts, funny hats, banjos and square-dancing – then jitterbug – and a mass of approximate American accents that got in the way of Shakespeare's full-ranging and demanding verse – all produced a sheep-shearing that did not belong to anywhere or to anyone, that didn't emerge out of any real culture: this was showbiz as superficial fancy dress. Like Hytner's over-clean Glastonbury/Bohemia, Warchus's corny cowboy Bohemia felt entirely 'produced'. Some empty husks that somehow *remembered* a real festival were there, but nothing of 'holy day' substance, nothing attached to the ceremonies that convey the deep spiritual meanings that are bound into a performance – like this sheep-shearing – that *enacts* a ritual, a ritual connecting real working lives to the cyclical turning of the seasons, the rhythms of the calendar, the astonishing mystery of human redemption, life-from-death.

By contrast, Complicité in 1992 grounded the sheep-shearing in a simple, stylized ritual. 'Bohemia' was a pile of earth centre stage (which would double, in the following scene, back in Sicilia, as Hermione's grave). Swearing their vows, the young lovers cupped earth in their hands and threw it into the air. By contrast, too, Propeller in 2005 got right under the skin of the sheep-shearing – literally. Sicilians (among them, Leontes) returned in balaclavas (so, black-face) and on all fours in woolly fleeces to *play* the sheep. There was something profoundly true in the impersonation: not just because they were completely winning in looking as bored and as daft as sheep look, but because, 'silly' in the medieval sense of the word, they were realizing on stage what Polixenes' metaphors recalled of childhood innocence back in the opening scene. These sheep connected nostalgia for the 'boy eternal' to the hard grind of rural life that, at the sheep-shearing festival, was on *holiday*. (Propeller's sheep, then, worked just the reverse of Warchus's falcon: it, a true thing, exposed the artificiality of the world it circled; they, 'mockeries', pointed to a world of profoundly 'true things'.) This Bohemia was full of flowers, garlands, song, English folk music, country dances, laughter, jollity, ribaldry – but no sleaze, no anxiety, no guilt. Inhabiting a little lost world that hadn't found its way out of the nineteenth century, Bohemia's peasant culture at the sheep-shearing was taking time out from back-breaking labour to celebrate its own 'triumph of time'. The shepherds were men of the land, simple but not mean. Autolycus (Tony Bell) was a big, wonderful rogue, a swaggering boozer in purple velvet trousers who lived his strut – but whose troubadour 'turn' was clearly stuck in the provinces, and in the northern ones at that. His gig had never played further south than Stoke-on-Trent. This ageing rocker (who, wrote John Peter, would make 'Rod Stewart look like St Francis of Assisi', *Sunday Times*, 5 February 2005) managed to fleece James Tucker's Young Shepherd of his entire wardrobe, an 'idiotic sight' – Tucker 'unwittingly (but avidly) co-operating' in his own striptease – that had Paul Taylor, for one, weeping with laughter (*Independent*, 4 February 2005). Florizel was a privileged toff out on a jaunt who had been surprised by simplicity, captured by lowliness – and evidently fascinated by an 'alternative' life that was teaching him to break out of his father's court's claustrophobia. Looking at Perdita, he saw freedom. Life. And so did spectators. Because Perdita was Tam Williams, Mamillius in a simple floral frock, returned to double his own sister. If Autolycus was the fascinating outsider, Williams's Perdita was the adored insider. *She was loved* – she was everybody's special child. And while she held modestly aside from the exuberant circle dances that went on during all the wholesomely bawdy banter – skirts raised, faces slapped, men mocked by earthy women displaying their sexuality – Perdita clearly belonged to this culture. Their native accents were also hers.

What was remarkable about Propeller's sheep-shearing was

not just the way it brought *The Winter's Tale* home (as Shakespeare's script would have it) to England, but the way it achieved a sense of lives minutely observed, of the earth, and somehow also of eternity – precious qualities it had in common with Noble's in 1992, where the emotional honesty and authenticity that Propeller produced on a tiny stage, Noble delivered in the vast barn of the Royal Shakespeare Theatre. Noble's inspiration was Stanley Spencer, the artist who lived his entire life in the small Berkshire village that was the background for almost all his work. Spencer's paintings of Cookham between the wars preserve an image of an England that somehow never was – and yet will always be: illustrations of a community, rural scenes, children gingerly stepping across barbed wire to retrieve a ball, hulls lined up in a boatyard, chicken coops against a yellow sky, mechanics manhandling tyres at a garage, a sow gazing at her litter through a makeshift fence, a woman scooping milk into the mouth of an orphan calf. But Cookham, too, was background to Spencer's sacred paintings. The Bible, for Spencer, was happening here and now – its incidents were the stuff of daily life. So he painted the New Testament on Cookham High Street: Christ, headed for crucifixion, drags his cross past local shop-fronts, watched by local carpenters in modern dress and housewives hanging out of upstairs windows; Christ resurrected explodes from a tomb in the village churchyard; Christ preaches at the Cookham regatta; St Francis talks to the birds in Ovey's farmyard. Seeding Noble's directorial imagination, Spencer offered a way of thinking about Englishness, about human particularity, storytelling, and, perhaps most significantly, the immanence of the miraculous in the everyday. Noble's sheep-shearing was set at a village fête, around 1953, coronation year: there was bunting, trestle tables loaded with plates of sandwiches curling in the sun, mismatched chairs dragged out from various kitchens, an oompah-pah band (featuring the vicar on drums), and, bobbing over the scene, a huge clutch of party balloons – remembering Mamillius. Everywhere spectators looked, they saw village stories. The Clown had scrubbed up for the occasion – in his Sunday best, his hair slicked back. And so had Autolycus: he had nicked a clean shirt and braces from some hedge somewhere and tied his greasy hair into a ponytail. A woman in an apron and house slippers wandered through the scene, handbagging the stranger who got fresh with her daughter. Two lads in short trousers – one pint-sized, the other a seven-foot-tall giant – blew soap bubbles. The Old Shepherd was in vintage tweeds, Perdita in a crown made of flowers and a dress printed with a cherry motif. Mopsa and Dorcas – the one in Fair Isle jumper, knit skirt, sagging petticoat; the other in ankle socks, Mary Janes, and plastic poppa-bead jewellery – played out their rivalry for the Clown's attentions over ice cream cones more and more furiously licked. Then, seduced by the pedlar who arrived in an overcoat that opened out like a cabinet of curiosities, they plonked themselves on the ground, skirts over thighs, knickers showing, to pore over the treasures he proffered before snatching at his ballads and launching into a hilariously off-key trio of 'Whither? O whither?' This deliciously lewd triangular 'wooing' in the foreground travestied the holy wooing between Florizel and Perdita behind, and its instincts were replayed in the dance of 'satyrs': local lads in clogs, red balloons (over tweed trousers) for testicles (inflated aspirationally), with broom handles phallically wielded in a choreography that both celebrated fertility and lampooned male anxiety. The scene was perfectly pitched. And it was absolutely right – once the disguises came off, once patriarchal violence exploded, threats flew, the crowd, abashed, dispersed, and the scene emptied, leaving the sad wreck of the summer party to desolation – that, somewhere in the far distance, a crack of thunder was heard.

'Dear life redeems you'

Returning to Sicilia, all of these productions found Leontes devastated by his history: John Nettles (RSC, 1992) sat in a wheelchair; Antony Sher (RSC, 1999) huddled against a wall; Alex Jennings (NT, 2001) sat beside Hermione's black marble tomb beneath smiling portraits of his wife and son; Kevin Costello (Leicester Haymarket, 1991) was nannied by Paulina. As before, Complicité (1992) staged the voyage: behind the toy galleon held aloft, a procession – all the Bohemians – wound around the stage, shedding Bohemian clothes as snow began to fall, transforming themselves into a moving sculpture enacting grief. Out of its centre, McBurney's Leontes crawled on bleeding knees: his daily circuit across the 'wide gap of time' was, evidently, an act of penance. And all of these productions caught the wonder of Hermione's statue. Gilbreath (RSC, 1999) stood in the same dock where she had protested her innocence; Hille stood on a plinth, hand extended (RSC, 2002); Skinner was revealed from behind a curtain (NT, 2001); Bond (RSC, 1992) was magically 'set' by means of a *trompe l'oeil* move that deposited her, centre stage, back to the audience, after the whole court – a gossiping, jostling, noisy parade swirling through the scene on their way to see the wonder promised at Paulina's – simply passed on, magically leaving the 'statue' behind. Reentering upstage, the court found themselves caught in the gauze box (which had returned from the production's opening moments), all gazing downstage at the statue. This production, then, wrote the wonder of the statue's animation on the faces of the onstage spectators, watching it happen. Dominic Cooke's production (RSC, 2006) gave perhaps the sunniest ending: Anton Lesser's Leontes laughed with amazement as Hermione reached out and touched his cheek. Complicité's (1992) gave the nerviest ending: McBurney's Leontes recoiled as the statue moved, then tentatively reached out a hand – crying, *roaring*, as his touch connected to flesh, 'O, she's warm!' Simon Usher's (1991) gave undoubtedly the bleakest ending: the Giulio Romano statue that Leontes and the rest gazed upon was – plaster. It didn't come to life. There was no 'miracle'. Instead, the living Hermione entered behind the crowd of miracle-seekers who turned to see a cripple on crutches, nothing like her statue stand-in; a body that bore the brunt of not just what Leontes had unleashed but the sixteen years since; and a face disfigured with scar tissue. So: no miracle – unless it was the couple's exchange of looks and their miraculous final embrace.

Making choices, all of the productions surveyed in this chapter have plumbed the emotional depths of a play that tests the endurance of the human heart. This is 'a great, puzzling, searching play', as John Peter in the *Sunday Times* has called *The Winter's Tale* (27 May 2001); a play whose effects his fellow reviewers constantly describe in terms of their traumatic physiology: its 'heart-stopping imagery' (Alastair Macaulay, *Financial Times*, 21 June 2005); its ability 'to crack the hardest heart' (Lyn Gardner, *Guardian*, 25 June 1993), 'to pierce the heart' (Charles Spencer, *Daily Telegraph*, 8 January 1999), to make 'your heart crack or your bones turn to silk' (Lyn Gardner, *Guardian*, 20 June 2005), to 'open up the conduits to the heart' (Benedict Nightingale, *The Times*, 3 July 1992). Nightingale quotes the play: 'My heart wept blood' (3 July 1992). Charles Spencer defies 'the hardest-hearted' to 'sit through' the play's 'magnificently moving conclusion' – a conclusion 'full of grace and forgiveness' – 'without blinking back tears' (*Daily Telegraph*, 3 July 1992). Breaking the heart, *The Winter's Tale* (it appears) strangely opens the heart, giving spectators at the millennium not so much a choice between 'a world ransomed, or one destroyed' as a recognition that, paradoxically, our costly world is ransomed by ruin. At the end of Hytner's *Tale*, Hermione and Perdita, mother and daughter, did not depart with Leontes and the rest of the court. 'Clutching each other like shipwreck survivors', they remained behind 'in a grave tableau', a reminder of 'those things that Time cannot redeem' (Paul Taylor, *Independent*, 26 May 2001). At the end of Propeller's *Tale*, reconciliation unravelled. Hermione pointedly spoke nothing to Leontes, and his courtiers peeled away, leaving the couple silently facing each other, then, when Hermione exited, stranding Leontes alone on stage. Almost immediately Perdita returned, but now no longer the daughter. Her dress shed, once again in pyjamas, Perdita was Mamillius, 'the son who is conspicuous by his absence in this reunion' (Paul Taylor, *Independent*, 4 February 2005). The candle Mamillius held recalled the beginning – the boy gazed at his father, then blew out the flame, returning this *Winter's Tale* to darkness. One ending, then, offered an embrace that was somehow also numb; the other, a gaze that closed off recognition with darkness. Ambiguous both, they demonstrate how productions of *The Winter's Tale* at the millennium finally – and finely – sustain a vision of this play that honours both its 'deal of wonder' and its sorrows 'waded in tears'.

NOTES

Introduction

1 Dryden's statement is from his 'Defence of the Epilogue ...' to *The Conquest of Grenada*, Part II, 1672, vol. 11, p. 206, in *The Works of John Dryden*, H. T. Swedenberg, Jr, et al., eds, and is part of his attack on the supposed faults of Elizabethan and Jacobean drama. For brief historical summaries of negative criticism of *The Winter's Tale*, see the editions by Orgel, Introduction, 1–2, and by Turner and Haas, New Variorum, 702–3.

2 For excellent accounts of the major renewal of interest in *The Winter's Tale* in twentieth-century criticism see Maurice Hunt, 'The Critical Legacy', in his edition of *'The Winter's Tale': Critical Essays*, 3–56, and Charles Frey, in *Shakespeare's Vast Romance*, 1–48. J. H. P. Pafford, in his 1963 Arden edition of the play, notes the 'growing appreciation of the quality and power' of the late plays, especially in structure (xliii–xliv). The preponderance of the evidence from 'General Assessments' of *The Winter's Tale* in Turner and Haas, 702–17, shows that the majority of critics since the second half of the twentieth century began have moved toward positive appraisal of the play's dramatic art and vision.

3 Two significant studies focusing on genre and dramatic conventions in Shakespeare's late plays are by Barbara Mowat (*The Dramaturgy of Shakespeare's Romances*, 1976) and Joan Hartwig (*Shakespeare's Tragicomic Vision*, 1972). Among other important books of the 1970s on the late plays are Douglas Peterson's fine study of philosophical patterns, grounded in the history of ideas, *Time, Tide, and Tempest*, 1973, and Hallett Smith's *Shakespeare's Romances: A Study of Some Ways of the Imagination*, 1972.

4 Sarah Grand, 'the pseudonym of Mrs. Frances Elizabeth McFall', as Karl Beckson points out, 'is generally credited with first using the term "new woman", in "The New Aspect of the Woman Question", *North American Review* (March 1894)'. Grand, author of a popular 'new woman' novel, *The Heavenly Twins*, 'became mayor of Bath six times' (Beckson, 141).

5 About the time of Barker's production of *The Winter's Tale* – 'a year or two before the war' – wrote McCarthy, she had been invited to No. 10 Downing Street to play for the King and Queen. At a rehearsal at No. 10, she found herself alone in Prime Minister Asquith's Cabinet Room: 'I felt like a Joan of Arc of the ballot-box. Martyrdom or not, the occasion must be seized. I opened my box of grease paints, took out the reddest stick I could find, and wrote across the blotting paper "Votes for Women."' She recalled the animated conversation with her friend Asquith that followed: 'He asked: "why do you think women should have the vote?" By Heaven, I told him!' (McCarthy, 149).

6 From Sara Pia Anderson's discussion with the cast and with me (19 June 1990), when I served as Dramaturg for the Shakespeare/Santa Cruz production of *The Winter's Tale*, University of California at Santa Cruz. Anderson has directed for both the Royal Shakespeare Company and the Royal National Theatre.

7 On these gender issues see Adelman, *Suffocating Mothers*, 220–36; Neely, *Broken Nuptials in Shakespeare's Plays*, 191–209; Traub, *Desire and Anxiety*, 42–9; and Erickson, *Patriarchal Structures in Shakespeare's Drama*, 148–72.

8 See John F. Danby's *Elizabethan and Jacobean Poets: Studies in Sidney, Shakespeare, Beaumont and Fletcher*, to connect the late plays to Sidney's *Arcadia*, for example, and Carol Gesner's *Shakespeare and the Greek Romance: A Study of Origins*.

9 For historical perspectives on political issues see Constance Jordan, *Shakespeare's Monarchies: Ruler and Subject in the Romances*, 1–34, 107–46; Stuart M. Kurland's article, '"We need no more of your advice": Political Realism in *The Winter's Tale*'; William R. Morse's article, 'Metacriticism and Materiality: the Case of Shakespeare's *The Winter's Tale*'; Stephen Orgel, in his Oxford edition of *The Winter's Tale*, 12–16; and Donna Hamilton's article, 'Shakespeare's Romances and Jacobean Political Discourse'.

10 J. H. P. Pafford, in his Arden edition, says Autolycus 'is to some extent modelled on Capnio [in *Pandosto*], who is an old servant of Dorastus described as being "a wily fellow"' (lxxix). (Dorastus is the prince in love with Fawnia, who is a prototype for Perdita.) But the resemblances of Autolycus and Capnio are both scant and superficial and have mainly to do with the servant's arranging transportation by sea for Dorastus and Fawnia. Furthermore, Capnio is not 'out of service' with the Prince (unlike Autolycus, IV.iii.14) and is neither a multiple role-playing con artist nor comically disruptive.

11 In the debate concerning the idea, put forward by Gerald Bentley, that the late plays differ from Shakespeare's earlier work because they were written for the Blackfriars, Andrew Gurr's view is that the 'company did not radically alter its repertory when it moved into Blackfriars'. Though, as Gurr says, the late plays make different demands on the company in staging, he believes they were played at both theatres 'unchanged' (*Playgoing*, 172–3).

Chapter I

1 Barker's first use of an apron was for a performance of *Iphigenia in Tauris* at His Majesty's Theatre early in 1912 (Mazer, *Shakespeare Refashioned*, 134). Barker's sole Shakespearean production prior to *The Winter's Tale* was *The Two Gentlemen of Verona* in 1904 at the Court Theatre; Dymkowski states that it 'by all accounts, was traditionally staged' (31; 241, n. 1). Among reformers attempting supposed 'Elizabethan' staging, William Poel (1852–1934) had the greatest impact upon Barker. Poel in 1910 (at the invitation of Beerbohm Tree, despite his differences from

Poel) had presented *The Two Gentlemen of Verona* at His Majesty's, with an 'apron' covering the orchestra pit – for the first time at that theatre (Speaight, 121).

2 Lewis Casson and Sybil Thorndike's 'Recollections of Harley Granville-Barker' originated as a radio broadcast on the British Broadcasting Corporation Third Programme, 20 November 1967. I cite from my transcription of key portions made while listening to the recording (NSA 1111) in the National Sound Archive, London.

3 This Barker letter was titled 'The Golden Thoughts of Granville Barker, Author, Mime, and Producer' when published in *Play Pictorial*, January 1913; Eric Salmon, ed., *Granville Barker and His Correspondents*, gives the date this letter was written as 'November, 1912' (529).

4 Barker's phrase 'perfectly white light' is from a newspaper article entitled '"Winter's Tale", Mr. Granville Barker on his Defence. Reply to Criticism', presumably from 1912 but bearing no specific date or source (Harvard Theatre Collection, *The Winter's Tale* fragile clippings file). The Scene and Light Plot (in the [W.T.] Account Book, Savoy Theatre Productions, 1912–13, Theatre Museum, London) shows the frequency of white lights, as well as circle lights, on full (e.g., I.i, ii; III.i, ii; IV.ii, iii, iv, v; V.ii and iii). One can understand Bridges-Adams's perception that Barker had 'swept shadows from the stage as if they harboured germs' (*The Lost Leader*, 12). Bridges-Adams believed that the 'hygienic whiteness of the setting' and the welcome 'absence of vegetation in the pastoral scenes' were 'part of an endeavour to recapture the daylight' of the Globe by modern means ('Granville-Barker and the Savoy', 30). But Barker also varied the lighting for particular dramatic purposes. The Scene and Light Plot shows that for Act II, scene ii, played in half-light in front of a cloth suggesting a prison, a blue light was used, as it was in III.ii, the trial scene. For II.iii, the stage was almost solely lit by the brazier, except for two blue lights, one of which, a circle light, was a dark and particularly dim blue (Scene and Light Plot, Account Book). Furthermore, a reviewer in the *Observer*, though aware of the dominance of white light in many scenes, noted 'the cunningly slanted sunlight, which does not (to our great relief) dispel all the shadows' (22 September 1912, 9). Though approving Barker's reforms, the reviewer did not want to eliminate fully what was residual from older traditions of stage lighting.

5 As Dennis Kennedy points out, the front-of-house lighting 'was not as innovative as the commentators assumed: Barker used a similar method at the Kingsway; Reinhardt and others had preceded him; and even Poel tried a form of horizontal illumination in 1910' (*Granville Barker*, 129). Mazer points out that Norman Marshall (*The Producer and the Play*, 149) 'erroneously calls Barker the first to use front-of-house lighting in England, a mistake repeated by many scholars including Styan' (*Shakespeare Refashioned*, 135; see also 227, n. 11, and 233, n. 60).

6 *The Winter's Tale* 1912 production's well-kept, detailed Account Book is listed as the [W.T.] Account Book, Savoy Theatre Productions, 1912–13, in the Theatre Museum, London, which holds part of the Victoria and Albert Museum collections. The Account Book contains not only the production's Scene and Light Plot but lists for scenery, properties,

wardrobe (costumes), and lists of expenditures relevant to construction of the *mise en scène*.

7 Only five short passages are marked with square brackets in Barker's 1912 acting edition that seem to indicate cuts: three in I.ii: acting ed. pp. 5, 13, and 18 (taken from parts of lines I.ii.12–14, 199–204, and 321 [Orgel ed.]); and two in IV.iv: acting ed. pp. 92 and 96 (taken from parts of lines IV.iv.605–9 and 718–23 [Orgel ed.]; the acting edition does not have line numbers). See Dymkowski, 216 n. 19 for a summary of scholarly estimates of cuts varying from six to twenty lines. See Laurie Osborne, 'Rethinking the Performance Editions', in Bulman, ed., *Shakespeare, Theory, and Performance* (168–86), for the important point that acting editions do not give transparent and indisputable evidence upon which to base a documentary account of a production. I use Barker's acting edition as I do promptbooks for other productions discussed in this volume, and as I do other theatrical records: I use them all with caution, and I compare acting editions and promptbooks to printed and recorded interviews, reviews at the time of the production, photographs, archival materials like costume drawings and lighting plots, account books, diaries, and other theatrical records.

8 For the convenience of readers who have no access to Barker's 1912 acting edition, I cite Barker's preface to *The Winter's Tale* from the posthumous *More Prefaces to Shakespeare*, edited by Edward M. Moore, Princeton, 1974, which includes Barker's prefaces to his acting editions for all three of his Savoy Shakespeare productions. However, my citations to Barker's text of *The Winter's Tale*, which is not contained in *More Prefaces*, are from the acting edition published in London by Heinemann, 1912. When my citations concern prefaces by Barker to Shakespeare plays other than *The Winter's Tale*, I refer to the illustrated four-volume edition of his *Prefaces to Shakespeare*, Princeton University Press, 1963.

9 The majority of actors who have spoken or written about their work with Barker as a director praise his methods (as well as his interpretative ideas). In 'Actors or Gramophones: the Paradoxes of Granville Barker', *Theatre Journal*, 36 (1984), 5–23, Mazer queries this majority opinion, making special use of an article entitled 'Mr. Granville Barker's Gramophones', *New Age*, 9 January 1913, in which an anonymous actor claiming to have been a member of the cast of Barker's *The Winter's Tale* complains of Barker's 'drilling' (quoted in Mazer, 'Actors or Gramophones', 10).

10 Barker's argument anticipates that of later critics seeking to understand the structure and tragicomic art of Shakespeare's late plays in light of Renaissance dramatic conventions; see Mowat's *The Dramaturgy of Shakespeare's Romances* (1976), for example, and Hartwig's *Shakespeare's Tragicomic Vision* (1972).

11 According to J. P. Wearing, Barker's *The Winter's Tale* ran for fifty-eight performances: 21 September to 2 November 1912 for the full run, and nine subsequent matinées in November: 5–7, 13, 14, 20, 21, 27, and 28. See his *The London Stage 1910–1919*.

12 Such objections show what Barker was up against. C. Lewis Hind

declared: 'Shakespeare is not for the stage. His words are too good, his plots too poor' ('The Public, the Play, and the Producer', 4 October 1912, Griffiths Collection, Birmingham Shakespeare Library, Birmingham Libraries). Another reviewer of the time opined that *Winter's Tale* 'reads far better than it acts. When Shakespeare wrote it he could no longer be bothered by thinking of the theatre, and in representation the flaws are emphasized' (Harvard Theatre Collection, fragile clippings file). The question of Shakespeare in performance, like the play's critical estimation, was in great dispute at the time of Barker's production. Desmond MacCarthy represents an emerging view: 'The performance of *The Winter's Tale* at the Savoy proves that we need no longer whisper to ourselves that Shakespeare reads better than he acts, and that it is not necessary to cut and dovetail his work in order to give it a unity' (*Eye-Witness*, 3 October 1912, 500).

13 Winthrop Ames, at the New Theatre in 1910, produced *The Winter's Tale* using an apron, a permanent set (of 'Elizabethan'-style panelling), and relatively continuous action, except for the interval. But he made numerous textual cuts. See Bartholomeusz (132–9), who also points out partial parallels to Barker's work in productions on the continent (143). Mazer emphasizes Barker's 'ability to integrate the varied and disparate features of the stagecraft of his day', combining traditionalist elements with his reforms (*Shakespeare Refashioned*, 150).

14 Lewis Casson's productions of *Julius Caesar* at Manchester (1914) and *Cymbeline* in London at the New Theatre (1923) had affinities with Barker's methods, as did Nigel Playfair's production of *As You Like It* at Stratford (1920); see Marshall (165–6). See also Dymkowski (77 and 219, n. 45) on other Barker actors who became directors, and Richard David (57 and 61). For a summary of how Barker's productions and prefaces have influenced subsequent Shakespeare productions, see M. St Clare Byrne, 'Introduction to the Illustrations' in Granville Barker's *Prefaces to Shakespeare* (1946), vol. 2 of the four-volume illustrated edition (Princeton, 1963), xlii–xlvi.

15 Dymkowski suggests Barker's part in the 1940 *King Lear* production was so substantial that he was in effect its director; her detailed study is based in part on 'extensive notes' taken at rehearsals by Hallam Fordham, in a typescript at the Folger Shakespeare Library to which Gielgud's own notes are appended (Dymkowski, 139).

16 See note 2, above.

Chapter II

1 According to Bartholomeusz (180), by 27 November 1951, Brook's production had run 167 performances; there may have been performances after that date, and the figure may not include the performances at Edinburgh, Brighton, and Coventry. Bartholomeusz states that the production nearest to this record, Mary Anderson's at the Lyceum in 1887 with Forbes-Robertson as Leontes, had run for 164 performances, making it 'the longest-running production of *The Winter's Tale* in Britain and America in the nineteenth century' (117).

2 Brook saw the structure of the play as tripartite, rather than (as is commonly argued) divided into two parts. In twentieth-century theatrical production, the play was commonly divided by an interval after the end of Act III (after the infant Perdita is found in Bohemia) and resumed with Time's speech at the beginning of Act IV. Arthur Colby Sprague reported that, when he saw Brook's production on 14 and 24 July 1951, the first of two intervals was placed after III.iii. On 8 September, however, he noted a change: the first interval now came earlier, at the end of the trial scene, III.ii, when Leontes asks Paulina to 'lead me to these sorrows' (Bartholomeusz, 175–6, from Sprague's letter to him of 29 November 1971). This change is confirmed by Gordon Crosse (MS Diaries, vol. 20, pp. 72–3); his notes suggest he saw the production at the Phoenix 'August 1951' and that it had an uncommon placement of intervals, which 'fell after III.ii & IV.iii': the 'purpose was to divide the play into "Sicilia-Bohemia-Sicilia"'. Brook's final choice, unusual in theatre practice of that time, exactly accorded with his idea of the play's structure that he subsequently expressed in *The Empty Space* (1968).

3 Angus McBean's 1951 *Winter's Tale* photographs to which I refer in this chapter may be seen as prints in the Theatre Museum, London. They can also be seen in the Harvard Theatre Collection (Houghton Library, Harvard University), which contains a large special collection of McBean photographs, has the negatives, and holds permissions rights.

4 The promptbook for Brook's production (promptbook S 219–1983) is in the Enthoven collection, held by the Theatre Museum, London (which is administered by the Victoria and Albert Museum). I am particularly grateful to librarian Claire Hudson, who retrieved the Phoenix Theatre archival box from storage for my use; the promptbook would have otherwise remained unavailable for my research.

5 In *Shakespeare – Hit or Miss?* (1991), Gielgud also stated, 'I had seen *The Winter's Tale* only once before, at Stratford' (83). Earlier, in *Stage Directions* (1963), he had remembered differently: 'I had seen *The Winter's Tale* several times at the Old Vic and Stratford' (44). Contemporary newspaper accounts state that he 'has long wanted to satisfy an ambition to act in "The Winter's Tale"' (*Daily Telegraph*, 27 June 1951; cf. *Evening Standard*, 26 May 1951). As these articles point out, Mamillius was the first speaking part performed by Gielgud's great-aunt Ellen Terry, in Charles Kean's 1856 production (in which Gielgud's grandmother Kate Terry played one of Hermione's waiting gentlewomen); in her fiftieth (jubilee) year of acting, Ellen Terry performed Hermione in Beerbohm Tree's 1906 production.

6 Similarly, Philip Hope-Wallace (*Manchester Guardian*, 29 June 1951) wrote that 'John Gielgud at once started Leontes' insane jealousy', sustaining it 'powerfully through the early scenes'. And the critic of *Time and Tide*, 7 July 1951, wrote that 'John Gielgud started Leontes' lunatic jealousy on so high and exciting a note that we had no chance to cavil'. But it is not possible to tell with certainty from either of these comments whether the jealousy these critics perceived started on a high note from Leontes' entrance or only when he first made his jealousy known within the opening sequence.

7 The Shakespeare Recording Society's recording number 214 was released on a set of three audiotape cassettes (180 minutes) by Caedmon in 1961 (CAE 16). Directed by Peter Wood, it used Christopher Fry's music. With the notable exception of George Rose as Autolycus, most actors in the cast surrounding Gielgud's Leontes in this recording were not the same as those in Brook's 1951 production. The Shakespeare Recording Society cast included William Squire (Polixenes), Robert Hardy (Camillo), Ernest Thesiger (Antigonus), Rachel Gurney (Hermione), Peggy Ashcroft (Paulina), Judith Stott (Perdita), Alan Bates (Florizel), Nigel Stock (Old Shepherd), and Alec McCowen (Clown [Young Shepherd]).

Chapter III

1 Cited from my interview with Trevor Nunn on 17 July 1988, tape-recorded in his office in Covent Garden, London. Except where otherwise noted, all quotations from Trevor Nunn in this chapter are taken from this interview.
2 Nunn's production of *The Winter's Tale* opened at the Royal Shakespeare Theatre 15 May 1969, toured Japan and Australia January to April, 1970, and was brought to the Aldwych (London) where it opened 2 July 1970 and remained in repertory until 15 February 1971. I draw in this chapter on archival materials in the Shakespeare Centre Library, Stratford-upon-Avon: the 1969 Royal Shakespeare Theatre promptbook and the 1970 Aldwych Theatre promptbook, distinguishing them by date only if using evidence with any significant differences between the two; the Stage Manager's Script (Aldwych 1970–71); the Music Cues Book (Stratford/Tokyo, 1969–70); and Production Files, including Sound Plots.
3 Peter Brook's *The Empty Space* (copyright 1968) antedates Nunn's 1969 season of late plays. Nunn said to me in interview, 'I don't say this in a competitive sense at all, but I think many people do perhaps forget that *The Winter's Tale* (and indeed the production of *Pericles* that happened in the same season) was the year before [Brook's production of] *A Midsummer Night's Dream*, and not the year after. I know, because Peter [Brook] saw the work' and his comments were 'very, very enthusiastic and generous'.
4 Irving Wardle seemed aware of this formalist influence in his review: 'Time is the central personage in the production, which takes the play as a poem on death and rebirth, nature versus art, with all its elements passing through the conditioning temporal medium. This is the usual academic reading, which Trevor Nunn has translated into exquisitely apt visual imagery.' See Wardle, 'Apt Imagery and Triumphant Design' (*The Times*, 16 May 1969).
5 Beauman adds that Nunn, in his 1966 *The Revenger's Tragedy*, broke from the style she calls 'Brechtian neo-realism' (291) designed by John Bury for the history plays presented by the Royal Shakespeare Company between 1963 and 1966. Nunn's *Revenger's Tragedy* used what Beauman calls 'thematic costumes, schematic staging' (292), and thus was in some ways comparable to his stylization of *The Winter's Tale*.

6 This quotation from Nunn, in interview with me in 1988, accords with his interview by Peter Ansorge ('Director in Interview'), in which Nunn states that the company 'set out to do *Pericles*, *The Winter's Tale*, and *Henry VIII* as three plays which dealt with a man – a representative individual – who lost or destroyed everything positive around him, and who had then to regenerate those positives, be reborn again. Consequently each of the productions began with an image of the individual: that vast Renaissance man at the beginning of *Pericles*; the spinning man at the beginning of *The Winter's Tale*; the Holbein-like portrait of Henry VIII' (17).

7 See *Encyclopedia of World Art*, Vol. 3: Leonardo's drawing was 'proclaimed the perfect proportional measurement by Luca Pacioli, a friend of Leonardo' (842). The Leonardo drawing of human proportions founded partially on the writings of Vitruvius is reproduced (from a copy in Venice, Gallerie dell'Accademia) in Plate 344 of Vol. 11 of the *Encyclopedia*.

8 Grady is using Joseph Frank's phrase from Frank's 1945 essay 'Spatial Form in Modern Literature'. Frank, over thirty years later, wrote (foreword to *Spatial Form in Narrative*, 8; see Grady, 100) of the relation between his own seminal essay and G. Wilson Knight's *The Wheel of Fire* (1930), particularly Knight's frequently cited assertions that Shakespeare's plays are 'set spatially as well as temporally in the mind', having 'a set of correspondences which are related to each other independently of the time-sequence which is the story' (Knight, *Wheel of Fire*, 3).

9 Cited from my interview with Barrie Ingham on 24 April 1993, tape-recorded in San Francisco, near the Curran Theatre in which he was performing in *Aspects of Love* (directed by Robin Phillips). Unless otherwise noted, all quotations from Barrie Ingham are taken from this interview.

10 Cited from my interview with Judi Dench on 13 September 1988, tape-recorded in her home in London. Unless otherwise noted, all quotations from Judi Dench are taken from this interview.

11 For my reference to Terry Hands's perception of the importance of Dench's breakthrough performance, I am indebted to Terry Hands, who allowed me to attend rehearsals at the Barbican prior to the revival (opened 14 October 1987) in London of his production of *The Winter's Tale* that had opened in Stratford-upon-Avon (30 April 1986).

Chapter IV

1 Productions of *The Winter's Tale* at the Oregon Shakespearean Festival (since 1988, renamed Oregon Shakespeare Festival), with dates of premiere, are as follows: 2 August 1954, directed by Paul Kliss; 18 July 1965, a fine production with an uncut text directed by Hugh Evans (Bartholomeusz, 190–1); 14 February 1975, directed by Audrey Stanley (reopened 22 June – 20 September for the main Festival season); 14 June 1984, directed by Hugh Evans, with Barry Kraft as Leontes; 17 June 1990, directed by Libby Appel, with performances of Leontes by Rex

Rabold, after whose death the role was played (from 27 July onward) by Henry Woronicz; 24 February 1996, directed by Fontaine Syer; 11 June 2002, directed by Michael Edwards; 24 February 2006, directed by Libby Appel.

2 Audrey Stanley's lecture/presentation was at Vanderbilt University, Nashville, Tennessee, September 1990 (hereafter cited as Vanderbilt lecture); I am indebted to her for a typescript of it.

3 In 'Notes from Audrey Stanley, Director of the Festival Production of *The Winter's Tale*', in a photocopied and bound typescript by David Laing entitled 'Study Guide for William Shakespeare's *The Winter's Tale*', Ashland, OR: Oregon Shakespearean Festival Association, n.d. [1975], 42–4.

4 Audrey Stanley gave me interviews on 16 July 1979, 30 April 1983, 15 August 1998, and 15 August 2002. Since her comments in these interviews are congruent with each other (as well as with her other comments from 1975 onward about the production), I do not give dates when citing these interviews. To avoid a cumbersome number of in-text citations, I make it clear when I am quoting from interviews with her but do not repeat the word 'interview' except where necessary for clarity of reference. When citing her from sources other than these interviews, I give in-text citations.

5 James Edmondson gave me interviews on 17 July 1979, 27 July 1990, 1 March 1994, and 28 June 1996. Since his comments in these interviews are congruent with each other, I do not give dates when citing them. To avoid a cumbersome number of in-text citations, I make it clear when I am quoting him but do not repeat the word 'interview' except where necessary. Edmondson, a director, actor, and teacher (the latter first at a college and then at a conservatory), holds an MA from the University of Colorado at Boulder; before the 1975 Ashland season, he acted in five seasons at the Colorado Shakespeare Festival, where his mentor, James Sandoe, like Audrey Stanley, made extensive use of Folio and quarto texts. In directing *The Winter's Tale* in 1975 at Ashland, Stanley frequently consulted the First Folio text of the play.

6 Le Clanché du Rand gave answers to my questions both in writing (24 September 1998) and in a subsequent telephone interview 28 September 1998. All my citations of her words are from these sources. Le Clanché du Rand played Hermione once before 1975, at the Colorado Shakespeare Festival in 1972, and once after 1975, at Pacific Conservatory for the Performing Arts in 1978, directed by Laird Williamson. She studied at the University of Rhodes in South Africa (BA, 1963) and at the University of California, Berkeley (MA in Dramatic Art, 1967). A professional actress in film and theatre, her explorations of Jungian thought have continued in her acting as well as her work as a playwright and a drama therapist (MA in Drama Therapy, New York University, 1990).

7 This analysis of staging and acting (including verse speaking) in I.ii is based, as is this chapter, not only on interviews with Stanley, du Rand, and Edmondson, cited above (notes 4, 5, and 6) but also on materials in the Oregon Shakespeare Festival Theatre Archives: the 1975 production promptbook; photographs and slides by Hank Kranzler; a 1975 audio

tape of scenes from the production recorded in the Bowmer Theatre (not during a full performance but done specially for broadcast as a sixty-minute radio cut version), narrated by Audrey Stanley; press cuttings; stage manager's files; lighting and sound plots; costume designs by Jeannie Davidson; set designs by Richard Hay; the 1975 Festival Programme; and information related to the Festival's history and its other productions of *The Winter's Tale*.

Chapter V

1 Cited from Jane Howell's letter to Mary Maher in which Howell commented on a paper I wrote for a seminar (2 April 1988) chaired by Maher on 'Shakespeare and Television: the Work of Jane Howell', at the Shakespeare Association of America annual meeting in Boston, 31 March – 2 April 1988. The letter is undated but would have been written in March or early April 1988. I am grateful to Howell for her comments and to Maher for making the exchange of ideas possible with Howell.

2 The terms 'realism' and 'naturalism' as applied to production styles for theatre and television are often used interchangeably, as Howell uses them in her two statements just cited, and as do others I cite in this chapter. Both terms are also frequently indicated in contemporary criticism by the term 'illusionism'. These complex and interrelated terms change their meanings in differing times and cultural contexts; I therefore use the terms particularly within the context in which the artists involved and critics have discussed the BBC production of *The Winter's Tale*. Furthermore, these terms can be ambiguous. The term 'naturalism', for example, as Ronald Gaskell points out, can be used 'to refer either to dramatic form or to a philosophic outlook on the world' (12). My use of the terms relates to dramatic form as well as to styles of theatrical and television production (especially in scenography) that attempt supposedly 'accurate' representation of detailed environments or kinds of behaviour, whether those are deemed to be like everyday life or drawn from a particular time and place. These styles have the appearance of verisimilitude, but their life-likeness is the result of artistic illusion. (See entries for 'Illusion', vol. 1, 617, and for 'Naturalism', vol. 2, 925–7, and for 'Realism and Reality', vol. 2, 1114–15, in Kennedy, ed., *The Oxford Encyclopedia of Theatre and Performance*.) Raymond Williams identifies several emphases television has adapted from naturalist theatre: 'the enclosed internal atmosphere; the local interpersonal conflict; the close-up on private feeling' (*Television*, 56).

3 Mary Maher recorded an interview in London with Jane Howell on 14 March 1988, in which Howell commented on the papers written for Maher's seminar (2 April 1988) at the Shakespeare Association of America annual meeting in Boston, 31 March–2 April 1988. By arrangement with Howell, Maher transcribed the interview and gave copies of it to seminar participants.

4 I cite these stage directions for the trial scene from the BBC TV Shakespeare volume on *The Winter's Tale*, pp. 56–7, which uses Peter

Alexander's 1951 edition of the *Complete Works*. Changes from the Alexander text (cuts, emendations, stage directions, and minor redistribution of lines among the Sicilian Lords and Gentlemen in II.i and V.ii) are carefully noted in the margins of the text in the BBC *Winter's Tale* volume. I have used the BBC volume as a resource, but unless noted differently, in order to maintain consistency throughout this book, I otherwise cite lines as they are numbered and appear in the Oxford Shakespeare edition of *The Winter's Tale* edited by Stephen Orgel.

5 I am indebted to Abbe Blum for the point that it is only 'Hermione who appears alone in this scene' ('Awakening', 3), her careful argumentation about ways Howell's presentation of the statue scene creates a sense of community, and her ideas exchanged in discussion in the seminar (2 April 1988) chaired by Mary Maher on 'Shakespeare and Television: the Work of Jane Howell', at the Shakespeare Association of America annual meeting, Boston, 31 March–2 April 1988.

Chapter VI

1 Peter Hall gave me the opportunity to be present in December 1987 for two weeks of workshops (especially on verse speaking) and rehearsals for his season of three of Shakespeare's late plays, as well as for additional rehearsals in August 1988, the month the plays transferred from the National Theatre's small Cottesloe theatre to its much larger Olivier theatre. The same actors and production team worked together to present all three plays. I am grateful to Peter Hall for an interview on 11 August 1988, as well as to members of the company for interviews in 1988: designer Alison Chitty, 12 August; Tim Pigott-Smith, 28 July, followed up on 11 August; Eileen Atkins, 26 July; Tony Church, 16 July; Ken Stott, 13 August; and Basil Henson, 13 August. Their quoted comments are from these interviews, unless otherwise indicated. London Weekend Television, for its 1988 South Bank Show on the National Theatre season of Shakespeare's late plays, filmed selections from rehearsals during the months from December 1987 until shortly before the opening of the late plays season in May 1988. This show was produced and directed by Chris Hunt and edited and presented by Melvyn Bragg. When my references are to the South Bank Show, they are so credited. In October, 1988, the National Theatre was given the title Royal National Theatre.

2 I refer to the interviews generously given me by Susan Wright, Paulina in *The Winter's Tale* directed by David William for the 1986 Canadian Shakespeare Festival, Stratford, Ontario (interview in Stratford, 5 October 1986), and by Tamu Gray, Paulina in *The Winter's Tale* directed by Fontaine Syer for the 1996 Oregon Shakespeare Festival (interview in Ashland, Oregon, 26 April 1996). My analysis also springs from my experience of seeing multiple performances of their work in the role of Paulina in these productions.

3 Roger Warren and I had many valuable exchanges of ideas during December 1987 and July and August 1988 about rehearsals and perform-

ances of the National Theatre's season of late plays. He was able to be present during the entire season from the first workshop through the last performance and drew on this experience in writing his excellent *Staging Shakespeare's Late Plays*, 1990.

4 Emily Dickinson's poem to which I refer is number 341 (p. 162) in Thomas H. Johnson's edition of *The Complete Poems of Emily Dickinson*.

Chapter VII

1 Bergman's *The Winter's Tale* transferred to the Brooklyn Academy of Music in 1995, where I saw the production in each of its four performances 31 May to 3 June. Audience members could choose to listen via headphones to a simultaneous English translation provided by interpreters from Stockholm. According to Ingemar Unge, when such translation is given, it is 'filtered through Swedish: the English version heard in the headphones follows the Swedish translation' (*Dramat*, 37).

2 Marker and Marker (p. 311, n. 44) give their source as 'a letter questioning Törnqvist's method and quoted by him in *Bergman och Strindberg*, p. 11'. The full title of Egil Törnqvist's book is *Bergman och Strindberg: Spöksonaten – drama och iscensättning, Dramaten 1973* (Stockholm: Prisma [Seelig], 1973). On Bergman's approach to text see also Marker and Marker, 141 and 271.

3 Bergman's comment is from an article, 'When Do You Quit, Ingmar?', supposedly an interview with one Anna Salander, but quite possibly written by Bergman himself, printed in *Dramat*, 13. Lennart Mörk kindly gave insights about the set in an interview with me on 1 June 1995 at the Brooklyn Academy of Music.

4 'Fifty of his [Almqvist's] seventy to eighty musical poems were published under the title *"Songes"* (= Dreams) in the imperial octavo edition of *The Book of the Wild Rose* II (1849)' though most of them were composed in the 1820s and 1830s (Romberg, 67). The bibliographical history of *The Book of the Wild Rose* is complex. According to Romberg (18), 'it was published between 1833 and 1851 in seventeen parts and two series: the first, the duodecimo edition, consisting of fourteen small-sized volumes from the years 1833 to 1851, and the second, the imperial octavo edition, consisting of three magnificent closely printed volumes from 1839 to 1850. The long tale, "The Hunting Seat", provides the framework for this vast and imposing collection of novels, short stories, lyrics, drama, music, essays, and tracts.'

5 Quotations from the Swedish programme were translated into English for me by Pia Kamlan, along with titles of Almqvist's *Songes*. I am grateful to her also for helpful information about Swedish cultural contexts and artistic traditions relevant to this production.

6 This quotation from the Swedish programme is quoted in English as printed in Romberg (73), who gives a reference to Almqvist's *Collected Works*, vol. 14, p. 12. Romberg's reference to the *Collected Works* is to *Samlade skrifter*, Stockholm, 1921–38. Romberg's book was translated from the Swedish by Sten Lidén.

7 One of Sweden's most important literary figures, Almqvist produced work in a wide range, from his early poems and stories influenced by German and Swedish romantic philosophy and literature and by Swedenborgian and Moravian mysticism, to his later work (after the mid-1830s), concerned with social and political questions. His novel *Sara Videbeck* (1839), striking in its stylistic realism, attacked conventional marriages. In his work for the newspaper *Aftonbladet*, known for its liberal perspectives, Almqvist showed his interest in women's rights. In 1837 he received ordination, but was critically alert to the conservatism of the Cathedral chapter, which cautioned him in 1840 for his views (see Romberg, 9–10, 14–26).

8 There is no indication in the Swedish programme of Bergman's authorship of the playbill or letter, though there is in fine print a note that he has 'translated' – '*övers.*' [sic] – the letter. I was told in my interview (2 June 1995) with the Dramaturg at Dramaten, Ulla Åberg, that the authorship is Bergman's. (All quotations from Ulla Åberg, unless otherwise indicated, are from this interview.) Even with the absence of Bergman's fictive letter and playbill in the Brooklyn Academy of Music printed programme, US audiences were aware that the framing device was a Bergman fiction, since they were told by narrative voice-over that those gathered onstage for the birthday celebration of 'Miss Ulricke Sofia' would perform Shakespeare's *The Winter's Tale*.

9 I cite lines from Almqvist's songs from the translation by Paul Britten-Austin that was used in creating the surtitles projected above the stage for the Swedish production as presented at the Brooklyn Academy of Music (BAM) 31 May and 1–3 June 1995. My source for these English surtitles is a copy of the 'Lyric Opera Surtitles Program Script File Header' used at BAM, given me by Dramaten's Ann-Christine Jernberg (Publicity officer) and Dramaturg Ulla Åberg. I am indebted to them both and to Ulla Åberg for help in arranging interviews and for answers to a number of queries. Technical design and presentation of the surtitles at BAM were by Michael Panayos. A cassette tape was released by the Royal Dramatic Theatre of Sweden with a number of Almqvist's songs used in the production (as well as other Almqvist songs and music): 'Irene Lindh sjunger "*Songes*" av C. J. L. Almqvist' (Dramaten, n.d.).

10 Unless otherwise indicated, all quotations, direct or indirect, from Feuer are taken from her interview with me on 3 June 1995 at the Brooklyn Academy of Music. Donya Feuer, who was born in Philadelphia and studied at Juilliard, was a member of Martha Graham's Company in 1955–56 and Artistic Director of the Studio for Dance with Paul Sansardo, New York, 1956–63. She has been a director at Dramaten in her own right, as well as a choreographer, and she has directed a number of productions elsewhere. Ted Hughes dedicated his *Shakespeare and the Goddess of Complete Being* to her.

11 Pernilla August gave me this interview on 2 June 1995 at the Brooklyn Academy of Music; unless otherwise indicated, all my citations of her comments are from this interview. Bibi Andersson also gave me an interview on 2 June 1995 in Brooklyn, from which I do not cite directly or in paraphrase but which helped my understanding of her fine performance.

[255]

12 At the time of Bergman's production, the theatrical representation of Time as a woman in productions of *The Winter's Tale* was relatively rare; other instances of which I am aware were in Oregon Shakespeare Festival productions directed by Libby Appel, 1990, and Fontaine Syer, 1996, and in the production by the Maly Drama Theatre, St Petersburg, 1997.

13 These linguistic changes are documented in a copy of the English text of *The Winter's Tale* as cut for the production. I am grateful to Dramaturg Ulla Åberg for a photocopy of this text (based on J. H. P. Pafford's edition, Arden Shakespeare, 1963).

14 As marked in the copy of the English text as cut for the production (see note 13), cuts to Act V were as follows: from V.i, approximately 153 lines out of the scene's total of 232; from V.ii approximately 100 lines out of 175; from V.iii, approximately 85 lines out of 155.

Chapter VIII

1 Naum Pinkhasik tape-recorded his interview with Lev Dodin in St Petersburg, 3 October 2004, using questions I had prepared; Katherine Kuskova translated the interview into English; Olga Kuskova helped facilitate both the interview and its translation. Quotations from Dodin are taken from this interview unless otherwise indicated.

2 Such achievement, as Maria Shevstova suggests, would hardly have been predictable given the Maly's origins (its name in Russian means 'small') by government decree in 1944 as a '35-seat theatre'. In 1973 Roman Malkin was made 'managing director' and Efim Padve became 'artistic director'. While increasing its 'artistic and technical standard of productions', Padve continued the Maly's social project as a people's theatre and expanded the repertoire to include contemporary drama. Lev Dodin's work had since the 1960s been associated with 'daring productions' of plays whose authors 'disclosed grim realities usually beautified in the official media' (Shevstova, *Dodin*, 3–5). His legendary production of Abramov's *Brothers and Sisters* in 1985, his first as head of the Maly, made clear his prominent position among Russian theatre artists whose work probed socio-political problems that made evident the need for *glasnost* (which Shevstova says is 'usually translated "openness"', and 'literally means "giving voice"'); those artists had long struggled for it (see Shevstova, *Dodin*, 7, 10–13).

3 According to the Maly's archivist, a Shakespeare play had only once before been staged in the Maly Drama Theatre (*Much Ado About Nothing*, directed by Yakov Khamarmer, which premiered 12 December 1964). But that was a minor production at a time before the Maly's reinvigoration under Padve (Artistic Director 1973–83) and before it became the theatre home of Lev Dodin as Artistic Director in 1983 (see Shevstova, *Dodin*, 4–6).

4 Olga Kuskova looked closely at the production script in Gnedich's Russian translation; I use her English translations of this script, of other Russian documents, and of reviews. I give key words or phrases in Russian, in her transliterations from the Cyrillic, only when needed in

order to discuss their connotations. In doing extensive research and translation for me, Olga Kuskova, a native speaker of Russian, drew on her bilingual fluency in Russian and English as well as her university degree work in English literature.

5 On my behalf, Karina Chumakova (formerly Magzoumova) interviewed Natalia Kolotova, Company Manager of the Maly Drama Theatre and Assistant Director of *The Winter's Tale*, using questions I had prepared; Chumakova translated that interview (held in St Petersburg, 7 April 2001) and related materials from Russian into English. Natalia Kolotova sent me a copy of the Russian script prepared for the production, copies of photographs, programmes, and her sketches of key scenes. Quotations from Natalia Kolotova are from the English translation of her 7 April 2001 interview unless otherwise indicated.

6 Professor Karen Fox of Santa Clara University wrote this letter to me after she had seen *The Winter's Tale* at the Maly in St Petersburg in 2001; she sent additional clarifications in her email of 23 June 2007. Professor Natalia Alexandrova in the Department of Foreign Languages, Russian Academy of Sciences, St Petersburg, reported that as of 2007 the internal passport documentation necessary in St Petersburg was 'a stamp in the passport if the residence is permanent and a special paper which one keeps in the passport if the registration is temporary' (Alexandrova, email message to the author, 25 June 2007). Professor Alexandrova did wide-ranging, crucial research in Russian archives for me and translated the necessary documents into English. She received helpful assistance from Alex Gorshkov. Professors Fox and Alexandrova, as well as Alex Gorshkov, answered many questions for me about the Maly production of *The Winter's Tale* based on their multiple viewings of it.

Chapter IX

1 *The Winter's Tale* is not, technically, a 'problem play'; certainly, it was not among the plays F. S. Boas identified as 'problem plays' when he coined the term at the end of the nineteenth century. That actors (like Antony Sher in 1999), directors, and reviewers are now regularly describing it as such is not so much a sign of a genre stretching as an indication that plays the theatre used to consider unproblematic – *The Taming of the Shrew*, *The Merchant of Venice*, *The Tempest* (to name just three) – are, on today's stage, distinctly problematic. It's to recognize, too, that, as we negotiate Shakespeare in the theatre, the nature of the 'problem' is constantly under review.

2 I am very grateful to Peter J. Smith for sharing with me his thick back files on *The Winter's Tale* – including viewing notes and production reviews – and equally grateful to Peter Scoggins for remembering Propeller's *Tale* for me. They will recognize themselves in this chapter, which could not have been written without their help.

APPENDIX

Major actors and staff for productions discussed in this volume

Savoy Theatre, London, 21 September 1912
Director: Harley Granville Barker   Designer: Norman Wilkinson
Costume designer: Albert Rothenstein [Rutherston]

Leontes	Henry Ainley	Polixenes	Charles Graham
Hermione	Lillah McCarthy	Paulina	Esmé Beringer
Mamillius	Eric Rae	Antigonus	Guy Rathbone
Perdita	Cathleen Nesbitt	Florizel	Dennis Neilson-Terry
Camillo	Stanley Drewitt	Autolycus	Arthur Whitby
Old Shepherd	H. O. Nicholson	Clown (Young Shepherd)	Leon Quartermaine

Phoenix Theatre, London, 27 June 1951
Director: Peter Brook
Set and costume designer: Sophie Fedorovitch   Music: Christopher Fry

Leontes	John Gielgud	Polixenes	Brewster Mason
Hermione	Diana Wynyard	Paulina	Flora Robson
Mamillius	Robert Anderson	Antigonus	Lewis Casson
Perdita	Virginia McKenna	Florizel	Richard Gale
Camillo	Michael Goodliffe	Autolycus	George Rose
Old Shepherd	George Howe	Clown (Young Shepherd)	Philip Guard

Royal Shakespeare Company at the Royal Shakespeare Theatre 15 May 1969
Director: Trevor Nunn
Set and costume designer: Christopher Morley   Music: Guy Woolfenden

Leontes	Barrie Ingham	Polixenes	Richard Pasco
Hermione	Judi Dench	Paulina	Brenda Bruce / Elizabeth Spriggs
Mamillius	Jeremy Richardson	Antigonus	Morgan Sheppard
Perdita	Judi Dench	Florizel	David Bailie
Camillo	Nicholas Selby	Autolycus	Derek Smith
Old Shepherd	Sydney Bromley	Clown (Young Shepherd)	Geoffrey Hutchings

The Oregon Shakespearean Festival at the Bowmer Theatre, Ashland
14 February 1975
Director: Audrey Stanley
Set designer: Richard L. Hay   Costume designer: Jeannie Davidson

Leontes	James Edmondson	*Polixenes*	Peter Silbert
Hermione	Le Clanché du Rand	*Paulina*	Randi Douglas
Mamillius	Brad O'Neil Todd Reichenbach	*Antigonus*	David L. Boushey
Perdita	Carmi Boushey	*Florizel*	Michael Horton
Camillo	Larry R. Ballard	*Autolycus*	Mark D. Murphey
Old Shepherd	Philip L. Jones	*Clown (Young Shepherd)*	Allen Nause

British Broadcasting Corporation, London, recorded 9–15 April 1980
Director: Jane Howell
Set designer: Don Homfray   Costume designer: John Peacock

Leontes	Jeremy Kemp	*Polixenes*	Robert Stephens
Hermione	Anna Calder-Marshall	*Paulina*	Margaret Tyzack
Mamillius	Jeremy Dimmick	*Antigonus*	Cyril Luckham
Perdita	Debbie Farrington	*Florizel*	Robin Kermode
Camillo	David Burke	*Autolycus*	Rikki Fulton
Old Shepherd	Arthur Hewlett	*Clown (Young Shepherd)*	Paul Jesson

National Theatre, London, at the Cottesloe, 18 May 1988
at the Olivier, 13 August 1988
Director: Peter Hall Set and costume designer: Alison Chitty

Leontes	Tim Pigott-Smith	*Polixenes*	Peter Woodward
Hermione	Sally Dexter	*Paulina*	Eileen Atkins
Mamillius	James Goodwin William Puttock	*Antigonus*	Tony Church
Perdita	Shirley Henderson	*Florizel*	Steven Mackintosh
Camillo	Basil Henson	*Autolycus*	Ken Stott
Old Shepherd	Michael Bryant	*Clown (Young Shepherd)*	Jeremy Flynn

Leicester Haymarket, Leicester, 21 January 1991
Director: Simon Usher   Designer: Anthony Lamble

Leontes	Kevin Costello	*Polixenes*	Neal Swettenham
Hermione	Valerie Gogan	*Paulina*	Judy Liebert
Mamillius	Oliver Payne	*Antigonus*	Robert Langdon Lloyd
	Kevin O'Reilly		
Perdita	Valerie Gogan	*Florizel*	Martin McKellan
Camillo	Tom Dunn	*Autolycus*	Robert Langdon Lloyd
Old Shepherd	Tom Dunn	*Clown (Young Shepherd)*	Kelly Hunter

Theatre de Complicité, Sydney Festival, 8 January 1992
(then on UK tour)
Director: Annabel Arden   Designer: Ariane Gastambide

Leontes	Simon McBurney	*Polixenes*	Dhobi Oparei
Hermione	Gabrielle Reidy	*Paulina*	Kathryn Hunter
Mamillius	Kathryn Hunter	*Antigonus*	Mark Lewis Jones
Perdita	Lilo Baur	*Florizel*	Mark Lewis Jones
Camillo	Leo Wringer	*Autolycus*	Marcello Magni
Old Shepherd	Kathryn Hunter	*Clown (Young Shepherd)*	Simon McBurney

Royal Shakespeare Company at the Royal Shakespeare Theatre
1 July 1992
Director: Adrian Noble   Designer: Anthony Ward

Leontes	John Nettles	*Polixenes*	Paul Jesson
Hermione	Samantha Bond	*Paulina*	Gemma Jones
Mamillius	Marc Elliott Stefan Weclawek	*Antigonus*	Andrew Jarvis
Perdita	Phyllida Hancock	*Florizel*	Alan Cox
Camillo	Benjamin Whitrow	*Autolycus*	Richard McCabe
Old Shepherd	Jeffery Dench	*Clown (Young Shepherd)*	Graham Turner

The Royal Dramatic Theatre of Sweden, Stockholm, 23 April 1994
Director: Ingmar Bergman
Set and costume designer: Lennart Mörk   Choreography: Donya Feuer
Songs and music: Carl Jonas Love Almqvist   Singer: Irene Lindh

Leontes	Börje Ahlstedt	*Polixenes*	Krister Henriksson
Hermione	Pernilla August	*Paulina*	Bibi Andersson
Mamillius	Anna Björk	*Antigonus*	Ingvar Kjellson
Perdita	Kristina Törnqvist	*Florizel*	Jakob Eklund
Camillo	Gösta Prüzelius	*Autolycus*	Reine Brynolfsson
Old Shepherd	Tord Peterson	*Clown (Young Shepherd)*	Per Mattsson

Maly Drama Theatre, St Petersburg, 30 October 1997
Director: Declan Donnellan   Set and costume designer: Nick Ormerod

Leontes	Pyotr Semak	*Polixenes*	Vladimir Zakharyev
Hermione	Natalia Akimova	*Paulina*	Vera Bykova
Mamillius	Nikolai Zakharov	*Antigonus*	Felix Rayevsky
			Alexei Zubarev
Perdita	Angelika Nevolina	*Florizel*	Alexander Koshkarev
			Sergei Diatchkov
Camillo	Mikhail Samochko	*Autolycus*	Sergei Vlasov
	Anatoly Kolibyanov		
Old Shepherd	Nikolai Lavrov	*Clown (Young Shepherd)*	Sergei Bekhterev

Royal Shakespeare Company at the Royal Shakespeare Theatre
6 January 1999
Director: Gregory Doran   Designer: Robert Jones

Leontes	Antony Sher	*Polixenes*	Ken Bones
Hermione	Alexandra Gilbreath	*Paulina*	Estelle Kohler
Mamillius	Emily Bruni	*Antigonus*	Jeffry Wickham
Perdita	Emily Bruni	*Florizel*	Ryan McCluskey
Camillo	Geoffrey Freshwater	*Autolycus*	Ian Hughes
Old Shepherd	James Hayes	*Clown (Young Shepherd)*	Christopher Brand

National Theatre, London, at the Olivier, 23 May 2001
Director: Nicholas Hytner   Set designer: Ashley Martin-Davis
Costume designer: Jon Morrell

Leontes	Alex Jennings	*Polixenes*	Julian Wadham
Hermione	Claire Skinner	*Paulina*	Deborah Findlay
Mamillius	Thomas Brown-Lowe		
	Liam Hess	*Antigonus*	Geoffrey Beevers
Perdita	Melanie Clark Pullen	*Florizel*	Daniel Roberts
Camillo	Joe Dixon	*Autolycus*	Phil Daniels
Old Shepherd	John Normington	*Clown (Young Shepherd)*	Iain Robertson

Royal Shakespeare Company at the Roundhouse, London, 12 April 2002
Director: Matthew Warchus   Designer: Vicky Mortimer

Leontes	Douglas Hodge	*Polixenes*	Rolf Saxon
Hermione Taylor	Anastasia Hille	*Paulina*	Myra Lucretia
Mamillius	Toby Parkes	*Antigonus*	Jude Akuwudike
	Jacob Parsons		
Perdita	Lauren Ward	*Florizel*	Alan Turkington
Camillo	Brian Protheroe	*Autolycus*	Felix Dexter
Old Shepherd	Keith Bartlett	*Clown (Young Shepherd)*	Dylan Charles

Propeller at the Watermill Theatre, Newbury, Berkshire
24 January 2005
Director: Edward Hall   Designer: Michael Pavelka

Leontes	Richard Clothier	*Polixenes*	Vince Leigh
Hermione	Simon Scardifield	*Paulina*	Adam Levy
Mamillius	Tam Williams	*Antigonus*	Dugald Bruce Lockhart
Perdita	Tam Williams	*Florizel*	Dugald Bruce Lockhart
Camillo	Bob Barrett	*Autolycus*	Tony Bell
Old Shepherd	Chris Myles	*Clown (Young Shepherd)*	James Tucker

Royal Shakespeare Company at the Swan, Stratford-upon-Avon
15 November 2006
Director: Dominic Cooke   Designer: Mike Britton

Leontes	Anton Lesser	*Polixenes*	Nigel Cooke
Hermione	Kate Fleetwood	*Paulina*	Linda Basset
Mamillius	Jonathan Clowes / Edward Statham	*Antigonus*	Ben Onwukwe
Perdita	Michelle Terry	*Florizel*	Simon Harrison
Camillo	Joseph Mydell	*Autolycus*	Richard Katz
Old Shepherd	Richard Moore	*Clown (Young Shepherd)*	Trystan Gravelle

BIBLIOGRAPHY

Addenbrooke, David, *The Royal Shakespeare Company: The Peter Hall Years*, London: William Kimber, 1974.
Adelman, Janet, *Suffocating Mothers: Fantasies of Maternal Origin in Shakespeare's Plays, 'Hamlet' to 'The Tempest'*, New York: Routledge, 1992.
Alexander, Peter, ed., *The Alexander Text of the Complete Works of William Shakespeare*, London: Collins, 1951.
Almqvist, C. J. L., *12 Songes*, Stockholm: Albert Bonniers Förlag, 1966.
Ansorge, Peter, 'Director in Interview', *Plays and Players* (September 1970), 16–17, 21.
Asp, Carolyn, 'Shakespeare's Paulina and the *Consolatio* Tradition', *Shakespeare Studies* 11 (1978), 145–58.
BBC TV Shakespeare, *The Winter's Tale*, London: British Broadcasting Corporation, 1981.
Barber, C. L., *Shakespeare's Festive Comedy: A Study of Dramatic Form and Its Relation to Social Custom*, Princeton: Princeton University Press, 1959.
——, and Richard Wheeler, *The Whole Journey: Shakespeare's Power of Development*, Berkeley and Los Angeles: University of California Press, 1986.
Barker, Harley Granville, *Associating with Shakespeare*. An address delivered at King's College, London, on 25 November 1931. London: for the Shakespeare Association by Humphrey Milford, Oxford University Press, 1932, 1–31.
——, *The Exemplary Theatre*, Boston: Little, Brown, 1922.
——, *More Prefaces to Shakespeare*, Edward M. Moore, ed., Princeton: Princeton University Press, 1974.
——, *Prefaces to Shakespeare* (1946); Illustrated edition, 4 vols with Illustrations and Notes by M. St Clare Byrne, Princeton: Princeton University Press, 1963 [vol. 2 also includes 'Introduction to the Illustrations' by M. St Clare Byrne].
——, ed., *The Winter's Tale: An Acting Edition*. Prepared with a Preface by Granville Barker, London: Heinemann, 1912.
Bartholomeusz, Dennis, *'The Winter's Tale' in Performance in England and America 1611–1976*, Cambridge: Cambridge University Press, 1982.
Barton, Anne, 'Leontes and the Spider: Language and Speaker in Shakespeare's Last Plays', in Philip Edwards, Inga-Stina Ewbank,

and G. K. Hunter, eds, *Shakespeare's Styles: Essays in Honour of Kenneth Muir*, Cambridge: Cambridge University Press, 1980, 131–50.

Barton, John, *Playing Shakespeare*, London: Methuen, 1984.

Bate, Jonathan, and Russell Jackson, eds, *Shakespeare: An Illustrated Stage History*, Oxford: Oxford University Press, 1996.

Beauman, Sally, *The Royal Shakespeare Company: A History of Ten Decades*, Oxford: Oxford University Press, 1982.

Beckerman, Bernard, *Shakespeare at the Globe 1599–1609*, New York: Macmillan, 1962.

Beckson, Karl, *London in the 1890's: A Cultural History*, New York: Norton, 1992.

Belsey, Catherine, 'Disrupting Sexual Difference: Meaning and Gender in the Comedies', in John Drakakis, ed., *Alternative Shakespeares*, London: Methuen, 1985, 166–90.

Bergman, Ingmar, *Images: My Life in Film*, Marianne Ruuth, trans. (from *Bilder*, Stockholm, 1990), New York: Arcade Publishing, 1994.

——, *The Magic Lantern*, Joan Tate, trans. (from *Laterna Magica*, Stockholm, 1987), New York: Viking Penguin, 1988.

Berry, Ralph, *On Directing Shakespeare*: *Interviews with Contemporary Directors*, London: Hamish Hamilton, 1989.

Bethell, S. L., *'The Winter's Tale': A Study*, London: Staples Press, 1946.

Bicks, Caroline, *Midwiving Subjects in Shakespeare's England. Women and Gender in the Early Modern World*, Aldershot: Ashgate, 2003.

——, 'Midwiving Virility in Early Modern England', in Naomi J. Miller and Naomi Yavneh, eds, *Maternal Measures: Figuring Caregiving in the Early Modern Period*, Aldershot: Ashgate, 2000, 49–64.

Biggins, Dennis, '"Exit Pursued by a Beare": A Problem in *The Winter's Tale*', *Shakespeare Quarterly* 13 (1962), 3–13.

Billington, Michael, 'Shakespeare and the modern British theatre', in Stanley Wells and Lena Cowen Orlin, eds, *Shakespeare: An Oxford Guide*, Oxford: Oxford University Press, 2003, 595–606.

Björkman, Stig, Torsten Manns, and Jonas Sima, *Bergman on Bergman: Interviews with Ingmar Bergman*, Paul Britten Austin, trans., New York: Simon and Schuster, 1973.

Blum, Abbe, 'Awakening Faith in Television: Act Five Scene Three of the BBC *The Winter's Tale* and the Question of Audience Participation', 1–8. Paper presented to the seminar (2 April 1988), chaired by Mary Z. Maher, on 'Shakespeare and Television: the Work of Jane Howell', Shakespeare Association of America Annual Meeting, Boston, 31 March – 2 April 1988.

——, '"Strike all that Look Upon with Mar[b]le": Monumentalizing Women in Shakespeare's Plays', in Anne M. Haselkorn and Betty S. Travitsky, eds, *The Renaissance Englishwoman in Print: Counterbalancing the Canon*, Amherst: University of Massachusetts Press, 1990, 99–118.

Bradbrook, M. C., *The Living Monument: Shakespeare and the Theatre of His Time*, Cambridge: Cambridge University Press, 1976.

Bridges-Adams, W., 'Granville-Barker and the Savoy', *Drama* n.s. 52 (1959), 28–31.

——, *The Lost Leader*, London: Sidgwick and Jackson, 1954.

Brook, Peter, 'Style in Shakespeare Production', in John Lehmann, ed., *Orpheus*, vol. 1, New York: New Directions, 1948, 139–46.

——, *The Empty Space*, New York: Atheneum, 1968.

——, *The Open Door: Thoughts on Acting and Theatre*, New York: Pantheon, 1993.

——, *The Shifting Point: Forty Years of Theatrical Exploration 1946–1987*, New York: Harper and Row, 1987.

——, *Threads of Time: Recollections*, Washington: Counterpoint, 1998.

Bulman, James C., 'The BBC Shakespeare and "House Style"', in J. C. Bulman and H. R. Coursen, eds, *Shakespeare on Television: An Anthology of Essays and Reviews*, Hanover, NH: University Press of New England, 1988, 50–60.

——, ed., *Shakespeare, Theory, and Performance*, London: Routledge, 1996.

——, and H. R. Coursen, eds, *Shakespeare on Television: An Anthology of Essays and Reviews*, Hanover, NH: University Press of New England, 1988.

Butler, Judith, 'Performative Acts and Gender Constitution: An Essay in Phenomenology and Feminist Theory', in Sue-Ellen Case, ed., *Performing Feminisms: Feminist Critical Theory and Theatre*, Baltimore: Johns Hopkins University Press, 1990, 270–82.

Byrne, Muriel St Clare, 'Fifty Years of Shakespearian Production: 1898–1948', *Shakespeare Survey* 2 (1949), 1–20.

——, Introduction, Illustrations and Notes to Harley Granville-Barker's *Prefaces to Shakespeare* (1946); Illustrated edition, 4 vols, Princeton: Princeton University Press, 1963, vol. 2, xiii–xlvi.

Caine, Barbara, *English Feminism, 1780–1980*, Oxford: Oxford University Press, 1997.

Calder-Marshall, Anna, '*The Winter's Tale*', in Roger Sales, ed., *Shakespeare in Perspective*, vol. 1, London: British Broadcasting Corporation, 1982, 241–9.

Cardullo, Bert, 'Ingmar Bergman's Concept for His 1973 Production of *The Ghost Sonata*: a Dramaturg's Response', *Essays in Arts and Sciences* 14 (1985), 33–48.
Carlson, Harry G., 'Bergman's *Vintersagan* in New York', *Tijdschrift voor Skandinavistiek* 20.1 (1999), 103–10.
Carter, Huntly, *The Theatre of Max Reinhardt*, 1914; repr., New York: Benjamin Blom, 1964.
Clubb, Louise G., 'The Tragicomic Bear', *Comparative Literature Studies* 9 (1972), 17–30.
Coghill, Nevill, 'Six Points of Stage-craft in *The Winter's Tale*', *Shakespeare Survey* 11 (1958), 31–41.
Conquest, Robert, *The Great Terror: A Reassessment*, New York: Oxford University Press, 1990.
Cook, Ann Jennalie, 'Jane Howell's Manipulation of Distance in *The Winter's Tale* (BBC-TV)', *Shakespeare Bulletin* 11 (1993), 37–9.
Cook, Judith, *Director's Theatre*, London: Harrap, 1974.
Craig, Edward Gordon, *On the Art of the Theatre* (1911); repr., New York: Theatre Books, 1960. [Includes reprint of *The First Dialogue*, 1905.]
Crosse, Gordon, 'Shakespearean performances which I have seen', MS Diaries, 21 vols., 1890–1953, Birmingham Shakespeare Library, Birmingham Libraries. [Also available as 'The Gordon Crosse Theatrical Diaries', published by Thomson Gale on the Arden subscription website The Shakespeare Collection.]
——, *Fifty Years of Shakespearean Playgoing*, London: Mowbray, 1940.
Cunningham, J. V., *Tradition and Poetic Structure*, Denver: Alan Swallow, 1960.
Danby, John, *Elizabethan and Jacobean Poets: Studies in Sidney, Shakespeare, Beaumont and Fletcher*, London: Faber and Faber, 1964 (originally published as *Poets on Fortune's Hill*, London: Faber and Faber, 1952).
David, Richard, *Shakespeare in the Theatre*, Cambridge: Cambridge University Press, 1978.
Dench, Judi, 'A Career in Shakespeare', in Jonathan Bate and Russell Jackson, eds, *Shakespeare: An Illustrated Stage History*, Oxford: Oxford University Press, 1996, 197–210.
——, 'Judi Dench Talks to Gareth Lloyd Evans', *see* Evans, Gareth Lloyd.
Dessen, Alan C., *Elizabethan Stage Conventions and Modern Interpreters*, Cambridge: Cambridge University Press, 1984.
——, 'Massed Entries and Theatrical Options in *The Winter's Tale*', *Medieval and Renaissance Drama in England* 8 (1996), 119–27.
——, 'The Oregon Shakespearean Festival, 1975', *Shakespeare Quarterly* 27 (1976), 83–93.

——, 'Reviewing Shakespeare for the Record', *Shakespeare Quarterly* 36 (1985), 602–8.
Dickinson, Emily, *The Complete Poems of Emily Dickinson*, Thomas H. Johnson, ed., Boston: Little, Brown, 1960.
Dolan, Jill, *The Feminist Spectator as Critic*, Ann Arbor: UMI Research Press, 1988.
Dollimore, Jonathan and Alan Sinfield, eds, *Political Shakrespeare: New Essays in Cultural Materialism*, Manchester: Manchester University Press, 1985.
Dramat [Ingmar Bergman Festival (New York) edition], Stockholm: The Royal Dramatic Theatre of Sweden, 1995.
Draper, R. P., *'The Winter's Tale': Text and Performance*, Houndmills, Basingstoke, and London: Macmillan, 1985.
Dryden, John, 'Defence of the Epilogue. Or, An Essay on the Dramatique Poetry *of the last Age', The Conquest of Granada*, Part II, 1672, *The Works of John Dryden*, H. T. Swedenberg, Jr, et al., eds, 20 vols, Berkeley and Los Angeles: University of California Press, 1956–2000; *The Conquest of Granada, Marriage A-la-Mode, The Assignation*, John Loftis, David Stuart Rodes, et al., eds, vol. 11 (1978), 203–18.
Dymkowski, Christine, *Harley Granville-Barker: A Preface to Modern Shakespeare*, Washington: Folger Shakespeare Library; London: Associated University Presses, 1986.
Eagleton, Terry, *Criticism and Ideology: A Study in Marxist Literary Theory*, 1975; Verso edition, London: Verso, 1978.
Elliott, Michael, 'Cathleen Nesbitt Talks to Michael Elliott about Harley Granville-Barker', *Listener*, 13 January 1972, 51–3.
Elsom, John, ed., *Is Shakespeare Still Our Contemporary?*, London: Routledge, 1989.
Encyclopedia of World Art, vol. 3, New York: McGraw-Hill, 1960.
Erickson, Peter, *Patriarchal Structures in Shakespeare's Drama*, Berkeley and Los Angeles: University of California Press, 1985.
Evans, Gareth Lloyd, 'Interpretation or Experience? Shakespeare at Stratford', *Shakespeare Survey* 23 (1970), 131–5.
——, 'Judi Dench Talks to Gareth Lloyd Evans', *Shakespeare Survey* 27 (1974), 137–42.
Ewbank, Inga-Stina, 'From Narrative to Dramatic Language: *The Winter's Tale* and Its Source', in Marvin and Ruth Thompson, eds, *Shakespeare and the Sense of Performance: Essays in the Tradition of Performance Criticism in Honor of Bernard Beckerman*, Newark, NJ: University of Delaware Press; London: Associated University Presses, 1989, 29–47.
Faucit, Helena (Lady Martin), *On Some of Shakespeare's Female Characters*, 5th ed., 1893; repr., New York: AMS, 1970. [First

published in part as 'Shakespeare's Women. . . . Hermione', *Blackwood's Edinburgh Magazine* 149 (1891), 1–37.]

Fenwick, Henry, 'The Production', in *The Winter's Tale*, The BBC TV Shakespeare, London: British Broadcasting Corporation, 1981, 17–27.

Ferguson, Margaret, Maureen Quilligan, and Nancy J. Vickers, eds, *Rewriting the Renaissance: The Discourses of Sexual Difference in Early Modern Europe*, Chicago: University of Chicago Press, 1986.

Feuer, Donya, 'On Bergman', *Dramat* [Ingmar Bergman Festival (New York) edition], Stockholm: The Royal Dramatic Theatre of Sweden, 1995, 15.

Foakes, R. A., ed., *Coleridge's Criticism of Shakespeare*, Detroit, MI: Wayne State University Press, 1989.

Frank, Joseph, 'Spatial Form in Modern Literature', in Mark Schorer, Josephine Miles, and Gordon McKenzie, eds, *Criticism: The Foundations of Modern Literary Judgment*, rev. ed., New York: Harcourt, 1958, 379–92. First published in the *Sewanee Review* 53 (Spring, Summer, and Autumn 1945).

——, 'Spatial Form: Thirty Years After', in Jeffrey R. Smitten and Ann Daghistany, eds, *Spatial Form in Narrative*, Ithaca, NY: Cornell University Press, 1981.

French, A. L., *Shakespeare and the Critics*, Cambridge: Cambridge University Press, 1972.

Frey, Charles, *Shakespeare's Vast Romance: A Study of 'The Winter's Tale'*, Columbia: University of Missouri Press, 1980.

Garber, Marjorie, *Shakespeare After All*, New York: Pantheon Books, 2004.

Garrick, David, *Florizel and Perdita. A Dramatic Pastoral, In Three Acts. Alter'd from 'The Winter's Tale' of Shakespear*, London: J. and R. Tonson, 1758; facsimile ed., London: Cornmarket Press, 1969.

Gaskell, Ronald, *Drama and Reality: The European Theatre since Ibsen*, London: Routledge and Kegan Paul, 1972.

Gesner, Carol, *Shakespeare and the Greek Romance: A Study of Origins*, Lexington: University Press of Kentucky, 1970.

Gielgud, John, *An Actor and His Time*, in collaboration with John Miller and John Powell, New York: Clarkson N. Potter, 1979.

——, *Shakespeare – Hit or Miss?*, with John Miller, London: Sidgwick and Jackson, 1991.

——, *Stage Directions*, New York: Random House, 1963.

Gnedich, Pyotr, trans., *Zimniaya Skaska* [*The Winter's Tale*], in vol. 4 of *Vilyam Shekspir: Sobraniye Sochineniy* [*William Shakespeare: The Collected Works*], St Petersburg: izdatelstvo KEM, 1997 [KEM Publishing House; first translated by Pyotr Gnedich from the English, St Petersburg: Brokhaus-Efron, 1904].

Godard, Jean-Luc, 'Bergmanorama', in Roger W. Oliver, ed., *Ingmar Bergman: An Artist's Journey on Stage, on Screen, in Print*, New York: Arcade Publishing, 1995, 37–41.

Grady, Hugh, *The Modernist Shakespeare: Critical Texts in a Material World*, Oxford: Clarendon Press, 1991.

Granville Barker, Harley, *see* Barker, Harley Granville.

Greenblatt, Stephen, *Will in the World: How Shakespeare Became Shakespeare*, New York: Norton, 2004.

Greenwald, Michael L., *Directions by Indirections: John Barton of the Royal Shakespeare Company*, Newark, NJ: University of Delaware Press; London: Associated University Presses, 1985.

Greif, Karen, '"If This Were Play'd upon a Stage": Harley Granville Barker's Shakespeare Productions at the Savoy Theatre, 1912–1914', *Harvard Library Bulletin* 28 (April 1980), 117–45.

Gurr, Andrew, *Playgoing in Shakespeare's London*, 2nd ed., Cambridge: Cambridge University Press, 1996.

——, 'The Shakespearean Stage', in *The Norton Shakespeare*, 2nd ed., based on the Oxford Edition, General Editor, Stephen Greenblatt, New York and London: Norton, 2008, 79–99.

——, and Mariko Ichikawa, *Staging in Shakespeare's Theatres*, Oxford Shakespeare Topics, Oxford: Oxford University Press, 2000.

——, with John Orrell, *Rebuilding Shakespeare's Globe*, New York: Routledge, 1989.

Hall, Joan Lord, *'The Winter's Tale': A Guide to the Play*, Greenwood Guides to Shakespeare, Westport, CT: Greenwood Press, 2005.

Hall, Peter, *Peter Hall's Diaries*, John Goodwin, ed., London: Hamish Hamilton, 1983.

Hamilton, Donna, 'Shakespeare's Romances and Jacobean Political Discourse', in Maurice Hunt, ed., *Approaches to Teaching Shakespeare's 'The Tempest' and Other Late Romances*, New York: Modern Language Association of America, 1992, 64–71.

Hardman, Christopher, *The Winter's Tale*, Penguin Critical Studies, Harmondsworth: Penguin, 1988.

Hartman, Geoffrey, and Patricia Parker, eds, *Shakespeare and the Question of Theory*, New York: Methuen, 1985.

Hartwig, Joan, *Shakespeare's Tragicomic Vision*, Baton Rouge: Louisiana State University Press, 1972.

——, 'The Tragicomic Perspective of *The Winter's Tale*', *ELH* 37 (1970), 12–36.

Hazlitt, William, *The Collected Works of William Hazlitt*, A. R. Waller and Arnold Glover, eds, with an introd. by W. E. Henley, 12 vols, London: Dent, 1902–4; vol. 1 (1902); vol. 11 (1904).

Hedrick, Donald, 'The Shakespeare Plays on TV: *The Winter's Tale*',

Shakespeare on Film Newsletter 6 (1982), 4, 6.

Helms, Lorraine, 'Playing the Woman's Part: Feminist Criticism and Shakespearean Performance', in Sue-Ellen Case, ed., *Performing Feminisms: Feminist Critical Theory and Theatre*, Baltimore: Johns Hopkins University Press, 1990, 196–206.

Hodgdon, Barbara, 'Absent Bodies, Present Voices: Performance Work and the Close of Romeo and Juliet's Golden Story', *Theater Journal* 42 (1989), 341–59.

——, *The Shakespeare Trade: Performances and Appropriations*, Philadelphia: University of Pennsylvania Press, 1998.

Holderness, Graham, 'Radical Potentiality and Institutional Closure: Shakespeare on Film and Television', in Jonathan Dollimore and Alan Sinfield, eds, *Political Shakespeare: New Essays in Cultural Materialism*, Ithaca, NY: Cornell University Press, 1985, 182–201.

——, ed., *The Shakespeare Myth*, Manchester: Manchester University Press, 1988.

Howard, Jean E., 'Scholarship, Theory, and More New Readings', in Georgianna Ziegler, ed., *Shakespeare Study Today* (The Horace Howard Furness Memorial Lectures), New York: AMS Press, 1988, 127–51.

——, *Shakespeare's Art of Orchestration: Stage Technique and Audience Response*, Chicago: University of Chicago Press, 1984.

——, *The Stage and Social Struggle in Early Modern England*, London: Routledge, 1994.

——, and Marion F. O'Connor, eds, *Shakespeare Reproduced: The Text in History and Ideology*, New York: Methuen, 1987.

Hughes, Ted, *Shakespeare and the Goddess of Complete Being*, London: Faber and Faber, 1992.

Hunt, Maurice, ed., *Approaches to Teaching Shakespeare's 'The Tempest' and Other Late Romances*, New York: Modern Language Association of America, 1992.

——, ed., *'The Winter's Tale': Critical Essays*, New York: Garland, 1995.

Jacobs, Gerald, *Judi Dench: A Great Deal of Laughter: An Authorized Biography*, London: Futura, 1986.

Johns, Eric, 'Gielgud in a New Role', *Theatre World* 47:319 (August 1951), 7–8.

Jones, David Richard, *Great Directors at Work: Stanislavsky, Brecht, Kazan, Brook*, Berkeley and Los Angeles: University of California Press, 1986.

Jordan, Constance, *Renaissance Feminism: Literary Texts and Political Models*, Ithaca, NY: Cornell University Press, 1990.

——, *Shakespeare's Monarchies: Ruler and Subject in the Romances*,

Ithaca, NY: Cornell University Press, 1997.
Kennedy, Dennis, *Granville Barker and the Dream of Theatre*, Cambridge: Cambridge University Press, 1985.
——, *Looking at Shakespeare: A Visual History of Twentieth-century Performance*, 2nd ed., Cambridge: Cambridge University Press, 2001.
——, ed., *Foreign Shakespeare*, Cambridge: Cambridge University Press, 1993.
——, ed., *The Oxford Encyclopedia of Theatre and Performance*, 2 vols, Oxford: Oxford University Press, 2003.
Kitto, H. D. F., *Form and Meaning in Drama*, London: Methuen, 1964.
——, *Greek Tragedy: A Literary Study*, 3rd ed., London: Methuen, 1961.
Knappman, Edward W., ed., *Great World Trials*, Detroit: Gale Research, 1997.
Knight, G. Wilson, *The Crown of Life: Essays in Interpretation of Shakespeare's Final Plays*, London: Oxford University Press, 1947; repr., with corrections, London: Methuen, 1958; repr., New York: Barnes and Noble, 1966.
——, *The Wheel of Fire: Interpretations of Shakespeare's Tragedy* (first published Oxford: Oxford University Press, 1930); 4th ed., London: Methuen, 1949; rev., repr., 1960.
Kraft, Barry, 'On the Theatrical Worth of Discarded Words', *On Stage Studies* 14 (1991), 8–15.
Kurland, Stuart M., '"We need no more of your advice": Political Realism in *The Winter's Tale*', *Studies in English Literature* 31 (1991), 365–86.
Lahr, John, 'Winter Songs', *The New Yorker*, 3 October 1994, 105–8.
Laing, David, *see* Stanley, Audrey.
Lenz, Carolyn Ruth Swift, Gayle Greene, and Carol Thomas Neely, eds, *The Woman's Part: Feminist Criticism of Shakespeare*, Urbana: University of Illinois Press, 1980.
Loman, Rikard, 'Bergman's *Vintersagan* at the Royal Dramatic Theatre', *Tijdschrift voor Skandinavistiek* 20.1 (1999), 111–20.
McCarthy, Lillah (Lady Keeble), *Myself and My Friends*, with an aside by Bernard Shaw, New York: E. P. Dutton, 1933.
McDonald, Jan, *The 'New Drama' 1900–1914*, Grove Press Modern Dramatists. London: Macmillan, 1986.
McDonald, Russ, *The Bedford Companion to Shakespeare: An Introduction with Documents*, Boston: Bedford Books, 1996.
McGuire, Philip C., *Shakespeare: The Jacobean Plays*, New York: St Martin's Press, 1994.
——, *Speechless Dialect: Shakespeare's Open Silences*, Berkeley and

Los Angeles: University of California Press, 1985.
Maguire, Laurie E., 'Feminist Editing and the Body of the Text', in Dympna Callaghan, ed., *A Feminist Companion to Shakespeare*, Oxford: Blackwell, 2000, 59–79.
Male, David, *The Winter's Tale*, Cambridge: Cambridge University Press, 1984.
Marker, Frederick J., and Lise-Lone Marker, *Ingmar Bergman: A Life in the Theatre*, Cambridge: Cambridge University Press, 1992 (rev. ed. of *Ingmar Bergman: Four Decades in the Theater*, Cambridge: Cambridge University Press, 1982).
Marshall, Norman, *The Producer and the Play*, London: Davis-Poynter, 1975.
Martin, Helena Faucit, *see* Faucit, Helena (Lady Martin).
Mazer, Cary M., 'Actors or Gramophones: the Paradoxes of Granville Barker', *Theatre Journal* 36 (1984), 5–23.
——, *Shakespeare Refashioned: Elizabethan Plays on Edwardian Stages*, Ann Arbor: University of Michigan Research Press, 1981.
Miller, John, *Judi Dench: With a Crack in Her Voice*, London: Weidenfeld and Nicolson, 1998.
Miller, Jonathan, *Subsequent Performances*, New York: E. Sifton Books/Viking, 1986.
Moore, Edward M., ed., *see* Barker, Harley Granville, *More Prefaces to Shakespeare*.
Morse, William R., 'Metacriticism and Materiality: the Case of Shakespeare's *The Winter's Tale*', *English Literary History* 58 (1991), 283–304.
Mowat, Barbara, *The Dramaturgy of Shakespeare's Romances*, Athens: University of Georgia Press, 1976.
Muir, Kenneth, *Shakespeare's Sources I*, London: Methuen, 1957.
——, ed., *Shakespeare: The Winter's Tale*, Casebook Series, London: Macmillan, 1968.
Mulryne, J. R., and Margaret Shewring, eds, *Shakespeare's Globe Rebuilt*, Cambridge: Cambridge University Press, 1997.
Mulvey, Laura, 'Visual Pleasure and Narrative Cinema', in Gerald Mast and Marshall Cohen, eds, *Film Theory and Criticism: Introductory Readings*, 3rd edition, New York: Oxford University Press, 1985, 803–16.
Neely, Carol Thomas, *Broken Nuptials in Shakespeare's Plays*, New Haven: Yale University Press, 1985.
Nesbitt, Cathleen, 'Cathleen Nesbitt Talks to Michael Elliott about Harley Granville-Barker', *see* Elliott, Michael.
——, *A Little Love and Good Company*, London: Faber and Faber, 1975.
Nuttall, A. D., *William Shakespeare: 'The Winter's Tale'*, London: Edward Arnold, 1966.

Oliver, Roger W., ed., *Ingmar Bergman: An Artist's Journey, on Stage, on Screen, in Print*, New York: Arcade Publishing, 1995.
Orgel, Stephen, 'The Poetics of Incomprehensibility', *Shakespeare Quarterly* 41 (1991), 431–7.
——, ed., *The Winter's Tale*, The Oxford Shakespeare, Oxford: Clarendon Press, 1996.
——, ed., *The Tempest*, The Oxford Shakespeare, Oxford: Clarendon Press, 1987.
Orrell, John, 'Designing the Globe: Reading the Documents', in J. R. Mulryne and Margaret Shewring, eds, *Shakespeare's Globe Rebuilt*, Cambridge: Cambridge University Press, 1997, 51–65.
Osborne, Laurie, 'Rethinking the Performance Editions: Theatrical and Textual Productions of Shakespeare', in James C. Bulman, ed., *Shakespeare, Theory, and Performance*, London: Routledge, 1996, 168–86.
Otten, Elizabeth, 'Jane Howell's *Winter's Tale*: the Message, Not the Medium', *Shakespeare on Film Newsletter* 14 (1989), 5.
Overton, Bill, *The Winter's Tale*, The Critics Debate. Atlantic Highlands, NJ: Humanities Press International, 1989.
Pafford, J. H. P., ed., *The Winter's Tale*, Arden Shakespeare. London: Methuen, 1963.
Palmer, Daryl L., 'Jacobean Muscovites: Winter, Tyranny, and Knowledge in *The Winter's Tale*', *Shakespeare Quarterly* 46 (1995), 323–9.
Paster, Gail Kern, *The Body Embarrassed: Drama and the Disciplines of Shame in Early Modern England*, Ithaca, NY: Cornell University Press, 1993.
Pavis, Patrice, 'Problems of Translation for the Stage: Interculturalism and Post-modern Theatre', in Hanna Scolnicov and Peter Holland, eds, *The Play out of Context: Transferring Plays from Culture to Culture*, Cambridge: Cambridge University Press, 1989, 25–44.
Pearce, Brian, 'Granville Barker's Production of *The Winter's Tale* (1912)', *Comparative Drama* 30 (1996), 395–411.
Pechter, Edward, ed., *Textual and Theatrical Shakespeare: Questions of Evidence*, Studies in Theatre History and Culture. Iowa City: University of Iowa Press, 1996.
Peterson, Douglas, *Time, Tide, and Tempest*, San Marino, CA: Huntington Library Publications, 1973.
Postlewait, Thomas, and Bruce A. McConachie, *Interpreting the Theatrical Past: Essays in the Historiography of Performance*, Iowa City: University of Iowa Press, 1989.
Pyle, Fitzroy, *'The Winter's Tale': A Commentary on the Structure*, London: Routledge and Kegan Paul, 1969.

Quiller-Couch, Arthur, and John Dover Wilson, eds, *The Winter's Tale*, The New Cambridge Shakespeare, Cambridge: Cambridge University Press, 1931; repr., 1959.
Roberts, Peter, 'The Winter's Tale', *Plays and Players* (July 1969), 30–3.
Robson, Flora, Introduction to *The Winter's Tale*, designs by Carl Toms, London: Folio Society, 1975.
Romberg, Bertil, *Carl Jonas Love Almqvist*, Sten Lidén, trans., Boston: Twayne Publishers, 1977.
Rothenstein, Albert, *see* Rutherston, Albert [name under which his work was published].
Rothwell, Kenneth, '"The Shakespeare Plays": *Hamlet* and the Five Plays of Season Three', *Shakespeare Quarterly* 32 (1981), 395–401.
Rutherston, Albert, 'Decoration in the Art of the Theatre', *Monthly Chapbook* 1:2 (August 1919), 7–28.
——, *Sixteen Designs for the Theatre*, with an Introduction, London: Oxford University Press, 1928.
Rutherston, Max, *Albert Rutherston 1881–1953*. An appreciation written on the occasion of an exhibition of the artist's work, 17 May–17 June 1988, n.p. [London], n.d. [1988].
Rutter, Carol Chillington, *Enter the Body: Women and Representation on Shakespeare's Stage*, London: Routledge, 2001.
——, *Shakespeare and Child's Play: Performing Lost Boys on Stage and Screen*, London: Routledge, 2007.
——, ed., *Documents of the Rose Playhouse*, The Revels Plays Companion Library. Manchester: Manchester University Press, 1984.
Rylands, George, 'Festival Shakespeare in the West End', *Shakespeare Survey* 6 (1953), 140–6.
Salander, Anna, 'When Do You Quit, Ingmar?' *Dramat* [Ingmar Bergman Festival (New York) edition], Stockholm: The Royal Dramatic Theatre of Sweden, 1995, 8–13. [Presented as an interview with Bergman but possibly authored by him.]
Salmon, Eric, ed., *Granville Barker and His Correspondents*, Detroit, MI: Wayne State University Press, 1986.
Sanders, Wilbur, *The Winter's Tale*, Twayne's New Critical Introductions to Shakespeare. Boston: Twayne, 1987.
Schanzer, Ernest, ed., *The Winter's Tale*, New Penguin Shakespeare. Harmondsworth: Penguin, 1969.
Self, David, *Television Drama: An Introduction*, London: Macmillan Education, 1984.
Seltzer, Daniel, 'The Staging of the Last Plays', in John Russell Brown and Bernard Harris, eds, *Later Shakespeare*, Stratford-upon-Avon Studies 8. London: Edward Arnold, 1966, 127–65.
Shakespeare, William, *The Norton Facsimile: The First Folio of Shakespeare*, 2nd ed., based on folios in the Folger Shakespeare

Library Collection, prepared by Charlton Hinman, with a new introd. by Peter W. M. Blayney, New York: Norton, 1996.
——, *The Norton Shakespeare*, 2nd ed., based on the Oxford Edition, General Editor, Stephen Greenblatt, New York and London: Norton, 2008.
——, *The Winter's Tale*, The Oxford Shakespeare, *see* Orgel, Stephen, ed.
Shattuck, Charles H., 'Shakespeare's Plays in Performance from 1660 to 1971', Appendix A in G. Blakemore Evans, ed., *The Riverside Shakespeare*, 2nd ed., Boston: Houghton Mifflin, 1997, 1905–31.
——, ed., *John Philip Kemble Promptbooks*, 11 vols, Charlottesville: University Press of Virginia, 1974, vol. 9: *Twelfth Night, Two Gentlemen, Winter's Tale* [1811].
Shevstova, Maria, *Dodin and the Maly Drama Theatre: Process to Performance*, London: Routledge, 2004.
——, 'Resistance and Resilience: an Overview of the Maly Drama Theatre of St. Petersburg', *New Theatre Quarterly* 13 (1997), 299–317.
Showalter, Elaine, 'Representing Ophelia: Women, Madness, and the Responsibilities of Feminist Criticism', in Patricia Parker and Geoffrey Hartman, eds, *Shakespeare and the Question of Theory*, London: Routledge, 1991, 77–94.
Smith, Hallett, *Shakespeare's Romances: A Study of Some Ways of the Imagination*, San Marino, CA: Huntington Library Publications, 1972.
Speaight, Robert, *William Poel and the Elizabethan Revival*, London: Heinemann, 1954.
Spender, Stephen, '*The Winter's Tale*', in Roger Sales, ed., *Shakespeare in Perspective*, vol. 1, London: British Broadcasting Company Press, 1982, 234–40.
Sprague, Arthur Colby, *Shakespearian Players and Performances*, Cambridge, MA: Harvard University Press, 1953; repr., New York: Greenwood Press, 1969.
Stanley, Audrey, 'Notes from Audrey Stanley, Director of the Festival Production of *The Winter's Tale*', in David Laing, 'Study Guide for William Shakespeare's *The Winter's Tale*', Ashland, OR: Oregon Shakespearean Festival Association, n.d. [1975], 42–4.
Styan, J. L., *Shakespeare's Stagecraft*, Cambridge: Cambridge University Press, 1967.
Tatspaugh, Patricia, 'Performance History: Shakespeare on the Stage, 1660–2001', in Stanley Wells and Lena Cowen Orlin, eds, *Shakespeare: An Oxford Guide*, Oxford: Oxford University Press, 2003, 525–49.

——, *The Winter's Tale*, Shakespeare at Stratford. London: Arden Shakespeare, 2002.
Taylor, Gary, and Michael Warren, eds, *The Division of the Kingdoms: Shakespeare's Two Versions of 'King Lear'*, Oxford: Clarendon Press, 1983.
Taylor, Neil, 'Two Types of Television Shakespeare', *Shakespeare Survey* 39 (1987), 103–11.
Terry, Ellen, *Ellen Terry's Memoirs*, with a Preface, Notes and Additional Biographical Chapters by Edith Craig and Christopher St John, New York: G. P. Putnam's Sons, 1932.
Terry, J. E. Harold, '*The Winter's Tale*', *Oxford and Cambridge Review*, No. 25 (November 1912), 168–74.
Tinkler, F. C., '*The Winter's Tale*', *Scrutiny* 5 (1937), 344–64.
Tolkein, J. R. R., *Tree and Leaf*, Boston: Houghton Mifflin, 1965.
Tollini, Frederick, *The Shakespeare Productions of Max Reinhardt*, Studies in Theatre Arts, vol. 31. Lewiston, NY: Edwin Mellen Press, 2004.
Törnqvist, Egil, *Bergman och Strindberg: Spöksonaten – drama och iscensättning, Dramaten 1973*, Stockholm: Prisma [Seelig], 1973.
Traub, Valerie, *Desire and Anxiety: Circulations of Sexuality in Shakespearean Drama*, London: Routledge, 1992.
Traversi, Derek A., *Shakespeare: The Last Phase*, Stanford: Stanford University Press, 1965.
Trewin, J. C., *Going to Shakespeare*, London: G. Allen and Unwin, 1978.
——, *Peter Brook: A Biography*, London: Macdonald, 1971.
——, *Shakespeare on the English Stage 1900–1964*, London: Barrie and Rockliff, 1964.
Trienens, Roger J., 'The Inception of Leontes' Jealousy in *The Winter's Tale*', *Shakespeare Quarterly* 4 (1953), 321–6.
Trousdale, Marion, 'The Question of Harley Granville-Barker and Shakespeare on Stage', *Renaissance Drama* n.s. 4 (1971), 3–36.
——, 'Style in *The Winter's Tale*', *Critical Quarterly* 18 (1976), 25–32.
Turner, Robert Kean, and Virginia Westling Haas, eds, *The Winter's Tale*, A New Variorum Edition of Shakespeare, with Robert A. Jones, Andrew J. Sabol, Patricia E. Tatspaugh, New York: Modern Language Association of America, 2005.
Unge, Ingemar, 'Swedish Spoken Here', *Dramat* [Ingmar Bergman Festival (New York) edition], Stockholm: The Royal Dramatic Theatre of Sweden, 1995, 37.
Waller, Gary, 'The Late Plays as Family Romance', in Maurice Hunt, ed., *Approaches to Teaching Shakespeare's 'The Tempest' and Other Late Romances*, New York: Modern Language Association of America, 1992, 57–63.

Warren, Roger, *Staging Shakespeare's Late Plays*, Oxford: Clarendon Press, 1990.

Wearing, J. P., *The London Stage 1910-1919: A Calendar of Plays and Players*, Metuchen, NJ: Scarecrow Press, 1982.

Weimann, Robert, 'Mimesis in *Hamlet*', in Geoffrey Hartman and Patricia Parker, eds, *Shakespeare and the Question of Theory*, New York: Methuen, 1985, 275-309.

——, 'Representation and Performance: the Uses of Authority in Shakespeare's Theater', *PMLA* 107 (1992), 497-510.

——, *Shakespeare and the Popular Tradition in the Theater*, Baltimore: Johns Hopkins University Press, 1978.

Wells, Stanley, 'Goes Out, Followed by a Furry Animal', *Times Literary Supplement*, 20 February 1981, 197.

——, 'Shakespeare and Romance', in John Russell Brown and Bernard Harris, eds, *Later Shakespeare*, Stratford-upon-Avon Studies 8, London: Edward Arnold, 1966, 49-79.

——, 'Shakespeare Performances in England, 1987-88', *Shakespeare Survey* 42 (1990), 129-48.

——, 'Television Shakespeare', *Shakespeare Quarterly* 33 (1981), 261-77.

——, and Gary Taylor, eds, *William Shakespeare: The Complete Works*, Oxford: Clarendon Press, 1986.

——, and Lena Cowen Orlin, eds, *Shakespeare: An Oxford Guide*, Oxford: Oxford University Press, 2003.

Werner, Sarah, *Shakespeare and Feminist Performance: Ideology on Stage*, London: Routledge, 2001.

Wilders, John, 'Adjusting the Set', *Times Higher Education Supplement*, 10 July 1981, 13.

Willems, Michèle, 'Entretien avec Jane Howell, Réalisatrice de la première Tetralogie, de *The Winter's Tale* et de *Titus Andronicus*' [Interview with Jane Howell, Director of the first Tetralogy, of *The Winter's Tale*, and of *Titus Andronicus*], in Michèle Willems, *Shakespeare à la Télévision*, Rouen: Publications de l'Université de Rouen, No. 123, 1987, 79-91. [Interview is in English.]

——, 'Verbal-Visual, Verbal-Pictorial, or Textual-Televisual? Reflections on the BBC Shakespeare Series', *Shakespeare Survey* 39 (1987), 91-102.

Williams, David, compiler, *Peter Brook: A Theatrical Casebook*, London: Methuen, 1988.

Williams, Raymond, 'Afterword', in Jonathan Dollimore and Alan Sinfield, eds, *Political Shakespeare: New Essays in Cultural Materialism*, Manchester: Manchester University Press, 1985, 231-9.

——, *Drama from Ibsen to Eliot*, London: Chatto and Windus, 1961.

——, *Drama in Performance*, New York: Basic Books, 1968.

———, *Television: Technology and Cultural Form*, New York: Schocken Books, 1975.

Williamson, Marilyn L., 'Doubling, Women's Anger, and Genre', *Women's Studies* 9 (1982), 107–19.

Willis, Susan, *The BBC Shakespeare Plays: Making the Televised Canon*, Chapel Hill: University of North Carolina Press, 1991.

Wineke, Donald R., 'Internalizing Passion: Leontes in the BBC *Winter's Tale*', [1–12]. Paper presented to the seminar (2 April 1988), chaired by Mary Z. Maher, on 'Shakespeare and Television: the Work of Jane Howell', Shakespeare Association of America Annual Meeting, Cambridge, MA, 31 March – 2 April 1988.

Worthen, W. B., 'Deeper Meanings and Theatrical Technique: the Rhetoric of Performance Criticism', *Shakespeare Quarterly* 40 (1989), 441–55.

———, *Shakespeare and the Authority of Performance*, Cambridge: Cambridge University Press, 1997.

———, *Shakespeare and the Force of Modern Performance*, Cambridge: Cambridge University Press, 2003.

Zitner, Sheldon, 'Wooden O's in Plastic Boxes: Shakespeare and Television', *University of Toronto Quarterly* 51 (1981), 1–12.

Zlobina, Alyona, 'The Truth of the Tale', *Znamya* 10 (1999).

INDEX

Note: Illustrations are indicated by page numbers in italics; 'n.' or 'nn.' after a page reference indicates the number of a note or notes on the page(s) referenced.

Åberg, Ulla, 180, 255nn.8–9, 256n.13
absolutism, 162
  Jacobean, 196, 198, 203
  monarchical, 15–16, 152
  political, 152
  see also political issues; tyrannical use of power; tyranny
actors, presentational modes of, 19, 20
  direct address, 72, 113, 134, 139, 140–1, 144, 145, 150, 184
  adaptations, 25–6
  see also textual cuts
Adelman, Janet, 6
Adolphson, Kristina, 187, *188*
Ahlstedt, Börje, 177, 180, 182, 183–5, 192
Ainley, Henry, 40, 42, 43, 45, 55, 57, 70
Akimova, Natalia, 202, 204, *205*
Alekseyevna, Yelena, 203
Alexander, Peter, 252–3n.4
Alexandrinsky Theatre, 196
Alexandrova, Natalia, 257n.6
Almqvist, Carl Jonas Love, 176, 178–82, 189
  Book of the Wild Rose, The (*Törnrosens bok*, sometimes translated *The Book of the Thornrose*), 179, 254n.4
  Collected Works, 254n.6
  Improvisations for the pianoforte (*Fria fantasier för piano-forte*), 178
  metafictional framing device, 179, 185, 186–7, 193
  range of work, 255n.7
  Sara Videbeck, 255n.7
  Songes, 178, 179, 180–1, 182, 192, 254nn.4–5; 'The Grave' ('*Graven*', *Songe* XXV), 181; 'Heart's flower' ('*Hjärtats blomma*', *Songe* XV), 180; 'The Listening Mary' ('*Den Lyssnande Maria*', *Songe* I), 193; 'My galleon' ('*Min gälar*', *Songe* XXVII), 181; translations, 255n.9; 'Why have you come to the meadow?' ('*Varför kom du på ängen?*', *Songe* XXIV), 189; 'World's End' ('*Världens slut*', *Songe* L), 189
Ames, Winthrop, 42, 247n.13
Anderson, Mary, 39, 48, 54, 99, 247n.1
Anderson, Sara Pia, 5, 6, 244n.6
Andersson, Bibi, 255n.11
  as Paulina, 177, 185, 190, 191–2

[279]

Angus Bowmer Theatre, 112–13
Anikst, Aleksandr Abramovich, 212
Ansorge, Peter, 87, 88, 89, 250n.6
Appel, Libby, 250–1n.1, 256n.12
Archer, William, 58
Arden, Annabel, *see* Theatre de Complicité
Ashcroft, Peggy, 4, 44, 74, 249n.7
Asquith, Herbert Henry, Prime Minister, 4, 243n.5
Atkins, Eileen, 156, 171, 253n.1
 as Paulina, 4, 154, 162, 163–4, *165*
Atkins, Robert, 60
August, Pernilla, 255n.11
 as Hermione, 177, 180, 183–5

Bailie, David, 102, *102*
Barber, C. L., 112, 123, 132
Barber, John, 66, 70, 104
Barclay, Sam, 137
Barker, Harley Granville, 2–4, 101, 121, 123, 155, 245n.3, 246n.9
 Account Book (*Winter's Tale* production), 36, 42, 49–50, 51, 53, 56, 245n.4, 245n.6
 acting edition (*Winter's Tale* production), 2, 39, 40, 41–2, 55, 246nn.7–8
 books: *Associating with Shakespeare*, 33, 34; *The Exemplary Theatre*, 33; *More Prefaces to Shakespeare*, 34, 36, 37, 39, 40, 41, 44, 46, 47, 48, 49, 51, 55, 56, 70, 246n.8; *Prefaces to Shakespeare*, 40, 41, 60
 break from illusionism, 2, 33–5
 influence of, 59–61
 plays: *The Marrying of Ann Leete*, 3, 47; *Waste*, 47
 predecessors and contemporary parallels, 58–60
 stage productions: *Iphigenia in Tauris*, 244n.1; *King Lear*, directing rehearsals of, 61, 247n.15; *A Midsummer Night's Dream*, 35; *Twelfth Night*, 35, 56; *The Two Gentlemen of Verona*, 244n.1; *Votes for Women!*, 3–4
 strength of women's parts supported by, 46–9
 Winter's Tale production at Savoy Theatre (1912), 31, 32–61, 70; continuity of action, 38–9; costume design, 37–8, 51; critical interpretation, 40–1; critical reception of, 55–8, 246n.12; dance, 51–3; decorative style, 36–8; eclecticism of, 32, 38, 51, 59; lighting, 33, 35, 245nn.4–5; music, 53; pace of speaking in, 43–5; presentation of Bohemia, 51; restoration of V.ii, 54–5; run of, 246n.11; set design, 35–6; stage architecture and apron staging, 33–6, 56, 244n.1; textual cuts, minimal, 39–40, 174–5, 246n.7
Bartholomeusz, Dennis, 22, 58, 66, 72, 74, 77, 81, 103
 productions discussed: Ames, 42; Barker, 37, 46, 54, 247n.13; Brook, 65, 70, 75, 76, 78, 82, 247n.1; Kean, 30–1; Kemble, 26; Macready, 28–9; Nunn, 98; Quayle, 84; Stanley, 113, 121

Barton, John, 86, 97, 155, 158
Bates, Alan, 249n.7
BBC, *see* British Broadcasting Corporation, 'BBC TV Shakespeare' series
bear(s)
  actors as, 22, 49–50, 78, 98, 122, 165, 186, 187, 230
  dramaturgy and, 13, 17, 22
  in productions: Arden, Complicité, 230; Barker, 49–50; Bergman, 186–7; Brook, 77, 78; Donnellan, 200; Doran, 230; Hall (Edward), Propeller, 230–1; Hall (Peter), 164–6; Howell, 144; Noble, 231, 232; Nunn, 97–8; Stanley, 122–3; Warchus, 232–3
  stage directions: *Beare* (First Folio), 9, 134, 230; *bear* (Orgel edition), 97
Beauman, Sally, 249n.5
Beevers, Geoffrey, 229
Behterev, Sergei, 206
Bell, Tony, 238
Bentley, Gerald, 244n.11
Bergman, Ingmar, 9, 170, 173, 254n.1, 254n.3, 255n.8
  background, 175–6
  films: *Cries and Whispers*, 183; *Fanny and Alexander*, 174, 175, 177, 183, 185; *Smiles of a Summer Night*, 177
  stage productions: *A Doll's House*, 177; *Hamlet*, 177, 183; *Madame de Sade*, 181, 183; *Peer Gynt*, 177
  Winter's Tale production with Royal Dramatic Theatre of Sweden (1994–95), 174–93; alteration of religious language, 190–1; catalyst to produce, 178; choreography, 176–7, 181–3; *figuranter* in, 176, 181–3, 184; framing device, 255n.8; music, 177–81, 189, 192, 193; rescripting, 193; set design, 176, 177; structural movements, 189–93; Swedish artistic and social culture reflected in, 176–7; teamwork, 177; text as 'raw material' for reinventing Shakespeare, 175; textual cuts, 174, 175, 190–1, 256n.14
Beringer, Esmé, 48, *57*
Berry, Cicely, 101
Bethell, S. L., 62
Bicks, Caroline, 7–8
Biggins, Dennis, 22
Billington, Michael, 20, 153–4, 157, 216, 234
Binyon, Laurence, 39
Björk, Anna, 185–6
Blackfriars theatre, 19, 20, 21, 23–4, 153, 244n.11
Blum, Abbe, 253n.5
Boas, F. S., 257n.1
Bohemia scenes (IV.ii–IV.iv), 9
  in productions: Barker, 51, 53; Bergman, 177, 187–9; Brook, 65, 66, 79; Donnellan, 204–7; Hall (Peter), 154, 166–8; sheep-shearing sequence in English *Tales* at the millennium, 235–40; Stanley, 113, 114, 123–4
  see also pastoral scene (IV.iv)
Boleyn, Anne, 17, 76
Bond, Samantha, 241
  as Hermione, 217, 223–4
Bones, Ken, 214, *226*
Boushey, Carmi, *130*
Bowmer Theatre, 112–13

Bradbrook, Muriel C., 22, 81–2
Bradley, John, 91
Bridges-Adams, W., 37, 60, 245n.4
British Broadcasting Corporation, 'BBC TV Shakespeare' series, 134–5
  house style, 135
  naturalistic mode, 150
  series policy, 136
  see also under Howell, Jane
Britten-Austin, Paul, 255n.9
Brook, Peter, 53, 58, 61, 162
  books: *The Empty Space*, 64–5, 77, 80, 81, 84, 85, 87, 248n.2, 249n.3; *The Open Door*, 83; *The Shifting Point*, 62, 83, 84; *Threads of Time*, 63, 68, 83
  on Maly Drama Theatre, 195
  promptbook (*Winter's Tale* production), 72, 76–7, 78, 81–2, 248n.4
  stage productions: *Boris Godunov*, 63; *Love's Labour's Lost*, 62, 63, 67; *Measure for Measure*, 63–4, 68; *A Midsummer Night's Dream*, 67, 84, 85, 249n.3; *Ring Round the Moon*, 64; *Romeo and Juliet*, 63; *Salome*, 63; *Titus Andronicus*, 62, 63; *Venice Preserved*, 68
  Winter's Tale production at Phoenix Theatre (1951), 62–84; cast, 64; costume design, 66; 'double image' design and blocking, 67–8; music, 64, 79; run of, 247n.1; set design, 65–6; structure of play, Brook's view of, 64–5, 248n.2; textual cuts, 76–7
Brooklyn Academy of Music, 181, 188, 254n.1, 255nn.8–9
Broome, John, 102

Brown-Lowe, Thomas, 219
Bruce, Brenda, 4, 95–6, 108
Bruneau, Lise, 82
Bruni, Emily, 216, *226*
Bryant, Michael, 167
Bryden, Ronald, 91–2, 96, 104
Bulman, James C., 135
Burke, David, 150
Bury, John, 86, 249n.5
Byrne, Muriel St Clare, 59, 247n.14

Calder-Marshall, Anna, 141–2, 148, 150
Canadian Shakespeare Festival, 253n.2
Carter, Michael, 154
Casson, Lewis, 33, 61, 162, 245n.2
  as Antigonus, 64, *74*, 79
  as director, 247n.14
Chaplin, Nellie, 53
Cheek by Jowl, 195
childhood, cultural valuation of, 218
Chitty, Alison, 152, 253n.1
choreography, *see* dance; Feuer, Donya
Chumakova, Karina, 257n.5
Church, Tony, 253n.1
  as Antigonus, 156, 161–2, 166
Citizen Kane (film), 217
Clapp, Susannah, 213
Clothier, Richard, 219–20
Clowes, Jonathan, 217
Clubb, Louise, 22
Coghill, Nevill, 22
Coleridge, Samuel Taylor, 11, 28
Colorado Shakespeare Festival, 115
Complicité, *see* Theatre de Complicité
Cook, Ann Jennalie, 140
Cooke, Dominic, *Winter's Tale* production with RSC at the Swan (2006), 216–17, 224, 241

Cookman, Anthony, 73
Costello, Kevin, 219, 240
costume design
  Barker production, 37–8, 51
  Bergman production, 174, 180, 187, 191
  Brook production, 66
  Donnellan production, 198–9, 205, 207, 212
  English *Tales* at the millennium, 214, 215, 217, 220, 224, 231, 232, 237, 239–40
  Hall (Peter) production, 152, 163
  Howell production, 137–8
  Nunn production, 101, 102
  Stanley production, 114, 116, 123
Cottesloe theatre, 23, 152, 153, 163, 166, 253n.1
Coveney, Michael, 157
Craig, Edward Gordon, 59
Crosse, Gordon, productions discussed
  Barker, 44, 49, 58, 248n.2
  Brook, 62, 66, 70, 77, 78, 79, 248n.2
  Tree, 31
cultural translation, reinvention and, 175, 176, 194, 196–8, 206
  in Bergman production's pastoral scenes, 189
  linguistic differences, 197–8
  see also Bergman, Ingmar; Donnellan, Declan

Dalí, Salvador, 63
dance
  Barker production, 51–3
  Bergman production, 176–7, 181–3
  Stanley production, 124
  see also satyrs' dance
Daniels, Phil, 236

Davidson, Jeannie, 114–15, 252n.7
da Vinci, Leonardo, 88, 89, 250n.7
Dench, Jeffery, 231, 232
Dench, Judi, 250nn.10–11
  doubling as Hermione and Perdita, 99–101, 103–6, 108; challenges of, 104; critical reception of, 104
  as Hermione, *91*, 92, 94, 99–100, 104, 105, 222
  as Perdita, 100–1, *102*, 103–4; use of Yorkshire accent, 101
Dessen, Alan, 21, 120, 121, 122, 126, 129, 131–2
Dexter, Felix, 237
Dexter, Sally, 154, 163, 169–70
Diaghilev, Sergei, 54
Dickinson, Emily, 169, 254n.4
direct address convention, 72, 113, 184
  television adaptation of, 134, 139, 140–1, 144, 145, 150
Dixon, Joe, *226*
Dodin, Lev, 194, 195, 197, 211, 212, 256nn.1–3
Donnellan, Declan, 194
  on jealousy, 201
  on Leontes' journey, 208, 212
  stage productions: *As You Like It*, *195*; *Measure for Measure*, 195; *Othello*, 195
  Winter's Tale production with Maly Drama Theatre, St Petersburg (1997), 194–212, 219; awarded Russia's Golden Mask for Best Production, 194; break from Russian romantic 'fairy-tale' assumptions, 212; costume design, 198–9, 205, 207, 212; critical

[283]

Donnellan, Declan (*continued*)
  reception of, 203–4, 206, 212; Gnedich translation used in, 196–8, 209; music, 209; prominence of play's political critique, 196, 197–8, 202–4, 205–7, 212; set design, 199–200, 212; textual cuts, 197, 207, 209, 210; tour, 195
Doran, Gregory, *Winter's Tale* production with RSC (1999), 214–15, 222, 224, 225, 230, 231, 234, 240
Douglas, Randi, 121, 125, *128*
Dowden, Edward, 11, 41, 172
Downie, Pennie, 101
Dramat, 175, 176, 181, 254n.1, 254n.3
Dramaten, *see* Royal Dramatic Theatre of Sweden, The
Draper, R. P., 2, 104
Drewitt, Stanley, 52, 57
Dryden, John, 1, 2, 24, 243n.1
du Rand, Le Clanché, 251n.6
  as Hermione, 112; Leontes' jealousy scene, 115–16, 117, *118*, 119–20; statue scene, 125–31, *128*, *130*, 133; trial scene, 121–2
Dymkowski, Christine, 59, 60, 61, 244n.1, 246n.7, 247nn.14–15

Eagleton, Terry, 10
Edmondson, James, 157, 251n.5
  as Leontes, 112, 115–22, *118*, 126, *128*, *130*; building 'tender side', 121; jealousy scene, building tension in, 116–21; repentance, 122, 124; statue scene, 126, 127–31, 133; trial scene, 121–2
  'physicality' of acting, 115, 120

Edwards, Christopher, 172
Edwards, Michael Donald, 251n.1
Eklund, Jakob, *188*
Elgar, Edward, 57
Elizabeth I, 16, 17, 76
Elliott, Marc, 217
Elliott, Steven, *226*
English *Tale*s at the millennium, 213–42
  bold stage images opening productions, 214–19
  double design explored, 213–14, 242
  Hermione as good Queen, 222–8
  'infection' and Leontes' jealousy, 219–21
  sheep-shearing sequence, 235–40
  statue scene and redemption, 240–2
  transitions in middle of *Winter's Tale*, 228–35; Autolycus' entrance, 234–5; bear, 230–1; Old Shepherd, 231–2; Time as Chorus, 232–3
Erickson, Peter, 6
Evans, Gareth Lloyd, 96, 103
Evans, Hugh, 250n.1
Eyre, Ronald, 160

Fanshawe, Simon, 201, 202, 208
Farjeon, Herbert, 50, 54
Faucit, Helena (Lady Martin), 29–30, 82
Fedorovitch, Sophie, 64, 65, 66, 78
feminism, *see under* gender relations
Fenwick, Henry, 135, 136, 137, 142, 143, 144, 149
Feuer, Donya, 175, 177, 181–3, 255n.10
figuranter, Swedish

nineteenth-century theatrical tradition of, 176, 181–3, 184
Findlay, Deborah, 225
Fleetwood, Kate, 217, 224
Fletcher, John, *The Faithful Shepherdess*, 11
Foakes, R. A., 28
Fogerty, Elsie, 44
formalism, 85–6, 90, 97, 98–9, 155, 249n.4
Forman, Simon, 18
Fox, Karen, 257n.6
Frank, Joseph, 250n.8
Freshwater, Geoffrey, 226
Frey, Charles, 1
Fry, Charles, 59
Fry, Christopher, 64, 249n.7
Fulton, Rikki, 150

Garber, Marjorie, 1
Gardner, Lyn, 200, 201, 208, 211, 241
Garrick, David, 29, 82
  Florizel and Perdita, a Dramatic Pastoral, In Three Acts, 25
Gaskell, Ronald, 252n.2
gender relations, 244n.7
  conflicts in, 143
  feminism, 3, 29, 46, 75, 225; feminist criticism, 5, 132; Stanley's production and, 110, 112
  misogyny, 7–8, 16, 74, 111, 161
  'new woman' movement, 3, 243n.4
  patriarchal, 5, 6–7, 8, 16, 191, 215, 225, 240
  suffrage and suffragettes, 3–4, 48, 243n.5
  women's resistance to tyranny, 5, 6–8, 16, 107, 121, 161–2, 225
  women's roles, 2–9, 16;

Barker production, 46–9; Bergman production, 190, 191; Brook production, 73–7; Garrick's rewritten statue scene, 25–6; Nunn production, 95–7, 106–8, 109; Paulina as political and spiritual counsellor, 4, 5, 16, 107, 124, 190, 191; Stanley production, 111–12, 124
Women's Social and Political Union (WSPU), 3, 4
see also political issues; power relations
genre, 1, 10–13, 14, 70, 134, 179, 243n.3, 257n.1
  comedy, 1, 10, 12, 14, 48, 55, 74, 78, 113, 123, 132, 157, 158, 160, 171, 230, 231
  Renaissance conceptions of, 11
  romance, 1, 8, 11–12, 13, 70, 75, 134, 172, 213
  theatrical issues and question of, 10–13
  tragicomedy, 1, 11–13, 18, 41, 45, 50, 172
Gielgud, John, 44, 63–4, 75, 99, 117
  Barker and, 61
  books: *An Actor and His Time*, 44; *Shakespeare – Hit or Miss?*, 68, 248n.5; *Stage Directions*, 248n.5
  stage roles: Angelo in *Measure for Measure*, 63, 69; Hamlet, 70; Lear, 61; Leontes, 62, 64, 66, 68–73, 74, 81–2, 83, 121, 127, 248n.6, 249n.7; Othello, 68–9
Gilbreath, Alexandra, 214, 220–1, 222, 224–5, 226, 240–1

[285]

Glastonbury Festival, 236
Globe theatre, performance at, 18, 19, 20–4, 153
Gnedich, Pyotr, 196–8, 209, 256n.4
Godard, Jean-Luc, 192
Goldblatt, Harold, 145
Goodbody, Buzz, 101
Gorshkov, Alex, 257n.6
Gouge, William, *Domesticall Duties*, 8
Grady, Hugh, 90, 250n.8
Graham, Charles, 57
Grand, Sarah, 243n.4
Granville-Barker, Harley, *see* Barker, Harley Granville
Gray, Tamu, 253n.2
  as Paulina, 4, 164
Greene, Robert, 19
  Pandosto, 11, 19, 24, 71, 244n.10; Shakespeare's transformation of, 14–18, 244n.10
Grevenius, Herbert, 181
Guarini, Giovan Battista, *Il Pastor Fido*, 12
Gurney, Rachel, 249n.7
Gurr, Andrew, 20, 23, 244n.11
Guthrie, Tyrone, 61

Hair (musical), 103
Hall, Edward, *Winter's Tale* production with Propeller at Watermill Theatre (2005), 218–20, 222, 223, 233, 237–9, 242, 257n.2
Hall, Peter, 23, 84, 86, 192
  books: *Peter Hall's Diaries*, 86
  National Theatre's season of late plays, 253n.1; compared to Nunn's season of late plays with RSC, 151–2
  stage productions, 9;
    Cymbeline, 151, 152, 157;
    The Tempest, 151, 152
Winter's Tale production at National Theatre (1988), 7, 127, 129, 151–73, 175; ambiguous ending, 170–2; costume design, 152, 163; critical reception, 156, 172–3; emphasis on verse and prose structures, 155–7, 159–60; lighting and colour palette, 153; 'Renaissance' visual references, 152; set design, 153, 166; textual cuts, 155; tour of, 152–4
Halqvist, Britt G., 174
Hancock, Sheila, 4
Hands, Terry, 100, 169, 250n.11
Harding, Esther, 112
Hardy, Robert, 249n.7
Harris, Joanna G., 124
Hartwig, Joan, 12, 243n.3, 246n.10
Hay, Richard L., 113, 114, 122, 124, 252n.7
Hayes, James, 231, 232
Hazlitt, William
  Characters of Shakespear's Plays, 27
  on Kemble, 27
Hedrick, Donald, 149, 150
Henriksson, Krister, 180
Henry VIII, 76
Henson, Basil, 166, 171, 253n.1
Hermione
  Barker production: inception of Leontes' jealousy, 42; statue scene, 46, 47, 55; trial scene, 46
  Bergman production: Almqvist's *Songes* and, 180–1; inception of Leontes' jealousy, 183–6; statue scene, 190, 191–3
  Brook production: inception of Leontes' jealousy, 71–2;

[286]

statue scene, 66, 80, 81–2, 83; trial scene, 76 as counterforce to Leontes, 5, 6–7, 8
Donnellan production, 199, 202; inception of Leontes' jealousy, 201; statue scene, 200, 208–10; trial scene, 197–8, 202, 204, *205*
English *Tales* at the millennium, 214, 215, 217, 222, *226*, 230; bear scene, 230, 231; inception of Leontes' jealousy, 219–221; pregnancy, 222–3; statue scene, 240, 241, 242; trial scene, 223–5, 228
Hall (Peter) production, 154, 157, 158; inception of Leontes' jealousy, 158, 159; statue scene, 169–72; trial scene, 162–3
Howell production: inception of Leontes' jealousy, 138–9, 140; statue scene, 145, 146–9; trial scene, 141–3
Nunn production, 98–100; doubling parts of Perdita and, 98–9, 103–4, 106; inception of Leontes' jealousy, 90–4; statue scene, 90, 95, 98, 103–4, 105, 106–7
performance history: early seventeenth century, 21, 23, 24; nineteenth century, 29, 30; Restoration and eighteenth century, 25–6
rethinking of women's roles and, 2
Stanley production, 111, 112, 115–16, 123; inception of

Leontes' jealousy, 117–21, *118*; statue scene, 114, 115, 125–31, *128*, *130*; trial scene, 121–2, 131
Hewetson, Herbert, *50*, 50–1
Hille, Anastasia, 241
  as Hermione, 215, 222, 223, 224
Hind, C. Lewis, 246–7n.12
Hodge, Douglas, 215
Holderness, Graham, 136
Homfray, Don, 136, 137
Hope-Wallace, Philip, 72, 79, 248n.6
Howell, Jane, 134, 252n.1, 252n.3
television productions: *Henry VI*, 135, 150; *Richard III*, 135; *Titus Andronicus*, 135, 150
Winter's Tale television production for BBC (1980), 134–50; adaptation of theatrical conventions to television, 138–9, 145; camera close-ups and direct address to camera, 139–45, 147, 150; costume design, 137–8; critical reception, 139–40, 149–50; Howell's critique of, 149–50; lighting, 136–7, 146; non-illusionism of, 135, 136, 137, 138, 144, 150; priority given to verbal life of drama, 140, 149; production style, 135–6; set design, 135–8; textual cuts, 149; vision of *Winter's Tale*, 137
Hughes, Ian, 234
Hughes, Ted, 255n.10
Hunt, Hugh, 46
Hunt, Maurice, 1

[287]

Hunter, Kathryn, 225
Hyde, Rupert, 42, 53
Hytner, Nicholas, *Winter's Tale* production at National Theatre (2001), 213, 215, 218, 219, 223, 224, 225, 229, 232, 233, 236–7, 240, 241, 242

Ibsen, Henrik
 Doll's House, A, 3
 Hedda Gabler, 4, 115
Ichikawa, Mariko, 20, 23
illusionism, 31, 58, 63
 break with: by Barker, 2, 33–5, 51; Bergman's strategies for, 186–8; by Howell, 135, 136
 use of term, 252n.2
 see also naturalism; non-illusionism; realism
improvisation
 by Autolycus in Bergman production, 188–9
 in Nunn rehearsals, 92
Ingham, Barrie, 250n.9
 as Leontes, 89, *91*, 92–3, 94–5, 96, 97, 99
Irving, Henry, 43, 44

Jackson, Barry, 59–60, 63
Jacobean absolutism, 196, 198, 203
Jacobs, Gerald, 99
James I, 15, 17, 19, 22
Jarvis, Andrew, 230, 231
jealousy, *see under* Leontes
Jennings, Alex, as Leontes, 215, 216, 224, 240
Jesson, Paul, 233
Johns, Eric, 62, 67–8
Johnson, Phillip, 120
Johnson, Samuel, 79
Jones, Gemma, 163
Jonson, Ben, 41
 Masque of Augurs, 22

Jungian psychology, 112

Kean, Charles, 24, 38, 117, 127, 248n.5
 scenography, 30–1
Kean, Mrs Charles (Ellen Tree), 30–1
Kemble, John Philip, 26–7, 28
Kemp, Jeremy, 138, 139–40, 143–4, 147, 150
Kennedy, Dennis
 productions discussed:
 Barker, 2, 32, 35, 39, 42, 46, 56, 57, 60, 61; Donnellan, 194, 199, 245n.5; in languages other than English, 176
Kingston, Jeremy, 200, 202, 208
Kitto, H. D. F., 110
Kliss, Paul, 250n.1
Knight, G. Wilson, 250n.8
Kohler, Estelle, 4, 225, 228
Kolotova, Natalia, 198, 199, 201, 203, 206, 208–9, 210, 257n.5
Konody, P. G., 37, 38, 58
Kraft, Barry, 250n.1
Kumalo, Alton, 98
Kuskova, Katherine, 256n.1
Kuskova, Olga, 256n.1, 256–7n.4
 on linguistic differences between Russian and Shakespearean text, 197–8

Lahr, John, 180, 185, 192, 193
Lambert, J. W., 96
late plays other than *The Winter's Tale*, 244n.11
 Cymbeline, 151, 152, 157, 247n.14
 family in, 8–9
 Henry VIII, 76, 88, 152, 250n.6
 Pericles, 88, 89, 92, 152,

[288]

249n.3, 250n.6
reappraisal of, 1–3, 243n.2
studies focusing on genre and dramatic conventions in, 243n.3
Tempest, The, 11, 151, 152, 173, 257n.1
as understood by: Hall (Peter), 151–2, 154; Nunn, 151
Lavrov, Nikolai, 206
Leavis, F. R., 85–6, 155
Leigh-Hunt, Barbara, 4, 99
Leonardo da Vinci, 88, 89, 250n.7
Leontes
  jealousy, inception of (I.ii), 6, 9, 16, 17, 27, 28, 29; Barker production, 41–3, 45; Bergman production, 183–6; Brook production, 70–2, 248n.6; Donnellan production, 200–2, 208; Hall (Peter) production, 157–60; Howell production, 138–40; 'infection' in English *Tale*s at the millennium, 219–21; Nunn production, 92–4; Stanley production, 115, 116–21
  misogyny of, 7–8, 16, 74, 111, 161
  Nunn's emphasis on inner psychological conflict in, 89–97
  repentance (III.ii), 9; Autolycus' repentance as parodic of, in Hall (Peter) production, 167; Barker production, 48; Brook production, 72–3, 82; Hall (Peter) production, 163–4; Howell production, 141, 143–4; Nunn production, 95, 97;
Stanley production, 115, 124
reunion of Perdita and (V.ii), 191
see also tyrannical use of power, tyranny
see also under statue scene (V.iii), Hall (Peter)
Lesser, Anton, 217, 224, 241
Liebert, Judy, 225
lighting
  Barker production, 33, 35, 245nn.4–5
  Hall (Peter) production, 153
  Howell production, 136–7, 146
  Nunn production, 87–8, 91–3, 94–5, 97–8, 108
  Stanley production, 114, 115, 122, 124
Lindh, Irene, 178, 180, 193
Lloyd, Robert Langdon, 234–5
Lloyd George, David, Prime Minister, 4
Löfgren, Lars, 176

Macaulay, Alastair, 200, 241
McBean, Angus, 65, 66, 82, 248n.3
McBurney, Simon, 240
  as Leontes, 216, 219, 241
McCabe, Richard, *228*, 234
MacCarthy, Desmond, 32, 38, 51, 57, 247n.12
McCarthy, Lillah, 3, 243n.5
  as Ann Whitefield in *Man and Superman*, 3
  as Hermione, 2, 37, 46–7, 55, 57
  in *Votes for Women!*, 3–4
McCowen, Alec, 249n.7
McDonagh, Martin, *The Pillowman*, 218
McGuire, Philip, 133
McKellen, Ian, 158
McLellan, Joseph, 140

Macready, William Charles, 28–9, 42, 82, 127
Magni, Marcello, 235
Maher, Mary, 252n.1, 252n.3, 253n.5
Malkin, Roman, 256n.2
Maly Drama Theatre, 194–5, 256n.3, 256n.12
   awarded title of 'Théâtre de l'Europe' (1998), 195
   origins of, 256n.2
   see also under Donnellan, Declan
Marker, Frederick J. and Lise-Lone Marker, 175, 176, 177, 182, 254n.2
Marshall, Norman, 36, 43, 245n.5
Martin, Helena Faucit, *see* Faucit, Helena (Lady Martin)
Masefield, John, 32
Mason, Brewster, 79
Masters, Anthony, 140
Maze, Steven, 122
Mazer, Cary, 33, 35, 245n.5, 247n.13
Messina, Cedric, 135
metatheatrical, 13, 20–1, 50, 150, 176, 179, 187
Mies van der Rohe, Ludwig, 200
Mikoyan, Sergo, 203
millennium, English *Tale*s at the, *see* English *Tale*s at the millennium
Miller, Jonathan, 135, 136
Miller, Neville, 96
Mishima, Yukio, *Madame de Sade*, 181, 183
Moffatt, John, 79, 80
monarchical absolutism, 15–16, 152
   see also absolutism
Morgan, Macnamara, *The Sheep-Shearing: Or Florizel and Perdita*, 25

Mörk, Lennart, 177
Morley, Christopher, 85, 87, 91
Mowat, Barbara, 12, 243n.3, 246n.10
Mucedorus (anonymous), 22
Muir, Kenneth, 25
Murphey, Mark D., 124
music, 24, 249n.7, 254n.4, 255n.9
   Barker production, 53
   Bergman production, 177–81, 189, 192, 193
   Brook production, 64, 79
   Donnellan production, 209
   English *Tale*s at the millennium, 217, 220, 238, 263
   Howell production, 146
   Nunn production, 101–3
   Stanley production, 125, 131

National Theatre production (1988), *see under* Hall, Peter
naturalism
   break away from, 86, 87–8, 108, 135, 136, 138, 144, 150, 200
   television's tendencies toward, 134, 135
   use of term, 252n.2
Neal, Mary, 53
Neely, Carol, 6
Neilson-Terry, Dennis, 52, 57
neo-classicism, 24, 25, 28
Nesbitt, Cathleen, 55
   as Perdita, 43, 44, 47–8, 52, 57, 101
Nettles, John, 219, 223, 240
'new woman' movement, *see under* gender relations
Nicholson, H. O., 52
Nightingale, Benedict, 220, 241–2
9/11 (terrorist attacks in New York [2001]), 218
Noble, Adrian, *Winter's Tale*

production with RSC (1992), 217, 219, 223, 230, 231, 232, 233, 234, 239–40, 241
non-illusionism
  Barker production, 32, 35, 56
  Howell production, 135, 136, 137, 138, 144, 150
  Nunn production, 87, 97–8
  Stanley production, 113
  see also illusionism
Nunn, Trevor, 84, 155, 158, 160, 201, 249n.1
  comparison to Peter Hall's season of late plays at the National Theatre, 151–2
  promptbook, 93, 97, 249n.2
  stage productions: *Henry VIII*, 88, 250n.6; *Pericles*, 88, 89, 92, 249n.3, 250n.6; *The Revenger's Tragedy*, 249n.5
  view of late plays, 151
  Winter's Tale production with RSC (1969–71), 85–109; affinities with Brook's 'empty space', 85, 86, 87; costumes, music, and movement, 101–3; doubling parts of Hermione and Perdita, 98–9; dreams as central motif in, 91, 93–4; focus on psychological microcosm, 88–9; lighting design and changes, 87–8, 91–3, 94–5, 97–8, 108; move away from naturalism, 87–8, 108; move away from the political, 89; non-illusionist methods, 87, 97–8; set design (white box), 87, 88; spatialization of images, 90–1; textual cuts, 105–8, 109; tour of, 249n.2; view of play as allegorical, 106

O'Connor, John J., 140
Oliver, Roger W., 175
Olivier, Laurence, 44
Olivier theatre
  Hall (Peter) production, 153, 166, 253n.1
  Hytner production, 215
O'Mahony, John, 202
Onwukwe, Ben, 229–30
Oparei, Dhobi, 230
oracle, 8, 12, 15, 21, 25
  Barker production, 38
  Bergman production, 190, 192
  Brook production, 72, 73 75, 77
  Donnellan production, 204
  English *Tale*s at the millennium, 225
  Hall (Peter) production, 160, 162
  Howell production, 143
  Nunn production, 94, 95
  Stanley production, 122, 123, 124, 129
Oregon Shakespeare Festival (Oregon Shakespearean Festival before 1988), 9, 49, 82, 166, 253n.2, 256n.12
  productions of *Winter's Tale* at, 250–1n.1
  Theatre Archives, 251–2n.7
  see also under Stanley, Audrey, *Winter's Tale* production with Oregon Shakespearean Festival (1975)
Orgel, Stephen, 1, 18, 253n.4
  edition of *The Tempest*, 151, 173
  on Leontes' jealousy, 159
  on Leontes' tyranny, 15

Orgel, Stephen (*continued*)
  on topicality of *Winter's Tale*, 17
  on tragicomedy, 11, 12
Ormcrod, Nick, 194, 195, 199–200, 212
Orrell, John, 21
Osborne, Charles, 156
Osborne, Laurie, 246n.7
Otten, Elizabeth, 145

Pachelbel, Johann, Canon in D, 125, 131
Padve, Efim, 195, 256n.2
Pafford, J. H. P., 174, 243n.2, 244n.10
Palmer, John, 33–4, 46
Pandosto, *see* Greene, Robert
Pankhurst family, 3, 4
Parkes, Toby, 216
Parsons, Gordon, 100
Pasco, Richard, *91*, 92, 99
Paster, Gail, 8
pastoral scene (IV.iv), 9
  Barker production, 36, 51–5, 58; music in, 53; satyrs' dance, 53–4
  Bergman production, 187–9
  Brook production, 79
  Donnellan production, 204–7
  Hall (Peter) production, 167–8; satyrs' dance, 154, 168
  Howell production, 136–7
  Nunn production, 101–3; satyrs and shepherds, 102
  sheep-shearing sequence in English *Tale*s at the millennium, 235–40
  Stanley production, 123–4
  see also Bohemia scenes (IV.ii–IV.iv)
Paulina
  Barker production, 48–9, 55; statue scene, *57*; trial scene, 43
  Bergman production, 177, 185, 190, 191; statue scene, 191–3
  Brook production, 64, 66, 73–7, *74*; fidelity to oracle, 75–6; omission of betrothal to Camillo, 76–7; statue scene, 81, 82
  as counterforce to Leontes, 5–6, 15–16, 107, 121
  Donnellan production, 209, 210
  English *Tale*s at the millennium, 220, 221, 223, 225, 228, 240, 241
  Hall (Peter) production, 154, 156, 160–2; Leontes' repentance, 163–4, *165*; proposed betrothal to Camillo, 171; statue scene, 170, 171
  Howell production, 141, 150; statue scene, 146–9
  Leontes' misogynist attacks on, 7–8, 16
  Nunn production, 95, 96–7, 106; lines cut, 106, 107–8; statue scene, 104; trial scene, 97
  performance history: early seventeenth century, 23, 24; nineteenth century, 29; Restoration and eighteenth century, 25
  rethinking of women's roles and, 2, 3, 4
  as spiritual and political counsellor, 5–6, 95, 96–7, 107, 111
  Stanley production, 111, 121, 123; conflict with lords, 124; Leontes' repentance, 122; proposed betrothal to Camillo, 129, 132–3; statue scene, 125, 126–7, *128*

Pavis, Patrice, 194, 196
Payne, Maggi, 124
Payne, Oliver, 216
Peacock, John, 137–8
Peele, George, *Old Wives Tale*, 12
performance history of *The Winter's Tale*
  early seventeenth century, 18–24
  nineteenth century, 22, 26–31, 38, 56
  Restoration and eighteenth century, 24–6
  twentieth century, 1–4, 9–10, 31, 58–61, 213–14, 241–2
  twenty-first century, 213–14, 241–2
Pesochinsky, Nikolai, 202, 204
Peter, John, 201, 202, 206, 208, 210–11, 215, 221, 233, 238, 241
Peterson, Douglas, 243n.3
Phoenix Theatre, *see under* Brook, Peter
pictorialism
  Barker's break from, 51
  Brook's use of, 63, 67, 84
  Edwardian, 33
  Howell's avoidance of, 135, 136
Pigott-Smith, Tim, 156, 158, 160, 253n.1
  on ending to *Winter's Tale*, 171, 172
  as Leontes, 7, 154, 157–62, 163, 164, *165*; in statue scene, 170; suddenness of jealousy, 158, 159; *tremor cordis* and mental state, 160
Pinkhasik, Naum, 256n.1
Planché, J. R., 58
Playfair, Nigel, 54–5, 247n.14
Poel, William, 34, 39, 59, 244–5n.1, 245n.5

political issues, 75, 244n.9
  connection of the personal with the political, 7, 17, 202; political consequences of Leontes' delusions, 160–6
  monarchical absolutism, 15–16, 152
  political absolutism, 152
  political critique prominent in Donnellan production, 196, 197–8, 202–4, 205–7, 212
  royal succession, 6, 16–17, 107, 124, 191
  suffrage, 3–4, 48, 243n.5
  see also power relations; tyrannical use of power, tyranny
Popov, Leonid, 196, 202, 204
Porter, Eric, 99
power relations, 5–9
  Bergman production, 190, 191
  Brook production, 76
  Donnellan production, 202–4
  Hall (Peter) production, 160–6
  Howell production, 142
  Stanley production, 111, 124
  textual cuts in Nunn production and loss of social nuances of, 107–8, 109
  see also gender relations; political issues; tyrannical use of power, tyranny
pregnancy, 116, 220, 222
pregnant belly, 94
pregnant body, 222
pregnant life, 100
prerogative, royal, 15
  see also absolutism; political issues; tyrannical use of power, tyranny

[293]

problem plays, 213, 257n.1
Propeller's *Winter's Tale* production at Watermill Theatre (2005), *see* Hall, Edward
Pushkin, Alexander, 204

Quayle, Anthony, 58, 81, 84

Rabold, Rex, 250–1n.1
Rashbrook, Stephen, *226*
realism
 break away from, 36, 51, 59, 81, 249n.5
 pictorial realism, 33–4
 spectacular realism, 31
 use of term, 252n.2
 see also illusionism; naturalism
Reichenbach, Todd, *118*
Reinhardt, Max, 58, 245n.5
repentance, *see under* Leontes
revaluation of *The Winter's Tale*, 1–2, 243n.2
 in recent performance history, 2
 rethinking women's roles, 2–9
 in scholarship and criticism, 1
Rich, Adrienne, 7
Richardson, Joy, 164
ritual theatre, idea of, 85, 86
 ritual action in Nunn's statue scene, 105, 107
 ritual in Stanley production, 125
 television's emphasis on individual responses rather than participation in ritual action, 145, 147
Roberts, Peter, 96
Robins, Elizabeth, *Votes for Women!*, 3–4
Robson, Flora, 64, 69, 162
 on *Henry VIII*, 76
 as Paulina, 4, 73–7, *74*, 81

Romano, Giulio, 37, 241
Romberg, Bertil, 179, 180, 254n.4, 254n.6, 255n.7
Rose, George, 64, 79, 249n.7
Rothenstein, Albert, 35–8, 51
Rothwell, Kenneth, 140, 149
Royal Dramatic Theatre of Sweden, The, 175
 model of, as Mamillius' toy in Bergman production, 185
 as set for Bergman production, 176, 177
 see also under Bergman, Ingmar
Royal Shakespeare Company (RSC), 155
 see also Cooke, Dominic; Doran, Gregory; Noble, Adrian; Warchus, Matthew
 see also under Nunn, Trevor
Rutherston, Albert, *see* Rothenstein, Albert
Rylands, George, 71, 72, 78, 79

Salander, Anna, 254n.3
Sampson, Nick, *226*
Sartre, Jean-Paul, 80–1
satyrs' dance, 24, 31
 Barker production, 53, 54
 cut from productions, 77, 149, 207
 Hall (Edward) production, 239
 Hall (Peter) production, 154, 168
 Nunn production, 101–2
 stage direction (First Folio), 53
Savoy Theatre, *see under* Barker, Harley Granville
Scardifield, Simon, 220, 222, 223
Schaar, Claes, 174
Schanzer, Ernst, 1, 10, 12–13, 22, 157

Schmidt, Michael, 213
Scoggins, Peter, 257n.2
Selby, Nicholas, 92
Self, David, 134
Semak, Pyotr, 194, 200–2, 208, 212
Semple, Goldie, 163
set design, 58–9
  Barker production, 35–6
  Bergman production, 176, 177
  Brook production, 65–6
  Donnellan production, 199–200, 212
  English *Tales* at the millennium, 214–20, 222, 229, 233, 236, 237, 239, 240–1
  Hall (Peter) production, 153, 166
  Howell production, 135–8
  Nunn production, 87, 88
  Stanley production, 113–14, 122, 123, 124, 125
sexuality, 3, 238
  in Hall (Peter) production of Bohemia scenes, 154
  and Hermione's pregnant body, 222
  Leontes' jealousy and feeling of sexual betrayal, 115
  sexual energies of satyrs' dance, 102, 168
Shakespeare Recording Society recording (1961), 249n.7
Shaw, George Bernard, 3
  on Barker's production, 32, 33, 57
  on McCarthy, 46
  Man and Superman, 3
  sheep-shearing sequence, 235–40
  see also pastoral scene (IV.iv)
Sher, Antony, 216, 240, 257n.1
  as Leontes, 208, 214, 220–1, 224, *226*

Shevstova, Maria, 202, 207, 209, 211, 212, 256n.2
Shorter, John, 104
Shulman, Milton, 98, 104
Shuttleworth, Ian, 201, 206
Sidney, Philip, *The Arcadia*, 12, 244n.8
Silbert, Peter, 116, *118*
Skinner, Claire, 215, 223, 224, 241
Smith, Derek, 101
Smith, Hallett, 243n.3
Smith, Peter J., 257n.2
Spencer, Charles, 201, 204, 208, 210, 211, 216, 241, 242
Spencer, Stanley, 239
Spenser, Edmund, *The Faerie Queene*, 12
Sprague, Arthur Colby, 66, 69–70, 71, 72, 74, 77, 248n.2
Spriggs, Elizabeth, 4, 95–6, 108
Squire, William, 249n.7
Stalin, Josef, 199
  'Great Terror', 203
  show trials of 1930s under, 202–3
Stanley, Audrey, 9, 49, 160, 250n.1, 251nn.4–5, 252n.7
  background, 110–11
  Vanderbilt University lecture (1990), 111, 113–14, 115, 132, 251n.2
  Winter's Tale production with Oregon Shakespearean Festival (1975), 110–33, 157; acute awareness of heightened moments involving references to gods, 111, 112, 122, 129, 131; affinity with Brook's production, 121; bear in, 122–3; close textual work, 115–17, 125, 132; costume designs, 114, 116, 123; critical

[295]

response to, 120–1;
dance, 124; ending, 9, 49;
lighting, 114, 115, 122,
124; music, 125, 131;
representation of the
feminine, 111–12; ritual,
strong use of, 125; set
design, 113–14, 122, 123,
124, 125; symbolic
images in, 123; 'three
worlds' in two main
parts, 113; visual
patterns, 131
see also under statue scene
(V.iii)
statue scene (V.iii), 6, 9, 17–18,
22–4, 29
Barker production, 46, 55–6
Bergman production, 191–3
Brook production, 66, 80–2
Donnellan production,
208–12; last visual
sequence with Mamillius,
210–11
English *Tale*s at the
millennium, 240–2
Garrick's revision, 25–6
Hall (Peter) production,
168–72; as primarily
about Leontes' journey,
169
Howell production, 145–9,
253n.5; reaction shots,
147
music in, 23–4
Nunn production, 98, 103–5,
106; ritual action in, 105,
107
Stanley production, 9, 111,
113–15, 125–32, *128*, *130*,
133; forgiveness at heart
of, 127–8; proposed
betrothal of Camillo and
Paulina in, 49, 129, 132–3
Stewart, Patrick, 97
Stock, Nigel, 249n.7

Stott, Judith, 249n.7
Stott, Ken, 154, 166–8, 253n.1
Stravinsky, Igor, 54
suffrage and suffragettes, *see
under* gender relations
Syer, Fontaine, 82, 251n.1,
253n.2, 256n.12
symbolic visual presentation,
conventions of, 21–2

Taylor, Myra Lucretia, 225
Taylor, Paul, 199, 211, 234, 238,
242
television production
challenges of, 134, 139–40,
144, 145, 150
production styles, 252n.2
see also under Howell, Jane
Terry, Ellen, 30, 248n.5
Terry, J. E. Harold, 43
Terry, Kate, 248n.5
textual cuts
Barker production, 39–40,
246n.7
Bergman production, 174,
175, 190–1, 256n.14
Brook production, 76–7
Donnellan production, 197,
207, 209, 210
Hall (Peter) production, 155
Howell production, 149
Nunn production, 105–8, 109
Theatre de Complicité, *Winter's
Tale* production by Annabel
Arden at Lyric
Hammersmith (1992), 216,
217, 219, 225, 229, 235,
237, 240, 241
Thesiger, Ernest, 249n.7
Thorndike, Sybil, 33, 245n.2
Time as Chorus (IV.i), 9, 26
dramaturgy and, 14, 17, 19,
24, 134, 232
iconographic figure, 24
in productions: Arden, 225;
Barker, 38, *50*, 50–1;

Bergman, 174, 187–8, *188*, 193, 256n.12; Brook, 77, 78; Donnellan, 199, 200, 210; English *Tales* at the millennium, 232–3; Hall (Edward), 233; Hall (Peter), 154, 166; Howell, 144–5; Hytner, 219, 232, 233; Noble, 233; Nunn, 89–90, 98, 105, 249n.4; Stanley, 123
as woman, 256n.12
Tollini, Frederick, 58
Tolstoy, Alexei, 207
Golden Key, or The Adventures of Buratino, The, 207
Törnqvist, Egil, 254n.2
Törnqvist, Kristina, *188*
Traub, Valerie, 6
Traversi, Derek, 119, 151
Tree, Ellen, *see* Kean, Mrs Charles
Tree, Herbert Beerbohm, 31, 54, 58, 59, 244n.1, 248n.5
Trewin, J. C., 63, 68, 70, 78, 80, 100–1
trial scene (III.ii), 5, 8, 9, 13, 16, 21, 26–7, 30
  Barker production, 36, 46
  Bergman production, 182, 190
  Brook production, 76, 82
  comparison to trial scene in *Henry VIII*, 76
  Donnellan production, 197–8, 202–4; reminder of Stalinist show trials, 202–3, 205
  English *Tales* at the millennium, 222, 223–5
  Hall (Peter) production, 162–4, 166
  Howell production, 136, 141–4, 252n.4
  Nunn production, 97, 100
  Stanley production, 121–2,

123, 131
Tucker, James, *229*, 238
Turlock, C., 120, 121
Turner, Graham, 232
tyrannical use of power, tyranny, 15–16, 25, 66, 70
  absolutism, 15, 152, 196, 203; dangers of, 7, 160–2, 199, 202–4; Stalinist show trials, evocation of, 202–4; violations of due process, 204
  Gielgud on Leontes as tyrant, 69
  of Leontes in trial scene, 16, 142, 198
  Leontes' jealousy and, 6, 16, 71, 94, 121, 160
  psychological and domestic consequences of, 152
  transtemporal recurrence in history, 203
  women's resistance to, 5, 6–8, 16, 107, 121, 161–2, 225
  see also political issues; power relations
Tyzack, Margaret, 150

Usher, Simon, *Winter's Tale* production at Leicester Haymarket (1991), 213, 215, 216, 219, 225, 234, 240, 241
Utah Shakespearean Festival, 115

Vitruvian man, Nunn's representation of Leonardo da Vinci's, 88, 89–90
Vlasov, Sergei, 206
von Franz, Marie-Louise, 112

Walkley, A. B., 51–3
Wall, Stephen, 172
Waller, Gary, 8–9
Walpole, Horace, 76

[297]

Warchus, Matthew, *Winter's Tale* production with RSC at the Roundhouse (2002), 215, 216, 218, 222, 223, 224, 225, 232–3, 237, 238, 241
Wardle, Irving, 105, 154, 158, 249n.4
Warren, Roger, 95, 96, 99, 104, 152, 153, 159, 160, 164, 166–7, 168, 173, 253–4n.3
Staging Shakespeare's Late Plays, 13, 254n.3
Webster, Benjamin, 58
Wells, Stanley, 11, 139–40, 141, 144, 145, 156–7, 168, 169, 172
Werson, Gerald, 157
Whitby, Arthur, 52–3
Whitrow, Benjamin, 233
Wilders, John, 150
Wilkinson, Norman, 35–7, 51
Willems, Michèle, 135–6
William, David, 173, 253n.2
Williams, David, 62
Williams, Harcourt, 60
Williams, Raymond, 10, 134, 135, 252n.2
Williams, Tam
 as Mamillius, 218–19, *227*, 233
 as Perdita, 238
Willis, Susan, 135, 137
Wilson, Cecil, 66
Wilson, John Dover, 71, 72
Wineke, Donald, 140
women's bodies, 185, 221, 222, 223, 224, 241
 patriarchal efforts to control, 6–8, 16
 see also gender relations; pregnancy
Wood, Peter, 99, 249n.7
Woodward, Peter, 158, 166, 168
Woolfenden, Guy, 101, 103
Woronicz, Henry, 251n.1
Worthen, W. B., 10
Wright, Susan, 4, 164, 253n.2
Wyckham, Glynne, 110
Wynyard, Diana, 64, 81, 82, *83*

Yeltsin, Boris, 207

Ziegler, Joe, 167
Zitner, Sheldon, 140